MW01041139

STCW

INCLUDING 2010 MANILA AMENDMENTS

STCW Convention and STCW Code

2017 EDITION

International Convention on
Standards of Training, Certification
and Watchkeeping for Seafarers

Published by the
INTERNATIONAL MARITIME ORGANIZATION
4 Albert Embankment, London SE1 7SR
www.imo.org

Printed and bound by CPI Group (UK) Ltd,
Croydon, CR0 4YY

ISBN: 978-92-801-1635-9

IMO PUBLICATION
Sales number: ID938E

Contents

Foreword

A comprehensive review of the 1978 STCW Convention commenced in January 2006 and culminated in a Conference of Parties to the STCW Convention, held in Manila, Philippines, from 21 to 25 June 2010, that adopted a significant number of amendments to the STCW Convention and STCW Code. The amendments update standards of competence required, particularly in light of emerging technologies, introduce new training and certification requirements and methodologies, improve mechanisms for enforcement of its provisions, and detail requirements on hours of work and rest, prevention of drug and alcohol abuse, and medical fitness standards for seafarers.

This publication contains the Final Act of the 2010 Conference of Parties to the 1978 STCW Convention, resolutions adopted by that Conference, and a complete, consolidated text of the STCW Convention, including its original articles, revised Annex and supporting STCW Code.

The Convention articles and annex provide the legal framework within which mandatory technical standards contained in part A of the STCW Code are applied. Part B of the Code provides guidance to assist those involved in educating, training or assessing the competence of seafarers or who are otherwise involved in applying STCW Convention provisions. While not mandatory, the guidance given has been harmonized through discussions within IMO, involving, where appropriate, consultation with the International Labour Organization. Observance of this guidance will contribute to achieving a more uniform application of Convention requirements.

All parts of this publication must be studied to understand the intent of the Convention fully and to give complete effect to the minimum global standards of knowledge, understanding, experience and professional competence desired by the States that are Parties to it, the industry itself and the general public.

The Convention and part A of the Code form a binding treaty between States, the interpretation of which is governed by the Vienna Convention on the Law of Treaties. The revision aims to bring the Convention and Code up to date with developments since the last full revision and to enable them to address issues that are anticipated to emerge in the foreseeable future in an effort to raise the standards of competence and professionalism of seafarers, upon whom the safety of life, property and the environment depends.

STCW Convention

International Convention on Standards of Training, Certification and Watchkeeping for Seafarers, 1978, as amended

including the Final Act of the 2010 Conference of Parties to the International Convention on Standards of Training, Certification and Watchkeeping for Seafarers, 1978, and resolutions 1 and 3 to 19 of the Conference

Contents

Foreword

The International Convention on Standards of Training, Certification and Watchkeeping for Seafarers (STCW), 1978, was adopted by the International Conference on Training and Certification of Seafarers on 7 July 1978.

The 1978 STCW Convention entered into force on 28 April 1984. Since then, amendments thereto have been adopted, in 1991, 1994, 1995, 1997, 1998, 2004, 2006 and 2010.

The 1991 amendments, relating to the global maritime distress and safety system (GMDSS) and conduct of trials, were adopted by resolution MSC.21(59) and entered into force on 1 December 1992.

The 1994 amendments on special training requirements for personnel on tankers were adopted by resolution MSC.33(63) and entered into force on 1 January 1996.

The 1995 amendments were adopted by resolution 1 of a Conference of Parties to the International Convention on Standards of Training, Certification and Watchkeeping for Seafarers, which was convened by the International Maritime Organization and met at the Headquarters of the Organization from 26 June to 7 July 1995 (1995 STCW Conference). The 1995 STCW Conference adopted the Seafarers' Training, Certification and Watchkeeping (STCW) Code.*

The STCW Code contains, in:

- ***Part A,*** mandatory provisions to which specific reference is made in the annex to the STCW Convention and which give, in detail, the minimum standards required to be maintained by Parties in order to give full and complete effect to the provisions of the STCW Convention; and, in

- ***Part B,*** recommended guidance to assist Parties to the STCW Convention and those involved in implementing, applying or enforcing its measures to give the STCW Convention full and complete effect in a uniform manner.

The 1997 amendments, to the Convention and to part A of the Code, relating to training of personnel on passenger and ro–ro passenger ships, were adopted by resolutions MSC.66(68) and MSC.67(68) and entered into force on 1 January 1999.

The 1998 amendments, to part A of the Code, relating to enhanced competence in cargo handling and stowage, particularly in respect of bulk cargoes, were adopted by resolution MSC.78(70) and entered into force on 1 January 2003.

The May 2004 amendments, to part A of the Code, adjusting certificates and endorsements, were adopted by resolution MSC.156(78). **The December 2004 amendments**, to part A of the Code, taking into account on-load and off-load devices in the competence relating to survival crafts and rescue boats other than fast rescue boats, were adopted by resolution MSC.180(79). Both amendments entered into force on 1 July 2006.

The 2006 amendments, to part A of the Code, introducing, *inter alia*, new measures pertaining to ship security officers, were adopted by resolution MSC.209(81) and entered into force on 1 January 2008.

---

* The STCW Code was circulated under cover of STCW.6/Circ.1 and STCW.6/Circ.1/Corr.1; amendments to the STCW Code are also circulated as STCW.6 circulars.

The 2010 amendments (the Manila Amendments) to the Convention and the Code were adopted by resolutions 1 and 2, respectively, of a Conference of Parties to the STCW Convention, held in Manila, Philippines, from 21 to 25 June 2010 (2010 STCW Conference). The amendments update standards of competence required, particularly in light of emerging technologies, introduced new training and certification requirements and methodologies, improve mechanisms for enforcement of its provisions, and provide detailed requirements on hours of work and rest, prevention of drug and alcohol abuse, and medical fitness standards for seafarers.

The 2014 amendments were adopted by MSC.373(93) and MSC.374(93). The amendments updated Chapter 1, General provisions, to the STCW Convention and Chapter I: Standards regarding general provisions, to the STCW Code, Part A: Mandatory standards regarding provisions of the Annex to the STCW Convention, and entered into force on 1 January 2016.

The 2015 amendments were adopted by MSC.396(95) and MSC.397(95). The amendments updated Chapter 1, General provisions, Regulations I/1 and I/II, Chapter V: Special training requirements for personnel on certain types of ships, new Section V/3, to the STCW Convention and Chapter V: Standards regarding special training requirements for personnel on certain types of ships to the STCW Code, Part A: Mandatory standards regarding provisions of the Annex to the STCW Convention, and entered into force on 1 January 2017.

The 2016 amendments were adopted by MSC.416(97) and MSC.417(97). The amendments updated Chapter 1, General provisions, Chapter V, Regulation V/2, Regulation V/4, and Chapter V, Table A-V/2, Table A-V/2-1, Table A-V/2-2, Table A-V/4-1 and Table A-V/4-2 to the STCW Code, Chapter I, General provisions, and enter into force on 1 July 2018.

Amendments to part B of the Code were adopted at the 69th, 72nd, 77th, 80th, 81st, 95th, 96th and 97th sessions of the Maritime Safety Committee (MSC) and have been promulgated by STCW circulars: STCW.6/Circ.3 (1998), Circ.4 (1998), Circ.5 (2000), Circ.6 (2003), Circ.7 (2005), Circs.8–10 (2006), STCW.6/Circ.11 (2015), STCW.6/Circ.12 (2016) and STCW.6/Circ.13 (2017).

This part of the publication contains the text of:

- the Final Act of the 2010 STCW Conference;
- the articles of the 1978 STCW Convention;
- resolution 1 of the 2010 STCW Conference and the annexed 2010 amendments, which completely replace the annex to the 1978 STCW Convention and the amendments thereto; and
- resolutions 3 to 19 of the 2010 STCW Conference.

Resolution 2 of the 2010 STCW Conference and the amendments annexed thereto, which completely replace the STCW Code, are contained in the latter part of this publication.

The footnotes to the text of the regulations of the STCW Convention, which have been added by the IMO Secretariat, have been inserted for ease of reference and do not form part of that Convention. The IMO Secretariat has been instructed to update these references as and when appropriate. In all cases, the reader must make use of the latest editions of the referenced texts, bearing in mind that such texts may have been revised or superseded by updated material since the publication of this consolidated edition of the STCW Convention and 2010 STCW Conference resolutions.

Final Act of the Conference of Parties to the International Convention on Standards of Training, Certification and Watchkeeping for Seafarers (STCW), 1978

1 Pursuant to the request of Parties to the International Convention on Standards of Training, Certification and Watchkeeping for Seafarers, 1978 (hereafter referred to as the 1978 STCW Convention), at the eighty-fourth session of the Maritime Safety Committee of the International Maritime Organization and subsequent decisions by the Council of the Organization at its one hundredth session and the Assembly of the Organization at its twenty-sixth session, and in accordance with article XII(1)(b) of the 1978 STCW Convention, a Conference of Parties to the 1978 STCW Convention was convened, in consultation with the Director-General of the International Labour Office, to consider amendments to the annex to the 1978 STCW Convention and the Seafarers' Training, Certification and Watchkeeping (STCW) Code.

2 The Conference was held at the Philippine International Convention Centre in Manila, the Philippines, from 21 to 25 June 2010.

3 Representatives of 85 States Parties to the 1978 STCW Convention participated in the Conference, namely the representatives of:

Angola
Antigua and Barbuda
Argentina
Australia
Azerbaijan
Bahamas
Bangladesh
Belgium
Belize
Brazil
Brunei Darussalam
Canada
Chile
China
Congo
Cook Islands
Côte D'ivoire
Croatia
Cyprus
Democratic People's Republic of Korea
Denmark
Estonia
Fiji
Finland
France
Georgia
Germany
Ghana
Greece
India
Indonesia
Iran (Islamic Republic of)
Iraq
Ireland
Israel
Italy
Jamaica
Japan
Kenya
Latvia
Lebanon
Liberia
Libyan Arab Jamahiriya
Lithuania
Luxembourg
Malaysia

Malta
Marshall Islands
Mexico
Morocco
Mozambique
Myanmar
Netherlands
Nigeria
Norway
Panama
Papua New Guinea
Philippines
Poland
Portugal
Qatar
Republic of Korea
Romania
Russian Federation
Saint Kitts and Nevis
Saudi Arabia
Singapore
Slovenia
South Africa
Spain
Sri Lanka
Sweden
Switzerland
Syrian Arab Republic
Thailand
Tunisia
Turkey
Tuvalu
Ukraine
United Arab Emirates
United Kingdom of Great Britain and Northern Ireland
United Republic of Tanzania
United States of America
Vanuatu
Viet Nam

4 The following State sent observers to the Conference:

Suriname

5 The following Associate Members of the Organization sent observers to the Conference:

Faroes
Hong Kong, China
Macao, China

6 The following organization of the United Nations system sent observers to the Conference:

International Labour Organization (ILO)

7 The following intergovernmental organizations sent observers to the Conference:

European Commission (EC)
League Of Arab States

8 The following non-governmental organizations sent observers to the Conference:

International Chamber Of Shipping (ICS)
International Shipping Federation (ISF)
International Transport Workers' Federation (ITF)
BIMCO
Oil Companies International Marine Forum (OCIMF)
International Association Of Drilling Contractors (IADC)
International Federation Of Shipmasters' Associations (IFSMA)
International Association Of Independent Tanker Owners (INTERTANKO)
Cruise Lines International Association (CLIA)
International Association Of Dry Cargo Shipowners (INTERCARGO)

International Maritime Lecturers Association (IMLA)
The Institute Of Marine Engineering, Science And Technology (IMarEST)
International Ship Managers' Association (InterManager)
Interferry
International Maritime Health Association (IMHA)
International Association Of Maritime Universities (IAMU)
Global Maritime Education And Training Association (GlobalMET)
The Nautical Institute (NI)

9 The Conference was opened by Mr. E.E. Mitropoulos, Secretary-General of the International Maritime Organization.

10 H.E. Mr. Noli de Castro, Vice President of the Republic of the Philippines, delivered a welcome address at the opening session of the Conference.

11 A message from Mr. Ban Ki-moon, Secretary-General of the United Nations, was read out at the opening session of the Conference.

12 The Conference elected Mr. Neil Frank R. Ferrer, of the Philippines, President of the Conference.

13 The Vice-Presidents elected by the Conference were:
H.E. Mr. Dwight C.R. Gardiner (Antigua and Barbuda)
Mr. Koffi Bertin Tano (Côte d'Ivoire)
Mr. Rajeev Gupta (India)
Rear Admiral Giancarlo Olimbo (Italy)
Mr. Abdel Hafiz El Kaissi (Lebanon)

14 The Secretariat of the Conference consisted of the following officers:

Secretary-General:	Mr. E.E. Mitropoulos Secretary-General of the Organization
Executive Secretary:	Mr. K. Sekimizu Director, Maritime Safety Division
Deputy Executive Secretary:	Mr. H. Hesse Senior Deputy Director, Maritime Safety Division
Assistant Deputy Executive Secretary:	Mr. A. Mahapatra Head, Maritime Training and Human Element Section, Maritime Safety Division

15 The Conference established the following Committees and elected respective officers:

Committee of the Whole

Chairman:	Rear Admiral P. Brady (Jamaica)
First Vice-Chairman:	Mr. S. Hassing (Netherlands)
Second Vice-Chairman:	Mr. Zheng Heping (China)

Drafting Committee

Chairman:	Ms. M. Medina (United States)
First Vice-Chairman:	Mr. B. Groves (Australia)
Second Vice-Chairman:	Capt. M.A. Shahba (Islamic Republic of Iran)

Credentials Committee

Chairman:	Mr. L. Chichinadze (Georgia)

16 The Drafting Committee was composed of representatives of the following States:

Argentina
Australia
China
France
Iran (Islamic Republic of)
Russian Federation
Spain
United States

17 The Credentials Committee was composed of representatives of the following States:

Georgia
Ireland
Nigeria
Panama
Thailand

18 The Conference used as the basis of its work the draft texts of amendments to the annex to the International Convention on Standards of Training, Certification and Watchkeeping for Seafarers, 1978, and the Seafarers' Training, Certification and Watchkeeping (STCW) Code prepared by the Sub-Committee on Standards of Training and Watchkeeping (STW), at its forty-first session, and endorsed by the Maritime Safety Committee, at its eighty-seventh session, of the Organization.

19 The Conference also considered proposals and comments submitted to the Conference by Parties to the 1978 STCW Convention and international organizations.

20 As a result of its deliberations, the Conference adopted:

- amendments to the annex to the International Convention on Standards of Training, Certification and Watchkeeping for Seafarers, 1978, together with resolution 1 on adoption of the amendments to the annex to the Convention, which constitute attachment 1 to this Final Act; and
- amendments to the Seafarers' Training, Certification and Watchkeeping (STCW) Code, together with resolution 2 on adoption of the amendments to the Code, which constitute attachment 2 to this Final Act.

21 The Conference also adopted the following resolutions set forth in attachment 3 to this Final Act:

Resolution 3: Expression of appreciation to the host Government;

Resolution 4: Transitional provisions and early implementation;

Resolution 5: Verification of certificates of competency and endorsements;

Resolution 6: Standards of training and certification and ships' manning levels;

Resolution 7: Promotion of technical knowledge, skills and professionalism of seafarers;

Resolution 8: Development of guidelines to implement international standards of medical fitness for seafarers;

Resolution 9: Revision of existing model courses published by the International Maritime Organization and development of new model courses;

Resolution 10: Promotion of technical co-operation;

Resolution 11: Measures to ensure the competency of masters and officers of ships operating in polar waters;

Resolution 12: Attracting new entrants to, and retaining seafarers in, the maritime profession;

Resolution 13: Accommodation for trainees;

Resolution 14: Promotion of the participation of women in the maritime industry;

Resolution 15: Future amendments and review of the STCW Convention and Code;

Resolution 16: Contribution of the International Labour Organization;

Resolution 17: Role of the World Maritime University, the IMO International Maritime Law Institute and the International Maritime Safety, Security and Environment Academy (IMSSEA) in promoting enhanced maritime standards;

Resolution 18: Year of the Seafarer; and

Resolution 19: Day of the Seafarer.

22 This Final Act is established in a single original text in the Arabic, Chinese, English, French, Russian and Spanish languages and is deposited with the Secretary-General of the International Maritime Organization.

23 The Secretary-General shall send:

(a) certified copies of this Final Act, with its attachments, to the Governments of the States invited to be represented at the Conference; and

(b) certified copies of the authentic texts of the amendments to the 1978 STCW Convention and the STCW Code, as referred to in paragraph 20 above, to all Parties to the 1978 STCW Convention, in conformity with article XII(1)(b)(ii) thereof.

DONE AT MANILA this twenty-fifth day of June, two thousand and ten.

IN WITNESS WHEREOF the undersigned have affixed their signatures to this Final Act.*

* Signatures omitted.

International Convention on Standards of Training, Certification and Watchkeeping for Seafarers, 1978

THE PARTIES TO THIS CONVENTION,

DESIRING to promote safety of life and property at sea and the protection of the marine environment by establishing in common agreement international standards of training, certification and watchkeeping for seafarers,

CONSIDERING that this end may best be achieved by the conclusion of an International Convention on Standards of Training, Certification and Watchkeeping for Seafarers,

HAVE AGREED as follows:

Article I
General obligations under the Convention

(1) The Parties undertake to give effect to the provisions of the Convention and the annex thereto, which shall constitute an integral part of the Convention. Every reference to the Convention constitutes at the same time a reference to the annex.

(2) The Parties undertake to promulgate all laws, decrees, orders and regulations and to take all other steps which may be necessary to give the Convention full and complete effect, so as to ensure that, from the point of view of safety of life and property at sea and the protection of the marine environment, seafarers on board ships are qualified and fit for their duties.

Article II
Definitions

For the purpose of the Convention, unless expressly provided otherwise:

- **(a)** *Party* means a State for which the Convention has entered into force;
- **(b)** *Administration* means the Government of the Party whose flag the ship is entitled to fly;
- **(c)** *Certificate* means a valid document, by whatever name it may be known, issued by or under the authority of the Administration or recognized by the Administration authorizing the holder to serve as stated in this document or as authorized by national regulations;
- **(d)** *Certificated* means properly holding a certificate;
- **(e)** *Organization* means the Inter-Governmental Maritime Consultative Organization (IMCO);*
- **(f)** *Secretary-General* means the Secretary-General of the Organization;
- **(g)** *Seagoing ship* means a ship other than those which navigate exclusively in inland waters or in waters within, or closely adjacent to, sheltered waters or areas where port regulations apply;

* The name of the Organization was changed to "International Maritime Organization (IMO)" by virtue of amendments to the Organization's Convention which entered into force on 22 May 1982.

(h) *Fishing vessel* means a vessel used for catching fish, whales, seals, walrus or other living resources of the sea;

(i) *Radio Regulations* means the Radio Regulations annexed to, or regarded as being annexed to, the most recent International Telecommunication Convention which may be in force at any time.

Article III
Application

The Convention shall apply to seafarers serving on board seagoing ships entitled to fly the flag of a Party except to those serving on board:

(a) warships, naval auxiliaries or other ships owned or operated by a State and engaged only on governmental non-commercial service; however, each Party shall ensure, by the adoption of appropriate measures not impairing the operations or operational capabilities of such ships owned or operated by it, that the persons serving on board such ships meet the requirements of the Convention so far as is reasonable and practicable;

(b) fishing vessels;

(c) pleasure yachts not engaged in trade; or

(d) wooden ships of primitive build.

Article IV
Communication of information

(1) The Parties shall communicate as soon as practicable to the Secretary-General:

(a) the text of laws, decrees, orders, regulations and instruments promulgated on the various matters within the scope of the Convention;

(b) full details, where appropriate, of contents and duration of study courses, together with their national examination and other requirements for each certificate issued in compliance with the Convention;

(c) a sufficient number of specimen certificates issued in compliance with the Convention.

(2) The Secretary-General shall notify all Parties of the receipt of any communication under paragraph (1)(a) and, *inter alia,* for the purposes of articles IX and X, shall, on request, provide them with any information communicated to him under paragraphs (1)(b) and (c).

Article V
Other treaties and interpretation

(1) All prior treaties, conventions and arrangements relating to standards of training, certification and watchkeeping for seafarers in force between the Parties shall continue to have full and complete effect during the terms thereof as regards:

(a) seafarers to whom this Convention does not apply;

(b) seafarers to whom this Convention applies, in respect of matters for which it has not expressly provided.

(2) To the extent, however, that such treaties, conventions or arrangements conflict with the provisions of the Convention, the Parties shall review their commitments under such treaties, conventions and arrangements with a view to ensuring that there is no conflict between these commitments and their obligations under the Convention.

(3) All matters which are not expressly provided for in the Convention remain subject to the legislation of Parties.

(4) Nothing in the Convention shall prejudice the codification and development of the law of the sea by the United Nations Conference on the Law of the Sea convened pursuant to resolution 2750 C(XXV) of the General Assembly of the United Nations, nor the present or future claims and legal views of any State concerning the law of the sea and the nature and extent of coastal and flag State jurisdiction.

Article VI
Certificates

(1) Certificates for masters, officers or ratings shall be issued to those candidates who, to the satisfaction of the Administration, meet the requirements for service, age, medical fitness, training, qualification and examinations in accordance with the appropriate provisions of the Annex to the Convention.

(2) Certificates for masters and officers issued in compliance with this article shall be endorsed by the issuing Administration in the form as prescribed in regulation I/2 of the Annex. If the language used is not English, the endorsement shall include a translation into that language.

Article VII
Transitional provisions

(1) A certificate of competency or of service in a capacity for which the Convention requires a certificate and which before entry into force of the Convention for a Party is issued in accordance with the laws of that Party or the Radio Regulations shall be recognized as valid for service after entry into force of the Convention for that Party.

(2) After the entry into force of the Convention for a Party, its Administration may continue to issue certificates of competency in accordance with its previous practices for a period not exceeding five years. Such certificates shall be recognized as valid for the purpose of the Convention. During this transitional period such certificates shall be issued only to seafarers who had commenced their sea service before entry into force of the Convention for that Party within the specific ship department to which those certificates relate. The Administration shall ensure that all other candidates for certification shall be examined and certificated in accordance with the Convention.

(3) A Party may, within two years after entry into force of the Convention for that Party, issue a certificate of service to seafarers who hold neither an appropriate certificate under the Convention nor a certificate of competency issued under its laws before entry into force of the Convention for that Party but who have:

- **(a)** served in the capacity for which they seek a certificate of service for not less than three years at sea within the last seven years preceding entry into force of the Convention for that Party;
- **(b)** produced evidence that they have performed that service satisfactorily;
- **(c)** satisfied the Administration as to medical fitness, including eyesight and hearing, taking into account their age at the time of application.

For the purpose of the Convention, a certificate of service issued under this paragraph shall be regarded as the equivalent of a certificate issued under the Convention.

Article VIII
Dispensation

(1) In circumstances of exceptional necessity, Administrations, if in their opinion this does not cause danger to persons, property or the environment, may issue a dispensation permitting a specified seafarer to serve in a specified ship for a specified period not exceeding six months in a capacity, other than that of the radio officer or radiotelephone operator, except as provided by the relevant Radio Regulations, for which he does not hold the appropriate certificate, provided that the person to whom the dispensation is issued shall be adequately qualified to fill the vacant post in a safe manner, to the satisfaction of the Administration. However, dispensations shall not be granted to a master or chief engineer officer except in circumstances of *force majeure* and then only for the shortest possible period.

(2) Any dispensation granted for a post shall be granted only to a person properly certificated to fill the post immediately below. Where certification of the post below is not required by the Convention, a dispensation may be issued to a person whose qualification and experience are, in the opinion of the Administration, of a clear equivalence to the requirements for the post to be filled, provided that, if such a person holds no appropriate certificate, he shall be required to pass a test accepted by the Administration as demonstrating that such a dispensation may safely be issued. In addition, Administrations shall ensure that the post in question is filled by the holder of an appropriate certificate as soon as possible.

(3) Parties shall, as soon as possible after 1 January of each year, send a report to the Secretary-General giving information of the total number of dispensations in respect of each capacity for which a certificate is required that have been issued during the year to seagoing ships, together with information as to the numbers of those ships above and below 1,600 gross register tons respectively.

Article IX
Equivalents

(1) The Convention shall not prevent an Administration from retaining or adopting other educational and training arrangements, including those involving seagoing service and shipboard organization especially adapted to technical developments and to special types of ships and trades, provided that the level of seagoing service, knowledge and efficiency as regards navigational and technical handling of ship and cargo ensures a degree of safety at sea and has a preventive effect as regards pollution at least equivalent to the requirements of the Convention.

(2) Details of such arrangements shall be reported as early as practicable to the Secretary-General who shall circulate such particulars to all Parties.

Article X
Control

(1) Ships, except those excluded by article III, are subject, while in the ports of a Party, to control by officers duly authorized by that Party to verify that all seafarers serving on board who are required to be certificated by the Convention are so certificated or hold an appropriate dispensation. Such certificates shall be accepted unless there are clear grounds for believing that a certificate has been fraudulently obtained or that the holder of a certificate is not the person to whom that certificate was originally issued.

(2) In the event that any deficiencies are found under paragraph (1) or under the procedures specified in regulation I/4, "Control procedures", the officer carrying out the control shall forthwith inform, in writing, the master of the ship and the Consul or, in his absence, the nearest diplomatic representative or the maritime authority of the State whose flag the ship is entitled to fly, so that appropriate action may be taken. Such notification shall specify the details of the deficiencies found and the grounds on which the Party determines that these deficiencies pose a danger to persons, property or the environment.

(3) In exercising the control under paragraph (1), if, taking into account the size and type of the ship and the length and nature of the voyage, the deficiencies referred to in paragraph (3) of regulation I/4 are not corrected and it is determined that this fact poses a danger to persons, property or the environment, the Party carrying out the control shall take steps to ensure that the ship will not sail unless and until these requirements are met to the extent that the danger has been removed. The facts concerning the action taken shall be reported promptly to the Secretary-General.

(4) When exercising control under this article, all possible efforts shall be made to avoid a ship being unduly detained or delayed. If a ship is so detained or delayed it shall be entitled to compensation for any loss or damage resulting therefrom.

(5) This article shall be applied as may be necessary to ensure that no more favourable treatment is given to ships entitled to fly the flag of a non-Party than is given to ships entitled to fly the flag of a Party.

Article XI
Promotion of technical co-operation

(1) Parties to the Convention shall promote, in consultation with, and with the assistance of, the Organization, support for those Parties which request technical assistance for:

- **(a)** training of administrative and technical personnel;
- **(b)** establishment of institutions for the training of seafarers;
- **(c)** supply of equipment and facilities for training institutions;
- **(d)** development of adequate training programmes, including practical training on seagoing ships; and
- **(e)** facilitation of other measures and arrangements to enhance the qualifications of seafarers;

preferably on a national, sub-regional or regional basis, to further the aims and purposes of the Convention, taking into account the special needs of developing countries in this regard.

(2) On its part, the Organization shall pursue the aforesaid efforts, as appropriate, in consultation or association with other international organizations, particularly the International Labour Organisation.

Article XII
Amendments

(1) The Convention may be amended by either of the following procedures:

- **(a)** amendments after consideration within the Organization:
  - **(i)** any amendment proposed by a Party shall be submitted to the Secretary-General, who shall then circulate it to all Members of the Organization, all Parties and the Director-General of the International Labour Office at least six months prior to its consideration;
  - **(ii)** any amendment so proposed and circulated shall be referred to the Maritime Safety Committee of the Organization for consideration;
  - **(iii)** Parties, whether or not Members of the Organization, shall be entitled to participate in the proceedings of the Maritime Safety Committee for consideration and adoption of amendments;
  - **(iv)** amendments shall be adopted by a two-thirds majority of the Parties present and voting in the Maritime Safety Committee expanded as provided for in sub-paragraph (a)(iii) (hereinafter referred to as the "expanded Maritime Safety Committee") on condition that at least one third of the Parties shall be present at the time of voting;
  - **(v)** amendments so adopted shall be communicated by the Secretary-General to all Parties for acceptance;

(vi) an amendment to an article shall be deemed to have been accepted on the date on which it is accepted by two thirds of the Parties;

(vii) an amendment to the annex shall be deemed to have been accepted:

1 at the end of two years from the date on which it is communicated to the Parties for acceptance; or

2 at the end of a different period, which shall be not less than one year, if so determined at the time of its adoption by a two-thirds majority of the Parties present and voting in the expanded Maritime Safety Committee;

however, the amendments shall be deemed not to have been accepted if, within the specified period, either more than one third of Parties or Parties the combined merchant fleets of which constitute not less than 50% of the gross tonnage of the world's merchant shipping of ships of 100 gross register tons or more notify the Secretary-General that they object to the amendment;

(viii) an amendment to an article shall enter into force with respect to those Parties which have accepted it six months after the date on which it is deemed to have been accepted, and with respect to each Party which accepts it after that date, six months after the date of that Party's acceptance;

(ix) an amendment to the annex shall enter into force with respect to all Parties, except those which have objected to the amendment under sub-paragraph (a)(vii) and which have not withdrawn such objections, six months after the date on which it is deemed to have been accepted. Before the date determined for entry into force, any Party may give notice to the Secretary-General that it exempts itself from giving effect to that amendment for a period not longer than one year from the date of its entry into force, or for such longer period as may be determined by a two-thirds majority of the Parties present and voting in the expanded Maritime Safety Committee at the time of the adoption of the amendment; or

(b) amendment by a conference:

(i) upon the request of a Party concurred in by at least one third of the Parties, the Organization shall convene, in association or consultation with the Director-General of the International Labour Office, a conference of Parties to consider amendments to the Convention;

(ii) every amendment adopted by such a conference by a two-thirds majority of the Parties present and voting shall be communicated by the Secretary-General to all Parties for acceptance;

(iii) unless the conference decides otherwise, the amendment shall be deemed to have been accepted and shall enter into force in accordance with the procedures specified in sub-paragraphs (a)(vi) and (a)(viii) or sub-paragraphs (a)(vii) and (a)(ix) respectively, provided that references in these sub-paragraphs to the expanded Maritime Safety Committee shall be taken to mean references to the conference.

(2) Any declaration of acceptance of, or objection to, an amendment or any notice given under paragraph (1)(a)(ix) shall be submitted in writing to the Secretary-General, who shall inform all Parties of any such submission and the date of its receipt.

(3) The Secretary-General shall inform all Parties of any amendments which enter into force, together with the date on which each such amendment enters into force.

Article XIII
Signature, ratification, acceptance, approval and accession

(1) The Convention shall remain open for signature at the Headquarters of the Organization from 1 December 1978 until 30 November 1979 and shall thereafter remain open for accession. Any State may become a Party by:

- **(a)** signature without reservation as to ratification, acceptance or approval; or
- **(b)** signature subject to ratification, acceptance or approval, followed by ratification, acceptance or approval; or
- **(c)** accession.

(2) Ratification, acceptance, approval or accession shall be effected by the deposit of an instrument to that effect with the Secretary-General.

(3) The Secretary-General shall inform all States that have signed the Convention or acceded to it and the Director-General of the International Labour Office of any signature or of the deposit of any instrument of ratification, acceptance, approval or accession and the date of its deposit.

Article XIV
Entry into force

(1) The Convention shall enter into force 12 months after the date on which not less than 25 States, the combined merchant fleets of which constitute not less than 50% of the gross tonnage of the world's merchant shipping of ships of 100 gross register tons or more, have either signed it without reservation as to ratification, acceptance or approval or deposited the requisite instruments of ratification, acceptance, approval or accession in accordance with article XIII.

(2) The Secretary-General shall inform all States that have signed the Convention or acceded to it of the date on which it enters into force.

(3) Any instrument of ratification, acceptance, approval or accession deposited during the 12 months referred to in paragraph (1) shall take effect on the coming into force of the Convention or three months after the deposit of such instrument, whichever is the later date.

(4) Any instrument of ratification, acceptance, approval or accession deposited after the date on which the Convention enters into force shall take effect three months after the date of deposit.

(5) After the date on which an amendment is deemed to have been accepted under article XII, any instrument of ratification, acceptance, approval or accession deposited shall apply to the Convention as amended.

Article XV
Denunciation

(1) The Convention may be denounced by any Party at any time after five years from the date on which the Convention entered into force for that Party.

(2) Denunciation shall be effected by notification in writing to the Secretary-General who shall inform all other Parties and the Director-General of the International Labour Office of any such notification received and of the date of its receipt as well as the date on which such denunciation takes effect.

(3) A denunciation shall take effect 12 months after receipt of the notification of denunciation by the Secretary-General or after any longer period which may be indicated in the notification.

Article XVI
Deposit and registration

(1) The Convention shall be deposited with the Secretary-General who shall transmit certified true copies thereof to all States that have signed the Convention or acceded to it.

(2) As soon as the Convention enters into force, the Secretary-General shall transmit the text to the Secretary-General of the United Nations for registration and publication, in accordance with Article 102 of the Charter of the United Nations.

Article XVII
Languages

The Convention is established in a single copy in the Chinese, English, French, Russian and Spanish languages, each text being equally authentic. Official translations in the Arabic and German languages shall be prepared and deposited with the signed original.

IN WITNESS WHEREOF the undersigned, being duly authorized by their respective Governments for that purpose, have signed the Convention.*

DONE AT LONDON this seventh day of July, one thousand nine hundred and seventy-eight.

* Signatures omitted.

Attachment 1 to the Final Act of the 2010 STCW Conference

Resolution 1

The Manila Amendments to the Annex to the International Convention on Standards of Training, Certification and Watchkeeping for Seafarers (STCW), 1978

THE 2010 MANILA CONFERENCE,

RECALLING Article XII(1)(b) of the International Convention on Standards of Training, Certification and Watchkeeping for Seafarers, 1978 (hereinafter referred to as "the Convention"), concerning the procedure for amendment by a Conference of Parties,

HAVING CONSIDERED the Manila amendments to the Annex to the Convention proposed and circulated to the Members of the Organization and to all Parties to the Convention,

1. ADOPTS, in accordance with article XII(1)(b)(ii) of the Convention, amendments to the annex to the Convention, the text of which is set out in the annex to the present resolution;

2. DETERMINES, in accordance with article XII(1)(a)(vii) of the Convention, that the amendments annexed hereto shall be deemed to have been accepted on 1 July 2011, unless, prior to that date, more than one third of Parties to the Convention or Parties the combined merchant fleets of which constitute not less than 50% of the gross tonnage of the world's merchant shipping of ships of 100 gross register tons or more have notified the Secretary-General that they object to the amendments;

3. INVITES Parties to note that, in accordance with article XII(1)(a)(ix) of the Convention, the amendments annexed hereto shall enter into force on 1 January 2012 upon being deemed to have been accepted in accordance with paragraph 2 above;

4. REQUESTS the Secretary-General of the Organization to transmit certified copies of the present resolution and the text of the amendments contained in the annex to all Parties to the Convention;

5. FURTHER REQUESTS the Secretary-General to transmit copies of this resolution and its annex to all Members of the Organization which are not Parties to the Convention.

Annex

The Manila Amendments to the Annex to the International Convention on Standards of Training, Certification and Watchkeeping for Seafarers, 1978

Chapter I
General provisions

Regulation I/1
Definitions and clarifications

1 For the purpose of the Convention, unless expressly provided otherwise:

.1 *Regulations* means regulations contained in the Annex to the Convention;

.2 *Approved* means approved by the Party in accordance with these regulations;

.3 *Master* means the person having command of a ship;

.4 *Officer* means a member of the crew, other than the master, designated as such by national law or regulations or, in the absence of such designation, by collective agreement or custom;

.5 *Deck officer* means an officer qualified in accordance with the provisions of chapter II of the Convention;

.6 *Chief mate* means the officer next in rank to the master and upon whom the command of the ship will fall in the event of the incapacity of the master;

.7 *Engineer officer* means an officer qualified in accordance with the provisions of regulation III/1, III/2 or III/3 of the Convention;

.8 *Chief engineer officer* means the senior engineer officer responsible for the mechanical propulsion and the operation and maintenance of the mechanical and electrical installations of the ship;

.9 *Second engineer officer* means the engineer officer next in rank to the chief engineer officer and upon whom the responsibility for the mechanical propulsion and the operation and maintenance of the mechanical and electrical installations of the ship will fall in the event of the incapacity of the chief engineer officer;

.10 *Assistant engineer officer* means a person under training to become an engineer officer and designated as such by national law or regulations;

.11 *Radio operator* means a person holding an appropriate certificate issued or recognized by the Administration under the provisions of the Radio Regulations;

.12 *GMDSS radio operator* means a person who is qualified in accordance with the provisions of chapter IV of the Convention;

.13 *Rating* means a member of the ship's crew other than the master or an officer;

.14 *Near-coastal voyages* means voyages in the vicinity of a Party as defined by that Party;

.15 *Propulsion power* means the total maximum continuous rated output power, in kilowatts, of all the ship's main propulsion machinery which appears on the ship's certificate of registry or other official document;

.16 *Radio duties* include, as appropriate, watchkeeping and technical maintenance and repairs conducted in accordance with the Radio Regulations, the International Convention for the Safety of Life at Sea, 1974 (SOLAS), as amended, and, at the discretion of each Administration, the relevant recommendations of the Organization;

.17 *Oil tanker* means a ship constructed and used for the carriage of petroleum and petroleum products in bulk;

.18 *Chemical tanker* means a ship constructed or adapted and used for the carriage in bulk of any liquid product listed in chapter 17 of the International Bulk Chemical Code;

.19 *Liquefied gas tanker* means a ship constructed or adapted and used for the carriage in bulk of any liquefied gas or other product listed in chapter 19 of the International Gas Carrier Code;

.20 *Passenger ship* means a ship as defined in the International Convention for the Safety of Life at Sea, 1974, as amended;

.21 *Ro–ro passenger ship* means a passenger ship with ro–ro spaces or special category spaces as defined in the International Convention for the Safety of Life at Sea, 1974 (SOLAS), as amended;

.22 *Month* means a calendar month or 30 days made up of periods of less than one month;

.23 *STCW Code* means the Seafarers' Training, Certification and Watchkeeping (STCW) Code as adopted by the 1995 Conference resolution 2, as it may be amended by the Organization;

.24 *Function* means a group of tasks, duties and responsibilities, as specified in the STCW Code, necessary for ship operation, safety of life at sea or protection of the marine environment;

.25 *Company* means the owner of the ship or any other organization or person such as the manager, or the bareboat charterer, who has assumed the responsibility for operation of the ship from the shipowner and who, on assuming such responsibility, has agreed to take over all the duties and responsibilities imposed on the company by these regulations;

.26 *Seagoing service* means service on board a ship relevant to the issue or revalidation of a certificate or other qualification;

.27 *ISPS Code* means the International Ship and Port Facility Security (ISPS) Code adopted on 12 December 2002 by resolution 2 of the Conference of Contracting Governments to the International Convention for the Safety of Life at Sea, 1974 (SOLAS), as may be amended by the Organization;

.28 *Ship security officer* means the person on board the ship, accountable to the master, designated by the company as responsible for the security of the ship including implementation and maintenance of the ship security plan and liaison with the company security officer and port facility security officers;

.29 *Security duties* include all security tasks and duties on board ships as defined by chapter XI-2 of the International Convention for the Safety of Life at Sea, 1974 (SOLAS), as amended, and the International Ship and Port Facility Security (ISPS) Code;

.30 *Certificate of competency* means a certificate issued and endorsed for masters, officers and GMDSS radio operators in accordance with the provisions of chapters II, III, IV or VII of this annex and entitling the lawful holder thereof to serve in the capacity and perform the functions involved at the level of responsibility specified therein;

.31 *Certificate of proficiency* means a certificate, other than a certificate of competency issued to a seafarer, stating that the relevant requirements of training, competencies or seagoing service in the Convention have been met;

.32 *Documentary evidence* means documentation, other than a certificate of competency or certificate of proficiency, used to establish that the relevant requirements of the Convention have been met;

.33 *Electro-technical officer* means an officer qualified in accordance with the provisions of regulation III/6 of the Convention;

.34 *Able seafarer deck* means a rating qualified in accordance with the provisions of regulation II/5 of the Convention;

.35 *Able seafarer engine* means a rating qualified in accordance with the provisions of regulation III/5 of the Convention;

.36 *Electro-technical rating* means a rating qualified in accordance with the provisions of regulation III/7 of the Convention;

.37 *Audit* means a systematic, independent and documented process for obtaining audit evidence and evaluating it objectively to determine the extent to which audit criteria are fulfilled;

.38 *Audit Scheme* means the IMO Member State Audit Scheme established by the Organization and taking into account the guidelines developed by the Organization;*

.39 *Code for Implementation* means the IMO Instruments Implementation Code (III Code) adopted by the Organization by resolution A.1070(28);

.40 *Audit Standard* means the Code for Implementation;

.41 *The IGF Code* means the International Code of safety for ships using gases or other low-flashpoint fuels, as defined in SOLAS regulation II-1/2.29;

.42 *Polar Code* means the International Code for Ships Operating in Polar Waters, as defined in SOLAS regulation XIV/1.1; and

.43 *Polar waters* means Arctic waters and/or the Antarctic area, as defined in SOLAS regulations XIV/1.2 to XIV/1.4.

2 These regulations are supplemented by the mandatory provisions contained in part A of the STCW Code and:

.1 any reference to a requirement in a regulation also constitutes a reference to the corresponding section of part A of the STCW Code;

.2 in applying these regulations, the related guidance and explanatory material contained in part B of the STCW Code should be taken into account to the greatest degree possible in order to achieve a more uniform implementation of the Convention provisions on a global basis;

.3 amendments to part A of the STCW Code shall be adopted, brought into force and take effect in accordance with the provisions of article XII of the Convention concerning the amendment procedure applicable to the annex; and

.4 part B of the STCW Code shall be amended by the Maritime Safety Committee in accordance with its rules of procedure.

3 The references made in article VI of the Convention to "the Administration" and "the issuing Administration" shall not be construed as preventing any Party from issuing and endorsing certificates under the provisions of these regulations.

Regulation I/2
Certificates and endorsements

1 Certificates of competency shall be issued only by the Administration, following verification of the authenticity and validity of any necessary documentary evidence.

2 Certificates issued in accordance with the provisions of regulations V/1-1 and V/1-2 to masters and officers shall only be issued by an Administration.

---

* Refer to the *Framework and Procedures for the IMO Member State Audit Scheme*, adopted by the Organization by resolution A.1067(28).

3 Certificates shall be in the official language or languages of the issuing country. If the language used is not English, the text shall include a translation into that language.

4 In respect of radio operators, Parties may:

.1 include the additional knowledge required by the relevant regulations in the examination for the issue of a certificate complying with the Radio Regulations; or

.2 issue a separate certificate indicating that the holder has the additional knowledge required by the relevant regulations.

5 The endorsement required by article VI of the Convention to attest the issue of a certificate shall only be issued if all the requirements of the Convention have been complied with.

6 At the discretion of a Party, endorsements may be incorporated in the format of the certificates being issued as provided for in section A-I/2 of the STCW Code. If so incorporated, the form used shall be that set forth in section A-I/2, paragraph 1. If issued otherwise, the form of endorsements used shall be that set forth in paragraph 2 of that section.

7 An Administration which recognizes under regulation I/10:

.1 a certificate of competency; or

.2 a certificate of proficiency issued to masters and officers in accordance with the provisions of regulations V/1-1 and V/1-2

shall endorse such certificate to attest its recognition only after ensuring the authenticity and validity of the certificate. The endorsement shall only be issued if all requirements of the Convention have been complied with. The form of the endorsement used shall be that set forth in paragraph 3 of section A-I/2 of the STCW Code.

8 The endorsements referred to in paragraphs 5, 6 and 7:

.1 may be issued as separate documents;

.2 shall be issued by the Administration only;

.3 shall each be assigned a unique number, except that endorsements attesting the issue of a certificate may be assigned the same number as the certificate concerned, provided that number is unique; and

.4 shall expire as soon as the certificate endorsed expires or is withdrawn, suspended or cancelled by the Party which issued it and, in any case, not more than five years after their date of issue.

9 The capacity in which the holder of a certificate is authorized to serve shall be identified in the form of endorsement in terms identical to those used in the applicable safe manning requirements of the Administration.

10 Administrations may use a format different from the format given in section A-I/2 of the STCW Code, provided that, as a minimum, the required information is provided in Roman characters and Arabic figures, taking into account the variations permitted under section A-I/2.

11 Subject to the provisions of regulation I/10, paragraph 5, any certificate required by the Convention must be kept available in its original form on board the ship on which the holder is serving.

12 Each Party shall ensure that certificates are issued only to candidates who comply with the requirements of this regulation.

13 Candidates for certification shall provide satisfactory proof:

.1 of their identity;

.2 that their age is not less than that prescribed in the regulation relevant to the certificate applied for;

.3 that they meet the standards of medical fitness specified in section A-I/9 of the STCW Code;

.4 of having completed the seagoing service and any related compulsory training required by these regulations for the certificate applied for; and

.5 that they meet the standards of competence prescribed by these regulations for the capacities, functions and levels that are to be identified in the endorsement to the certificate.

14 Each Party undertakes to maintain a register or registers of all certificates and endorsements for masters, officers, and, as applicable, ratings which are issued, have expired or have been revalidated, suspended, cancelled or reported lost or destroyed and of dispensations issued.

15 Each Party undertakes to make available information on the status of such certificates of competency, endorsements and dispensations to other Parties and companies which request verification of the authenticity and validity of certificates produced to them by seafarers seeking recognition of their certificates under regulation I/10 or employment on board ship.

16 As of 1 January 2017, the information on the status of information required to be available in accordance with paragraph 15 of this regulation shall be made available, in the English language, through electronic means.

Regulation I/3

Principles governing near-coastal voyages

1 Any Party defining near-coastal voyages for the purpose of the Convention shall not impose training, experience or certification requirements on the seafarers serving on board the ships entitled to fly the flag of another Party and engaged on such voyages in a manner resulting in more stringent requirements for such seafarers than for seafarers serving on board ships entitled to fly its own flag. In no case shall any such Party impose requirements in respect of seafarers serving on board ships entitled to fly the flag of another Party in excess of those of the Convention in respect of ships not engaged on near-coastal voyages.

2 A Party that, for ships afforded the benefits of the near-coastal voyage provisions of the Convention, which includes voyages off the coast of other Parties within the limits of their near-coastal definition, shall enter into an undertaking with the Parties concerned specifying the details of both involved trading areas and other relevant conditions.

3 With respect to ships entitled to fly the flag of a Party regularly engaged on near-coastal voyages off the coast of another Party, the Party whose flag the ship is entitled to fly shall prescribe training, experience and certification requirements for seafarers serving on such ships at least equal to those of the Party off whose coast the ship is engaged, provided that they do not exceed the requirements of the Convention in respect of ships not engaged on near-coastal voyages. Seafarers serving on a ship which extends its voyage beyond what is defined as a near-coastal voyage by a Party and enters waters not covered by that definition shall fulfil the appropriate competency requirements of the Convention.

4 A Party may afford a ship which is entitled to fly its flag the benefits of the near-coastal voyage provisions of the Convention when it is regularly engaged off the coast of a non-Party on near-coastal voyages as defined by the Party.

5 The certificates of seafarers issued by a Party for its defined near-coastal voyages limits may be accepted by other Parties for service in their defined near-coastal voyages limits, provided the Parties concerned enter into an undertaking specifying the details of involved trading areas and other relevant conditions thereof.

6 Parties defining near-coastal voyages, in accordance with the requirements of this regulation, shall:

.1 meet the principles governing near-coastal voyages specified in section A-I/3;

.2 communicate to the Secretary-General, in conformity with the requirements of regulation I/7, the details of the provisions adopted; and

.3 incorporate the near-coastal voyages limits in the endorsements issued pursuant to regulation I/2, paragraphs 5, 6 or 7.

7 Nothing in this regulation shall, in any way, limit the jurisdiction of any State, whether or not a Party to the Convention.

Regulation I/4
Control procedures

1 Control exercised by a duly authorized control officer under article X shall be limited to the following:

.1 verification in accordance with article X(1) that all seafarers serving on board who are required to be certificated in accordance with the Convention hold an appropriate certificate or a valid dispensation, or provide documentary proof that an application for an endorsement has been submitted to the Administration in accordance with regulation I/10, paragraph 5;

.2 verification that the numbers and certificates of the seafarers serving on board are in conformity with the applicable safe manning requirements of the Administration; and

.3 assessment, in accordance with section A-I/4 of the STCW Code, of the ability of the seafarers of the ship to maintain watchkeeping and security standards, as appropriate, as required by the Convention if there are clear grounds for believing that such standards are not being maintained because any of the following have occurred:

.3.1 the ship has been involved in a collision, grounding or stranding, or

.3.2 there has been a discharge of substances from the ship when under way, at anchor or at berth which is illegal under any international convention, or

.3.3 the ship has been manoeuvred in an erratic or unsafe manner whereby routeing measures adopted by the Organization or safe navigation practices and procedures have not been followed, or

.3.4 the ship is otherwise being operated in such a manner as to pose a danger to persons, property, the environment, or a compromise to security.

2 Deficiencies which may be deemed to pose a danger to persons, property or the environment include the following:

.1 failure of seafarers to hold a certificate, to have an appropriate certificate, to have a valid dispensation or to provide documentary proof that an application for an endorsement has been submitted to the Administration in accordance with regulation I/10, paragraph 5;

.2 failure to comply with the applicable safe manning requirements of the Administration;

.3 failure of navigational or engineering watch arrangements to conform to the requirements specified for the ship by the Administration;

.4 absence in a watch of a person qualified to operate equipment essential to safe navigation, safety radiocommunications or the prevention of marine pollution; and

.5 inability to provide, for the first watch at the commencement of a voyage and for subsequent relieving watches, persons who are sufficiently rested and otherwise fit for duty.

3 Failure to correct any of the deficiencies referred to in paragraph 2, in so far as it has been determined by the Party carrying out the control that they pose a danger to persons, property or the environment, shall be the only grounds under article X on which a Party may detain a ship.

Regulation I/5
National provisions

1 Each Party shall establish processes and procedures for the impartial investigation of any reported incompetency, act, omission or compromise to security that may pose a direct threat to safety of life or property at sea or to the marine environment by the holders of certificates or endorsements issued by that Party in connection with their performance of duties related to their certificates and for the withdrawal, suspension and cancellation of such certificates for such cause and for the prevention of fraud.

2 Each Party shall take and enforce appropriate measures to prevent fraud and other unlawful practices involving certificates and endorsements issued.

3 Each Party shall prescribe penalties or disciplinary measures for cases in which the provisions of its national legislation giving effect to the Convention are not complied with in respect of ships entitled to fly its flag or of seafarers duly certificated by that Party.

4 In particular, such penalties or disciplinary measures shall be prescribed and enforced in cases in which:

.1 a company or a master has engaged a person not holding a certificate as required by the Convention;

.2 a master has allowed any function or service in any capacity required by these regulations to be performed by a person holding an appropriate certificate to be performed by a person not holding the required certificate, a valid dispensation or having the documentary proof required by regulation I/10, paragraph 5; or

.3 a person has obtained by fraud or forged documents an engagement to perform any function or serve in any capacity required by these regulations to be performed or filled by a person holding a certificate or dispensation.

5 A Party, within whose jurisdiction there is located any company which, or any person who, is believed on clear grounds to have been responsible for, or to have knowledge of, any apparent non-compliance with the Convention specified in paragraph 4, shall extend all co-operation possible to any Party which advises it of its intention to initiate proceedings under its jurisdiction.

Regulation I/6
Training and assessment

Each Party shall ensure that:

.1 the training and assessment of seafarers, as required under the Convention, are administered, supervised and monitored in accordance with the provisions of section A-I/6 of the STCW Code; and

.2 those responsible for the training and assessment of competence of seafarers, as required under the Convention, are appropriately qualified in accordance with the provisions of section A-I/6 of the STCW Code for the type and level of training or assessment involved.

Regulation I/7
Communication of information

1 In addition to the information required to be communicated by article IV, each Party shall provide to the Secretary-General, within the time periods prescribed and in the format specified in section A-I/7 of the STCW Code, such other information as may be required by the Code on other steps taken by the Party to give the Convention full and complete effect.

2 When complete information as prescribed in article IV and section A-I/7 of the STCW Code has been received and such information confirms that full and complete effect is given to the provisions of the Convention, the Secretary-General shall submit a report to this effect to the Maritime Safety Committee.

3 Following subsequent confirmation by the Maritime Safety Committee, in accordance with procedures adopted by the Committee, that the information which has been provided demonstrates that full and complete effect is given to the provisions of the Convention:

.1 the Maritime Safety Committee shall identify the Parties so concerned;

.2 shall review the list of Parties which communicated information that demonstrated that they give full and complete effect to the relevant provisions of the Convention, to retain in this list only the Parties so concerned; and

.3 other Parties shall be entitled, subject to the provisions of regulations I/4 and I/10, to accept, in principle, that certificates issued by or on behalf of the Parties identified in paragraph 3.1 are in compliance with the Convention.

4 Amendments to the Convention and STCW Code, with dates of entry into force later than the date information has been, or will be, communicated to the Secretary-General in accordance with the provisions of paragraph 1, are not subject to the provisions of section A-I/7, paragraphs 1 and 2.

Regulation I/8

Quality standards

1 Each Party shall ensure that:

.1 in accordance with the provisions of section A-I/8 of the STCW Code, all training, assessment of competence, certification, including medical certification, endorsement and revalidation activities carried out by non-governmental agencies or entities under its authority are continuously monitored through a quality standards system to ensure achievement of defined objectives, including those concerning the qualifications and experience of instructors and assessors; and

.2 where governmental agencies or entities perform such activities, there shall be a quality standards system.

2 Each Party shall also ensure that an evaluation is periodically undertaken, in accordance with the provisions of section A-I/8 of the STCW Code, by qualified persons who are not themselves involved in the activities concerned. This evaluation shall include all changes to national regulations and procedures in compliance with the amendments to the Convention and STCW Code, with dates of entry into force later than the date information was communicated to the Secretary-General.

3 A report containing the results of the evaluation required by paragraph 2 shall be communicated to the Secretary-General in accordance with the format specified in section A-I/7 of the STCW Code.

Regulation I/9

Medical standards

1 Each Party shall establish standards of medical fitness for seafarers and procedures for the issue of a medical certificate in accordance with the provisions of this regulation and of section A-I/9 of the STCW Code.

2 Each Party shall ensure that those responsible for assessing the medical fitness of seafarers are medical practitioners recognized by the Party for the purpose of seafarer medical examinations, in accordance with the provisions of section A-I/9 of the STCW Code.

3 Every seafarer holding a certificate issued under the provisions of the Convention, who is serving at sea, shall also hold a valid medical certificate issued in accordance with the provisions of this regulation and of section A-I/9 of the STCW Code.

4 Every candidate for certification shall:

.1 be not less than 16 years of age;

.2 provide satisfactory proof of his/her identity; and

.3 meet the applicable medical fitness standards established by the Party.

5 Medical certificates shall remain valid for a maximum period of two years unless the seafarer is under the age of 18, in which case the maximum period of validity shall be one year.

6 If the period of validity of a medical certificate expires in the course of a voyage, then the medical certificate shall continue in force until the next port of call where a medical practitioner recognized by the Party is available, provided that the period shall not exceed three months.

7 In urgent cases the Administration may permit a seafarer to work without a valid medical certificate until the next port of call where a medical practitioner recognized by the Party is available, provided that:

.1 the period of such permission does not exceed three months; and

.2 the seafarer concerned is in possession of an expired medical certificate of recent date.

Regulation I/10
Recognition of certificates

1 Each Administration shall ensure that the provisions of this regulation are complied with, in order to recognize, by endorsement in accordance with regulation I/2, paragraph 7, a certificate issued by or under the authority of another Party to a master, officer or radio operator and that:

.1 the Administration has confirmed, through an evaluation of that Party, which may include inspection of facilities and procedures, that the requirements of the Convention regarding standards of competence, training and certification and quality standards are fully complied with; and

.2 an undertaking is agreed with the Party concerned that prompt notification will be given of any significant change in the arrangements for training and certification provided in compliance with the Convention.

2 Measures shall be established to ensure that seafarers who present, for recognition, certificates issued under the provisions of regulations II/2, III/2 or III/3, or issued under regulation VII/1 at the management level, as defined in the STCW Code, have an appropriate knowledge of the maritime legislation of the Administration relevant to the functions they are permitted to perform.

3 Information provided and measures agreed upon under this regulation shall be communicated to the Secretary-General in conformity with the requirements of regulation I/7.

4 Certificates issued by or under the authority of a non-Party shall not be recognized.

5 Notwithstanding the requirement of regulation I/2, paragraph 7, an Administration may, if circumstances require, subject to the provisions of paragraph 1, allow a seafarer to serve for a period not exceeding three months on board a ship entitled to fly its flag, while holding an appropriate and valid certificate issued and endorsed as required by another Party for use on board that Party's ships but which has not yet been endorsed so as to render it appropriate for service on board ships entitled to fly the flag of the Administration. Documentary proof shall be readily available that application for an endorsement has been submitted to the Administration.

6 Certificates and endorsements issued by an Administration under the provisions of this regulation in recognition of, or attesting the recognition of, a certificate issued by another Party shall not be used as the basis for further recognition by another Administration.

Regulation I/11
Revalidation of certificates

1 Every master, officer and radio operator holding a certificate issued or recognized under any chapter of the Convention other than regulation V/3 or chapter VI, who is serving at sea or intends to return to sea after a period ashore, shall, in order to continue to qualify for seagoing service, be required, at intervals not exceeding five years, to:

.1 meet the standards of medical fitness prescribed by regulation I/9; and

.2 establish continued professional competence in accordance with section A-I/11 of the STCW Code.

2 Every master, officer and radio operator shall, for continuing seagoing service on board ships for which special training requirements have been internationally agreed upon, successfully complete approved relevant training.

3 Every master and officer shall, for continuing seagoing service on board tankers, meet the requirements in paragraph 1 of this regulation and be required, at intervals not exceeding five years, to establish continued professional competence for tankers in accordance with section A-I/11, paragraph 3 of the STCW Code.

4 Every master or officer shall, for continuing seagoing service on board ships operating in polar waters, meet the requirements of paragraph 1 of this regulation and be required, at intervals not exceeding five years, to establish continued professional competence for ships operating in polar waters in accordance with section A-1/11, paragraph 4 of the STCW Code.

5 Each Party shall compare the standards of competence which it required of candidates for certificates issued before 1 January 2017 with those specified for the appropriate certificate in part A of the STCW Code, and shall determine the need for requiring the holders of such certificates to undergo appropriate refresher and updating training or assessment.

6 The Party shall, in consultation with those concerned, formulate or promote the formulation of a structure of refresher and updating courses as provided for in section A-I/11 of the STCW Code.

7 For the purpose of updating the knowledge of masters, officers and radio operators, each Administration shall ensure that the texts of recent changes in national and international regulations concerning the safety of life at sea, security and the protection of the marine environment are made available to ships entitled to fly its flag.

Regulation I/12

Use of simulators

1 The performance standards and other provisions set forth in section A-I/12 and such other requirements as are prescribed in part A of the STCW Code for any certificate concerned shall be complied with in respect of:

- **.1** all mandatory simulator-based training;
- **.2** any assessment of competency required by part A of the STCW Code which is carried out by means of a simulator; and
- **.3** any demonstration, by means of a simulator, of continued proficiency required by part A of the STCW Code.

Regulation I/13

Conduct of trials

1 These regulations shall not prevent an Administration from authorizing ships entitled to fly its flag to participate in trials.

2 For the purposes of this regulation, the term *trial* means an experiment or series of experiments, conducted over a limited period, which may involve the use of automated or integrated systems in order to evaluate alternative methods of performing specific duties or satisfying particular arrangements prescribed by the Convention, which would provide at least the same degree of safety, security and pollution prevention as provided by these regulations.

3 The Administration authorizing ships to participate in trials shall be satisfied that such trials are conducted in a manner that provides at least the same degree of safety, security and pollution prevention as provided by these regulations. Such trials shall be conducted in accordance with guidelines adopted by the Organization.

4 Details of such trials shall be reported to the Organization as early as practicable but not less than six months before the date on which the trials are scheduled to commence. The Organization shall circulate such particulars to all Parties.

5 The results of trials authorized under paragraph 1, and any recommendations the Administration may have regarding those results, shall be reported to the Organization, which shall circulate such results and recommendations to all Parties.

6 Any Party having any objection to particular trials authorized in accordance with this regulation should communicate such objection to the Organization as early as practicable. The Organization shall circulate details of the objection to all Parties.

7 An Administration which has authorized a trial shall respect objections received from other Parties relating to such trial by directing ships entitled to fly its flag not to engage in a trial while navigating in the waters of a coastal State which has communicated its objection to the Organization.

8 An Administration which concludes, on the basis of a trial, that a particular system will provide at least the same degree of safety, security and pollution prevention as provided by these regulations may authorize ships entitled to fly its flag to continue to operate with such a system indefinitely, subject to the following requirements:

- **.1** the Administration shall, after results of the trial have been submitted in accordance with paragraph 5, provide details of any such authorization, including identification of the specific ships which may be subject to the authorization, to the Organization, which will circulate this information to all Parties;
- **.2** any operations authorized under this paragraph shall be conducted in accordance with any guidelines developed by the Organization, to the same extent as they apply during a trial;
- **.3** such operations shall respect any objections received from other Parties in accordance with paragraph 7, to the extent such objections have not been withdrawn; and
- **.4** an operation authorized under this paragraph shall only be permitted pending a determination by the Maritime Safety Committee as to whether an amendment to the Convention would be appropriate, and, if so, whether the operation should be suspended or permitted to continue before the amendment enters into force.

9 At the request of any Party, the Maritime Safety Committee shall establish a date for the consideration of the trial results and for the appropriate determinations.

Regulation I/14

Responsibilities of companies

1 Each Administration shall, in accordance with the provisions of section A-I/14, hold companies responsible for the assignment of seafarers for service on their ships in accordance with the provisions of the present Convention, and shall require every such company to ensure that:

- **.1** each seafarer assigned to any of its ships holds an appropriate certificate in accordance with the provisions of the Convention and as established by the Administration;
- **.2** its ships are manned in compliance with the applicable safe manning requirements of the Administration;
- **.3** seafarers assigned to any of its ships have received refresher and updating training as required by the Convention;
- **.4** documentation and data relevant to all seafarers employed on its ships are maintained and readily accessible, and include, without being limited to, documentation and data on their experience, training, medical fitness and competency in assigned duties;

.5 seafarers, on being assigned to any of its ships, are familiarized with their specific duties and with all ship arrangements, installations, equipment, procedures and ship characteristics that are relevant to their routine or emergency duties;

.6 the ship's complement can effectively coordinate their activities in an emergency situation and in performing functions vital to safety, security and to the prevention or mitigation of pollution; and

.7 at all times on board its ships there shall be effective oral communication in accordance with chapter V, regulation 14, paragraphs 3 and 4 of the International Convention for the Safety of Life at Sea, 1974 (SOLAS), as amended.

Regulation I/15
Transitional provisions

1 Until 1 January 2017, a Party may continue to issue, recognize and endorse certificates in accordance with the provisions of the Convention which applied immediately prior to 1 January 2012 in respect of those seafarers who commenced approved seagoing service, an approved education and training programme or an approved training course before 1 July 2013.

2 Until 1 January 2017, a Party may continue to renew and revalidate certificates and endorsements in accordance with the provisions of the Convention which applied immediately prior to 1 January 2012.

Regulation I/16
Verification of compliance

1 Parties shall use the provisions of the Code for Implementation in the execution of their obligations and responsibilities contained in the present Convention.

2 Every Party shall be subject to periodic audits by the Organization in accordance with the audit standard to verify compliance with and implementation of the present Convention.

3 The Secretary-General of the Organization shall have responsibility for administering the Audit Scheme, based on the guidelines developed by the Organization.

4 Every Party shall have responsibility for facilitating the conduct of the audit and implementation of a programme of actions to address the findings, based on the guidelines developed by the Organization.*

5 Audit of all Parties shall be:

.1 based on an overall schedule developed by the Secretary-General of the Organization, taking into account the guidelines developed by the Organization; and

.2 conducted at periodic intervals, taking into account the guidelines developed by the Organization.*

* Refer to the *Framework and Procedures for the IMO Member State Audit Scheme*, adopted by the Organization by resolution A.1067(28).

Chapter II
Master and deck department

Regulation II/1
Mandatory minimum requirements for certification of officers in charge of a navigational watch on ships of 500 gross tonnage or more

1 Every officer in charge of a navigational watch serving on a seagoing ship of 500 gross tonnage or more shall hold a certificate of competency.

2 Every candidate for certification shall:

.1 be not less than 18 years of age;

.2 have approved seagoing service of not less than 12 months as part of an approved training programme which includes onboard training that meets the requirements of section A-II/1 of the STCW Code and is documented in an approved training record book, or otherwise have approved seagoing service of not less than 36 months;

.3 have performed, during the required seagoing service, bridge watchkeeping duties under the supervision of the master or a qualified officer for a period of not less than six months;

.4 meet the applicable requirements of the regulations in chapter IV, as appropriate, for performing designated radio duties in accordance with the Radio Regulations;

.5 have completed approved education and training and meet the standard of competence specified in section A-II/1 of the STCW Code; and

.6 meet the standard of competence specified in section A-VI/1, paragraph 2, section A-VI/2, paragraphs 1 to 4, section A-VI/3, paragraphs 1 to 4 and section A-VI/4, paragraphs 1 to 3 of the STCW Code.

Regulation II/2
Mandatory minimum requirements for certification of masters and chief mates on ships of 500 gross tonnage or more

Master and chief mate on ships of 3,000 gross tonnage or more

1 Every master and chief mate on a seagoing ship of 3,000 gross tonnage or more shall hold a certificate of competency.

2 Every candidate for certification shall:

.1 meet the requirements for certification as an officer in charge of a navigational watch on ships of 500 gross tonnage or more and have approved seagoing service in that capacity:

.1.1 for certification as chief mate, not less than 12 months, and

.1.2 for certification as master, not less than 36 months; however, this period may be reduced to not less than 24 months if not less than 12 months of such seagoing service has been served as chief mate; and

.2 have completed approved education and training and meet the standard of competence specified in section A-II/2 of the STCW Code for masters and chief mates on ships of 3,000 gross tonnage or more.

Master and chief mate on ships of between 500 and 3,000 gross tonnage

3 Every master and chief mate on a seagoing ship of between 500 and 3,000 gross tonnage shall hold a certificate of competency.

4 Every candidate for certification shall:

.1 for certification as chief mate, meet the requirements of an officer in charge of a navigational watch on ships of 500 gross tonnage or more;

.2 for certification as master, meet the requirements of an officer in charge of a navigational watch on ships of 500 gross tonnage or more and have approved seagoing service of not less than 36 months in that capacity; however, this period may be reduced to not less than 24 months if not less than 12 months of such seagoing service has been served as chief mate; and

.3 have completed approved training and meet the standard of competence specified in section A-II/2 of the STCW Code for masters and chief mates on ships of between 500 and 3,000 gross tonnage.

Regulation II/3

Mandatory minimum requirements for certification of officers in charge of a navigational watch and of masters on ships of less than 500 gross tonnage

Ships not engaged on near-coastal voyages

1 Every officer in charge of a navigational watch serving on a seagoing ship of less than 500 gross tonnage not engaged on near-coastal voyages shall hold a certificate of competency for ships of 500 gross tonnage or more.

deck dept.

2 Every master serving on a seagoing ship of less than 500 gross tonnage not engaged on near-coastal voyages shall hold a certificate of competency for service as master on ships of between 500 and 3,000 gross tonnage.

Ships engaged on near-coastal voyages

Officer in charge of a navigational watch

3 Every officer in charge of a navigational watch on a seagoing ship of less than 500 gross tonnage engaged on near-coastal voyages shall hold a certificate of competency.

4 Every candidate for certification as officer in charge of a navigational watch on a seagoing ship of less than 500 gross tonnage engaged on near-coastal voyages shall:

.1 be not less than 18 years of age;

.2 have completed:

.2.1 special training, including an adequate period of appropriate seagoing service as required by the Administration, or

.2.2 approved seagoing service in the deck department of not less than 36 months;

.3 meet the applicable requirements of the regulations in chapter IV, as appropriate, for performing designated radio duties in accordance with the Radio Regulations;

.4 have completed approved education and training and meet the standard of competence specified in section A-II/3 of the STCW Code for officers in charge of a navigational watch on ships of less than 500 gross tonnage engaged on near-coastal voyages; and

.5 meet the standard of competence specified in section A-VI/1, paragraph 2, section A-VI/2, paragraphs 1 to 4, section A-VI/3, paragraphs 1 to 4 and section A-VI/4, paragraphs 1 to 3 of the STCW Code.

Master

5 Every master serving on a seagoing ship of less than 500 gross tonnage engaged on near-coastal voyages shall hold a certificate of competency.

6 Every candidate for certification as master on a seagoing ship of less than 500 gross tonnage engaged on near-coastal voyages shall:

.1 be not less than 20 years of age;

.2 have approved seagoing service of not less than 12 months as officer in charge of a navigational watch;

.3 have completed approved education and training and meet the standard of competence specified in section A-II/3 of the STCW Code for masters on ships of less than 500 gross tonnage engaged on near-coastal voyages; and

.4 meet the standard of competence specified in section A-VI/1, paragraph 2, section A-VI/2, paragraphs 1 to 4, section A-VI/3, paragraphs 1 to 4 and section A-VI/4, paragraphs 1 to 3 of the STCW Code.

Exemptions

7 The Administration, if it considers that a ship's size and the conditions of its voyage are such as to render the application of the full requirements of this regulation and section A-II/3 of the STCW Code unreasonable or impracticable, may to that extent exempt the master and the officer in charge of a navigational watch on such a ship or class of ships from some of the requirements, bearing in mind the safety of all ships which may be operating in the same waters.

Regulation II/4

Mandatory minimum requirements for certification of ratings forming part of a navigational watch[*]

1 Every rating forming part of a navigational watch on a seagoing ship of 500 gross tonnage or more, other than ratings under training and ratings whose duties while on watch are of an unskilled nature, shall be duly certificated to perform such duties.

2 Every candidate for certification shall:

.1 be not less than 16 years of age;

.2 have completed:

.2.1 approved seagoing service including not less than six months of training and experience, or

.2.2 special training, either pre-sea or on board ship, including an approved period of seagoing service which shall not be less than two months; and

.3 meet the standard of competence specified in section A-II/4 of the STCW Code.

3 The seagoing service, training and experience required by subparagraphs 2.2.1 and 2.2.2 shall be associated with navigational watchkeeping functions and involve the performance of duties carried out under the direct supervision of the master, the officer in charge of the navigational watch or a qualified rating.

[*] These requirements are not those for certification of Able Seamen as contained in the ILO Certification of Able Seamen Convention, 1946, or any subsequent convention.

Regulation II/5

Mandatory minimum requirements for certification of ratings as able seafarer deck

1 Every able seafarer deck serving on a seagoing ship of 500 gross tonnage or more shall be duly certificated.

2 Every candidate for certification shall:

- **.1** be not less than 18 years of age;
- **.2** meet the requirements for certification as a rating forming part of a navigational watch;
- **.3** while qualified to serve as a rating forming part of a navigational watch, have approved seagoing service in the deck department of:
  - **.3.1** not less than 18 months, or
  - **.3.2** not less than 12 months and have completed approved training; and
- **.4** meet the standard of competence specified in section A-II/5 of the STCW Code.

3 Every Party shall compare the standards of competence which it required of Able Seamen for certificates issued before 1 January 2012 with those specified for the certificate in section A-II/5 of the STCW Code, and shall determine the need, if any, for requiring these personnel to update their qualifications.

4 Until 1 January 2012, a Party which is also a Party to the International Labour Organization Certification of Able Seamen Convention, 1946 (No. 74) may continue to issue, recognize and endorse certificates in accordance with the provisions of the aforesaid convention.

5 Until 1 January 2017, a Party which is also a Party to the International Labour Organization Certification of Able Seamen Convention, 1946 (No. 74) may continue to renew and revalidate certificates and endorsements in accordance with the provisions of the aforesaid convention.

6 Seafarers may be considered by the Party to have met the requirements of this regulation if they have served in a relevant capacity in the deck department for a period of not less than 12 months within the last 60 months preceding the entry into force of this regulation for that Party.

Chapter III
Engine department

Regulation III/1
Mandatory minimum requirements for certification of officers in charge of an engineering watch in a manned engine-room or designated duty engineers in a periodically unmanned engine-room

1 Every officer in charge of an engineering watch in a manned engine-room or designated duty engineer officer in a periodically unmanned engine-room on a seagoing ship powered by main propulsion machinery of 750 kW propulsion power or more shall hold a certificate of competency.

2 Every candidate for certification shall:

.1 be not less than 18 years of age;

.2 have completed combined workshop skills training and an approved seagoing service of not less than 12 months as part of an approved training programme which includes onboard training that meets the requirements of section A-III/1 of the STCW Code and is documented in an approved training record book, or otherwise have completed combined workshop skills training and an approved seagoing service of not less than 36 months of which not less than 30 months shall be seagoing service in the engine department;

.3 have performed, during the required seagoing service, engine-room watchkeeping duties under the supervision of the chief engineer officer or a qualified engineer officer for a period of not less than six months;

.4 have completed approved education and training and meet the standard of competence specified in section A-III/1 of the STCW Code; and

.5 meet the standard of competence specified in section A-VI/1, paragraph 2, section A-VI/2, paragraphs 1 to 4, section A-VI/3, paragraphs 1 to 4 and section A-VI/4, paragraphs 1 to 3 of the STCW Code.

Regulation III/2
Mandatory minimum requirements for certification of chief engineer officers and second engineer officers on ships powered by main propulsion machinery of 3,000 kW propulsion power or more

1 Every chief engineer officer and second engineer officer on a seagoing ship powered by main propulsion machinery of 3,000 kW propulsion power or more shall hold a certificate of competency.

2 Every candidate for certification shall:

.1 meet the requirements for certification as an officer in charge of an engineering watch on seagoing ships powered by main propulsion machinery of 750 kW propulsion power or more and have approved seagoing service in that capacity:

.1.1 for certification as second engineer officer, have not less than 12 months as qualified engineer officer, and

.1.2 for certification as chief engineer officer, have not less than 36 months; however, this period may be reduced to not less than 24 months if not less than 12 months of such seagoing service has been served as second engineer officer; and

.2 have completed approved education and training and meet the standard of competence specified in section A-III/2 of the STCW Code.

Regulation III/3

Mandatory minimum requirements for certification of chief engineer officers and second engineer officers on ships powered by main propulsion machinery of between 750 kW and 3,000 kW propulsion power

1 Every chief engineer officer and second engineer officer on a seagoing ship powered by main propulsion machinery of between 750 kW and 3,000 kW propulsion power shall hold a certificate of competency.

2 Every candidate for certification shall:

.1 meet the requirements for certification as an officer in charge of an engineering watch and:

.1.1 for certification as second engineer officer, have not less than 12 months of approved seagoing service as assistant engineer officer or engineer officer, and

.1.2 for certification as chief engineer officer, have not less than 24 months of approved seagoing service of which not less than 12 months shall be served while qualified to serve as second engineer officer; and

.2 have completed approved education and training and meet the standard of competence specified in section A-III/3 of the STCW Code.

3 Every engineer officer who is qualified to serve as second engineer officer on ships powered by main propulsion machinery of 3,000 kW propulsion power or more may serve as chief engineer officer on ships powered by main propulsion machinery of less than 3,000 kW propulsion power, provided the certificate is so endorsed.

Regulation III/4

Mandatory minimum requirements for certification of ratings forming part of a watch in a manned engine-room or designated to perform duties in a periodically unmanned engine-room

1 Every rating forming part of an engine-room watch or designated to perform duties in a periodically unmanned engine-room on a seagoing ship powered by main propulsion machinery of 750 kW propulsion power or more, other than ratings under training and ratings whose duties are of an unskilled nature, shall be duly certificated to perform such duties.

2 Every candidate for certification shall:

.1 be not less than 16 years of age;

.2 have completed:

.2.1 approved seagoing service including not less than six months of training and experience, or

.2.2 special training, either pre-sea or on board ship, including an approved period of seagoing service which shall not be less than two months; and

.3 meet the standard of competence specified in section A-III/4 of the STCW Code.

3 The seagoing service, training and experience required by subparagraphs 2.2.1 and 2.2.2 shall be associated with engine-room watchkeeping functions and involve the performance of duties carried out under the direct supervision of a qualified engineer officer or a qualified rating.

Regulation III/5

Mandatory minimum requirements for certification of ratings as able seafarer engine in a manned engine-room or designated to perform duties in a periodically unmanned engine-room

1 Every able seafarer engine serving on a seagoing ship powered by main propulsion machinery of 750 kW propulsion power or more shall be duly certificated.

2 Every candidate for certification shall:

.1 be not less than 18 years of age;

.2 meet the requirements for certification as a rating forming part of a watch in a manned engine-room or designated to perform duties in a periodically unmanned engine-room;

.3 while qualified to serve as a rating forming part of an engineering watch, have approved seagoing service in the engine department of:

.3.1 not less than 12 months, or

.3.2 not less than 6 months and have completed approved training; and

.4 meet the standard of competence specified in section A-III/5 of the STCW Code.

3 Every Party shall compare the standars of competence which it required of ratings in the engine department for certificates issued before 1 January 2012 with those specified for the certificate in section A-III/5 of the STCW Code, and shall determine the need, if any, for requiring these personnel to update their qualifications.

4 Seafarers may be considered by the Party to have met the requirements of this regulation if they have served in a relevant capacity in the engine department for a period of not less than 12 months within the last 60 months preceding the entry into force of this regulation for that Party.

Regulation III/6

Mandatory minimum requirements for certification of electro-technical officers

1 Every electro-technical officer serving on a seagoing ship powered by main propulsion machinery of 750 kW propulsion power or more shall hold a certificate of competency.

2 Every candidate for certification shall:

.1 be not less than 18 years of age;

.2 have completed not less than 12 months of combined workshop skills training and approved seagoing service of which not less than 6 months shall be seagoing service as part of an approved training programme which meets the requirements of section A-III/6 of the STCW Code and is documented in an approved training record book, or otherwise not less than 36 months of combined workshop skills training and approved seagoing service of which not less than 30 months shall be seagoing service in the engine department;

.3 have completed approved education and training and meet the standard of competence specified in section A-III/6 of the STCW Code; and

.4 meet the standard of competence specified in section A-VI/1, paragraph 2, section A-VI/2, paragraphs 1 to 4, section A-VI/3, paragraphs 1 to 4 and section A-VI/4, paragraphs 1 to 3 of the STCW Code.

3 Every Party shall compare the standard of competence which it required of electro-technical officers for certificates issued before 1 January 2012 with those specified for the certificate in section A-III/6 of the STCW Code, and shall determine the need for requiring those personnel to update their qualifications.

4 Seafarers may be considered by the Party to have met the requirements of this regulation if they have served in a relevant capacity on board a ship for a period of not less than 12 months within the last 60 months preceding the entry into force of this regulation for that Party and meet the standard of competence specified in section A-III/6 of the STCW Code.

5 Notwithstanding the above requirements of paragraphs 1 to 4, a suitably qualified person may be considered by a Party to be able to perform certain functions of section A-III/6.

Regulation III/7

Mandatory minimum requirements for certification of electro-technical ratings

1 Every electro-technical rating serving on a seagoing ship powered by main propulsion machinery of 750 kW propulsion power or more shall be duly certificated.

2 Every candidate for certification shall:

- **.1** be not less than 18 years of age;
- **.2** have:
  - **.2.1** completed approved seagoing service including not less than 12 months training and experience, or
  - **.2.2** completed approved training, including an approved period of seagoing service which shall not be less than 6 months, or
  - **.2.3** qualifications that meet the technical competences in table A-III/7 and an approved period of seagoing service, which shall not be less than 3 months; and
- **.3** meet the standard of competence specified in section A-III/7 of the STCW Code.

3 Every Party shall compare the standard of competence which it required of electro-technical ratings for certificates issued before 1 January 2012 with those specified for the certificate in section A-III/7 of the STCW Code, and shall determine the need, if any, for requiring these personnel to update their qualifications.

4 Seafarers may be considered by the Party to have met the requirements of this regulation if they have served in a relevant capacity on board a ship for a period of not less than 12 months within the last 60 months preceding the entry into force of this regulation for that Party and meet the standard of competence specified in section A-III/7 of the STCW Code.

5 Notwithstanding the above requirements of paragraphs 1 to 4, a suitably qualified person may be considered by a Party to be able to perform certain functions of section A-III/7.

Chapter IV
Radiocommunication and radio operators

Explanatory note

Mandatory provisions relating to radio watchkeeping are set forth in the Radio Regulations and in the International Convention for the Safety of Life at Sea, 1974 (SOLAS), as amended. Provisions for radio maintenance are set forth in the International Convention for the Safety of Life at Sea, 1974, as amended, and the guidelines adopted by the Organization.*

Regulation IV/1
Application

1 Except as provided in paragraph 2, the provisions of this chapter apply to radio operators on ships operating in the global maritime distress and safety system (GMDSS) as prescribed by the International Convention for the Safety of Life at Sea, 1974, as amended.

2 Radio operators on ships not required to comply with the provisions of the GMDSS in chapter IV of the SOLAS Convention are not required to meet the provisions of this chapter. Radio operators on these ships are, nevertheless, required to comply with the Radio Regulations. The Administration shall ensure that the appropriate certificates as prescribed by the Radio Regulations are issued to or recognized in respect of such radio operators.

Regulation IV/2
Mandatory minimum requirements for certification of GMDSS radio operators

1 Every person in charge of or performing radio duties on a ship required to participate in the GMDSS shall hold an appropriate certificate related to the GMDSS, issued or recognized by the Administration under the provisions of the Radio Regulations.

2 In addition, every candidate for certification of competency under this regulation for service on a ship, which is required by the International Convention for the Safety of Life at Sea, 1974, as amended, to have a radio installation, shall:

- **.1** be not less than 18 years of age; and
- **.2** have completed approved education and training and meet the standard of competence specified in section A-IV/2 of the STCW Code.

* Refer to the *Radio maintenance guidelines for the Global Maritime Distress and Safety System* (GMDSS) *related to sea areas A3 and A4* adopted by the Organization by resolution A.702(17), as amended.

Chapter V
Special training requirements for personnel on certain types of ships

Regulation V/1-1
Mandatory minimum requirements for the training and qualifications of masters, officers and ratings on oil and chemical tankers

1 Officers and ratings assigned specific duties and responsibilities related to cargo or cargo equipment on oil or chemical tankers shall hold a certificate in basic training for oil and chemical tanker cargo operations.

2 Every candidate for a certificate in basic training for oil and chemical tanker cargo operations shall have completed basic training in accordance with provisions of section A-VI/1 of the STCW Code and shall have completed:

.1 at least three months of approved seagoing service on oil or chemical tankers and meet the standard of competence specified in section A-V/1-1, paragraph 1 of the STCW Code; or

.2 an approved basic training for oil and chemical tanker cargo operations and meet the standard of competence specified in section A-V/1-1, paragraph 1 of the STCW Code.

3 Masters, chief engineer officers, chief mates, second engineer officers and any person with immediate responsibility for loading, discharging, care in transit, handling of cargo, tank cleaning or other cargo-related operations on oil tankers shall hold a certificate in advanced training for oil tanker cargo operations.

4 Every candidate for a certificate in advanced training for oil tanker cargo operations shall:

.1 meet the requirements for certification in basic training for oil and chemical tanker cargo operations; and

.2 while qualified for certification in basic training for oil and chemical tanker cargo operations, have:

.2.1 at least three months of approved seagoing service on oil tankers, or

.2.2 at least one month of approved onboard training on oil tankers, in a supernumerary capacity, which includes at least three loading and three unloading operations and is documented in an approved training record book taking into account guidance in section B-V/1; and

.3 have completed approved advanced training for oil tanker cargo operations and meet the standard of competence specified in section A-V/1-1, paragraph 2 of the STCW Code.

5 Masters, chief engineer officers, chief mates, second engineer officers and any person with immediate responsibility for loading, discharging, care in transit, handling of cargo, tank cleaning or other cargo-related operations on chemical tankers shall hold a certificate in advanced training for chemical tanker cargo operations.

6 Every candidate for a certificate in advanced training for chemical tanker cargo operations shall:

.1 meet the requirements for certification in basic training for oil and chemical tanker cargo operations; and

.2 while qualified for certification in basic training for oil and chemical tanker cargo operations, have:

.2.1 at least three months of approved seagoing service on chemical tankers, or

.2.2 at least one month of approved onboard training on chemical tankers, in a supernumerary capacity, which includes at least three loading and three unloading operations and is documented in an approved training record book taking into account guidance in section B-V/1; and

.3 have completed approved advanced training for chemical tanker cargo operations and meet the standard of competence specified in section A-V/1-1, paragraph 3 of the STCW Code.

7 Administrations shall ensure that a certificate of proficiency is issued to seafarers, who are qualified in accordance with paragraphs 2, 4 or 6 as appropriate, or that an existing certificate of competency or certificate of proficiency is duly endorsed.

Regulation V/1-2

Mandatory minimum requirements for the training and qualifications of masters, officers and ratings on liquefied gas tankers

1 Officers and ratings assigned specific duties and responsibilities related to cargo or cargo equipment on liquefied gas tankers shall hold a certificate in basic training for liquefied gas tanker cargo operations.

2 Every candidate for a certificate in basic training for liquefied gas tanker cargo operations shall have completed basic training in accordance with provisions of section A-VI/1 of the STCW Code and shall have completed:

.1 at least three months of approved seagoing service on liquefied gas tankers and meet the standard of competence specified in section A-V/1-2, paragraph 1 of the STCW Code; or

.2 an approved basic training for liquefied gas tanker cargo operations and meet the standard of competence specified in section A-V/1-2, paragraph 1 of the STCW Code.

3 Masters, chief engineer officers, chief mates, second engineer officers and any person with immediate responsibility for loading, discharging, care in transit, handling of cargo, tank cleaning or other cargo-related operations on liquefied gas tankers shall hold a certificate in advanced training for liquefied gas tanker cargo operations.

4 Every candidate for a certificate in advanced training for liquefied gas tanker cargo operations shall:

.1 meet the requirements for certification in basic training for liquefied gas tanker cargo operations; and

.2 while qualified for certification in basic training for liquefied gas tanker cargo operations, have:

.2.1 at least three months of approved seagoing service on liquefied gas tankers, or

.2.2 at least one month of approved onboard training on liquefied gas tankers, in a supernumerary capacity, which includes at least three loading and three unloading operations and is documented in an approved training record book taking into account guidance in section B-V/1; and

.3 have completed approved advanced training for liquefied gas tanker cargo operations and meet the standard of competence specified in section A-V/1-2, paragraph 2 of the STCW Code.

5 Administrations shall ensure that a certificate of proficiency is issued to seafarers, who are qualified in accordance with paragraphs 2 or 4 as appropriate, or that an existing certificate of competency or certificate of proficiency is duly endorsed.

Regulation V/2

Mandatory minimum requirements for the training and qualifications of masters, officers, ratings and other personnel on passenger ships

1 This regulation applies to masters, officers, ratings and other personnel serving on board passenger ships engaged on international voyages. Administrations shall determine the applicability of these requirements to personnel serving on passenger ships engaged on domestic voyages.

2 Before being assigned shipboard duties, all persons serving on a passenger ship shall meet the requirements of section A-VI/1, paragraph 1 of the STCW Code.

3 Masters, officers, ratings and other personnel serving on board passenger ships shall complete the training and familiarization required by paragraphs 5 to 9 below, in accordance with their capacity, duties and responsibilities.

4 Masters, officers, ratings and other personnel, who are required to be trained in accordance with paragraphs 7 to 9 below shall, at intervals not exceeding five years, undertake appropriate refresher training or be required to provide evidence of having achieved the required standard of competence within the previous five years.

5 Personnel serving on board passenger ships shall complete passenger ship emergency familiarization appropriate to their capacity, duties and responsibilities as specified in section A-V/2, paragraph 1 of the STCW Code.

6 Personnel providing direct service to passengers in passenger spaces on board passenger ships shall complete the safety training specified in section A-V/2, paragraph 2 of the STCW Code.

7 Masters, officers, ratings qualified in accordance with chapters II, III and VII and other personnel designated on the muster list to assist passengers in emergency situations on board passenger ships, shall complete passenger ship crowd management training as specified in section A-V/2, paragraph 3 of the STCW Code.

8 Masters, chief engineer officers, chief mates, second engineer officers and any person designated on the muster list of having responsibility for the safety of passengers in emergency situations on board passenger ships shall complete approved training in crisis management and human behaviour as specified in section A-V/2, paragraph 4 of the STCW Code.

9 Masters, chief engineer officers, chief mates, second engineer officers and every person assigned immediate responsibility for embarking and disembarking passengers, for loading, discharging or securing cargo, or for closing hull openings on board ro-ro passenger ships, shall complete approved training in passenger safety, cargo safety and hull integrity as specified in section A-V/2, paragraph 5 of the STCW Code.

10 Administrations shall ensure that documentary evidence of the training which has been completed is issued to every person found qualified in accordance with paragraphs 6 to 9 of this regulation.

Regulation V/3

Mandatory minimum requirements for the training and qualifications of masters, officers, ratings and other personnel on ships subject to the IGF Code

1 This regulation applies to masters, officers and ratings and other personnel serving on board ships subject to the IGF Code.

2 Prior to being assigned shipboard duties on board ships subject to the IGF Code, seafarers shall have completed the training required by paragraphs 4 to 9 below in accordance with their capacity, duties and responsibilities.

3 All seafarers serving on board ships subject to the IGF Code shall, prior to being assigned shipboard duties, receive appropriate ship and equipment specific familiarization as specified in regulation I/14, paragraph 1.5.

4 Seafarers responsible for designated safety duties associated with the care, use or in emergency response to the fuel on board ships subject to the IGF Code shall hold a certificate in basic training for service on ships subject to the IGF Code.

5 Every candidate for a certificate in basic training for service on ships subject to the IGF Code shall have completed basic training in accordance with provisions of section A-V/3, paragraph 1 of the STCW Code.

6 Seafarers responsible for designated safety duties associated with the care, use or in emergency response to the fuel on board ships subject to the IGF Code who have been qualified and certified according to regulation V/1-2, paragraphs 2 and 5, or regulation V/1-2, paragraphs 4 and 5 on liquefied gas tankers, are to be considered as having met the requirements specified in section A-V/3, paragraph 1 for basic training for service on ships subject to the IGF Code.

7 Masters, engineer officers and all personnel with immediate responsibility for the care and use of fuels and fuel systems on ships subject to the IGF Code shall hold a certificate in advanced training for service on ships subject to the IGF Code.

8 Every candidate for a certificate in advanced training for service on ships subject to the IGF Code shall, while holding the Certificate of Proficiency described in paragraph 4, have:

- **.1** completed approved advanced training for service on ships subject to the IGF Code and meet the standard of competence as specified in section A-V/3, paragraph 2 of the STCW Code; and
- **.2** completed at least one month of approved seagoing service that includes a minimum of three bunkering operations on board ships subject to the IGF Code. Two of the three bunkering operations may be replaced by approved simulator training on bunkering operations as part of the training in paragraph 8.1 above.

9 Masters, engineer officers and any person with immediate responsibility for the care and use of fuels on ships subject to the IGF Code who have been qualified and certified according to the standards of competence specified in section A–V/1-2, paragraph 2 for service on liquefied gas tankers are to be considered as having met the requirements specified in section A-V/3, paragraph 2 for advanced training for ships subject to the IGF Code, provided they have also:

- **.1** met the requirements of paragraph 6; and
- **.2** met the bunkering requirements of paragraph 8.2 or have participated in conducting three cargo operations on board the liquefied gas tanker; and
- **.3** have completed sea going service of three months in the previous five years on board:
  - **.1** ships subject to the IGF Code;
  - **.2** tankers carrying as cargo, fuels covered by the IGF Code; or
  - **.3** ships using gases or low flashpoint fuel as fuel.

10 Every Party shall compare the standards of competence which it required of persons serving on gas-fuelled ships before 1 January 2017 with the standards of competence in Section A-V/3 of the STCW Code, and shall determine the need, if any, for requiring these personnel to update their qualifications.

11 Administrations shall ensure that a Certificate of Proficiency is issued to seafarers, who are qualified in accordance with paragraphs 4 or 7, as appropriate.

12 Seafarers holding Certificates of Proficiency in accordance with paragraph 4 or 7 above shall, at intervals not exceeding five years, undertake appropriate refresher training or be required to provide evidence of having achieved the required standard of competence within the previous five years.

Regulation V/4

Mandatory minimum requirements for the training and qualifications of masters and deck officers on ships operating in polar waters

1 Masters, chief mates and officers in charge of a navigational watch on ships operating in polar waters shall hold a certificate in basic training for ships operating in polar waters, as required by the Polar Code.

2 Every candidate for a certificate in basic training for ships operating in polar waters shall have completed an approved basic training for ships operating in polar waters and meet the standard of competence specified in section A-V/4, paragraph 1, of the STCW Code.

3 Masters and chief mates on ships operating in polar waters, shall hold a certificate in advanced training for ships operating in polar waters, as required by the Polar Code.

4 Every candidate for a certificate in advanced training for ships operating in polar waters shall:

- **.1** meet the requirements for certification in basic training for ships in polar waters;
- **.2** have at least two (2) months of approved seagoing service in the deck department, at management level or while performing watchkeeping duties at the operational level, within polar waters or other equivalent approved seagoing service; and
- **.3** have completed approved advanced training for ships operating in polar waters and meet the standard of competence specified in section A-V/4, paragraph 2 of the STCW Code.

5 Administrations shall ensure that a Certificate of Proficiency is issued to seafarers who are qualified in accordance with paragraphs 2 or 4, as appropriate.

Transitional provisions

6 Until 1 July 2020, seafarers who commenced approved seagoing service in polar waters prior to 1 July 2018 shall be able to establish that they meet the requirements of paragraph 2 by:

- **.1** having completed approved seagoing service on board a ship operating in polar waters or equivalent approved seagoing service, performing duties in the deck department at the operational or management level, for a period of at least three months in total during the preceding five years; or
- **.2** having successfully completed a training course meeting the training guidance established by the Organization for ships operating in polar waters.*

7 Until 1 July 2020, seafarers who commenced approved seagoing service in polar waters prior to 1 July 2018 shall be able to establish that they meet the requirements of paragraph 4 by:

- **.1** having completed approved seagoing service on board a ship operating in polar waters or equivalent approved seagoing service, performing duties in the deck department at management level, for a period of at least three months in total during the preceding five years; or
- **.2** having successfully completed a training course meeting the training guidance established by the Organization for ships operating in polar waters* and having completed approved seagoing service on board a ship operating in polar waters or equivalent approved seagoing service, performing duties in the deck department at the management level, for a period of at least two months in total during the preceding five years.

* Refer to section B-V/g of the STCW Code.

Chapter VI
Emergency, occupational safety, security, medical care and survival functions

Regulation VI/1
Mandatory minimum requirements for safety familiarization, basic training and instruction for all seafarers

1 Seafarers shall receive safety familiarization and basic training or instruction in accordance with section A-VI/1 of the STCW Code and shall meet the appropriate standard of competence specified therein.

2 Where basic training is not included in the qualification for the certificate to be issued, a certificate of proficiency shall be issued, indicating that the holder has attended the course in basic training.

A. Chapter VI Regulation 1

Regulation VI/2
Mandatory minimum requirements for the issue of certificates of proficiency in survival craft, rescue boats and fast rescue boats

1 Every candidate for a certificate of proficiency in survival craft and rescue boats other than fast rescue boats shall:

- **.1** be not less than 18 years of age;
- **.2** have approved seagoing service of not less than 12 months or have attended an approved training course and have approved seagoing service of not less than six months; and
- **.3** meet the standard of competence for certificates of proficiency in survival craft and rescue boats, set out in section A-VI/2, paragraphs 1 to 4 of the STCW Code.

2 Every candidate for a certificate of proficiency in fast rescue boats shall:

- **.1** be the holder of a certificate of proficiency in survival craft and rescue boats other than fast rescue boats;
- **.2** have attended an approved training course; and
- **.3** meet the standard of competence for certificates of proficiency in fast rescue boats, set out in section A-VI/2, paragraphs 7 to 10 of the STCW Code.

Regulation VI/3
Mandatory minimum requirements for training in advanced fire fighting

1 Seafarers designated to control fire-fighting operations shall have successfully completed advanced training in techniques for fighting fire, with particular emphasis on organization, tactics and command, in accordance with the provisions of section A-VI/3, paragraphs 1 to 4 of the STCW Code and shall meet the standard of competence specified therein.

2 Where training in advanced fire fighting is not included in the qualifications for the certificate to be issued, a certificate of proficiency shall be issued indicating that the holder has attended a course of training in advanced fire fighting.

Regulation VI/4
Mandatory minimum requirements relating to medical first aid and medical care

1 Seafarers designated to provide medical first aid on board ship shall meet the standard of competence in medical first aid specified in section A-VI/4, paragraphs 1 to 3 of the STCW Code.

2 Seafarers designated to take charge of medical care on board ship shall meet the standard of competence in medical care on board ships specified in section A-VI/4, paragraphs 4 to 6 of the STCW Code.

3 Where training in medical first aid or medical care is not included in the qualifications for the certificate to be issued, a certificate of proficiency shall be issued indicating that the holder has attended a course of training in medical first aid or in medical care.

Regulation VI/5

Mandatory minimum requirements for the issue of certificates of proficiency for ship security officers

1 Every candidate for a certificate of proficiency as ship security officer shall:

- **.1** have approved seagoing service of not less than 12 months or appropriate seagoing service and knowledge of ship operations; and
- **.2** meet the standard of competence for certification of proficiency as ship security officer, set out in section A-VI/5, paragraphs 1 to 4 of the STCW Code.

2 Administrations shall ensure that every person found qualified under the provisions of this regulation is issued with a certificate of proficiency.

Regulation VI/6

Mandatory minimum requirements for security-related training and instruction for all seafarers

1 Seafarers shall receive security-related familiarization and security-awareness training or instruction in accordance with section A-VI/6, paragraphs 1 to 4 of the STCW Code and shall meet the appropriate standard of competence specified therein.

2 Where security awareness is not included in the qualification for the certificate to be issued, a certificate of proficiency shall be issued indicating that the holder has attended a course in security awareness training.

3 Every Party shall compare the security-related training or instruction it requires of seafarers who hold or can document qualifications before the entry into force of this regulation with those specified in section A-VI/6, paragraph 4 of the STCW Code, and shall determine the need for requiring these seafarers to update their qualifications.

Seafarers with designated security duties

4 Seafarers with designated security duties shall meet the standard of competence specified in section A-VI/6, paragraphs 6 to 8 of the STCW Code.

5 Where training in designated security duties is not included in the qualifications for the certificate to be issued, a certificate of proficiency shall be issued indicating that the holder has attended a course of training for designated security duties.

6 Every Party shall compare the security training standards required of seafarers with designated security duties who hold or can document qualifications before the entry into force of this regulation with those specified in section A-VI/6, paragraph 8 of the STCW Code, and shall determine the need for requiring these seafarers to update their qualifications.

Chapter VII
Alternative certification

Regulation VII/1
Issue of alternative certificates

1 Notwithstanding the requirements for certification laid down in chapters II and III of this annex, Parties may elect to issue or authorize the issue of certificates other than those mentioned in the regulations of those chapters, provided that:

.1 the associated functions and levels of responsibility to be stated on the certificates and in the endorsements are selected from and identical to those appearing in sections A-II/1, A-II/2, A-II/3, A-II/4, A-II/5, A-III/1, A-III/2, A-III/3, A-III/4, A-III/5 and A-IV/2 of the STCW Code;

.2 the candidates have completed approved education and training and meet the requirements for standards of competence, prescribed in the relevant sections of the STCW Code and as set forth in section A-VII/1 of this Code, for the functions and levels that are to be stated in the certificates and in the endorsements;

.3 the candidates have completed approved seagoing service appropriate to the performance of the functions and levels that are to be stated on the certificate. The minimum duration of seagoing service shall be equivalent to the duration of seagoing service prescribed in chapters II and III of this annex. However, the minimum duration of seagoing service shall be not less than as prescribed in section A-VII/2 of the STCW Code;

.4 the candidates for certification who are to perform the function of navigation at the operational level shall meet the applicable requirements of the regulations in chapter IV, as appropriate, for performing designated radio duties in accordance with the Radio Regulations; and

.5 the certificates are issued in accordance with the requirements of regulation I/2 and the provisions set forth in chapter VII of the STCW Code.

2 No certificate shall be issued under this chapter unless the Party has communicated information to the Organization in accordance with article IV and regulation I/7.

Regulation VII/2
Certification of seafarers

1 Every seafarer who performs any function or group of functions specified in tables A-II/1, A-II/2, A-II/3, A-II/4 or A-II/5 of chapter II or in tables A-III/1, A-III/2, A-III/3, A-III/4 or A-III/5 of chapter III or A-IV/2 of chapter IV of the STCW Code shall hold a certificate of competency or certificate of proficiency, as applicable.

Regulation VII/3
Principles governing the issue of alternative certificates

1 Any Party which elects to issue or authorize the issue of alternative certificates shall ensure that the following principles are observed:

.1 no alternative certification system shall be implemented unless it ensures a degree of safety at sea and has a preventive effect as regards pollution at least equivalent to that provided by the other chapters; and

.2 any arrangement for alternative certification issued under this chapter shall provide for the interchangeability of certificates with those issued under the other chapters.

2 The principle of interchangeability in paragraph 1 shall ensure that:

.1 seafarers certificated under the arrangements of chapters II and/or III and those certificated under chapter VII are able to serve on ships which have either traditional or other forms of shipboard organization; and

.2 seafarers are not trained for specific shipboard arrangements in such a way as would impair their ability to take their skills elsewhere.

3 In issuing any certificate under the provisions of this chapter, the following principles shall be taken into account:

.1 the issue of alternative certificates shall not be used in itself:

.1.1 to reduce the number of crew on board,

.1.2 to lower the integrity of the profession or "de-skill" seafarers, or

.1.3 to justify the assignment of the combined duties of the engine and deck watchkeeping officers to a single certificate holder during any particular watch; and

.2 the person in command shall be designated as the master; and the legal position and authority of the master and others shall not be adversely affected by the implementation of any arrangement for alternative certification.

4 The principles contained in paragraphs 1 and 2 of this regulation shall ensure that the competency of both deck and engineer officers is maintained.

Chapter VIII
Watchkeeping

Regulation VIII/1
Fitness for duty

1 Each Administration shall, for the purpose of preventing fatigue:

.1 establish and enforce rest periods for watchkeeping personnel and those whose duties involve designated safety, security and prevention of pollution duties in accordance with the provisions of section A-VIII/1 of the STCW Code; and

.2 require that watch systems are so arranged that the efficiency of all watchkeeping personnel is not impaired by fatigue and that duties are so organized that the first watch at the commencement of a voyage and subsequent relieving watches are sufficiently rested and otherwise fit for duty.

2 Each Administration shall, for the purpose of preventing drug and alcohol abuse, ensure that adequate measures are established in accordance with the provisions of section A-VIII/1 while taking into account the guidance given in section B-VIII/1 of the STCW Code.

Regulation VIII/2
Watchkeeping arrangements and principles to be observed

1 Administrations shall direct the attention of companies, masters, chief engineer officers and all watchkeeping personnel to the requirements, principles and guidance set out in the STCW Code which shall be observed to ensure that a safe continuous watch or watches appropriate to the prevailing circumstances and conditions are maintained on all seagoing ships at all times.

2 Administrations shall require the master of every ship to ensure that watchkeeping arrangements are adequate for maintaining a safe watch or watches, taking into account the prevailing circumstances and conditions and that, under the master's general direction:

.1 officers in charge of the navigational watch are responsible for navigating the ship safely during their periods of duty, when they shall be physically present on the navigating bridge or in a directly associated location such as the chartroom or bridge control room at all times;

.2 radio operators are responsible for maintaining a continuous radio watch on appropriate frequencies during their periods of duty;

.3 officers in charge of an engineering watch, as defined in the STCW Code, under the direction of the chief engineer officer, shall be immediately available and on call to attend the machinery spaces and, when required, shall be physically present in the machinery space during their periods of responsibility;

.4 an appropriate and effective watch or watches are maintained for the purpose of safety at all times, while the ship is at anchor or moored and, if the ship is carrying hazardous cargo, the organization of such watch or watches takes full account of the nature, quantity, packing and stowage of the hazardous cargo and of any special conditions prevailing on board, afloat or ashore; and

.5 as applicable, an appropriate and effective watch or watches are maintained for the purposes of security.

Attachment 3 to the Final Act of the 2010 STCW Conference

Resolution 3

Expression of appreciation to the host Government

THE 2010 MANILA CONFERENCE,

NOTING with appreciation the kind invitation of the Government of the Philippines to the International Maritime Organization to hold the International Conference to adopt amendments to the International Convention on Standards of Training, Certification and Watchkeeping for Seafarers, 1978, and the Seafarers Training, Certification and Watchkeeping Code,

ACKNOWLEDGING the generous financial and in-kind contribution and excellent arrangements made by the Government of the Philippines for the Conference, as well as the hospitality, courtesies and other amenities bestowed on the Participants to the Conference,

1. EXPRESSES its profound gratitude and thanks to the Government and the People of the Philippines for their valuable contribution to the success of the Conference;

2. DECIDES, in grateful recognition of this contribution, to designate the amendments adopted by the Conference as:

> "The Manila Amendments to the International Convention on Standards of Training, Certification and Watchkeeping for Seafarers, 1978".

Resolution 4

Transitional provisions and early implementation

THE 2010 MANILA CONFERENCE,

HAVING ADOPTED the Manila amendments to the International Convention on Standards of Training, Certification and Watchkeeping for Seafarers, 1978, and to the Seafarers' Training, Certification and Watchkeeping Code, as amended (STCW Convention and Code),

HAVING AGREED to include regulation I/15 on Transitional provisions, which allows for an interval of five years, or until the time of the next revalidation of certificate(s) of competency after the amendments have entered into force, whichever is later, before Parties will be required to issue, recognize and endorse certificates in accordance with the amendments adopted by the Conference,

RECOGNIZING that, in order to achieve full compliance by 1 January 2017, it is necessary for Parties to promptly begin taking appropriate measures to implement the STCW Convention and Code in their national training, certification and administration systems,

BEING CONCERNED that difficulties, which may arise in connection with the implementation of the requirements of the STCW Convention and Code, could undermine the objective of introducing the highest practicable standards of competence at the earliest possible time,

1. URGES each Party to keep the Maritime Safety Committee of the International Maritime Organization informed of progress made in respect of the transitional provisions of regulation I/15 under its national system to implement the requirements of the amendments to the STCW Convention and Code, adopted by the Conference, as well as any difficulties encountered in this regard;

2. FURTHER URGES each Party to take appropriate steps for early implementation of the amendments to the STCW Convention and Code adopted by the Conference;

3. INVITES the Maritime Safety Committee of the International Maritime Organization, in order to promote the introduction of the highest practicable standards of competence as soon as possible, to monitor progress toward implementation of the STCW Convention and Code by all Parties, with the aim of encouraging an orderly transition and anticipating complications, which could otherwise undermine full and effective implementation.

Resolution 5

Verification of certificates of competency and endorsements

THE 2010 MANILA CONFERENCE,

HAVING ADOPTED the Manila amendments to the International Convention on Standards of Training, Certification and Watchkeeping for Seafarers, 1978, and to the Seafarers' Training, Certification and Watchkeeping Code, as amended,

RECOGNIZING the importance of adequate education and training for, and experience acquired by, all seafarers,

RECOGNIZING ALSO the need for all ships to be manned and operated by properly trained and certified seafarers,

RECOGNIZING FURTHER that the verification of certificates of competency and endorsements issued to seafarers is essential also from the point of view of preventing unlawful practices associated with the issuance of such certificates as well as to supporting port State control activities,

RECOMMENDS that Administrations take appropriate steps to:

.1 establish electronic databases to assist in verifying the authenticity and validity of certificates of competency and endorsements they issue; and

.2 respond appropriately and in a timely manner to any request from other Administrations for verification of the authenticity and validity of certificates of competency and endorsements.

Resolution 6

Standards of training and certification and ships' manning levels

THE 2010 MANILA CONFERENCE,

HAVING ADOPTED the Manila amendments to the International Convention on Standards of Training, Certification and Watchkeeping for Seafarers, 1978, and to the Seafarers' Training, Certification and Watchkeeping Code, as amended (STCW Convention and Code),

RECOGNIZING the importance of adequate education and training for, and experience acquired by, all seafarers,

RECOGNIZING ALSO the need for all ships to be manned and operated by properly trained and certified seafarers,

NOTING that the STCW Convention and Code establish standards of training, certification and watchkeeping for seafarers,

1. REAFFIRMS that the STCW Convention and Code are instruments concerned with standards of training and certification and do not determine ships' manning levels;

2. REAFFIRMS ALSO that any decision relating to ships' manning levels is the responsibility of the Administrations and shipowners concerned taking into account the principles of safe manning* adopted by the International Maritime Organization.

Resolution 7

Promotion of technical knowledge, skills and professionalism of seafarers

THE 2010 MANILA CONFERENCE,

HAVING ADOPTED the Manila amendments to the International Convention on Standards of Training, Certification and Watchkeeping for Seafarers, 1978, and to the Seafarers' Training, Certification and Watchkeeping Code, as amended (STCW Convention and Code),

NOTING with concern the reported and anticipated shortage of qualified officers to effectively man and operate ships engaged in international trade,

APPRECIATING that the overall effectiveness of selection, training and certification processes can only be evaluated through the skills, abilities and competence exhibited by seafarers during the course of their service on board ship,

RECOMMENDS that Administrations make arrangements to ensure that shipping companies:

.1 establish criteria and processes for the selection of seafarers exhibiting the highest practicable standards of technical knowledge, skills and professionalism;

* Refers to resolution A.890(21), as amended, on *Principles of safe manning*, adopted by the Assembly of the International Maritime Organization on 25 November 1999.

.2 monitor the standards exhibited by ships' personnel in the performance of their duties;

.3 encourage all officers serving on their ships to participate actively in the training of junior personnel;

.4 monitor carefully and review frequently the progress made by junior personnel in the acquisition of knowledge and skills during their service on board ship;

.5 provide refresher and updating training at suitable intervals, as may be required; and

.6 take all appropriate measures to instil pride in the maritime profession and encourage the creation of a safety culture and environmental conscience among all those who serve on their ships.

Resolution 8

Development of guidelines to implement international standards of medical fitness for seafarers

THE 2010 MANILA CONFERENCE,

HAVING ADOPTED the Manila amendments to the International Convention on Standards of Training, Certification and Watchkeeping for Seafarers, 1978, and to the Seafarers' Training, Certification and Watchkeeping Code, as amended (STCW Convention and Code),

RECOGNIZING the importance of the overall medical fitness of masters and ships' crews to the safety of life and property at sea and the protection of the marine environment,

TAKING COGNIZANCE OF the international standards of medical fitness for seafarers included in the STCW Convention and Code and the Maritime Labour Convention, 2006,

INVITES the International Maritime Organization, in co-operation with the International Labour Organization and the World Health Organization, to develop guidelines to implement the aforementioned standards.

Resolution 9

Revision of existing model courses published by the International Maritime Organization and development of new model courses

THE 2010 MANILA CONFERENCE,

HAVING ADOPTED the Manila amendments to the International Convention on Standards of Training, Certification and Watchkeeping for Seafarers, 1978, and to the Seafarers' Training, Certification and Watchkeeping Code, as amended (STCW Convention and Code),

RECOGNIZING the significant contribution made to seafarers' training and certification through model courses, validated and published by the International Maritime Organization (IMO), providing core curricula based on the minimum requirements of the STCW Convention and Code,

APPRECIATING that the aforementioned model courses have assisted many training institutions to improve the quality of the training they provide and have been used to improve procedures for assessing competency,

DESIRING to achieve greater uniformity in the application of the training and assessment provisions of the STCW Convention and Code,

INVITES:

.1 IMO to take steps to revise and update existing model courses and develop new model courses, which provide guidance on the implementation of the training and assessment provisions of the STCW Convention and Code; and

.2 Governments and international organizations to provide funding for, and otherwise assist in, the revision, updating of existing model courses and development of new model courses.

Resolution 10

Promotion of technical co-operation

THE 2010 MANILA CONFERENCE,

HAVING ADOPTED the Manila amendments to the International Convention on Standards of Training, Certification and Watchkeeping for Seafarers, 1978, and to the Seafarers' Training, Certification and Watchkeeping Code, as amended (STCW Convention and Code),

RECALLING IMO Assembly resolution A.998(25) on Need for capacity building for the development and implementation of new, and amendments to existing instruments,

RECOGNIZING the importance of adequate education and training for, and experience acquired by, all seafarers,

RECOGNIZING FURTHER that, in some cases, there may be limited facilities for providing specialized training programmes and obtaining the required experience, particularly in developing countries,

BELIEVING that the promotion of technical co-operation will assist countries lacking adequate expertise or facilities in providing proper training and experience to implement the STCW Convention and Code,

1. STRONGLY URGES Parties to provide, or arrange to provide, in co-operation with the International Maritime Organization (IMO), assistance to those States which have difficulty in meeting the revised requirements of the STCW Convention and Code and which request such assistance;

2. INVITES IMO to intensify its endeavours to provide States with the assistance they may require and to make adequate provision for that purpose within its technical co-operation programme.

Resolution 11

Measures to ensure the competency of masters and officers of ships operating in polar waters

THE 2010 MANILA CONFERENCE,

HAVING ADOPTED the Manila amendments to the International Convention on Standards of Training, Certification and Watchkeeping for Seafarers, 1978, and to the Seafarers' Training, Certification and Watchkeeping Code, as amended (STCW Convention and Code),

NOTING that, as a result of the increase in maritime traffic in polar waters, several accidents have occurred there in recent years,

NOTING FURTHER the remoteness and the singular hydrographic, oceanographic, meteorological and glaciological characteristics of polar waters, to the extent that search and rescue, care and evacuation of persons and addressing the consequences of pollution entail considerable operational and logistical problems,

RECOGNIZING that the operation of ships sailing in polar waters calls for specific education, training, experience and related qualifications for masters and officers on board such ships,

RECOGNIZING ALSO the efforts made by governments to train masters and officers through courses dedicated to this particular class of navigation,

RECOGNIZING FURTHER both the Guidelines for ships operating in polar waters* and the need for mandatory training requirements when the Polar Code under development by the International Maritime Organization is adopted,

RECOMMENDS that governments adopt measures conducive to ensuring that masters and officers of ships which operate in polar waters have appropriate training and experience, so that they are able to:

.1 plan voyages to polar waters, taking into account glaciological, hydrographic, oceanographic and meteorological factors;

.2 navigate safely in polar waters, in particular in restricted ice-covered areas under adverse conditions of wind and visibility; and

.3 supervise and ensure compliance with the requirements deriving from intergovernmental agreements and with those relating to safety of life at sea and protection of the marine environment.

Resolution 12

Attracting new entrants to, and retaining seafarers in, the maritime profession

THE 2010 MANILA CONFERENCE,

HAVING ADOPTED the Manila amendments to the International Convention on Standards of Training, Certification and Watchkeeping for Seafarers, 1978, and to the Seafarers' Training, Certification and Watchkeeping Code, as amended (STCW Convention and Code),

BEING AWARE that more than 90% of world trade is carried by sea and that the shipping industry operates safely, securely, efficiently and in an environmentally sound manner,

RECOGNIZING the vital service seafarers provide to shipping, an industry that contributes significantly to global and sustainable development and prosperity,

RECOGNIZING ALSO the need for today's increasingly sophisticated ships to be entrusted to seafarers who are competent in all respects to operate them in a safe, secure, efficient and environmentally sound manner,

RECOGNIZING FURTHER that any discriminative legislation adopted and practices enacted have the potential to discourage young people from joining the profession and serving seafarers from remaining in it,

* Refer to resolution A.1024(26) – *Guidelines for ships operating in polar waters*, adopted by the Assembly of the International Maritime Organization on 2 December 2009.

NOTING with concern the reported and anticipated shortage of qualified officers to effectively man and operate ships,

NOTING ALSO with appreciation the "Go to Sea!" campaign launched, in November 2008, by the Secretary-General of the International Maritime Organization, in co-operation with the International Labour Organization, BIMCO, International Chamber of Shipping, International Shipping Federation, INTERCARGO, INTERTANKO and the International Transport Workers' Federation,

APPRECIATING the overall efforts of the shipping industry to promote among young persons a career at sea,

RECOMMENDS that Administrations, shipping companies, shipowner, ship manager and seafarer organizations and any other entities concerned do their utmost to promote among young persons a career at sea and to retain existing seafarers within the industry by:

.1 engendering a more favourable public perception, in particular among young people, of the maritime industry;

.2 promoting a greater awareness and knowledge among young people of the opportunities offered by a career at sea;

.3 improving the quality of life at sea by bringing it more closely in line with the career alternatives available ashore and by enhancing the facilities provided on board ships, including accessing the Internet;

.4 encouraging all officers serving on their ships to participate actively in the training and mentoring of junior personnel during their service on board ship;

.5 encouraging the provision of adequate accommodation for trainees on new buildings; and

.6 taking all appropriate measures to instil pride in the maritime profession and encourage the creation of a safety culture and environmental conscience among all those who serve on their ships.

Resolution 13

Accommodation for trainees

THE 2010 MANILA CONFERENCE,

HAVING ADOPTED the Manila amendments to the International Convention on Standards of Training, Certification and Watchkeeping for Seafarers, 1978, and to the Seafarers' Training, Certification and Watchkeeping Code, as amended (STCW Convention and Code),

NOTING with concern the reported and anticipated shortage of qualified officers to effectively man and operate ships engaged in international trade,

RECOGNIZING the need for today's increasingly sophisticated ships to be entrusted to seafarers who are competent in all respects to operate them in a safe, secure, efficient and environmentally sound manner,

RECOGNIZING ALSO that minimum mandatory seagoing service forms part of the requirements prescribed in the STCW Convention and Code for operational level and support level certification,

RECOGNIZING FURTHER that the lack of adequate accommodation for trainees on board ships constitutes a significant impediment to properly training them and subsequently retaining them at sea, thus adding to the aforementioned shortage,

URGES shipowners, ship managers and shipping companies to provide suitable accommodation for trainees on board their ships both existing and new.

Resolution 14

Promotion of the participation of women in the maritime industry

THE 2010 MANILA CONFERENCE,

HAVING ADOPTED the Manila amendments to the International Convention on Standards of Training, Certification and Watchkeeping for Seafarers, 1978, and to the Seafarers' Training, Certification and Watchkeeping Code, as amended,

NOTING the Long- and Medium-Term Plans for the Integration of Women in the Maritime Sector developed by the International Maritime Organization,

NOTING ALSO the resolution concerning the promotion of opportunities for women seafarers adopted by the International Labour Conference of the International Labour Organization on 22 February 2006,

EXPRESSING SUPPORT for the latter's aims to promote the training of women in the maritime sector,

CONSIDERING HIGHLY DESIRABLE that both men and women have equal access opportunities to maritime training and to employment on board ship,

1. INVITES Governments:

   .1 to give special consideration to securing equal access by men and women in all sectors of the maritime industry; and

   .2 to highlight the role of women in the seafaring profession and to promote their greater participation in maritime training and at all levels in the maritime industry;

2. FURTHER INVITES Governments and the industry:

   .1 to endeavour considering ways to identify and overcome, at international level, the existing constraints, such as the lack of facilities for women on board training vessels, so that women can participate fully and without hindrance in seafaring activities in order to facilitate effectively the achievement of Millennium Development Goals (MDG) 3 (Promote gender equality and empower women);

   .2 to support the provision of on-the-job-training opportunities so that women may acquire the appropriate level of practical experience required to enhance professional maritime skills.

Resolution 15

Future amendments and review of the STCW Convention and Code

THE 2010 MANILA CONFERENCE,

HAVING ADOPTED the Manila amendments to the International Convention on Standards of Training, Certification and Watchkeeping for Seafarers, 1978, and to the Seafarers' Training, Certification and Watchkeeping Code, as amended (STCW Convention and Code),

NOTING that rapidly evolving technology and training methodologies require a consistent approach towards reviewing, amending and updating the STCW Convention and Code,

NOTING FURTHER, however, that frequent amendments to the STCW Convention and Code may be problematic to Maritime Administrations, shipowners, maritime training and education institutions and/or seafarers and should, therefore, be avoided,

1. RECOMMENDS that significant and extensive amendments to the STCW Convention and Code should, as far as possible, be developed and adopted on a five-yearly cycle basis;

2. RECOMMENDS FURTHER that a comprehensive review of the STCW Convention and Code should, as far as possible, be carried out every ten years to address any inconsistencies identified in the interim, and to ensure that they are up to date with emerging technologies.

Resolution 16

Contribution of the International Labour Organization

THE 2010 MANILA CONFERENCE,

HAVING ADOPTED the Manila amendments to the International Convention on Standards of Training, Certification and Watchkeeping for Seafarers, 1978, and to the Seafarers' Training, Certification and Watchkeeping Code, as amended (STCW Convention and Code),

RECOGNIZING the role, competence and expertise of the International Labour Organization (ILO) on matters relating to the occupational safety and health of seafarers,

RECOGNIZING ALSO the significant benefit to the achievement of the objective of the International Maritime Organization and the shipping industry from the Maritime Labour Convention, 2006 (MLC 2006), once in force and implemented,

1. EXPRESSES its appreciation for the contribution made by ILO during the development of the aforementioned amendments to the STCW Convention and Code;

2. STRONGLY RECOMMENDS to Governments, which have not yet done so, to promptly ratify the MLC 2006 to enable its expeditious entry into force and, thereafter, to ensure its wide and effective implementation.

Resolution 17

Role of the World Maritime University, the IMO International Maritime Law Institute and the International Maritime Safety, Security and Environment Academy (IMSSEA) in promoting enhanced maritime standards

THE 2010 MANILA CONFERENCE,

HAVING ADOPTED the Manila amendments to the International Convention on Standards of Training, Certification and Watchkeeping for Seafarers, 1978, and to the Seafarers' Training, Certification and Watchkeeping Code, as amended (STCW Convention and Code),

BEING AWARE of the difficulties of countries, in particular developing countries, in achieving the standards of training and assessment required by the STCW Convention and Code,

RECOGNIZING the significant contribution made by graduates of the World Maritime University (WMU) and the IMO International Maritime Law Institute (IMLI) and the International Maritime Safety, Security and Environment Academy (IMSSEA) to the global and uniform implementation of standards incorporated in maritime safety and pollution prevention-related instruments adopted by the International Maritime Organization (IMO), including the STCW Convention and Code,

RECOGNIZING ALSO the need to maintain the required level of competence of personnel in the international maritime field in order to achieve the objectives of the Organization for safer, secure and efficient shipping in an environmentally sound manner worldwide,

RECOGNIZING FURTHER the leading role played by WMU, IMLI and IMSSEA in maritime education, training and research and the transfer of knowledge through their activities,

RECOGNIZING FURTHER the desirability of common and coordinated approaches in maritime education and training programmes of academic organizations and institutions in line with those of WMU, IMLI and IMSSEA for global implementation of the enhanced standards of the STCW Convention and Code,

APPRECIATING the generous contribution of various entities and donors (in particular, the Governments of China, Italy, Malta, Sweden and the Nippon Foundation of Japan), which have, over many years, been providing financial support and fellowships to candidates from developing countries enrolled in courses at WMU, IMLI and IMSSEA,

1. URGES IMO to continue promoting the role of WMU, IMLI and IMSSEA in maritime education, training and research in the context of the global implementation of IMO instruments, including the enhanced standards of the STCW Convention and Code;

2. RECOMMENDS STRONGLY that Governments, international organizations and shipping industry maintain and further develop their support to WMU, IMLI and IMSSEA to enable them both to continue to make available highly qualified maritime lecturers, administrators and lawyers; and to continue to provide maritime education, training and research to the benefit of maritime industry, especially candidates from developing countries;

3. COMMENDS the staff (both academic and administrative) of WMU, IMLI and IMSSEA for their dedication and commitment to their duties and their contribution to the attainment of the objectives of the institutions.

Resolution 18

Year of the Seafarer

THE 2010 MANILA CONFERENCE,

HAVING ADOPTED the Manila amendments to the International Convention on Standards of Training, Certification and Watchkeeping for Seafarers, 1978, and to the Seafarers' Training, Certification and Watchkeeping Code, as amended,

BEING AWARE of the decision of the International Maritime Organization (IMO) to name 2010 as the "Year of the Seafarer",

BEING EQUALLY AWARE of the contribution seafarers from all over the world make to international seaborne trade, the world economy and civil society as a whole,

RECOGNIZING FULLY the enormous risks seafarers shoulder in the execution of their daily tasks and duties in an often hostile environment,

MINDFUL of the deprivations to which seafarers are subject through spending long periods of their professional life at sea away from their families and friends,

BEING CONCERNED at reported instances in which seafarers were unfairly treated when their ships were involved in accidents; were abandoned in foreign ports; were refused shore leave for security purposes; and were subjected to serious risks while their ships were sailing through piracy-infested areas and to potentially harmful treatment while in the hands of pirates,

DESIRING to join in the celebrations of IMO and the maritime community to pay due tribute to seafarers for the contribution referred to above,

1. EXPRESSES DEEP APPRECIATION to IMO for its timely and appropriate decision to dedicate the current year to the Seafarer;

2. EXPRESSES ALSO DEEP APPRECIATION AND GRATITUDE to seafarers from all over the world for their unique contribution to international seaborne trade, the world economy and civil society as a whole;

3. EQUALLY EXPRESSES DEEP APPRECIATION to maritime pilots, VTS operators, seafarer welfare organizations and all others who contribute to assisting ships and seafarers to enter, stay at, or leave ports and offshore terminals and to navigate through hazardous waters safely and with due care for the marine environment;

4. URGES Governments, shipping organizations and companies and all other parties concerned to take appropriate action to recognize the contribution of seafarers as highlighted above, including by working together, under the auspices of IMO and the International Labour Organization (ILO), to promote seafaring as a career choice for young persons and encourage those already in the profession to continue serving the industry;

5. URGES ALSO Governments, shipping organizations and companies and all other parties concerned, working together under the auspices of IMO and ILO, to take appropriate action to promote and implement, as widely and effectively as possible:

.1 the IMO/ILO Guidelines on the fair treatment of seafarers in the event of a maritime accident;

.2 the IMO/ILO Guidelines on provision of financial security in case of abandonment of seafarers; and

.3 the IMO/ILO Guidelines on shipowners' responsibilities in respect of contractual claims for personal injury to, or death of, seafarers;

6. URGES FURTHER Governments and the shipping industry to take appropriate action to implement:

.1 the International Ship and Port Facility Security (ISPS) Code;

.2 the Guidelines adopted and promulgated by IMO to prevent and suppress acts of piracy and robbery against ships; and

.3 the Convention for the Suppression of Unlawful Acts Against the Safety of Maritime Navigation, 1988 (1988 SUA Convention), and the Protocol for the Suppression of Unlawful Acts Against the Safety of Fixed Platforms Located on the Continental Shelf, 1988 (1988 SUA Protocol), as amended by the 2005 Protocol to the 1988 SUA Convention and the 2005 Protocol to the 1988 SUA Protocol,

in a manner that, while ensuring that maximum protection is afforded to seafarers, does not subject them to any unfair treatment and unnecessary inconvenience;

7. URGES ALSO Governments to ratify, accept, approve or accede to, and thereafter effectively implement, the Maritime Labour Convention, 2006;

8. INVITES IMO, ILO and industry organizations to intensify their efforts to deliver the Year of the Seafarer Action Plan to the full and in the best interests of the seafarers.

Resolution 19

Day of the Seafarer

THE 2010 MANILA CONFERENCE,

HAVING ADOPTED the Manila amendments to the International Convention on Standards of Training, Certification and Watchkeeping for Seafarers (STCW), 1978, and to the Seafarers' Training, Certification and Watchkeeping Code, as amended,

RECOGNIZING FULLY the unique contribution seafarers from all over the world make to international seaborne trade, the world economy and civil society as a whole,

RECOGNIZING EQUALLY the considerable risks seafarers shoulder in the execution of their daily tasks and duties in an often hostile environment,

MINDFUL of the deprivations to which seafarers are subject through spending long periods of their professional life at sea away from their families and friends,

DEEPLY APPRECIATIVE that, in recognition of the above, the International Maritime Organization has named 2010 as the "Year of the Seafarer" in order for it and the maritime community as a whole to pay due tribute to seafarers in recognition of the above,

DESIRING to ensure the continued expression of this deep appreciation and gratitude to seafarers from all over the world for the reasons explained above on an annual basis,

RECOGNIZING that the adoption of the aforementioned amendments to the STCW Convention and Code on this, the 25th June 2010, makes this a very significant day for the maritime community and those who serve it on board ships,

1. RESOLVES to nominate the 25th June of each year hereafter as the **"Day of the Seafarer"**;

2. ENCOURAGES Governments, shipping organizations, companies, shipowners and all other parties concerned to duly and appropriately promote the Day of the Seafarer and take action to celebrate it meaningfully;

3. INVITES the Secretary-General of the International Maritime Organization to bring this resolution to the attention of the IMO Assembly for endorsement and for any other appropriate action it may deem necessary to promote the letter and spirit of the Day.

STCW Code

Seafarers' Training, Certification and Watchkeeping Code, as amended

including resolution 2 of the 2010 Conference of Parties to the International Convention on Standards of Training, Certification and Watchkeeping for Seafarers, 1978

Contents

Tables

Foreword

The Seafarers' Training, Certification and Watchkeeping (STCW) Code was adopted on 7 July 1995 by a Conference of Parties to the International Convention on Standards of Training, Certification and Watchkeeping for Seafarers. It was amended in 1997, 1998, 2000, 2003, 2004, 2005, 2006, 2014, 2015 and 2016.

In 2010, a Conference of Parties to the International Convention on Standards of Training, Certification and Watchkeeping for Seafarers was held in Manila, the Philippines (2010 STCW Conference). Resolution 2 of the 2010 STCW Conference and the annexed 2010 amendments, which completely replace the STCW Code and the amendments thereto, constitute attachment 2 to the Final Act of that Conference.

The STCW Code, which cross-refers directly to the articles and regulations of, and should be read in conjunction with, the STCW Convention, contains, in:

- ***Part A***, mandatory provisions to which specific reference is made in the Annex to the STCW Convention and which give, in detail, the minimum standards required to be maintained by Parties in order to give full and complete effect to the provisions of the STCW Convention; and, in

- ***Part B,*** recommended guidance to assist Parties to the STCW Convention and those involved in implementing, applying or enforcing its measures to give the STCW Convention full and complete effect in a uniform manner.

This part of the publication contains the text of:

- part A of the Code, as amended

- part B of the Code, as amended.

The footnotes to the text of the STCW Code, which have been added by the IMO Secretariat, do not form part of that Code and have been inserted for ease of reference. The IMO Secretariat has been requested to update these footnotes as and when appropriate. In all cases, the reader must make use of the latest editions of the referenced texts, bearing in mind that such texts may have been revised or superseded by updated material since publication of the Code.

Attachment 2 to the Final Act of the 2010 STCW Conference

Resolution 2

The Manila Amendments to the Seafarers' Training, Certification and Watchkeeping (STCW) Code

THE 2010 MANILA CONFERENCE,

HAVING ADOPTED resolution 1 on Adoption of the Manila amendments to the annex to the International Convention on Standards of Training, Certification and Watchkeeping for Seafarers (STCW), 1978,

RECOGNIZING the importance of establishing detailed mandatory standards of competence and other mandatory provisions necessary to ensure that all seafarers shall be properly educated and trained, adequately experienced, skilled and competent to perform their duties in a manner which provides for the safety of life, property and security at sea and the protection of the marine environment,

ALSO RECOGNIZING the need to allow for the timely amendment of such mandatory standards and provisions in order to effectively respond to changes in technology, operations, practices and procedures used on board ships,

RECALLING that a large percentage of maritime casualties and pollution incidents are caused by human error,

APPRECIATING that one effective means of reducing the risks associated with human error in the operation of seagoing ships is to ensure that the highest practicable standards of training, certification and competence are maintained in respect of the seafarers who are or will be employed on such ships,

DESIRING to achieve and maintain the highest practicable standards for the safety of life, property and security at sea and in port and for the protection of the environment,

HAVING CONSIDERED amendments to the Seafarers' Training, Certification and Watchkeeping (STCW) Code, comprised in part A – Mandatory standards regarding provisions of the annex to the 1978 STCW Convention, as amended, and part B – Recommended guidance regarding provisions of the 1978 STCW Convention, as amended, proposed and circulated to all Members of the Organization and all Parties to the Convention,

NOTING that regulation I/1, paragraph 2, of the annex to the 1978 STCW Convention provides that amendments to part A of the STCW Code shall be adopted, brought into force and take effect in accordance with the provisions of article XII of the Convention concerning the amendment procedure applicable to the annex,

HAVING CONSIDERED amendments to the STCW Code proposed and circulated to the Members of the Organization and to all Parties to the Convention,

1. ADOPTS amendments to the Seafarers' Training, Certification and Watchkeeping (STCW) Code, set out in annex to the present resolution;

2. DETERMINES, in accordance with article XII(1)(a)(vii) of the Convention, that the amendments to part A of the STCW Code shall be deemed to have been accepted on 1 July 2011, unless, prior to that date, more than one third of Parties or Parties the combined merchant fleets of which constitute not less than 50% of the gross tonnage of the world's merchant shipping of ships of 100 gross register tons or more have notified the Secretary-General that they object to the amendments;

3. INVITES Parties to note that, in accordance with article XII(1)(a)(ix) of the Convention, the amendments to part A of the STCW Code annexed hereto shall enter into force on 1 January 2012 upon being deemed to have been accepted in accordance with paragraph 2 above;

4. RECOMMENDS that the guidance contained in part B of the STCW Code, as amended, should be taken into account by all Parties to the 1978 STCW Convention as from the date of entry into force of the amendments to part A of the STCW Code;

5. REQUESTS the Maritime Safety Committee to keep the STCW Code under review and amend it, as appropriate;

6. ALSO REQUESTS the Secretary-General of the Organization to transmit certified copies of the present resolution and the text of amendments to the STCW Code contained in the annex to all Parties to the Convention;

7. FURTHER REQUESTS the Secretary-General to transmit copies of this resolution and its annex to all Members of the Organization which are not Parties to the Convention.

Annex

The Manila Amendments to the Seafarers' Training, Certification and Watchkeeping (STCW) Code

Part A

Mandatory standards regarding provisions of the annex to the STCW Convention

Introduction

1 This part of the STCW Code contains mandatory provisions to which specific reference is made in the annex to the International Convention on Standards of Training, Certification and Watchkeeping for Seafarers, 1978, as amended, hereinafter referred to as the STCW Convention. These provisions give in detail the minimum standards required to be maintained by Parties in order to give full and complete effect to the Convention.

2 Also contained in this part are standards of competence required to be demonstrated by candidates for the issue and revalidation of certificates of competency under the provisions of the STCW Convention. To clarify the linkage between the alternative certification provisions of chapter VII and the certification provisions of chapters II, III and IV, the abilities specified in the standards of competence are grouped, as appropriate, under the following seven functions:

- **.1** Navigation
- **.2** Cargo handling and stowage
- **.3** Controlling the operation of the ship and care for persons on board
- **.4** Marine engineering
- **.5** Electrical, electronic and control engineering
- **.6** Maintenance and repair
- **.7** Radiocommunications

at the following levels of responsibility:

- **.1** Management level
- **.2** Operational level
- **.3** Support level

Functions and levels of responsibility are identified by subtitle in the tables of standards of competence given in chapters II, III and IV of this part. The scope of the function at the level of responsibility stated in a subtitle is defined by the abilities listed under it in column 1 of the table. The meaning of "function" and "level of responsibility" is defined in general terms in section A-I/1 below.

3 The numbering of the sections of this part corresponds with the numbering of the regulations contained in the annex to the STCW Convention. The text of the sections may be divided into numbered parts and paragraphs, but such numbering is unique to that text alone.

Chapter I
Standards regarding general provisions

Section A-I/1
Definitions and clarifications

1 The definitions and clarifications contained in article II and regulation I/1 apply equally to the terms used in parts A and B of this Code. In addition, the following supplementary definitions apply only to this Code:

.1 *Standard of competence* means the level of proficiency to be achieved for the proper performance of functions on board ship in accordance with the internationally agreed criteria as set forth herein and incorporating prescribed standards or levels of knowledge, understanding and demonstrated skill;

.2 *Management level* means the level of responsibility associated with:

.2.1 serving as master, chief mate, chief engineer officer or second engineer officer on board a seagoing ship, and

.2.2 ensuring that all functions within the designated area of responsibility are properly performed;

.3 *Operational level* means the level of responsibility associated with:

.3.1 serving as officer in charge of a navigational or engineering watch or as designated duty engineer for periodically unmanned machinery spaces or as radio operator on board a seagoing ship, and

.3.2 maintaining direct control over the performance of all functions within the designated area of responsibility in accordance with proper procedures and under the direction of an individual serving in the management level for that area of responsibility;

.4 *Support level* means the level of responsibility associated with performing assigned tasks, duties or responsibilities on board a seagoing ship under the direction of an individual serving in the operational or management level;

.5 *Evaluation criteria* are the entries appearing in column 4 of the "Specification of Minimum Standard of Competence" tables in part A and provide the means for an assessor to judge whether or not a candidate can perform the related tasks, duties and responsibilities; and

.6 *Independent evaluation* means an evaluation by suitably qualified persons, independent of, or external to, the unit or activity being evaluated, to verify that the administrative and operational procedures at all levels are managed, organized, undertaken and monitored internally in order to ensure their fitness for purpose and achievement of stated objectives.

Section A-I/2
Certificates and endorsements

1 Where, as provided in regulation I/2, paragraph 6, the endorsement required by article VI of the Convention is incorporated in the wording of the certificate itself, the certificate shall be issued in the format shown hereunder, provided that the words "or until the date of expiry of any extension of the validity of this certificate as may be shown overleaf" appearing on the front of the form and the provisions for recording extension of the validity appearing on the back of the form shall be omitted where the certificate is required to be replaced upon its expiry. Guidance on completion of the form is contained in section B-I/2 of this Code.

(Official Seal)

(COUNTRY)

CERTIFICATE ISSUED UNDER THE PROVISIONS OF THE INTERNATIONAL CONVENTION ON STANDARDS OF TRAINING, CERTIFICATION AND WATCHKEEPING FOR SEAFARERS, 1978, AS AMENDED

The Government of . . . . certifies that . . . . has been found duly qualified in accordance with the provisions of regulation . . . . of the above Convention, as amended, and has been found competent to perform the following functions, at the levels specified, subject to any limitations indicated until . . . . or until the date of expiry of any extension of the validity of this certificate as may be shown overleaf:

FUNCTION	LEVEL	LIMITATIONS APPLYING (IF ANY)

The lawful holder of this certificate may serve in the following capacity or capacities specified in the applicable safe manning requirements of the Administration:

CAPACITY	LIMITATIONS APPLYING (IF ANY)

Certificate No. . . . . issued on . . . .

(Official Seal)

. . . .
Signature of duly authorized official

. . . .
Name of duly authorized official

The original of this certificate must be kept available in accordance with regulation I/2, paragraph 11, of the Convention while its holder is serving on a ship.

Date of birth of the holder of the certificate . . . .

Signature of the holder of the certificate . . . .

Photograph of the holder of the certificate

The validity of this certificate is hereby extended until	
(Official Seal)	.... *Signature of duly authorized official*
Date of revalidation	.... *Name of duly authorized official*
The validity of this certificate is hereby extended until	
(Official Seal)	.... *Signature of duly authorized official*
Date of revalidation	.... *Name of duly authorized official*

2 Except as provided in paragraph 1, the form used to attest the issue of a certificate shall be as shown hereunder, provided that the words "or until the date of expiry of any extension of the validity of this endorsement as may be shown overleaf" appearing on the front of the form and the provisions for recording extension of the validity appearing on the back of the form shall be omitted where the endorsement is required to be replaced upon its expiry. Guidance on completion of the form is contained in section B-I/2 of this Code.

(Official Seal)

(COUNTRY)

ENDORSEMENT ATTESTING THE ISSUE OF A CERTIFICATE UNDER THE PROVISIONS OF THE INTERNATIONAL CONVENTION ON STANDARDS OF TRAINING, CERTIFICATION AND WATCHKEEPING FOR SEAFARERS, 1978, AS AMENDED

The Government of .... certifies that certificate No. .... has been issued to .... who has been found duly qualified in accordance with the provisions of regulation .... of the above Convention, as amended, and has been found competent to perform the following functions, at the levels specified, subject to any limitations indicated until .... or until the date of expiry of any extension of the validity of this endorsement as may be shown overleaf:

FUNCTION	LEVEL	LIMITATIONS APPLYING (IF ANY)

The lawful holder of this endorsement may serve in the following capacity or capacities specified in the applicable safe manning requirements of the Administration:

CAPACITY	LIMITATIONS APPLYING (IF ANY)

Endorsement No. .... issued on ....

(Official Seal) ....

Signature of duly authorized official

....

Name of duly authorized official

The original of this endorsement must be kept available in accordance with regulation I/2, paragraph 11, of the Convention while its holder is serving on a ship.

Date of birth of the holder of the certificate ....

Signature of the holder of the certificate ....

Photograph of the holder of the certificate

The validity of this endorsement is hereby extended until	
(Official Seal)	. . . . *Signature of duly authorized official*
Date of revalidation	. . . . *Name of duly authorized official*
The validity of this endorsement is hereby extended until	
(Official Seal)	. . . . *Signature of duly authorized official*
Date of revalidation	. . . . *Name of duly authorized official*

3 The form used to attest the recognition of a certificate shall be as shown hereunder, except that the words "or until the date of expiry of any extension of the validity of this endorsement as may be shown overleaf" appearing on the front of the form and the provisions for recording extension of the validity appearing on the back of the form shall be omitted where the endorsement is required to be replaced upon its expiry. Guidance on completion of the form is contained in section B-I/2 of this Code.

(Official Seal)

(COUNTRY)

ENDORSEMENT ATTESTING THE RECOGNITION OF A CERTIFICATE UNDER THE PROVISIONS OF THE INTERNATIONAL CONVENTION ON STANDARDS OF TRAINING, CERTIFICATION AND WATCHKEEPING FOR SEAFARERS, 1978, AS AMENDED

The Government of .... certifies that certificate No. .... issued to .... by or on behalf of the Government of .... is duly recognized in accordance with the provisions of regulation I/10 of the above Convention, as amended, and the lawful holder is authorized to perform the following functions, at the levels specified, subject to any limitations indicated until .... or until the date of expiry of any extension of the validity of this endorsement as may be shown overleaf:

FUNCTION	LEVEL	LIMITATIONS APPLYING (IF ANY)

The lawful holder of this endorsement may serve in the following capacity or capacities specified in the applicable safe manning requirements of the Administration:

CAPACITY	LIMITATIONS APPLYING (IF ANY)

Endorsement No. .... issued on ....

(Official Seal) ....

Signature of duly authorized official

....

Name of duly authorized official

The original of this endorsement must be kept available in accordance with regulation I/2, paragraph 11, of the Convention while its holder is serving on a ship.

Date of birth of the holder of the certificate ....

Signature of the holder of the certificate ....

Photograph of the holder of the certificate

Section A-I/9

Medical standards

1 Parties, when establishing standards of medical fitness for seafarers as required by regulation I/9, shall adhere to the minimum in-service eyesight standards set out in table A-I/9 and take into account the criteria for physical and medical fitness set out in paragraph 2. They should also take into account the guidance given in section B-I/9 of this Code and table B-I/9 regarding assessment of minimum physical abilities.

These standards may, to the extent determined by the Party without prejudice to the safety of the seafarers or the ship, differentiate between those persons seeking to start a career at sea and those seafarers already serving at sea and between different functions on board, bearing in mind the different duties of seafarers. They shall also take into account any impairment or disease that will limit the ability of the seafarer to effectively perform his/her duties during the validity period of the medical certificate.

2 The standards of physical and medical fitness established by the Party shall ensure that seafarers satisfy the following criteria:

- **.1** have the physical capability, taking into account paragraph 5 below, to fulfil all the requirements of the basic training as required by section A-VI/1, paragraph 2;
- **.2** demonstrate adequate hearing and speech to communicate effectively and detect any audible alarms;
- **.3** have no medical condition, disorder or impairment that will prevent the effective and safe conduct of their routine and emergency duties on board during the validity period of the medical certificate;
- **.4** are not suffering from any medical condition likely to be aggravated by service at sea or to render the seafarer unfit for such service or to endanger the health and safety of other persons on board; and
- **.5** are not taking any medication that has side effects that will impair judgment, balance or any other requirements for effective and safe performance of routine and emergency duties on board.

3 Medical fitness examinations of seafarers shall be conducted by appropriately qualified and experienced medical practitioners recognized by the Party.

4 Each Party shall establish provisions for recognizing medical practitioners. A register of recognized medical practitioners shall be maintained by the Party and made available to other Parties, companies and seafarers on request.

5 Each Party shall provide guidance for the conduct of medical fitness examinations and issuing of medical certificates, taking into account provisions set out in section B-I/9 of this Code. Each Party shall determine the amount of discretion given to recognized medical practitioners on the application of the medical standards, bearing in mind the different duties of seafarers, except that there shall not be discretion with respect to the minimum eyesight standards for distance vision aided, near/immediate vision and colour vision in table A-I/9 for seafarers in the deck department required to undertake lookout duties. A Party may allow discretion on the application of these standards with regard to seafarers in the engine department, on the condition that seafarers' combined vision fulfils the requirements set out in table A-I/9.

6 Each Party shall establish processes and procedures to enable seafarers who, after examination, do not meet the medical fitness standards or have had a limitation imposed on their ability to work, in particular with respect to time, field of work or trading area, to have their case reviewed in line with that Party's provisions for appeal.

7 The medical certificate provided for in regulation I/9, paragraph 3, shall include the following information at a minimum:

.1 **Authorizing authority** and the requirements under which the document is issued

.2 **Seafarer information**

.2.1 Name: *(Last, first, middle)*

.2.2 Date of birth: *(Day/month/year)*

.2.3 Gender: *(Male/Female)*

.2.4 Nationality

.3 **Declaration of the recognized medical practitioner**

.3.1 Confirmation that identification documents were checked at the point of examination: *Y/N*

.3.2 Hearing meets the standards in section A-I/9? *Y/N*

.3.3 Unaided hearing satisfactory? *Y/N*

.3.4 Visual acuity meets standards in section A-I/9? *Y/N*

.3.5 Colour vision* meets standards in section A-I/9? *Y/N*

.3.5.1 Date of last colour vision test.

.3.6 Fit for lookout duties? *Y/N*

.3.7 No limitations or restrictions on fitness? *Y/N*

If "N", specify limitations or restrictions.

.3.8 Is the seafarer free from any medical condition likely to be aggravated by service at sea or to render the seafarer unfit for such service or to endanger the health of other persons on board? *Y/N*

.3.9 Date of examination: *(day/month/year)*

.3.10 Expiry date of certificate: *(day/month/year)*

.4 **Details of the issuing authority**

.4.1 Official stamp (including name) of the issuing authority

.4.2 Signature of the authorized person

.5 **Seafarer's signature** – *confirming that the seafarer has been informed of the content of the certificate and of the right to a review in accordance with paragraph 6 of section A-I/9*

8 Medical certificates shall be in the official language of the issuing country. If the language used is not English, the text shall include a translation into that language.

* Note: Colour vision assessment only needs to be conducted every six years.

Table A-I/9

Minimum in-service eyesight standards for seafarers

STCW Convention regulation	Category of seafarer	Distance vision aided[1]		Near/immediate vision	Colour vision[3]	Visual fields[4]	Night blindness[4]	Diplopia (double vision)[4]
		One eye	Other eye	Both eyes together, aided or unaided				
I/11 II/1 II/2 II/3 II/4 II/5 VII/2	Masters, deck officers and ratings required to undertake lookout duties	0.5[2]	0.5	Vision required for ship's navigation (e.g., chart and nautical publication reference, use of bridge instrumentation and equipment, and identification of aids to navigation)	See Note 6	Normal Visual fields	Vision required to perform all necessary functions in darkness without compromise	No significant condition evident
I/11 III/1 III/2 III/3 III/4 III/5 III/6 III/7 VII/2	All engineer officers, electro-technical officers, electro-technical ratings and ratings or others forming part of an engine-room watch	0.4[5]	0.4 (see Note 5)	Vision required to read instruments in close proximity, to operate equipment, and to identify systems/ components as necessary	See Note 7	Sufficient visual fields	Vision required to perform all necessary functions in darkness without compromise	No significant condition evident
I/11 IV/2	GMDSS Radio operators	0.4	0.4	Vision required to read instruments in close proximity, to operate equipment and to identify systems/ components as necessary	See Note 7	Sufficient visual fields	Vision required to perform all necessary functions in darkness without compromise	No significant condition evident

Notes:

[1] Values given in Snellen decimal notation.

[2] A value of at least 0.7 in one eye is recommended to reduce the risk of undetected underlying eye disease.

[3] As defined in the *International Recommendations for Colour Vision Requirements for Transport* by the Commission Internationale de l'Eclairage (CIE-143-2001 including any subsequent versions).

[4] Subject to assessment by a clinical vision specialist where indicated by initial examination findings.

[5] Engine department personnel shall have a combined eyesight vision of at least 0.4.

[6] CIE colour vision standard 1 or 2. Other equivalent confirmatory test methods currently recognized by the Administration may continue to be used.

[7] CIE colour vision standard 1, 2 or 3. Other equivalent confirmatory test methods currently recognized by the Administration may continue to be used.

Section A-I/10
Recognition of certificates

1 The provisions of regulation I/10, paragraph 4, regarding the non-recognition of certificates issued by a non-Party shall not be construed as preventing a Party, when issuing its own certificate, from accepting seagoing service, education and training acquired under the authority of a non-Party, provided the Party complies with regulation I/2 in issuing each such certificate and ensures that the requirements of the Convention relating to seagoing service, education, training and competence are complied with.

2 Where an Administration which has recognized a certificate withdraws its endorsement of recognition for disciplinary reasons, the Administration shall inform the Party that issued the certificate of the circumstances.

Section A-I/11
Revalidation of certificates

Professional competence

1 Continued professional competence as required under regulation I/11 shall be established by:

- **.1** approved seagoing service, performing functions appropriate to the certificate held, for a period of at least:
  - **.1.1** twelve months in total during the preceding five years, or
  - **.1.2** three months in total during the preceding six months immediately prior to revalidating; or
- **.2** having performed functions considered to be equivalent to the seagoing service required in paragraph 1.1; or
- **.3** passing an approved test; or
- **.4** successfully completing an approved training course or courses; or
- **.5** having completed approved seagoing service, performing functions appropriate to the certificate held, for a period of not less than three months in a supernumerary capacity, or in a lower officer rank than that for which the certificate held is valid immediately prior to taking up the rank for which it is valid.

2 The refresher and updating courses required by regulation I/11 shall be approved and include changes in relevant national and international regulations concerning the safety of life at sea, security and the protection of the marine environment and take account of any updating of the standard of competence concerned.

3 Continued professional competence for tankers as required under regulation I/11, paragraph 3, shall be established by:

- **.1** approved seagoing service, performing duties appropriate to the tanker certificate or endorsement held, for a period of at least three months in total during the preceding five years; or
- **.2** successfully completing an approved relevant training course or courses.

4 Continued professional competence for masters and officers on board ships operating in polar waters, as required under regulation I/11, shall be established by:

- **.1** approved seagoing service, performing functions appropriate to the certificate held, for a period of at least two months in total during the preceding five years; or
- **.2** having performed functions considered to be equivalent to the seagoing service required in paragraph 4.1; or
- **.3** passing an approved test; or
- **.4** successfully completing an approved training course or courses.

Section A-I/12
Standards governing the use of simulators

Part 1 – Performance standards

General performance standards for simulators used in training

1 Each Party shall ensure that any simulator used for mandatory simulator-based training shall:

.1 be suitable for the selected objectives and training tasks;

.2 be capable of simulating the operating capabilities of shipboard equipment concerned, to a level of physical realism appropriate to training objectives, and include the capabilities, limitations and possible errors of such equipment;

.3 have sufficient behavioural realism to allow a trainee to acquire the skills appropriate to the training objectives;

.4 provide a controlled operating environment, capable of producing a variety of conditions, which may include emergency, hazardous or unusual situations relevant to the training objectives;

.5 provide an interface through which a trainee can interact with the equipment, the simulated environment and, as appropriate, the instructor; and

.6 permit an instructor to control, monitor and record exercises for the effective debriefing of trainees.

General performance standards for simulators used in assessment of competence

2 Each Party shall ensure that any simulator used for the assessment of competence required under the Convention or for any demonstration of continued proficiency so required shall:

.1 be capable of satisfying the specified assessment objectives;

.2 be capable of simulating the operational capabilities of the shipboard equipment concerned to a level of physical realism appropriate to the assessment objectives, and include the capabilities, limitations and possible errors of such equipment;

.3 have sufficient behavioural realism to allow a candidate to exhibit the skills appropriate to the assessment objectives;

.4 provide an interface through which a candidate can interact with the equipment and simulated environment;

.5 provide a controlled operating environment, capable of producing a variety of conditions, which may include emergency, hazardous or unusual situations relevant to assessment objectives; and

.6 permit an assessor to control, monitor and record exercises for the effective assessment of the performance of candidates.

Additional performance standards

3 In addition to meeting the basic requirements set out in paragraphs 1 and 2, simulation equipment to which this section applies shall meet the performance standards given hereunder in accordance with their specific type.

Radar simulation

4 Radar simulation equipment shall be capable of simulating the operational capabilities of navigational radar equipment which meets all applicable performance standards adopted by the Organization* and incorporate facilities to:

.1 operate in the stabilized relative-motion mode and sea- and ground-stabilized true-motion modes;

.2 model weather, tidal streams, current, shadow sectors, spurious echoes and other propagation effects, and generate coastlines, navigational buoys and search and rescue transponders; and

.3 create a real-time operating environment incorporating at least two own-ship stations with ability to change own ship's course and speed, and include parameters for at least 20 target ships and appropriate communication facilities.

Automatic Radar Plotting Aid (ARPA) simulation

5 ARPA simulation equipment shall be capable of simulating the operational capabilities of ARPAs which meet all applicable performance standards adopted by the Organization,* and shall incorporate the facilities for:

.1 manual and automatic target acquisition;

.2 past track information;

.3 use of exclusion areas;

.4 vector/graphic time-scale and data display; and

.5 trial manoeuvres.

Part 2 – Other provisions

Simulator training objectives

6 Each Party shall ensure that the aims and objectives of simulator-based training are defined within an overall training programme and that specific training objectives and tasks are selected so as to relate as closely as possible to shipboard tasks and practices.

Training procedures

7 In conducting mandatory simulator-based training, instructors shall ensure that:

.1 trainees are adequately briefed beforehand on the exercise objectives and tasks and are given sufficient planning time before the exercise starts;

.2 trainees have adequate familiarization time on the simulator and with its equipment before any training or assessment exercise commences;

.3 guidance given and exercise stimuli are appropriate to the selected exercise objectives and tasks and to the level of trainee experience;

.4 exercises are effectively monitored, supported as appropriate by audio and visual observation of trainee activity and pre- and post-exercise evaluation reports;

.5 trainees are effectively debriefed to ensure that training objectives have been met and that operational skills demonstrated are of an acceptable standard;

.6 the use of peer assessment during debriefing is encouraged; and

.7 simulator exercises are designed and tested so as to ensure their suitability for the specified training objectives.

* See relevant/appropriate performance standards adopted by the Organization.

Assessment procedures

8 Where simulators are used to assess the ability of candidates to demonstrate levels of competency, assessors shall ensure that:

.1 performance criteria are identified clearly and explicitly and are valid and available to the candidates;

.2 assessment criteria are established clearly and are explicit to ensure reliability and uniformity of assessment and to optimize objective measurement and evaluation, so that subjective judgements are kept to the minimum;

.3 candidates are briefed clearly on the tasks and/or skills to be assessed and on the tasks and performance criteria by which their competency will be determined;

.4 assessment of performance takes into account normal operating procedures and any behavioural interaction with other candidates on the simulator or with simulator staff;

.5 scoring or grading methods to assess performance are used with caution until they have been validated; and

.6 the prime criterion is that a candidate demonstrates the ability to carry out a task safely and effectively to the satisfaction of the assessor.

Qualifications of instructors and assessors*

9 Each Party shall ensure that instructors and assessors are appropriately qualified and experienced for the particular types and levels of training and corresponding assessment of competence as specified in regulation I/6 and section A-I/6.

Section A-I/13
Conduct of trials

(No provisions)

Section A-I/14
Responsibilities of companies

1 Companies, masters and crew members each have responsibility for ensuring that the obligations set out in this section are given full and complete effect and that such other measures as may be necessary are taken to ensure that each crew member can make a knowledgeable and informed contribution to the safe operation of the ship.

2 The company shall provide written instructions to the master of each ship to which the Convention applies, setting forth the policies and the procedures to be followed to ensure that all seafarers who are newly employed on board the ship are given a reasonable opportunity to become familiar with the shipboard equipment, operating procedures and other arrangements needed for the proper performance of their duties, before being assigned to those duties. Such policies and procedures shall include:

.1 allocation of a reasonable period of time during which each newly employed seafarer will have an opportunity to become acquainted with:

.1.1 the specific equipment the seafarer will be using or operating;

* The relevant IMO Model Course(s) and resolution MSC.64(67), Recommendations on new and amended performance standards, may be of assistance in the preparation of courses.

.1.2 ship-specific watchkeeping, safety, environmental protection, security and emergency procedures and arrangements the seafarer needs to know to perform the assigned duties properly; and

.2 designation of a knowledgeable crew member who will be responsible for ensuring that an opportunity is provided to each newly employed seafarer to receive essential information in a language the seafarer understands.

3 Companies shall ensure that masters, officers and other personnel assigned specific duties and responsibilities on board their ro–ro passenger ships shall have completed familiarization training to attain the abilities that are appropriate to the capacity to be filled and duties and responsibilities to be taken up, taking into account the guidance given in section B-I/14 of this Code.

4 Companies shall ensure that masters and officers on board their passenger ships shall have completed familiarization training to attain the abilities that are appropriate to the capacity to be filled and duties and responsibilities to be taken up, taking into account the guidance given in section B-I/14, paragraph 3 of this Code.

Section A-I/15

Transitional provisions

(No provisions)

Section A-I/16

Verification of compliance

1 For the purpose of regulation I/16 the areas that shall be subject to audit are indicated in the table below:

Areas subject to be audited		
Reference	**Area**	**Remarks and summary description**
Initial communication of information		
Article IV, regulation I/7, and section A-I/7, paragraph 2	Initial communication of information	Has the Party communicated information pursuant to article IV and regulation I/7? If yes, has the Maritime Safety Committee confirmed that the information provided demonstrates that "full and complete effect" is given to the provisions of the STCW Convention?
Subsequent reports		
Article IX and section A-I/7, paragraph 3.1	Equivalents	Has the Administration retained/adopted any equivalent educational and training arrangements since communicating information pursuant to regulation I/7? If yes, have the details of such arrangements been reported to the Secretary-General?
Regulation I/10 and section A-I/7, paragraph 3.2	Recognition of certificates	Does the Administration recognize certificates issued by other Party in accordance with regulation I/10? If yes, has the Party submitted reports on the measures taken to ensure compliance with regulation I/10?
Regulation VII/1, section A-I/7, paragraph 3.3	Alternative certification	Does the Party authorize employment of seafarers holding alternative certificates issued under regulation VII/1 on ships entitled to fly its flag? If yes, has a copy of the type of minimum safe manning document issued to such ships been provided to the Secretary General?

Areas subject to be audited		
Reference	**Area**	**Remarks and summary description**
Regulation I/8.3 and section A-I/7, paragraph 4	Communication of information concerning the periodic independent evaluation	Has the Party communicated its report of independent evaluation pursuant to regulation I/8?
Regulation I/7.4, and section A-I/7 paragraphs 5 and 6	Communication of information concerning STCW amendments	Has the Party communicated a report concerning implementation of subsequent mandatory amendments to the STCW Convention and Code?
Regulation I/13, paragraphs 4 and 5	Conduct of trials	Has the Administration authorized ships entitle to fly its flag to participate in trials? If yes, have the details of such trials been reported to the Secretary-General (paragraph 4)?, and Have the details of results of the trials been reported to the Secretary-General (paragraph 5)?
Article VIII	Dispensations	Has the Administration issued any dispensation? If yes, are reports related to dispensations issued during each year sent to the Secretary General?
Control		
Article X and regulation I/4	Port State control	Has the Party exercised port State control? If yes, have control measures as required under article X been established?
Fitness for duty and watchkeeping arrangements		
Regulation VIII/1, paragraph 1 and section A-VIII/1	Fatigue prevention	Has the Administration established measures to enforce the STCW Convention and Code requirements in respect of fatigue prevention?
Regulation VIII/1, paragraph 2 and section A-VIII/1, paragraph 10	Prevention of drug and alcohol abuse	Has the Administration established measures to enforce STCW Convention and Code requirements for the purpose of preventing drug and alcohol abuse?
Regulation VIII/2	Watchkeeping arrangements and principles to be observed	Has the Administration directed the attention of companies, masters, chief engineer officers and all watchkeeping personnel to the requirements, principles and guidance set out in the STCW Code to ensure that safe continuous watches appropriate to prevailing circumstances and conditions are maintained in all seagoing ships at all times?

Chapter II
Standards regarding the master and deck department

Section A-II/1
Mandatory minimum requirements for certification of officers in charge of a navigational watch on ships of 500 gross tonnage or more

Standard of competence

1 Every candidate for certification shall:

- **.1** be required to demonstrate the competence to undertake, at the operational level, the tasks, duties and responsibilities listed in column 1 of table A-II/1;
- **.2** at least hold the appropriate certificate for performing VHF radiocommunications in accordance with the requirements of the Radio Regulations; and
- **.3** if designated to have primary responsibility for radiocommunications during distress incidents, hold the appropriate certificate issued or recognized under the provisions of the Radio Regulations.

2 The minimum knowledge, understanding and proficiency required for certification is listed in column 2 of table A-II/1.

3 The level of knowledge of the subjects listed in column 2 of table A-II/1 shall be sufficient for officers of the watch to carry out their watchkeeping duties.*

4 Training and experience to achieve the necessary level of theoretical knowledge, understanding and proficiency shall be based on section A-VIII/2, part 4-1 – Principles to be observed in keeping a navigational watch – and shall also take into account the relevant requirements of this part and the guidance given in part B of this Code.

5 Every candidate for certification shall be required to provide evidence of having achieved the required standard of competence in accordance with the methods for demonstrating competence and the criteria for evaluating competence tabulated in columns 3 and 4 of table A-II/1.

Onboard training

6 Every candidate for certification as officer in charge of a navigational watch of ships of 500 gross tonnage or more whose seagoing service, in accordance with paragraph 2.2 of regulation II/1, forms part of a training programme approved as meeting the requirements of this section shall follow an approved programme of onboard training which:

- **.1** ensures that, during the required period of seagoing service, the candidate receives systematic practical training and experience in the tasks, duties and responsibilities of an officer in charge of a navigational watch, taking into account the guidance given in section B-II/1 of this Code;
- **.2** is closely supervised and monitored by qualified officers aboard the ships in which the approved seagoing service is performed; and
- **.3** is adequately documented in a training record book or similar document.†

* The relevant IMO Model Course(s) may be of assistance in the preparation of courses.

† The relevant IMO Model Course(s) and a similar document produced by the International Shipping Federation may be of assistance in the preparation of training record books.

Near-coastal voyages

7 The following subjects may be omitted from those listed in column 2 of table A-II/1 for issue of restricted certificates for service on near-coastal voyages, bearing in mind the safety of all ships which may be operating in the same waters:

- **.1** celestial navigation; and
- **.2** those electronic systems of position fixing and navigation that do not cover the waters for which the certificate is to be valid.

Table A-II/1

Specification of minimum standard of competence for officers in charge of a navigational watch on ships of 500 gross tonnage or more

Function: Navigation at the operational level

Column 1	Column 2	Column 3	Column 4
Competence	**Knowledge, understanding and proficiency**	**Methods for demonstrating competence**	**Criteria for evaluating competence**
Plan and conduct a passage and determine position	*Celestial navigation* Ability to use celestial bodies to determine the ship's position *Terrestrial and coastal navigation* Ability to determine the ship's position by use of: .1 landmarks .2 aids to navigation, including lighthouses, beacons and buoys .3 dead reckoning, taking into account winds, tides, currents and estimated speed	Examination and assessment of evidence obtained from one or more of the following: .1 approved in-service experience .2 approved training ship experience .3 approved simulator training, where appropriate .4 approved laboratory equipment training using chart catalogues, charts, nautical publications, radio navigational warnings, sextant, azimuth mirror, electronic navigation equipment, echo-sounding equipment, compass	The information obtained from nautical charts and publications is relevant, interpreted correctly and properly applied. All potential navigational hazards are accurately identified The primary method of fixing the ship's position is the most appropriate to the prevailing circumstances and conditions The position is determined within the limits of acceptable instrument/system errors The reliability of the information obtained from the primary method of position fixing is checked at appropriate intervals Calculations and measurements of navigational information are accurate
	Thorough knowledge of and ability to use nautical charts, and publications, such as sailing directions, tide tables, notices to mariners, radio navigational warnings and ships' routeing information		The charts selected are the largest scale suitable for the area of navigation, and charts and publications are corrected in accordance with the latest information available
	Electronic systems of position fixing and navigation Ability to determine the ship's position by use of electronic navigational aids		Performance checks and tests to navigation systems comply with manufacturer's recommendations and good navigational practice
	Echo-sounders Ability to operate the equipment and apply the information correctly		

Table A-II/1 *(continued)*

Function: Navigation at the operational level *(continued)*

Column 1	Column 2	Column 3	Column 4
Competence	**Knowledge, understanding and proficiency**	**Methods for demonstrating competence**	**Criteria for evaluating competence**
Plan and conduct a passage and determine position *(continued)*	*Compass – magnetic and gyro* Knowledge of the principles of magnetic and gyro-compasses Ability to determine errors of the magnetic and gyro-compasses, using celestial and terrestrial means, and to allow for such errors *Steering control system* Knowledge of steering control systems, operational procedures and change-over from manual to automatic control and vice versa. Adjustment of controls for optimum performance *Meteorology* Ability to use and interpret information obtained from shipborne meteorological instruments Knowledge of the characteristics of the various weather systems, reporting procedures and recording systems Ability to apply the meteorological information available		Errors in magnetic and gyro-compasses are determined and correctly applied to courses and bearings The selection of the mode of steering is the most suitable for the prevailing weather, sea and traffic conditions and intended manoeuvres Measurements and observations of weather conditions are accurate and appropriate to the passage Meteorological information is correctly interpreted and applied

Table A-II/1 *(continued)*

Function: Navigation at the operational level *(continued)*

Column 1	Column 2	Column 3	Column 4
Competence	**Knowledge, understanding and proficiency**	**Methods for demonstrating competence**	**Criteria for evaluating competence**
Maintain a safe navigational watch	*Watchkeeping* Thorough knowledge of the content, application and intent of the International Regulations for Preventing Collisions at Sea, 1972, as amended Thorough knowledge of the Principles to be observed in keeping a navigational watch The use of routeing in accordance with the General Provisions on Ships' Routeing The use of information from navigational equipment for maintaining a safe navigational watch Knowledge of blind pilotage techniques The use of reporting in accordance with the General Principles for Ship Reporting Systems and with VTS procedures	Examination and assessment of evidence obtained from one or more of the following: .1 approved in-service experience; .2 approved training ship experience .3 approved simulator training, where appropriate .4 approved laboratory equipment training	The conduct, handover and relief of the watch conforms with accepted principles and procedures A proper lookout is maintained at all times and in such a way as to conform to accepted principles and procedures Lights, shapes and sound signals conform with the requirements contained in the International Regulations for Preventing Collisions at Sea, 1972, as amended, and are correctly recognized The frequency and extent of monitoring of traffic, the ship and the environment conform with accepted principles and procedures A proper record is maintained of the movements and activities relating to the navigation of the ship Responsibility for the safety of navigation is clearly defined at all times, including periods when the master is on the bridge and while under pilotage
	Bridge resource management Knowledge of bridge resource management principles, including: .1 allocation, assignment, and prioritization of resources .2 effective communication .3 assertiveness and leadership .4 obtaining and maintaining situational awareness .5 consideration of team experience	Assessment of evidence obtained from one or more of the following: .1 approved training .2 approved in-service experience .3 approved simulator training	Resources are allocated and assigned as needed in correct priority to perform necessary tasks Communication is clearly and unambiguously given and received Questionable decisions and/or actions result in appropriate challenge and response Effective leadership behaviours are identified Team member(s) share accurate understanding of current and predicted vessel state, navigation path, and external environment

Table A-II/1 *(continued)*

Function: Navigation at the operational level *(continued)*

Column 1	Column 2	Column 3	Column 4
Competence	**Knowledge, understanding and proficiency**	**Methods for demonstrating competence**	**Criteria for evaluating competence**
Use of radar and ARPA to maintain safety of navigation **Note:** Training and assessment in the use of ARPA is not required for those who serve exclusively on ships not fitted with ARPA. This limitation shall be reflected in the endorsement issued to the seafarer concerned	*Radar navigation* Knowledge of the fundamentals of radar and automatic radar plotting aids (ARPA) Ability to operate and to interpret and analyse information obtained from radar, including the following: Performance, including: .1 factors affecting performance and accuracy .2 setting up and maintaining displays .3 detection of misrepresentation of information, false echoes, sea return, etc., racons and SARTs Use, including: .1 range and bearing; course and speed of other ships; time and distance of closest approach of crossing, meeting overtaking ships .2 identification of critical echoes; detecting course and speed changes of other ships; effect of changes in own ship's course or speed or both .3 application of the International Regulations for Preventing Collisions at Sea, 1972, as amended .4 plotting techniques and relative- and true-motion concepts .5 parallel indexing	Assessment of evidence obtained from approved radar simulator and ARPA simulator plus in-service experience	Information obtained from radar and ARPA is correctly interpreted and analysed, taking into account the limitations of the equipment and prevailing circumstances and conditions Action taken to avoid a close encounter or collision with other vessels is in accordance with the International Regulations for Preventing Collisions at Sea, 1972, as amended Decisions to amend course and/or speed are both timely and in accordance with accepted navigation practice Adjustments made to the ship's course and speed maintain safety of navigation Communication is clear, concise and acknowledged at all times in a seamanlike manner Manoeuvring signals are made at the appropriate time and are in accordance with the International Regulations for Preventing Collisions at Sea, 1972, as amended

Table A-II/1 *(continued)*

Function: Navigation at the operational level *(continued)*

Column 1	Column 2	Column 3	Column 4
Competence	**Knowledge, understanding and proficiency**	**Methods for demonstrating competence**	**Criteria for evaluating competence**
Use of radar and ARPA to maintain safety of navigation (*continued*)	Principal types of ARPA, their display characteristics, performance standards and the dangers of over-reliance on ARPA Ability to operate and to interpret and analyse information obtained from ARPA, including: .1 system performance and accuracy, tracking capabilities and limitations, and processing delays .2 use of operational warnings and system tests .3 methods of target acquisition and their limitations .4 true and relative vectors, graphic representation of target information and danger areas .5 deriving and analysing information, critical echoes, exclusion areas and trial manoeuvres		

Table A-II/1 *(continued)*

Function: Navigation at the operational level *(continued)*

Column 1	Column 2	Column 3	Column 4
Competence	**Knowledge, understanding and proficiency**	**Methods for demonstrating competence**	**Criteria for evaluating competence**
Use of ECDIS to maintain the safety of navigation **Note:** Training and assessment in the use of ECDIS is not required for those who serve exclusively on ships not fitted with ECDIS. This limitation shall be reflected in the endorsements issued to the seafarer concerned	*Navigation using ECDIS* Knowledge of the capability and limitations of ECDIS operations, including: .1 a thorough understanding of Electronic Navigational Chart (ENC) data, data accuracy, presentation rules, display options and other chart data formats .2 the dangers of over-reliance .3 familiarity with the functions of ECDIS required by performance standards in force Proficiency in operation, interpretation, and analysis of information obtained from ECDIS, including: .1 use of functions that are integrated with other navigation systems in various installations, including proper functioning and adjustment to desired settings .2 safe monitoring and adjustment of information, including own position, sea area display, mode and orientation, chart data displayed, route monitoring, user-created information layers, contacts (when interfaced with AIS and/or radar tracking) and radar overlay functions (when interfaced) .3 confirmation of vessel position by alternative means .4 efficient use of settings to ensure conformance to operational procedures, including alarm parameters for anti-grounding, proximity to contacts and special areas, completeness of chart data and chart update status, and backup arrangements .5 adjustment of settings and values to suit the present conditions	Examination and assessment of evidence obtained from one or more of the following: .1 approved training ship experience .2 approved ECDIS simulator training	Monitors information on ECDIS in a manner that contributes to safe navigation Information obtained from ECDIS (including radar overlay and/or radar tracking functions, when fitted) is correctly interpreted and analysed, taking into account the limitations of the equipment, all connected sensors (including radar and AIS where interfaced), and prevailing circumstances and conditions Safety of navigation is maintained through adjustments made to the ship's course and speed through ECDIS-controlled track-keeping functions (when fitted) Communication is clear, concise and acknowledged at all times in a seamanlike manner

Table A-II/1 *(continued)*

Function: Navigation at the operational level *(continued)*

Column 1	**Column 2**	**Column 3**	**Column 4**
Competence	**Knowledge, understanding and proficiency**	**Methods for demonstrating competence**	**Criteria for evaluating competence**
Use of ECDIS to maintain the safety of navigation *(continued)*	.6 situational awareness while using ECDIS including safe water and proximity of hazards, set and drift, chart data and scale selection, suitability of route, contact detection and management, and integrity of sensors		
Respond to emergencies	*Emergency procedures* Precautions for the protection and safety of passengers in emergency situations Initial action to be taken following a collision or a grounding; initial damage assessment and control Appreciation of the procedures to be followed for rescuing persons from the sea, assisting a ship in distress, responding to emergencies which arise in port	Examination and assessment of evidence obtained from one or more of the following: .1 approved in-service experience .2 approved training ship experience .3 approved simulator training, where appropriate .4 practical training	The type and scale of the emergency is promptly identified Initial actions and, if appropriate, manoeuvring of the ship are in accordance with contingency plans and are appropriate to the urgency of the situation and nature of the emergency
Respond to a distress signal at sea	*Search and rescue* Knowledge of the contents of the International Aeronautical and Maritime Search and Rescue (IAMSAR) Manual	Examination and assessment of evidence obtained from practical instruction or approved simulator training, where appropriate	The distress or emergency signal is immediately recognized Contingency plans and instructions in standing orders are implemented and complied with
Use the IMO Standard Marine Communication Phrases and use English in written and oral form	*English language* Adequate knowledge of the English language to enable the officer to use charts and other nautical publications, to understand meteorological information and messages concerning ship's safety and operation, to communicate with other ships, coast stations and VTS centres and to perform the officer's duties also with a multilingual crew, including the ability to use and understand the IMO Standard Marine Communication Phrases (IMO SMCP)	Examination and assessment of evidence obtained from practical instruction	English language nautical publications and messages relevant to the safety of the ship are correctly interpreted or drafted Communications are clear and understood

Table A-II/1 *(continued)*

Function: Navigation at the operational level *(continued)*

Column 1	Column 2	Column 3	Column 4
Competence	**Knowledge, understanding and proficiency**	**Methods for demonstrating competence**	**Criteria for evaluating competence**
Transmit and receive information by visual signalling	*Visual signalling* Ability to use the International Code of Signals Ability to transmit and receive, by Morse light, distress signal SOS as specified in Annex IV of the International Regulations for Preventing Collisions at Sea, 1972, as amended, and appendix 1 of the International Code of Signals, and visual signalling of single-letter signals as also specified in the International Code of Signals	Assessment of evidence obtained from practical instruction and/or simulation	Communications within the operator's area of responsibility are consistently successful
Manoeuvre the ship	*Ship manoeuvring and handling* Knowledge of: .1 the effects of deadweight, draught, trim, speed and under-keel clearance on turning circles and stopping distances .2 the effects of wind and current on ship handling .3 manoeuvres and procedures for the rescue of person overboard .4 squat, shallow-water and similar effects .5 proper procedures for anchoring and mooring	Examination and assessment of evidence obtained from one or more of the following: .1 approved in-service experience .2 approved training ship experience .3 approved simulator training, where appropriate .4 approved training on a manned scale ship model, where appropriate	Safe operating limits of ship propulsion, steering and power systems are not exceeded in normal manoeuvres Adjustments made to the ship's course and speed to maintain safety of navigation

Table A-II/1 *(continued)*

Function: Cargo handling and stowage at the operational level

Column 1	Column 2	Column 3	Column 4
Competence	**Knowledge, understanding and proficiency**	**Methods for demonstrating competence**	**Criteria for evaluating competence**
Monitor the loading, stowage, securing, care during the voyage and the unloading of cargoes	*Cargo handling, stowage and securing* Knowledge of the effect of cargo, including heavy lifts, on the seaworthiness and stability of the ship Knowledge of safe handling, stowage and securing of cargoes, including dangerous, hazardous and harmful cargoes, and their effect on the safety of life and of the ship Ability to establish and maintain effective communications during loading and unloading	Examination and assessment of evidence obtained from one or more of the following: .1 approved in-service experience .2 approved training ship experience .3 approved simulator training, where appropriate	Cargo operations are carried out in accordance with the cargo plan or other documents and established safety rules/regulations, equipment operating instructions and shipboard stowage limitations The handling of dangerous, hazardous and harmful cargoes complies with international regulations and recognized standards and codes of safe practice Communications are clear, understood and consistently successful
Inspect and report defects and damage to cargo spaces, hatch covers and ballast tanks	Knowledge* and ability to explain where to look for damage and defects most commonly encountered due to: .1 loading and unloading operations .2 corrosion .3 severe weather conditions Ability to state which parts of the ship shall be inspected each time in order to cover all parts within a given period of time Identify those elements of the ship structure which are critical to the safety of the ship State the causes of corrosion in cargo spaces and ballast tanks and how corrosion can be identified and prevented Knowledge of procedures on how the inspections shall be carried out Ability to explain how to ensure reliable detection of defects and damages Understanding of the purpose of the "enhanced survey programme"	Examination and assessment of evidence obtained from one or more of the following: .1 approved in-service experience .2 approved training ship experience .3 approved simulator training, where appropriate	The inspections are carried out in accordance with laid-down procedures, and defects and damage are detected and properly reported Where no defects or damage are detected, the evidence from testing and examination clearly indicates adequate competence in adhering to procedures and ability to distinguish between normal and defective or damaged parts of the ship

* It should be understood that deck officers need not be qualified in the survey of ships.

Table A-II/1 *(continued)*

Function: Controlling the operation of the ship and care for persons on board at the operational level

Column 1	Column 2	Column 3	Column 4
Competence	**Knowledge, understanding and proficiency**	**Methods for demonstrating competence**	**Criteria for evaluating competence**
Ensure compliance with pollution-prevention requirements	*Prevention of pollution of the marine environment and anti-pollution procedures* Knowledge of the precautions to be taken to prevent pollution of the marine environment Anti-pollution procedures and all associated equipment Importance of proactive measures to protect the marine environment	Examination and assessment of evidence obtained from one or more of the following: .1 approved in-service experience .2 approved training ship experience .3 approved training	Procedures for monitoring shipboard operations and ensuring compliance with MARPOL requirements are fully observed Actions to ensure that a positive environmental reputation is maintained
Maintain seaworthiness of the ship	*Ship stability* Working knowledge and application of stability, trim and stress tables, diagrams and stress-calculating equipment Understanding of fundamental actions to be taken in the event of partial loss of intact buoyancy Understanding of the fundamentals of watertight integrity *Ship construction* General knowledge of the principal structural members of a ship and the proper names for the various parts	Examination and assessment of evidence obtained from one or more of the following: .1 approved in-service experience .2 approved training ship experience .3 approved simulator training, where appropriate .4 approved laboratory equipment training	The stability conditions comply with the IMO intact stability criteria under all conditions of loading Actions to ensure and maintain the watertight integrity of the ship are in accordance with accepted practice
Prevent, control and fight fires on board	*Fire prevention and fire-fighting appliances* Ability to organize fire drills Knowledge of classes and chemistry of fire Knowledge of fire-fighting systems Knowledge of action to be taken in the event of fire, including fires involving oil systems	Assessment of evidence obtained from approved fire-fighting training and experience as set out in section A-VI/3	The type and scale of the problem is promptly identified and initial actions conform with the emergency procedure and contingency plans for the ship Evacuation, emergency shutdown and isolation procedures are appropriate to the nature of the emergency and are implemented promptly The order of priority and the levels and time-scales of making reports and informing personnel on board are relevant to the nature of the emergency and reflect the urgency of the problem

Table A-II/1 *(continued)*

Function: Controlling the operation of the ship and care for persons on board at the operational level *(continued)*

Column 1	Column 2	Column 3	Column 4
Competence	**Knowledge, understanding and proficiency**	**Methods for demonstrating competence**	**Criteria for evaluating competence**
Operate life-saving appliances	*Life-saving* Ability to organize abandon ship drills and knowledge of the operation of survival craft and rescue boats, their launching appliances and arrangements, and their equipment, including radio life-saving appliances, satellite EPIRBs, SARTs, immersion suits and thermal protective aids	Assessment of evidence obtained from approved training and experience as set out in section A-VI/2, paragraphs 1 to 4	Actions in responding to abandon ship and survival situations are appropriate to the prevailing circumstances and conditions and comply with accepted safety practices and standards
Apply medical first aid on board ship	*Medical aid* Practical application of medical guides and advice by radio, including the ability to take effective action based on such knowledge in the case of accidents or illnesses that are likely to occur on board ship	Assessment of evidence obtained from approved training as set out in section A-VI/4, paragraphs 1 to 3	The identification of probable cause, nature and extent of injuries or conditions is prompt, and treatment minimizes immediate threat to life
Monitor compliance with legislative requirements	Basic working knowledge of the relevant IMO conventions concerning safety of life at sea, security and protection of the marine environment	Assessment of evidence obtained from examination or approved training	Legislative requirements relating to safety of life at sea, security and protection of the marine environment are correctly identified
Application of leadership and teamworking skills	Working knowledge of shipboard personnel management and training A knowledge of related international maritime conventions and recommendations, and national legislation Ability to apply task and workload management, including: .1 planning and co-ordination .2 personnel assignment .3 time and resource constraints .4 prioritization	Assessment of evidence obtained from one or more of the following: .1 approved training .2 approved in-service experience .3 practical demonstration	The crew are allocated duties and informed of expected standards of work and behaviour in a manner appropriate to the individuals concerned Training objectives and activities are based on assessment of current competence and capabilities and operational requirements Operations are demonstrated to be in accordance with applicable rules

Table A-II/1 *(continued)*

Function: Controlling the operation of the ship and care for persons on board at the operational level *(continued)*

Column 1	Column 2	Column 3	Column 4
Competence	**Knowledge, understanding and proficiency**	**Methods for demonstrating competence**	**Criteria for evaluating competence**
Application of leadership and teamworking skills *(continued)*	Knowledge and ability to apply effective resource management: .1 allocation, assignment and prioritization of resources .2 effective communication onboard and ashore .3 decisions reflect consideration of team experiences .4 assertiveness and leadership, including motivation .5 obtaining and maintaining situational awareness Knowledge and ability to apply decision-making techniques: .1 situation and risk assessment .2 identify and consider generated options .3 selecting course of action .4 evaluation of outcome effectiveness		Operations are planned and resources are allocated as needed in correct priority to perform necessary tasks Communication is clearly and unambiguously given and received Effective leadership behaviours are demonstrated Necessary team member(s) share accurate understanding of current and predicted vessel status and operational status and external environment Decisions are most effective for the situation
Contribute to the safety of personnel and ship	Knowledge of personal survival techniques Knowledge of fire prevention and ability to fight and extinguish fires Knowledge of elementary first aid Knowledge of personal safety and social responsibilities	Assessment of evidence obtained from approved training and experience as set out in section A-VI/1, paragraph 2	Appropriate safety and protective equipment is correctly used Procedures and safe working practices designed to safeguard personnel and the ship are observed at all times Procedures designed to safeguard the environment are observed at all times Initial and follow-up action on becoming aware of an emergency conforms with established emergency response procedures

Section A-II/2

Mandatory minimum requirements for certification of masters and chief mates on ships of 500 gross tonnage or more

Standard of competence

1 Every candidate for certification as master or chief mate of ships of 500 gross tonnage or more shall be required to demonstrate the competence to undertake, at the management level, the tasks, duties and responsibilities listed in column 1 of table A-II/2.

2 The minimum knowledge, understanding and proficiency required for certification is listed in column 2 of table A-II/2. This incorporates, expands and extends in depth the subjects listed in column 2 of table A-II/1 for officers in charge of a navigational watch.

3 Bearing in mind that the master has ultimate responsibility for the safety and security of the ship, its passengers, crew and cargo, and for the protection of the marine environment against pollution by the ship, and that a chief mate shall be in a position to assume that responsibility at any time, assessment in these subjects shall be designed to test their ability to assimilate all available information that affects the safety and security of the ship, its passengers, crew or cargo, or the protection of the marine environment.

4 The level of knowledge of the subjects listed in column 2 of table A-II/2 shall be sufficient to enable the candidate to serve in the capacity of master or chief mate.*

5 The level of theoretical knowledge, understanding and proficiency required under the different sections in column 2 of table A-II/2 may be varied according to whether the certificate is to be valid for ships of 3,000 gross tonnage or more or for ships of between 500 gross tonnage and 3,000 gross tonnage.

6 Training and experience to achieve the necessary level of theoretical knowledge, understanding and proficiency shall take into account the relevant requirements of this part and the guidance given in part B of this Code.

7 Every candidate for certification shall be required to provide evidence of having achieved the required standard of competence in accordance with the methods for demonstrating competence and criteria for evaluating competence tabulated in columns 3 and 4 of table A-II/2.

Near-coastal voyages

8 An Administration may issue a certificate restricted to service on ships engaged exclusively on near-coastal voyages and, for the issue of such a certificate, may exclude such subjects as are not applicable to the waters or ships concerned, bearing in mind the effect on the safety of all ships which may be operating in the same waters.

* The relevant IMO Model Course(s) may be of assistance in the preparation of courses.

Table A-II/2

Specification of minimum standard of competence for masters and chief mates on ships of 500 gross tonnage or more

Function: Navigation at the management level

Column 1	Column 2	Column 3	Column 4
Competence	**Knowledge, understanding and proficiency**	**Methods for demonstrating competence**	**Criteria for evaluating competence**
Plan a voyage and conduct navigation	Voyage planning and navigation for all conditions by acceptable methods of plotting ocean tracks, taking into account, e.g.: .1 restricted waters .2 meteorological conditions .3 ice .4 restricted visibility .5 traffic separation schemes .6 vessel traffic service (VTS) areas .7 areas of extensive tidal effects Routeing in accordance with the General Provisions on Ships' Routeing Reporting in accordance with the General principles for Ship Reporting Systems and with VTS procedures	Examination and assessment of evidence obtained from one or more of the following: .1 approved in-service experience .2 approved simulator training, where appropriate .3 approved laboratory equipment training using: chart catalogues, charts, nautical publications and ship particulars	The equipment, charts and nautical publications required for the voyage are enumerated and appropriate to the safe conduct of the voyage The reasons for the planned route are supported by facts and statistical data obtained from relevant sources and publications Positions, courses, distances and time calculations are correct within accepted accuracy standards for navigational equipment All potential navigational hazards are accurately identified
Determine position and the accuracy of resultant position fix by any means	Position determination in all conditions: .1 by celestial observations .2 by terrestrial observations, including the ability to use appropriate charts, notices to mariners and other publications to assess the accuracy of the resulting position fix .3 using modern electronic navigational aids, with specific knowledge of their operating principles, limitations, sources of error, detection of misrepresentation of information and methods of correction to obtain accurate position fixing	Examination and assessment of evidence obtained from one or more of the following: .1 approved in-service experience .2 approved simulator training, where appropriate .3 approved laboratory equipment training using: .3.1 charts, nautical almanac, plotting sheets, chronometer, sextant and a calculator .3.2 charts, nautical publications and navigational instruments (azimuth mirror, sextant, log, sounding equipment, compass) and manufacturers' manuals .3.3 radar, terrestrial electronic position-fixing systems, satellite navigation systems and appropriate nautical charts and publications	The primary method chosen for fixing the ship's position is the most appropriate to the prevailing circumstances and conditions The fix obtained by celestial observations is within accepted accuracy levels The fix obtained by terrestrial observations is within accepted accuracy levels The accuracy of the resulting fix is properly assessed The fix obtained by the use of electronic navigational aids is within the accuracy standards of the systems in use. The possible errors affecting the accuracy of the resulting position are stated and methods of minimizing the effects of system errors on the resulting position are properly applied

Table A-II/2 *(continued)*

Function: Navigation at the management level *(continued)*

Column 1	Column 2	Column 3	Column 4
Competence	**Knowledge, understanding and proficiency**	**Methods for demonstrating competence**	**Criteria for evaluating competence**
Determine and allow for compass errors	Ability to determine and allow for errors of the magnetic and gyro-compasses Knowledge of the principles of magnetic and gyro-compasses An understanding of systems under the control of the master gyro and a knowledge of the operation and care of the main types of gyro-compass	Examination and assessment of evidence obtained from one or more of the following: .1 approved in-service experience .2 approved simulator training, where appropriate .3 approved laboratory equipment training using: celestial observations, terrestrial bearings and comparison between magnetic and gyro-compasses	The method and frequency of checks for errors of magnetic and gyro-compasses ensures accuracy of information
Coordinate search and rescue operations	A thorough knowledge of and ability to apply the procedures contained in the International Aeronautical and Maritime Search and Rescue (IAMSAR) Manual	Examination and assessment of evidence obtained from one or more of the following: .1 approved in-service experience .2 approved simulator training, where appropriate .3 approved laboratory equipment training using: relevant publications, charts, meteorological data, particulars of ships involved, radiocommunication equipment and other available facilities and one or more of the following: .1 approved SAR training course .2 approved simulator training, where appropriate .3 approved laboratory equipment training	The plan for coordinating search and rescue operations is in accordance with international guidelines and standards Radiocommunications are established and correct communication procedures are followed at all stages of the search and rescue operations
Establish watchkeeping arrangements and procedures	Thorough knowledge of content, application and intent of the International Regulations for Preventing Collisions at Sea, 1972, as amended Thorough knowledge of the content, application and intent of the Principles to be observed in keeping a navigational watch	Examination and assessment of evidence obtained from one or more of the following: .1 approved in-service experience .2 approved simulator training, where appropriate	Watchkeeping arrangements and procedures are established and maintained in compliance with international regulations and guidelines so as to ensure the safety of navigation, protection of the marine environment and safety of the ship and persons on board

Table A-II/2 *(continued)*

Function: Navigation at the management level *(continued)*

Column 1	Column 2	Column 3	Column 4
Competence	**Knowledge, understanding and proficiency**	**Methods for demonstrating competence**	**Criteria for evaluating competence**
Maintain safe navigation through the use of information from navigation equipment and systems to assist command decision making **Note:** Training and assessment in the use of ARPA is not required for those who serve exclusively on ships not fitted with ARPA. This limitation shall be reflected in the endorsement issued to the seafarer concerned	An appreciation of system errors and thorough understanding of the operational aspects of navigational systems Blind pilotage planning Evaluation of navigational information derived from all sources, including radar and ARPA, in order to make and implement command decisions for collision avoidance and for directing the safe navigation of the ship The interrelationship and optimum use of all navigational data available for conducting navigation	Examination and assessment of evidence obtained from approved ARPA simulator and one or more of the following: .1 approved in-service experience .2 approved simulator training, where appropriate .3 approved laboratory equipment training	Information obtained from navigation equipment and systems is correctly interpreted and analysed, taking into account the limitations of the equipment and prevailing circumstances and conditions Action taken to avoid a close encounter or collision with another vessel is in accordance with the International Regulations for Preventing Collisions at Sea, 1972, as amended
Maintain the safety of navigation through the use of ECDIS and associated navigation systems to assist command decision making **Note:** Training and assessment in the use of ECDIS is not required for those who serve exclusively on ships not fitted with ECDIS. This limitation shall be reflected in the endorsement issued to the seafarer concerned	Management of operational procedures, system files and data, including: .1 manage procurement, licensing and updating of chart data and system software to conform to established procedures .2 system and information updating, including the ability to update ECDIS system version in accordance with vendor's product development .3 create and maintain system configuration and backup files .4 create and maintain log files in accordance with established procedures .5 create and maintain route plan files in accordance with established procedures .6 use ECDIS log-book and track history functions for inspection of system functions, alarm settings and user responses Use ECDIS playback functionality for passage review, route planning and review of system functions	Assessment of evidence obtained from one of the following: .1 approved in-service experience .2 approved training ship experience .3 approved ECDIS simulator training	Operational procedures for using ECDIS are established, applied and monitored Actions taken to minimize risk to safety of navigation

Table A-II/2 *(continued)*

Function: Navigation at the management level *(continued)*

Column 1	Column 2	Column 3	Column 4
Competence	**Knowledge, understanding and proficiency**	**Methods for demonstrating competence**	**Criteria for evaluating competence**
Forecast weather and oceanographic conditions	Ability to understand and interpret a synoptic chart and to forecast area weather, taking into account local weather conditions and information received by weather fax Knowledge of the characteristics of various weather systems, including tropical revolving storms and avoidance of storm centres and the dangerous quadrants Knowledge of ocean current systems Ability to calculate tidal conditions Use all appropriate nautical publications on tides and currents	Examination and assessment of evidence obtained from one or more of the following: .1 approved in-service experience .2 approved laboratory equipment training	The likely weather conditions predicted for a determined period are based on all available information Actions taken to maintain safety of navigation minimize any risk to safety of the ship Reasons for intended action are backed by statistical data and observations of the actual weather conditions
Respond to navigational emergencies	Precautions when beaching a ship Action to be taken if grounding is imminent, and after grounding Refloating a grounded ship with and without assistance Action to be taken if collision is imminent and following a collision or impairment of the watertight integrity of the hull by any cause Assessment of damage control Emergency steering Emergency towing arrangements and towing procedure	Examination and assessment of evidence obtained from practical instruction, in-service experience and practical drills in emergency procedures	The type and scale of any problem is promptly identified and decisions and actions minimize the effects of any malfunction of the ship's systems Communications are effective and comply with established procedures Decisions and actions maximize safety of persons on board

Table A-II/2 *(continued)*

Function: Navigation at the management level *(continued)*

Column 1	Column 2	Column 3	Column 4
Competence	**Knowledge, understanding and proficiency**	**Methods for demonstrating competence**	**Criteria for evaluating competence**
Manoeuvre and handle a ship in all conditions	Manoeuvring and handling a ship in all conditions, including: .1 manoeuvres when approaching pilot stations and embarking or disembarking pilots, with due regard to weather, tide, headreach and stopping distances .2 handling ship in rivers, estuaries and restricted waters, having regard to the effects of current, wind and restricted water on helm response .3 application of constant-rate-of-turn techniques .4 manoeuvring in shallow water, including the reduction in under-keel clearance caused by squat, rolling and pitching .5 interaction between passing ships and between own ship and nearby banks (canal effect) .6 berthing and unberthing under various conditions of wind, tide and current with and without tugs .7 ship and tug interaction .8 use of propulsion and manoeuvring systems .9 choice of anchorage; anchoring with one or two anchors in limited anchorages and factors involved in determining the length of anchor cable to be used .10 dragging anchor; clearing fouled anchors .11 dry-docking, both with and without damage .12 management and handling of ships in heavy weather, including assisting a ship or aircraft in distress; towing operations; means of keeping an unmanageable ship out of trough of the sea, lessening drift and use of oil .13 precautions in manoeuvring to launch rescue boats or survival craft in bad weather	Examination and assessment of evidence obtained from one or more of the following: .1 approved in-service experience .2 approved simulator training, where appropriate .3 approved manned scale ship model, where appropriate	All decisions concerning berthing and anchoring are based on a proper assessment of the ship's manoeuvring and engine characteristics and the forces to be expected while berthed alongside or lying at anchor While under way, a full assessment is made of possible effects of shallow and restricted waters, ice, banks, tidal conditions, passing ships and own ship's bow and stern wave so that the ship can be safely manoeuvred under various conditions of loading and weather

Table A-II/2 *(continued)*

Function: Navigation at the management level *(continued)*

Column 1	Column 2	Column 3	Column 4
Competence	**Knowledge, understanding and proficiency**	**Methods for demonstrating competence**	**Criteria for evaluating competence**
Manoeuvre and handle a ship in all conditions *(continued)*	.14 methods of taking on board survivors from rescue boats and survival craft .15 ability to determine the manoeuvring and propulsion characteristics of common types of ships, with special reference to stopping distances and turning circles at various draughts and speeds .16 importance of navigating at reduced speed to avoid damage caused by own ship's bow wave and stern wave .17 practical measures to be taken when navigating in or near ice or in conditions of ice accumulation on board .18 use of, and manoeuvring in and near, traffic separation schemes and in vessel traffic service (VTS) areas		
Operate remote controls of propulsion plant and engineering systems and services	Operating principles of marine power plants Ships' auxiliary machinery General knowledge of marine engineering terms	Examination and assessment of evidence obtained from one or more of the following: .1 approved in-service experience .2 approved simulator training, where appropriate	Plant, auxiliary machinery and equipment is operated in accordance with technical specifications and within safe operating limits at all times

Table A-II/2 *(continued)*

Function: Cargo handling and stowage at the management level

Column 1	Column 2	Column 3	Column 4
Competence	**Knowledge, understanding and proficiency**	**Methods for demonstrating competence**	**Criteria for evaluating competence**
Plan and ensure safe loading, stowage, securing, care during the voyage and unloading of cargoes	Knowledge of and ability to apply relevant international regulations, codes and standards concerning the safe handling, stowage, securing and transport of cargoes Knowledge of the effect on trim and stability of cargoes and cargo operations Use of stability and trim diagrams and stress-calculating equipment, including automatic data-based (ADB) equipment, and knowledge of loading cargoes and ballasting in order to keep hull stress within acceptable limits Stowage and securing of cargoes on board ships, including cargo-handling gear and securing and lashing equipment Loading and unloading operations, with special regard to the transport of cargoes identified in the Code of Safe Practice for Cargo Stowage and Securing General knowledge of tankers and tanker operations Knowledge of the operational and design limitations of bulk carriers Ability to use all available shipboard data related to loading, care and unloading of bulk cargoes Ability to establish procedures for safe cargo handling in accordance with the provisions of the relevant instruments such as IMDG Code, IMSBC Code, MARPOL 73/78 Annexes III and V and other relevant information Ability to explain the basic principles for establishing effective communications and improving working relationship between ship and terminal personnel	Examination and assessment of evidence obtained from one or more of the following: .1 approved in-service experience .2 approved simulator training, where appropriate using: stability, trim and stress tables, diagrams and stress-calculating equipment	The frequency and extent of cargo condition monitoring is appropriate to its nature and prevailing conditions Unacceptable or unforeseen variations in the condition or specification of the cargo are promptly recognized and remedial action is immediately taken and designed to safeguard the safety of the ship and those on board Cargo operations are planned and executed in accordance with established procedures and legislative requirements Stowage and securing of cargoes ensures that stability and stress conditions remain within safe limits at all times during the voyage

Table A-II/2 *(continued)*

Function: Cargo handling and stowage at the management level *(continued)*

Column 1	Column 2	Column 3	Column 4
Competence	**Knowledge, understanding and proficiency**	**Methods for demonstrating competence**	**Criteria for evaluating competence**
Assess reported defects and damage to cargo spaces, hatch covers and ballast tanks and take appropriate action	Knowledge of the limitations on strength of the vital constructional parts of a standard bulk carrier and ability to interpret given figures for bending moments and shear forces Ability to explain how to avoid the detrimental effects on bulk carriers of corrosion, fatigue and inadequate cargo handling	Examination and assessment of evidence obtained from one or more of the following: .1 approved in-service experience .2 approved simulator training, where appropriate using: stability, trim and stress tables, diagrams and stress-calculating equipment	Evaluations are based on accepted principles, well-founded arguments and correctly carried out. The decisions taken are acceptable, taking into consideration the safety of the ship and the prevailing conditions
Carriage of dangerous goods	International regulations, standards, codes and recommendations on the carriage of dangerous cargoes, including the International Maritime Dangerous Goods (IMDG) Code and the International Maritime Solid Bulk Cargoes (IMSBC) Code Carriage of dangerous, hazardous and harmful cargoes; precautions during loading and unloading and care during the voyage	Examination and assessment of evidence obtained from one or more of the following: .1 approved in-service experience .2 approved simulator training, where appropriate .3 approved specialist training	Planned distribution of cargo is based on reliable information and is in accordance with established guidelines and legislative requirements Information on dangers, hazards and special requirements is recorded in a format suitable for easy reference in the event of an incident

Hazmat training:
49 CFR 172.704
◦ recurrent: every 3 years

Table A-II/2 *(continued)*

Function: Controlling the operation of the ship and care for persons on board at the management level

Column 1	Column 2	Column 3	Column 4
Competence	**Knowledge, understanding and proficiency**	**Methods for demonstrating competence**	**Criteria for evaluating competence**
Control trim, stability and stress	Understanding of fundamental principles of ship construction and the theories and factors affecting trim and stability and measures necessary to preserve trim and stability Knowledge of the effect on trim and stability of a ship in the event of damage to and consequent flooding of a compartment and countermeasures to be taken Knowledge of IMO recommendations concerning ship stability	Examination and assessment of evidence obtained from one or more of the following: .1 approved in-service experience .2 approved training ship experience .3 approved simulator training, where appropriate	Stability and stress conditions are maintained within safe limits at all times
Monitor and control compliance with legislative requirements and measures to ensure safety of life at sea, security and the protection of the marine environment	Knowledge of international maritime law embodied in international agreements and conventions Regard shall be paid especially to the following subjects: .1 certificates and other documents required to be carried on board ships by international conventions, how they may be obtained and their period of validity .2 responsibilities under the relevant requirements of the International Convention on Load Lines, 1966, as amended .3 responsibilities under the relevant requirements of the International Convention for the Safety of Life at Sea, 1974, as amended .4 responsibilities under the International Convention for the Prevention of Pollution from Ships, as amended .5 maritime declarations of health and the requirements of the International Health Regulations .6 responsibilities under international instruments affecting the safety of the ship, passengers, crew and cargo .7 methods and aids to prevent pollution of the marine environment by ships .8 national legislation for implementing international agreements and conventions	Examination and assessment of evidence obtained from one or more of the following: .1 approved in-service experience .2 approved training ship experience .3 approved simulator training, where appropriate	Procedures for monitoring operations and maintenance comply with legislative requirements Potential non-compliance is promptly and fully identified Planned renewal and extension of certificates ensures continued validity of surveyed items and equipment

Table A-II/2 *(continued)*

Function: Controlling the operation of the ship and care for persons on board at the management level *(continued)*

Column 1	Column 2	Column 3	Column 4
Competence	**Knowledge, understanding and proficiency**	**Methods for demonstrating competence**	**Criteria for evaluating competence**
Maintain safety and security of the ship's crew and passengers and the operational condition of life-saving, fire-fighting and other safety systems	Thorough knowledge of life-saving appliance regulations (International Convention for the Safety of Life at Sea) Organization of fire drills and abandon ship drills Maintenance of operational condition of life-saving, fire-fighting and other safety systems Actions to be taken to protect and safeguard all persons on board in emergencies Actions to limit damage and salve the ship following a fire, explosion, collision or grounding	Examination and assessment of evidence obtained from practical instruction and approved in-service training and experience	Procedures for monitoring fire-detection and safety systems ensure that all alarms are detected promptly and acted upon in accordance with established emergency procedures
Develop emergency and damage control plans and handle emergency situations	Preparation of contingency plans for response to emergencies Ship construction, including damage control Methods and aids for fire prevention, detection and extinction Functions and use of life-saving appliances	Examination and assessment of evidence obtained from approved in-service training and experience	Emergency procedures are in accordance with the established plans for emergency situations

Table A-II/2 *(continued)*

Function: Controlling the operation of the ship and care for persons on board at the management level *(continued)*

Column 1	Column 2	Column 3	Column 4
Competence	**Knowledge, understanding and proficiency**	**Methods for demonstrating competence**	**Criteria for evaluating competence**
Use of leadership and managerial skill	Knowledge of shipboard personnel management and training A knowledge of related international maritime conventions and recommendations, and national legislation Ability to apply task and workload management, including: .1 planning and co-ordination .2 personnel assignment .3 time and resource constraints .4 prioritization Knowledge and ability to apply effective resource management: .1 allocation, assignment and prioritization of resources .2 effective communication on board and ashore .3 decisions reflect consideration of team experiences .4 assertiveness and leadership, including motivation .5 obtaining and maintaining situation awareness Knowledge and ability to apply decision-making techniques: .1 situation and risk assessment .2 identify and generate options .3 selecting course of action .4 evaluation of outcome effectiveness Development, implementation, and oversight of standard operating procedures	Assessment of evidence obtained from one or more of the following: .1 approved training .2 approved in-service experience .3 approved simulator training	The crew are allocated duties and informed of expected standards of work and behaviour in a manner appropriate to the individuals concerned Training objectives and activities are based on assessment of current competence and capabilities and operational requirements Operations are demonstrated to be in accordance with applicable rules Operations are planned and resources are allocated as needed in correct priority to perform necessary tasks Communication is clearly and unambiguously given and received Effective leadership behaviours are demonstrated Necessary team member(s) share accurate understanding of current and predicted vessel state and operational status and external environment Decisions are most effective for the situation Operations are demonstrated to be effective and in accordance with applicable rules

Table A-II/2 *(continued)*

Function: Controlling the operation of the ship and care for persons on board at the management level *(continued)*

Column 1	Column 2	Column 3	Column 4
Competence	**Knowledge, understanding and proficiency**	**Methods for demonstrating competence**	**Criteria for evaluating competence**
Organize and manage the provision of medical care on board	A thorough knowledge* of the use and contents of the following publications: .1 International Medical Guide for Ships or equivalent national publications .2 medical section of the International Code of Signals .3 Medical First Aid Guide for Use in Accidents Involving Dangerous Goods	Examination and assessment of evidence obtained from approved training	Actions taken and procedures followed correctly apply and make full use of advice available

* The relevant IMO Model Course(s) may be of assistance in the preparation of courses.

Section A-II/3

Mandatory minimum requirements for certification of officers in charge of a navigational watch and of masters on ships of less than 500 gross tonnage, engaged on near-coastal voyages

Officer in charge of a navigational watch

Standard of competence

1 Every candidate for certification shall:

- **.1** be required to demonstrate the competence to undertake, at operational level, the tasks, duties and responsibilities listed in column 1 of table A-II/3;
- **.2** at least hold the appropriate certificate for performing VHF radiocommunications in accordance with the requirements of the Radio Regulations; and
- **.3** if designated to have primary responsibility for radiocommunications during distress incidents, hold the appropriate certificate issued or recognized under the provisions of the Radio Regulations.

2 The minimum knowledge, understanding and proficiency required for certification is listed in column 2 of table A-II/3.

3 The level of knowledge of the subjects listed in column 2 of table A-II/3 shall be sufficient to enable the candidate to serve in the capacity of officer in charge of a navigational watch.

4 Training and experience to achieve the necessary level of theoretical knowledge, understanding and proficiency shall be based on section A-VIII/2, part 4-1 – Principles to be observed in keeping a navigational watch, and shall also take into account the relevant requirements of this part and the guidance given in part B of this Code.

5 Every candidate for certification shall be required to provide evidence of having achieved the required standard of competence in accordance with the methods for demonstrating competence and the criteria for evaluating competence tabulated in columns 3 and 4 of table A-II/3.

Special training

6 Every candidate for certification as officer in charge of a navigational watch on ships of less than 500 gross tonnage, engaged on near-coastal voyages, who, in accordance with paragraph 4.2.1 of regulation II/3, is required to have completed special training, shall follow an approved programme of onboard training which:

- **.1** ensures that, during the required period of seagoing service, the candidate receives systematic practical training and experience in the tasks, duties and responsibilities of an officer in charge of a navigational watch, taking into account the guidance given in section B-II/1 of this Code;
- **.2** is closely supervised and monitored by qualified officers on board the ships in which the approved seagoing service is performed; and
- **.3** is adequately documented in a training record book or similar document.*

Master

7 Every candidate for certification as master on ships of less than 500 gross tonnage, engaged on near-coastal voyages, shall meet the requirements for an officer in charge of a navigational watch set out below and, in addition, shall be required to provide evidence of knowledge and ability to carry out all the duties of such a master.

* The relevant IMO Model Course(s) and a similar document produced by the International Shipping Federation may be of assistance in the preparation of training record books.

Table A-II/3

Specification of minimum standard of competence for officers in charge of a navigational watch and for masters on ships of less than 500 gross tonnage engaged on near-coastal voyages

Function: Navigation at the operational level

Column 1	Column 2	Column 3	Column 4
Competence	**Knowledge, understanding and proficiency**	**Methods for demonstrating competence**	**Criteria for evaluating competence**
Plan and conduct a coastal passage and determine position **Note:** Training and assessment in the use of ECDIS is not required for those who serve exclusively on ships not fitted with ECDIS. This limitation shall be reflected in the endorsement issued to the seafarer concerned	*Navigation* Ability to determine the ship's position by the use of: .1 landmarks .2 aids to navigation, including lighthouses, beacons and buoys .3 dead reckoning, taking into account winds, tides, currents and estimated speed	Examination and assessment of evidence obtained from one or more of the following: .1 approved in-service experience .2 approved training ship experience .3 approved simulator training, where appropriate .4 approved laboratory equipment training using: chart catalogues, charts, nautical publications, radio navigational warnings, sextant, azimuth mirror, electronic navigation equipment, echo-sounding equipment, compass	Information obtained from nautical charts and publications is relevant, interpreted correctly and properly applied The primary method of fixing the ship's position is the most appropriate to the prevailing circumstances and conditions The position is determined within the limits of acceptable instrument/system errors The reliability of the information obtained from the primary method of position fixing is checked at appropriate intervals Calculations and measurements of navigational information are accurate
	Thorough knowledge of and ability to use nautical charts and publications, such as sailing directions, tide tables, notices to mariners, radio navigational warnings and ships' routeing information Reporting in accordance with General Principles for Ship Reporting Systems and with VTS procedures **Note:** This item is only required for certification as master		Charts and publications selected are the largest scale on board suitable for the area of navigation, and charts are corrected in accordance with the latest information available

Table A-II/3 *(continued)*

Function: Navigation at the operational level *(continued)*

Column 1	Column 2	Column 3	Column 4
Competence	**Knowledge, understanding and proficiency**	**Methods for demonstrating competence**	**Criteria for evaluating competence**
Plan and conduct a coastal passage and determine position *(continued)*	Voyage planning and navigation for all conditions by acceptable methods of plotting coastal tracks, taking into account, e.g.: .1 restricted waters .2 meteorological conditions .3 ice .4 restricted visibility .5 traffic separation schemes .6 vessel traffic service (VTS) areas .7 areas of extensive tidal effects **Note:** This item is only required for certification as master		
	Thorough knowledge of and ability to use ECDIS	Examination and assessment of evidence obtained from one or more of the following: .1 approved training ship experience .2 approved ECDIS simulator training	
	Navigational aids and equipment Ability to operate safely and determine the ship's position by use of all navigational aids and equipment commonly fitted on board the ships concerned	Assessment of evidence obtained from approved radar simulator	Performance checks and tests of navigation systems comply with manufacturer's recommendations, good navigational practice and IMO resolutions on performance standards for navigational equipment Interpretation and analysis of information obtained from radar is in accordance with accepted navigational practice and takes account of the limits and accuracy levels of radar
	Compasses Knowledge of the errors and corrections of magnetic compasses Ability to determine errors of the compass, using terrestrial means, and to allow for such errors		Errors in magnetic compasses are determined and applied correctly to courses and bearings
	Automatic pilot Knowledge of automatic pilot systems and procedures; change-over from manual to automatic control and vice versa; adjustment of controls for optimum performance		Selection of the mode of steering is the most suitable for prevailing weather, sea and traffic conditions and intended manoeuvres

Table A-II/3 *(continued)*

Function: Navigation at the operational level *(continued)*

Column 1	Column 2	Column 3	Column 4
Competence	**Knowledge, understanding and proficiency**	**Methods for demonstrating competence**	**Criteria for evaluating competence**
Plan and conduct a coastal passage and determine position *(continued)*	*Meteorology* Ability to use and interpret information obtained from shipborne meteorological instruments Knowledge of the characteristics of the various weather systems, reporting procedures and recording systems Ability to apply the meteorological information available		Measurements and observations of weather conditions are accurate and appropriate to the passage Meteorological information is evaluated and applied to maintain the safe passage of the vessel
Maintain a safe navigational watch	*Watchkeeping* Thorough knowledge of content, application and intent of the International Regulations for Preventing Collisions at Sea, 1972, as amended Knowledge of content of the Principles to be observed in keeping a navigational watch Use of routeing in accordance with the General Provisions on Ships' Routeing Use of reporting in accordance with the General Principles for Ship Reporting Systems and with VTS procedures	Examination and assessment of evidence obtained from one or more of the following: .1 approved in-service experience .2 approved training ship experience .3 approved simulator training, where appropriate .4 approved laboratory equipment training	The conduct, handover and relief of the watch conforms with accepted principles and procedures A proper lookout is maintained at all times and in conformity with accepted principles and procedures Lights, shapes and sound signals conform with the requirements contained in the International Regulations for Preventing Collisions at Sea, 1972, as amended and are correctly recognized The frequency and extent of monitoring of traffic, the ship and the environment conform with accepted principles and procedures Action to avoid close encounters and collision with other vessels is in accordance with the International Regulations for Preventing Collisions at Sea, 1972, as amended Decisions to adjust course and/or speed are both timely and in accordance with accepted navigation procedures A proper record is maintained of movements and activities relating to the navigation of the ship Responsibility for safe navigation is clearly defined at all times, including periods when the master is on the bridge and when under pilotage

Section A-II/4

Mandatory minimum requirements for certification of ratings forming part of a navigational watch

Standard of competence

1 Every rating forming part of a navigational watch on a seagoing ship of 500 gross tonnage or more shall be required to demonstrate the competence to perform the navigation function at the support level, as specified in column 1 of table A-II/4.

2 The minimum knowledge, understanding and proficiency required of ratings forming part of a navigational watch on a seagoing ship of 500 gross tonnage or more is listed in column 2 of table A-II/4.

3 Every candidate for certification shall be required to provide evidence of having achieved the required standard of competence in accordance with the methods for demonstrating competence and the criteria for evaluating competence specified in columns 3 and 4 of table A-II/4. The reference to "practical test" in column 3 may include approved shore-based training in which the trainees undergo practical testing.

4 Where there are no tables of competence for the support level with respect to certain functions, it remains the responsibility of the Administration to determine the appropriate training, assessment and certification requirements to be applied to personnel designated to perform those functions at the support level.

Table A-II/4

Specification of minimum standard of competence for ratings forming part of a navigational watch

Function: Navigation at the support level

Column 1	Column 2	Column 3	Column 4
Competence	**Knowledge, understanding and proficiency**	**Methods for demonstrating competence**	**Criteria for evaluating competence**
Steer the ship and also comply with helm orders in the English language	Use of magnetic and gyro-compasses Helm orders Change-over from automatic pilot to hand steering and vice versa	Assessment of evidence obtained from: .1 practical test, or .2 approved in-service experience, or .3 approved training ship experience	A steady course is steered within acceptable limits, having regard to the area of navigation and prevailing sea state. Alterations of course are smooth and controlled Communications are clear and concise at all times and orders are acknowledged in a seamanlike manner
Keep a proper look-out by sight and hearing	Responsibilities of a look-out, including reporting the approximate bearing of a sound signal, light or other object in degrees or points	Assessment of evidence obtained from: .1 practical test, or .2 approved in-service experience, or .3 approved training ship experience	Sound signals, lights and other objects are promptly detected and their approximate bearing, in degrees or points, is reported to the officer of the watch
Contribute to monitoring and controlling a safe watch	Shipboard terms and definitions Use of appropriate internal communication and alarm systems Ability to understand orders and to communicate with the officer of the watch on matters relevant to watchkeeping duties Procedures for the relief, maintenance and handover of a watch Information required to maintain a safe watch Basic environmental protection procedures	Assessment of evidence obtained from approved in-service experience or approved training ship experience	Communications are clear and concise and advice/clarification is sought from the officer on watch where watch information or instructions are not clearly understood Maintenance, handover and relief of the watch is in conformity with accepted practices and procedures
Operate emergency equipment and apply emergency procedures	Knowledge of emergency duties and alarm signals Knowledge of pyrotechnic distress signals; satellite EPIRBs and SARTs Avoidance of false distress alerts and action to be taken in event of accidental activation	Assessment of evidence obtained from demonstration and approved in-service experience or approved training ship experience	Initial action on becoming aware of an emergency or abnormal situation is in conformity with established practices and procedures Communications are clear and concise at all times and orders are acknowledged in a seamanlike manner The integrity of emergency and distress alerting systems is maintained at all times

Section A-II/5

Mandatory minimum requirements for certification of ratings as able seafarer deck

Standard of competence

1 Every able seafarer deck serving on a seagoing ship of 500 gross tonnage or more shall be required to demonstrate the competence to perform the functions at the support level, as specified in column 1 of table A-II/5.

2 The minimum knowledge, understanding and proficiency required of an able seafarer deck serving on a seagoing ship of 500 gross tonnage or more is listed in column 2 of table A-II/5.

3 Every candidate for certification shall be required to provide evidence of having achieved the required standard of competence in accordance with the methods for demonstrating competence and the criteria for evaluating competence specified in columns 3 and 4 of table A-II/5.

Table A-II/5

Specification of minimum standards of competence of ratings as able seafarer deck

Function: Navigation at the support level

Column 1	Column 2	Column 3	Column 4
Competence	**Knowledge, understanding and proficiency**	**Methods for demonstrating competence**	**Criteria for evaluating competence**
Contribute to a safe navigational watch	Ability to understand orders and to communicate with the officer of the watch on matters relevant to watchkeeping duties Procedures for the relief, maintenance and handover of a watch Information required to maintain a safe watch	Assessment of evidence obtained from in-service experience or practical test	Communications are clear and concise Maintenance, handover and relief of the watch is in conformity with acceptable practices and procedures
Contribute to berthing, anchoring and other mooring operations	Working knowledge of the mooring system and related procedures, including: .1 the function of mooring and tug lines and how each line functions as part of an overall system .2 the capacities, safe working loads and breaking strengths of mooring equipment, including mooring wires, synthetic and fibre lines, winches, anchor windlasses, capstans, bitts, chocks and bollards .3 the procedures and order of events for making fast and letting go mooring and tug lines and wires, including towing lines .4 the procedures and order of events for the use of anchors in various operations Working knowledge of the procedures and order of events associated with mooring to a buoy or buoys	Assessment of evidence obtained from one or more of the following: .1 approved in-service experience .2 practical training .3 examination .4 approved training ship experience .5 approved simulator training, where appropriate	Operations are carried out in accordance with established safety practices and equipment operating instructions

Table A-II/5 *(continued)*

Function: Cargo handling and stowage at the support level

Column 1	Column 2	Column 3	Column 4
Competence	**Knowledge, understanding and proficiency**	**Methods for demonstrating competence**	**Criteria for evaluating competence**
Contribute to the handling of cargo and stores	Knowledge of procedures for safe handling, stowage and securing of cargoes and stores, including dangerous, hazardous and harmful substances and liquids Basic knowledge of and precautions to observe in connection with particular types of cargo and identification of IMDG labelling	Assessment of evidence obtained from one or more of the following: .1 approved in-service experience .2 practical training .3 examination .4 approved training ship experience .5 approved simulator training, where appropriate	Cargo and stores operations are carried out in accordance with established safety procedures and equipment operating instructions The handling of dangerous, hazardous and harmful cargoes or stores complies with established safety practices

Table A-II/5 *(continued)*

Function: Controlling the operation of the ship and care for persons on board at the support level

Column 1	Column 2	Column 3	Column 4
Competence	**Knowledge, understanding and proficiency**	**Methods for demonstrating competence**	**Criteria for evaluating competence**
Contribute to the safe operation of deck equipment and machinery	Knowledge of deck equipment, including: .1 function and uses of valves and pumps, hoists, cranes, booms and related equipment .2 function and uses of winches, windlasses, capstans and related equipment .3 hatches, watertight doors, ports and related equipment .4 fibre and wire ropes, cables and chains, including their construction, use, markings, maintenance and proper stowage	Assessment of evidence obtained from one or more of the following: .1 approved in-service experience .2 practical training .3 examination .4 approved training ship experience	Operations are carried out in accordance with established safety practices and equipment operating instructions
	.5 ability to use and understand basic signals for the operation of equipment, including winches, windlasses, cranes and hoists	Assessment of evidence obtained from practical demonstration	Communications within the operator's area of responsibility are consistently successful
	.6 ability to operate anchoring equipment under various conditions, such as anchoring, weighing anchor, securing for sea, and in emergencies	Assessment of evidence obtained from practical demonstration	Equipment operation is safely carried out in accordance with established procedures
	Knowledge of the following procedures and ability to: .1 rig and unrig bosun's chairs and staging .2 rig and unrig pilot ladders, hoists, rat-guards and gangways	Assessment of evidence obtained from practical demonstration	Demonstrate the proper methods for rigging and unrigging in accordance with safe industry practice
	.3 use marlin spike seamanship skills, including the proper use of knots, splices and stoppers		Demonstrate the proper creation and use of knots, splices, stoppers, whippings, servings as well as proper canvas handling
	Use and handling of deck and cargo-handling gear and equipment: .1 access arrangements, hatches and hatch covers, ramps, side/bow/stern doors or elevators .2 pipeline systems – bilge and ballast suctions and wells		

Table A-II/5 *(continued)*

Function: Controlling the operation of the ship and care for persons on board at the support level *(continued)*

Column 1	Column 2	Column 3	Column 4
Competence	**Knowledge, understanding and proficiency**	**Methods for demonstrating competence**	**Criteria for evaluating competence**
Contribute to the safe operation of deck equipment and machinery *(continued)*	.3 cranes, derricks, winches Knowledge of hoisting and dipping flags and the main single-flag signals. (A, B, G, H, O, P, Q)		Demonstrate the proper use of blocks and tackle Demonstrate the proper methods for handling lines, wires, cables and chains
Apply occupational health and safety precautions	Working knowledge of safe working practices and personal shipboard safety including: .1 working aloft .2 working over the side .3 working in enclosed spaces .4 permit to work systems .5 line handling .6 lifting techniques and methods of preventing back injury .7 electrical safety .8 mechanical safety .9 chemical and biohazard safety .10 personal safety equipment	Assessment of evidence obtained from one or more of the following: .1 approved in-service experience .2 practical training .3 examination .4 approved training ship experience	Procedures designed to safeguard personnel and the ship are observed at all times Safe working practices are observed and appropriate safety and protective equipment is correctly used at all times
Apply precautions and contribute to the prevention of pollution of the marine environment	Knowledge of the precautions to be taken to prevent pollution of the marine environment Knowledge of the use and operation of anti-pollution equipment Knowledge of the approved methods for disposal of marine pollutants	Assessment of evidence obtained from one or more of the following: .1 approved in-service experience .2 practical training .3 examination .4 approved training ship experience	Procedures designed to safeguard the marine environment are observed at all times
Operate survival craft and rescue boats	Knowledge of the operation of survival craft and rescue boats, their launching appliances and arrangements, and their equipment Knowledge of survival at sea techniques	Assessment of evidence obtained from approved training and experience as set out in section A-VI/2, paragraphs 1 to 4	Actions in responding to abandon ship and survival situations are appropriate to the prevailing circumstances and conditions and comply with accepted safety practices and standards

Table A-II/5 *(continued)*

Function: Maintenance and repair at the support level

Column 1	Column 2	Column 3	Column 4
Competence	**Knowledge, understanding and proficiency**	**Methods for demonstrating competence**	**Criteria for evaluating competence**
Contribute to shipboard maintenance and repair	Ability to use painting, lubrication and cleaning materials and equipment Ability to understand and execute routine maintenance and repair procedures Knowledge of surface preparation techniques	Assessment of evidence obtained from practical demonstration	Maintenance and repair activities are carried out in accordance with technical, safety and procedural specifications
	Understanding manufacturer's safety guidelines and shipboard instructions Knowledge of safe disposal of waste materials Knowledge of the application, maintenance and use of hand and power tools	Assessment of evidence obtained from one or more of the following: .1 approved in-service experience .2 practical training .3 examination .4 approved training ship experience	

Chapter III
Standards regarding engine department

Section A-III/1
Mandatory minimum requirements for certification of officers in charge of an engineering watch in a manned engine-room or as designated duty engineers in a periodically unmanned engine-room

Training

1 The education and training required by paragraph 2.4 of regulation III/1 shall include training in mechanical and electrical workshop skills relevant to the duties of an engineer officer.

Onboard training

2 Every candidate for certification as officer in charge of an engineering watch in a manned engine-room or as designated duty engineer in a periodically unmanned engine-room of ships powered by main propulsion machinery of 750 kW or more whose seagoing service, in accordance with paragraph 2.2 of regulation III/1, forms part of a training programme approved as meeting the requirements of this section shall follow an approved programme of onboard training which:

- **.1** ensures that, during the required period of seagoing service, the candidate receives systematic practical training and experience in the tasks, duties and responsibilities of an officer in charge of an engine-room watch, taking into account the guidance given in section B-III/1 of this Code;
- **.2** is closely supervised and monitored by a qualified and certificated engineer officer aboard the ships in which the approved seagoing service is performed; and
- **.3** is adequately documented in a training record book.

Standard of competence

3 Every candidate for certification as officer in charge of an engineering watch in a manned engine-room or as designated duty engineer in a periodically unmanned engine-room on a seagoing ship powered by main propulsion machinery of 750 kW propulsion power or more shall be required to demonstrate ability to undertake, at the operational level, the tasks, duties and responsibilities listed in column 1 of table A-III/1.

4 The minimum knowledge, understanding and proficiency required for certification is listed in column 2 of table A-III/1.

5 The level of knowledge of the material listed in column 2 of table A-III/1 shall be sufficient for engineer officers to carry out their watchkeeping duties.[*]

6 Training and experience to achieve the necessary theoretical knowledge, understanding and proficiency shall be based on section A-VIII/2, part 4-2–Principles to be observed in keeping an engineering watch, and shall take into account the relevant requirements of this part and the guidance given in part B of this Code.

7 Candidates for certification for service in ships in which steam boilers do not form part of their machinery may omit the relevant requirements of table A-III/1. A certificate awarded on such a basis shall not be valid for service on ships in which steam boilers form part of a ship's machinery until the engineer officer meets the standard of competence in the items omitted from table A-III/1. Any such limitation shall be stated on the certificate and in the endorsement.

---
[*] The relevant IMO Model Course(s) may be of assistance in the preparation of courses.

8 The Administration may omit knowledge requirements for types of propulsion machinery other than those machinery installations for which the certificate to be awarded shall be valid. A certificate awarded on such a basis shall not be valid for any category of machinery installation which has been omitted until the engineer officer proves to be competent in these knowledge requirements. Any such limitation shall be stated on the certificate and in the endorsement.

9 Every candidate for certification shall be required to provide evidence of having achieved the required standard of competence in accordance with the methods for demonstrating competence and the criteria for evaluating competence tabulated in columns 3 and 4 of table A-III/1.

Near-coastal voyages

10 The requirements of paragraphs 2.2 to 2.5 of regulation III/1 relating to level of knowledge, understanding and proficiency required under the different sections listed in column 2 of table A-III/1 may be varied for engineer officers of ships powered by main propulsion machinery of less than 3,000 kW propulsion power engaged on near-coastal voyages, as considered necessary, bearing in mind the effect on the safety of all ships which may be operating in the same waters. Any such limitation shall be stated on the certificate and in the endorsement.

Table A-III/1 *(continued)*

Function: Controlling the operation of the ship and care for persons on board at the operational level *(continued)*

Column 1	Column 2	Column 3	Column 4
Competence	**Knowledge, understanding and proficiency**	**Methods for demonstrating competence**	**Criteria for evaluating competence**
Application of leadership and teamworking skills *(continued)*	Knowledge and ability to apply effective resource management: .1 allocation, assignment, and prioritization of resources .2 effective communication on board and ashore .3 decisions reflect consideration of team experiences .4 assertiveness and leadership, including motivation .5 obtaining and maintaining situational awareness Knowledge and ability to apply decision-making techniques: .1 situation and risk assessment .2 identify and consider generated options .3 selecting course of action .4 evaluation of outcome effectiveness		Operations are planned and resources are allocated as needed in correct priority to perform necessary tasks Communication is clearly and unambiguously given and received Effective leadership behaviours are demonstrated Necessary team member(s) share accurate understanding of current and predicted vessel state and operational status and external environment Decisions are most effective for the situation
Contribute to the safety of personnel and ship	Knowledge of personal survival techniques Knowledge of fire prevention and ability to fight and extinguish fires Knowledge of elementary first aid Knowledge of personal safety and social responsibilities	Assessment of evidence obtained from approved training and experience as set out in section A-VI/1, paragraph 2	Appropriate safety and protective equipment is correctly used Procedures and safe working practices designed to safeguard personnel and the ship are observed at all times Procedures designed to safeguard the environment are observed at all times Initial and follow-up actions on becoming aware of an emergency conform with established emergency response procedures

Section A-III/2

Mandatory minimum requirements for certification of chief engineer officers and second engineer officers on ships powered by main propulsion machinery of 3,000 kW propulsion power or more

Standard of competence

1 Every candidate for certification as chief engineer officer and second engineer officer of seagoing ships powered by main propulsion machinery of 3,000 kW power or more shall be required to demonstrate ability to undertake, at the management level, the tasks, duties and responsibilities listed in column 1 of table A-III/2.

2 The minimum knowledge, understanding and proficiency required for certification is listed in column 2 of table A-III/2. This incorporates, expands and extends in depth the subjects listed in column 2 of table A-III/1 for officers in charge of an engineering watch.

3 Bearing in mind that a second engineer officer shall be in a position to assume the responsibilities of the chief engineer officer at any time, assessment in these subjects shall be designed to test the candidate's ability to assimilate all available information that affects the safe operation of the ship's machinery and the protection of the marine environment.

4 The level of knowledge of the subjects listed in column 2 of table A-III/2 shall be sufficient to enable the candidate to serve in the capacity of chief engineer officer or second engineer officer.*

5 Training and experience to achieve the necessary level of theoretical knowledge, understanding and proficiency shall take into account the relevant requirements of this part and the guidance given in part B of this Code.

6 The Administration may omit knowledge requirements for types of propulsion machinery other than those machinery installations for which the certificate to be awarded shall be valid. A certificate awarded on such a basis shall not be valid for any category of machinery installation which has been omitted until the engineer officer proves to be competent in these knowledge requirements. Any such limitation shall be stated on the certificate and in the endorsement.

7 Every candidate for certification shall be required to provide evidence of having achieved the required standard of competence in accordance with the methods for demonstrating competence and the criteria for evaluating competence tabulated in columns 3 and 4 of table A-III/2.

Near-coastal voyages

8 The level of knowledge, understanding and proficiency required under the different sections listed in column 2 of table A-III/2 may be varied for engineer officers of ships powered by main propulsion machinery with limited propulsion power engaged on near-coastal voyages, as considered necessary, bearing in mind the effect on the safety of all ships which may be operating in the same waters. Any such limitation shall be stated on the certificate and in the endorsement.

* The relevant IMO Model Course(s) may be of assistance in the preparation of courses.

Table A-III/2

Specification of minimum standard of competence for chief engineer officers and second engineer officers on ships powered by main propulsion machinery of 3,000 kW propulsion power or more

Function: Marine engineering at the management level

Column 1	Column 2	Column 3	Column 4
Competence	**Knowledge, understanding and proficiency**	**Methods for demonstrating competence**	**Criteria for evaluating competence**
Manage the operation of propulsion plant machinery	Design features, and operative mechanism of the following machinery and associated auxiliaries: .1 marine diesel engine .2 marine steam turbine .3 marine gas turbine .4 marine steam boiler	Examination and assessment of evidence obtained from one or more of the following: .1 approved in-service experience .2 approved training ship experience .3 approved simulator training, where appropriate .4 approved laboratory equipment training	Explanation and understanding of design features and operating mechanisms are appropriate

Table A-III/2 *(continued)*

Function: Marine engineering at the management level *(continued)*

Column 1	Column 2	Column 3	Column 4
Competence	**Knowledge, understanding and proficiency**	**Methods for demonstrating competence**	**Criteria for evaluating competence**
Plan and schedule operations	*Theoretical knowledge* Thermodynamics and heat transmission Mechanics and hydromechanics Propulsive characteristics of diesel engines, steam and gas turbines, including speed, output and fuel consumption Heat cycle, thermal efficiency and heat balance of the following: .1 marine diesel engine .2 marine steam turbine .3 marine gas turbine .4 marine steam boiler Refrigerators and refrigeration cycle Physical and chemical properties of fuels and lubricants Technology of materials Naval architecture and ship construction, including damage control *Practical knowledge* Start up and shut down main propulsion and auxiliary machinery, including associated systems Operating limits of propulsion plant The efficient operation, surveillance, performance assessment and maintaining safety of propulsion plant and auxiliary machinery Functions and mechanism of automatic control for main engine Functions and mechanism of automatic control for auxiliary machinery including but not limited to: .1 generator distribution systems .2 steam boilers .3 oil purifier .4 refrigeration system .5 pumping and piping systems .6 steering gear system .7 cargo-handling equipment and deck machinery	Examination and assessment of evidence obtained from one or more of the following: .1 approved in-service experience .2 approved training ship experience .3 approved simulator training, where appropriate .4 approved laboratory equipment training	The planning and preparation of operations is suited to the design parameters of the power installation and to the requirements of the voyage
Operation, surveillance, performance assessment and maintaining safety of propulsion plant and auxiliary machinery		Examination and assessment of evidence obtained from one or more of the following: .1 approved in-service experience .2 approved training ship experience .3 approved simulator training, where appropriate .4 approved laboratory equipment training	The methods of preparing for the start-up and of making available fuels, lubricants, cooling water and air are the most appropriate Checks of pressures, temperatures and revolutions during the start-up and warm-up period are in accordance with technical specifications and agreed work plans Surveillance of main propulsion plant and auxiliary systems is sufficient to maintain safe operating conditions The methods of preparing the shutdown and of supervising the cooling down of the engine are the most appropriate The methods of measuring the load capacity of the engines are in accordance with technical specifications Performance is checked against bridge orders Performance levels are in accordance with technical specifications

Table A-III/2 *(continued)*

Function: Marine engineering at the management level *(continued)*

Column 1	Column 2	Column 3	Column 4
Competence	**Knowledge, understanding and proficiency**	**Methods for demonstrating competence**	**Criteria for evaluating competence**
Manage fuel, lubrication and ballast operations	Operation and maintenance of machinery, including pumps and piping systems	Examination and assessment of evidence obtained from one or more of the following: .1 approved in-service experience .2 approved training ship experience .3 approved simulator training, where appropriate	Fuel and ballast operations meet operational requirements and are carried out so as to prevent pollution of the marine environment

Table A-III/2 *(continued)*

Function: Electrical, electronic and control engineering at the management level

Column 1	Column 2	Column 3	Column 4
Competence	**Knowledge, understanding and proficiency**	**Methods for demonstrating competence**	**Criteria for evaluating competence**
Manage operation of electrical and electronic control equipment	*Theoretical knowledge* Marine electrotechnology, electronics, power electronics, automatic control engineering and safety devices Design features and system configurations of automatic control equipment and safety devices for the following: .1 main engine .2 generator and distribution system .3 steam boiler Design features and system configurations of operational control equipment for electrical motors Design features of high-voltage installations Features of hydraulic and pneumatic control equipment	Examination and assessment of evidence obtained from one or more of the following: .1 approved in-service experience .2 approved training ship experience .3 approved simulator training, where appropriate .4 approved laboratory equipment training	Operation of equipment and system is in accordance with operating manuals Performance levels are in accordance with technical specifications
Manage trouble-shooting, restoration of electrical and electronic control equipment to operating condition	*Practical knowledge* Troubleshooting of electrical and electronic control equipment Function test of electrical, electronic control equipment and safety devices Troubleshooting of monitoring systems Software version control	Examination and assessment of evidence obtained from one or more of the following: .1 approved in-service experience .2 approved training ship experience .3 approved simulator training, where appropriate .4 approved laboratory equipment training	Maintenance activities are correctly planned in accordance with technical, legislative, safety and procedural specifications Inspection, testing and troubleshooting of equipment are appropriate

Table A-III/2 *(continued)*

Function: Maintenance and repair at the management level

Column 1	Column 2	Column 3	Column 4
Competence	**Knowledge, understanding and proficiency**	**Methods for demonstrating competence**	**Criteria for evaluating competence**
Manage safe and effective maintenance and repair procedures	*Theoretical knowledge* Marine engineering practice *Practical knowledge* Manage safe and effective maintenance and repair procedures Planning maintenance, including statutory and class verifications Planning repairs	Examination and assessment of evidence obtained from one or more of the following: .1 approved in-service experience .2 approved training ship experience .3 approved workshop training	Maintenance activities are correctly planned and carried out in accordance with technical, legislative, safety and procedural specifications Appropriate plans, specifications, materials and equipment are available for maintenance and repair Action taken leads to the restoration of plant by the most suitable method
Detect and identify the cause of machinery malfunctions and correct faults	*Practical knowledge* Detection of machinery malfunction, location of faults and action to prevent damage Inspection and adjustment of equipment Non-destructive examination	Examination and assessment of evidence obtained from one or more of the following: .1 approved in-service experience .2 approved training ship experience .3 approved simulator training, where appropriate .4 approved laboratory equipment training	The methods of comparing actual operating conditions are in accordance with recommended practices and procedures Actions and decisions are in accordance with recommended operating specifications and limitations
Ensure safe working practices	*Practical knowledge* Safe working practices	Examination and assessment of evidence obtained from one or more of the following: .1 approved in-service experience .2 approved training ship experience .3 approved laboratory equipment training	Working practices are in accordance with legislative requirements, codes of practice, permits to work and environmental concerns

Table A-III/2 *(continued)*

Function: Controlling the operation of the ship and care for persons on board at the management level

Column 1	Column 2	Column 3	Column 4
Competence	**Knowledge, understanding and proficiency**	**Methods for demonstrating competence**	**Criteria for evaluating competence**
Control trim, stability and stress	Understanding of fundamental principles of ship construction and the theories and factors affecting trim and stability and measures necessary to preserve trim and stability Knowledge of the effect on trim and stability of a ship in the event of damage to, and consequent flooding of, a compartment and countermeasures to be taken Knowledge of IMO recommendations concerning ship stability	Examination and assessment of evidence obtained from one or more of the following: .1 approved in-service experience .2 approved training ship experience .3 approved simulator training, where appropriate	Stability and stress conditions are maintained within safety limits at all times
Monitor and control compliance with legislative requirements and measures to ensure safety of life at sea, security and protection of the marine environment	Knowledge of relevant international maritime law embodied in international agreements and conventions Regard shall be paid especially to the following subjects: .1 certificates and other documents required to be carried on board ships by international conventions, how they may be obtained and the period of their legal validity .2 responsibilities under the relevant requirements of the International Convention on Load Lines, 1966, as amended .3 responsibilities under the relevant requirements of the International Convention for the Safety of Life at Sea, 1974, as amended .4 responsibilities under the International Convention for the Prevention of Pollution from Ships, as amended .5 maritime declarations of health and the requirements of the International Health Regulations .6 responsibilities under international instruments affecting the safety of the ships, passengers, crew or cargo .7 methods and aids to prevent pollution of the environment by ships .8 knowledge of national legislation for implementing international agreements and conventions	Examination and assessment of evidence obtained from one or more of the following: .1 approved in-service experience .2 approved training ship experience .3 approved simulator training, where appropriate	Procedures for monitoring operations and maintenance comply with legislative requirements Potential non-compliance is promptly and fully identified Requirements for renewal and extension of certificates ensure continued validity of survey items and equipment

Table A-III/2 *(continued)*

Function: Controlling the operation of the ship and care for persons on board at the management level *(continued)*

Column 1	Column 2	Column 3	Column 4
Competence	**Knowledge, understanding and proficiency**	**Methods for demonstrating competence**	**Criteria for evaluating competence**
Maintain safety and security of the vessel, crew and passengers and the operational condition of life-saving, fire-fighting and other safety systems	A thorough knowledge of life-saving appliance regulations (International Convention for the Safety of Life at Sea) Organization of fire and abandon ship drills Maintenance of operational condition of life-saving, fire-fighting and other safety systems Actions to be taken to protect and safeguard all persons on board in emergencies Actions to limit damage and salve the ship following fire, explosion, collision or grounding	Examination and assessment of evidence obtained from practical instruction and approved in-service training and experience	Procedures for monitoring fire-detection and safety systems ensure that all alarms are detected promptly and acted upon in accordance with established emergency procedures
Develop emergency and damage control plans and handle emergency situations	Ship construction, including damage control Methods and aids for fire prevention, detection and extinction Functions and use of life-saving appliances	Examination and assessment of evidence obtained from approved in-service training and experience	Emergency procedures are in accordance with the established plans for emergency situations

Table A-III/2 *(continued)*

Function: Controlling the operation of the ship and care for persons on board at the management level *(continued)*

Column 1	Column 2	Column 3	Column 4
Competence	**Knowledge, understanding and proficiency**	**Methods for demonstrating competence**	**Criteria for evaluating competence**
Use leadership and managerial skills	Knowledge of shipboard personnel management and training A knowledge of international maritime conventions and recommendations, and related national legislation Ability to apply task and workload management, including: .1 planning and coordination .2 personnel assignment .3 time and resource constraints .4 prioritization Knowledge and ability to apply effective resource management: .1 allocation, assignment, and prioritization of resources .2 effective communication on board and ashore .3 decisions reflect consideration of team experience .4 assertiveness and leadership, including motivation .5 obtaining and maintaining situation awareness Knowledge and ability to apply decision-making techniques: .1 situation and risk assessment .2 identify and generate options .3 select course of action .4 evaluation of outcome effectiveness Development, implementation, and oversight of standard operating procedures	Assessment of evidence obtained from one or more of the following: .1 approved training .2 approved in-service experience .3 approved simulator training	The crew are allocated duties and informed of expected standards of work and behaviour in a manner appropriate to the individuals concerned Training objectives and activities are based on assessment of current competence and capabilities and operational requirements Operations are demonstrated to be in accordance with applicable rules Operations are planned and resources are allocated as needed in correct priority to perform necessary tasks Communication is clearly and unambiguously given and received Effective leadership behaviours are demonstrated Necessary team member(s) share accurate understanding of current and predicted vessel state and operational status and external environment Decisions are most effective for the situation Operations are demonstrated to be effective and in accordance with applicable rules

Section A-III/3

Mandatory minimum requirements for certification of chief engineer officers and second engineer officers on ships powered by main propulsion machinery of between 750 kW and 3,000 kW propulsion power

Standard of competence

1 Every candidate for certification as chief engineer officer and second engineer officer of seagoing ships powered by main propulsion machinery of between 750 kW and 3,000 kW power shall be required to demonstrate ability to undertake, at management level, the tasks, duties and responsibilities listed in column 1 of table A-III/2.

2 The minimum knowledge, understanding and proficiency required for certification is listed in column 2 of table A-III/2. This incorporates, expands and extends in depth the subjects listed in column 2 of table A-III/1 for officers in charge of an engineering watch in a manned engine-room or designated duty engineers in a periodically unmanned engine-room.

3 Bearing in mind that a second engineer officer shall be in a position to assume the responsibilities of the chief engineer officer at any time, assessment in these subjects shall be designed to test the candidate's ability to assimilate all available information that affects the safe operation of the ship's machinery and the protection of the marine environment.

4 The level of knowledge of the subjects listed in column 2 of table A-III/2 may be lowered but shall be sufficient to enable the candidate to serve in the capacity of chief engineer officer or second engineer officer at the range of propulsion power specified in this section.

5 Training and experience to achieve the necessary level of theoretical knowledge, understanding and proficiency shall take into account the relevant requirements of this part and the guidance given in part B of this Code.

6 The Administration may omit knowledge requirements for types of propulsion machinery other than those machinery installations for which the certificate to be awarded shall be valid. A certificate awarded on such a basis shall not be valid for any category of machinery installation which has been omitted until the engineer officer proves to be competent in these knowledge requirements. Any such limitation shall be stated on the certificate and in the endorsement.

7 Every candidate for certification shall be required to provide evidence of having achieved the required standard of competence in accordance with the methods for demonstrating competence and the criteria for evaluating competence tabulated in columns 3 and 4 of table A-III/2.

Near-coastal voyages

8 The level of knowledge, understanding and proficiency required under the different sections listed in column 2 of table A-III/2 and the requirements of paragraphs 2.1.1 and 2.1.2 of regulation III/3 may be varied for engineer officers of ships powered by main propulsion machinery of less than 3,000 kW main propulsion power engaged on near-coastal voyages, as considered necessary, bearing in mind the effect on the safety of all ships which may be operating in the same waters. Any such limitation shall be stated on the certificate and in the endorsement.

Section A-III/4

Mandatory minimum requirements for certification of ratings forming part of a watch in a manned engine-room or designated to perform duties in a periodically unmanned engine-room

Standard of competence

1 Every rating forming part of an engine-room watch on a seagoing ship shall be required to demonstrate the competence to perform the marine engineering function at the support level, as specified in column 1 of table A-III/4.

2 The minimum knowledge, understanding and proficiency required of ratings forming part of an engine-room watch is listed in column 2 of table A-III/4.

3 Every candidate for certification shall be required to provide evidence of having achieved the required standard of competence in accordance with the methods for demonstrating competence and the criteria for evaluating competence specified in columns 3 and 4 of table A-III/4. The reference to "practical test" in column 3 may include approved shore-based training in which the students undergo practical testing.

4 Where there are no tables of competence for the support level with respect to certain functions, it remains the responsibility of the Administration to determine the appropriate training, assessment and certification requirements to be applied to personnel designated to perform those functions at the support level.

Table A-III/4

Specification of minimum standard of competence for ratings forming part of an engineering watch

Function: Marine engineering at the support level

Column 1	Column 2	Column 3	Column 4
Competence	**Knowledge, understanding and proficiency**	**Methods for demonstrating competence**	**Criteria for evaluating competence**
Carry out a watch routine appropriate to the duties of a rating forming part of an engine-room watch Understand orders and be understood in matters relevant to watchkeeping duties	Terms used in machinery spaces and names of machinery and equipment Engine-room watchkeeping procedures Safe working practices as related to engine-room operations Basic environmental protection procedures Use of appropriate internal communication system Engine-room alarm systems and ability to distinguish between the various alarms, with special reference to fire-extinguishing gas alarms	Assessment of evidence obtained from one or more of the following: .1 approved in-service experience; .2 approved training ship experience; or .3 practical test	Communications are clear and concise, and advice or clarification is sought from the officer of the watch where watch information or instructions are not clearly understood Maintenance, handover and relief of the watch is in conformity with accepted principles and procedures
For keeping a boiler watch: Maintain the correct water levels and steam pressures	Safe operation of boilers	Assessment of evidence obtained from one or more of the following: .1 approved in-service experience; .2 approved training ship experience; .3 practical test; or .4 approved simulator training, where appropriate	Assessment of boiler condition is accurate and based on relevant information available from local and remote indicators and physical inspections The sequence and timing of adjustments maintains safety and optimum efficiency
Operate emergency equipment and apply emergency procedures	Knowledge of emergency duties Escape routes from machinery spaces Familiarity with the location and use of fire-fighting equipment in the machinery spaces	Assessment of evidence obtained from demonstration and approved in-service experience or approved training ship experience	Initial action on becoming aware of an emergency or abnormal situation conforms with established procedures Communications are clear and concise at all times and orders are acknowledged in a seamanlike manner

Section A-III/5

Mandatory minimum requirements for certification of ratings as able seafarer engine in a manned engine-room or designated to perform duties in a periodically unmanned engine-room

Standard of competence

1 Every able seafarer engine serving on a seagoing ship powered by main propulsion machinery of 750 kW propulsion power or more shall be required to demonstrate the competence to perform the functions at the support level, as specified in column 1 of table A-III/5.

2 The minimum knowledge, understanding and proficiency required of an able seafarer engine serving on a seagoing ship powered by main propulsion machinery of 750 kW propulsion power or more is listed in column 2 of table A-III/5.

3 Every candidate for certification shall be required to provide evidence of having achieved the required standard of competence in accordance with the methods for demonstrating competence and the criteria for evaluating competence specified in columns 3 and 4 of table A-III/5.

Table A-III/5

Specification of minimum standard of competence for ratings as able seafarer engine in a manned engine-room or designated to perform duties in a periodically unmanned engine-room

Function: Marine engineering at the support level

Column 1	Column 2	Column 3	Column 4
Competence	**Knowledge, understanding and proficiency**	**Methods for demonstrating competence**	**Criteria for evaluating competence**
Contribute to a safe engineering watch	Ability to understand orders and to communicate with the officer of the watch in matters relevant to watchkeeping duties Procedures for the relief, maintenance and handover of a watch Information required to maintain a safe watch	Assessment of evidence obtained from in-service experience or practical test	Communications are clear and concise Maintenance, handover and relief of the watch is in conformity with acceptable practices and procedures
Contribute to the monitoring and controlling of an engine-room watch	Basic knowledge of the function and operation of main propulsion and auxiliary machinery Basic understanding of main propulsion and auxiliary machinery control pressures, temperatures and levels	Assessment of evidence obtained from one or more of the following: .1 approved in-service experience; .2 approved training ship experience; or .3 practical test	The frequency and extent of monitoring of main propulsion and auxiliary machinery conforms with accepted principles and procedures Deviations from the norm are identified Unsafe conditions or potential hazards are promptly recognized, reported and rectified before work continues
Contribute to fuelling and oil transfer operations	Knowledge of the function and operation of fuel system and oil transfer operations, including: .1 preparations for fuelling and transfer operations .2 procedures for connecting and disconnecting fuelling and transfer hoses .3 procedures relating to incidents that may arise during fuelling or transferring operation .4 securing from fuelling and transfer operations .5 ability to correctly measure and report tank levels	Assessment of evidence obtained from one or more of the following: .1 approved in-service experience .2 practical training .3 examination .4 approved training ship experience Assessment of evidence obtained from practical demonstration	Transfer operations are carried out in accordance with established safety practices and equipment operating instructions The handling of dangerous, hazardous and harmful liquids complies with established safety practices Communications within the operator's area of responsibility are consistently successful

Table A-III/5 *(continued)*

Function: Marine engineering at the support level *(continued)*

Column 1	Column 2	Column 3	Column 4
Competence	**Knowledge, understanding and proficiency**	**Methods for demonstrating competence**	**Criteria for evaluating competence**
Contribute to bilge and ballast operations	Knowledge of the safe function, operation and maintenance of the bilge and ballast systems, including: .1 reporting incidents associated with transfer operations .2 ability to correctly measure and report tank levels	Assessment of evidence obtained from one or more of the following: .1 approved in-service experience .2 practical training .3 examination .4 approved training ship experience Assessment of evidence obtained from practical demonstration	Operations and maintenance are carried out in accordance with established safety practices and equipment operating instructions, and pollution of the marine environment is avoided Communications within the operator's area of responsibility are consistently successful
Contribute to the operation of equipment and machinery	Safe operation of equipment, including: .1 valves and pumps .2 hoists and lifting equipment .3 hatches, watertight doors, ports and related equipment Ability to use and understand basic crane, winch and hoist signals	Assessment of evidence obtained from one or more of the following: .1 approved in-service experience .2 practical training .3 examination .4 approved training ship experience Assessment of evidence obtained from practical demonstration	Operations are carried out in accordance with established safety practices and equipment operating instructions Communications within the operator's area of responsibility are consistently successful

Function: Electrical, electronic and control engineering at the support level

Column 1	Column 2	Column 3	Column 4
Competence	**Knowledge, understanding and proficiency**	**Methods for demonstrating competence**	**Criteria for evaluating competence**
Safe use of electrical equipment	Safe use and operation of electrical equipment, including: .1 safety precautions before commencing work or repair .2 isolation procedures .3 emergency procedures .4 different voltages on board Knowledge of the causes of electric shock and precautions to be observed to prevent shock	Assessment of evidence obtained from one or more of the following: .1 approved in-service experience .2 practical training .3 examination .4 approved training ship experience	Recognizes and reports electrical hazards and unsafe equipment Understands safe voltages for hand-held equipment Understands risks associated with high-voltage equipment and onboard work

Table A-III/5 *(continued)*

Function: Maintenance and repair at the support level

Column 1	Column 2	Column 3	Column 4
Competence	**Knowledge, understanding and proficiency**	**Methods for demonstrating competence**	**Criteria for evaluating competence**
Contribute to shipboard maintenance and repair	Ability to use painting, lubrication and cleaning materials and equipment Ability to understand and execute routine maintenance and repair procedures Knowledge of surface preparation techniques Knowledge of safe disposal of waste materials Understanding manufacturer's safety guidelines and shipboard instructions Knowledge of the application, maintenance and use of hand and power tools and measuring instruments and machine tools Knowledge of metalwork	Assessment of evidence obtained from practical demonstration Assessment of evidence obtained from one or more of the following: .1 approved in-service experience .2 practical training .3 examination .4 approved training ship experience	Maintenance activities are carried out in accordance with technical, safety and procedural specifications Selection and use of equipment and tools is appropriate

Table A-III/5 *(continued)*

Function: Controlling the operation of the ship and care for persons on board at the support level

Column 1	Column 2	Column 3	Column 4
Competence	**Knowledge, understanding and proficiency**	**Methods for demonstrating competence**	**Criteria for evaluating competence**
Contribute to the handling of stores	Knowledge of procedures for safe handling, stowage and securing of stores	Assessment of evidence obtained from one or more of the following: .1 approved in-service experience .2 practical training .3 examination .4 approved training ship experience	Stores operations are carried out in accordance with established safety practices and equipment operating instructions The handling of dangerous, hazardous and harmful stores complies with established safety practices Communications within the operator's area of responsibility are consistently successful
Apply precautions and contribute to the prevention of pollution of the marine environment	Knowledge of the precautions to be taken to prevent pollution of the marine environment Knowledge of use and operation of anti-pollution equipment Knowledge of approved methods for disposal of marine pollutants	Assessment of evidence obtained from one or more of the following: .1 approved in-service experience .2 practical training .3 examination .4 approved training ship experience	Procedures designed to safeguard the marine environment are observed at all times
Apply occupational health and safety procedures	Working knowledge of safe working practices and personal shipboard safety, including: .1 electrical safety .2 lockout/tag-out .3 mechanical safety .4 permit to work systems .5 working aloft .6 working in enclosed spaces .7 lifting techniques and methods of preventing back injury .8 chemical and biohazard safety .9 personal safety equipment	Assessment of evidence obtained from one or more of the following: .1 approved in-service experience .2 practical training .3 examination .4 approved training ship experience	Procedures designed to safeguard personnel and the ship are observed at all times Safe working practices are observed and appropriate safety and protective equipment is correctly used at all times

Section A-III/6

Mandatory minimum requirements for certification of electro-technical officers

Training

1 The education and training required by paragraph 2.3 of regulation III/6 shall include training in electronic and electrical workshop skills relevant to the duties of electro-technical officer.

Onboard training

2 Every candidate for certification as electro-technical officer shall follow an approved programme of onboard training which:

.1 ensures that, during the required period of seagoing service, the candidate receives systematic practical training and experience in the tasks, duties and responsibilities of an electro-technical officer;

.2 is closely supervised and monitored by qualified and certificated officers aboard the ships in which the approved seagoing service is performed; and

.3 is adequately documented in a training record book.

Standard of competence

3 Every candidate for certification as electro-technical officer shall be required to demonstrate the ability to undertake the tasks, duties and responsibilities listed in column 1 of table A-III/6.

4 The minimum knowledge, understanding and proficiency required for certification is listed in column 2 of table A-III/6, and it shall take into account the guidance given in part B of this Code.

5 Every candidate for certification shall be required to provide evidence of having achieved the required standard of competence tabulated in columns 3 and 4 of table A-III/6.

Table A-III/6

Specification of minimum standard of competence for electro-technical officers

Function: Electrical, electronic and control engineering at the operational level

Column 1	Column 2	Column 3	Column 4
Competence	**Knowledge, understanding and proficiency**	**Methods for demonstrating competence**	**Criteria for evaluating competence**
Monitor the operation of electrical, electronic and control systems	Basic understanding of the operation of mechanical engineering systems, including: .1 prime movers, including main propulsion plant .2 engine-room auxiliary machinery .3 steering systems .4 cargo handling systems .5 deck machinery .6 hotel systems Basic knowledge of heat transmission, mechanics and hydromechanics *Knowledge of:* Electro-technology and electrical machines theory Fundamentals of electronics and power electronics Electrical power distribution boards and electrical equipment Fundamentals of automation, automatic control systems and technology Instrumentation, alarm and monitoring systems Electrical drives Technology of electrical materials Electro-hydraulic and electro-pneumatic control systems Appreciation of the hazards and precautions required for the operation of power systems above 1,000 volts	Examination and assessment of evidence obtained from one or more of the following: .1 approved in-service experience .2 approved training ship experience .3 approved simulator training, where appropriate .4 approved laboratory equipment training	Operation of equipment and system is in accordance with operating manuals Performance levels are in accordance with technical specifications

Table A-III/6 *(continued)*

Function: Electrical, electronic and control engineering at the operational level *(continued)*

Column 1	Column 2	Column 3	Column 4
Competence	**Knowledge, understanding and proficiency**	**Methods for demonstrating competence**	**Criteria for evaluating competence**
Monitor the operation of automatic control systems of propulsion and auxiliary machinery	Preparation of control systems of propulsion and auxiliary machinery for operation	Examination and assessment of evidence obtained from one or more of the following: .1 approved in-service experience .2 approved training ship experience .3 approved simulator training, where appropriate .4 approved laboratory equipment training	Surveillance of main propulsion plant and auxiliary systems is sufficient to maintain safe operation condition
Operate generators and distribution systems	Coupling, load sharing and changing over generators Coupling and breaking connection between switchboards and distribution panels	Examination and assessment of evidence obtained from one or more of the following: .1 approved in-service experience .2 approved training ship experience .3 approved simulator training, where appropriate .4 approved laboratory equipment training	Operations are planned and carried out in accordance with operating manuals, established rules and procedures to ensure safety of operations Electrical distribution systems can be understood and explained with drawings/instructions
Operate and maintain power systems in excess of 1,000 volts	*Theoretical knowledge* High-voltage technology Safety precautions and procedures Electrical propulsion of the ships, electrical motors and control systems *Practical knowledge* Safe operation and maintenance of high-voltage systems, including knowledge of the special technical type of high-voltage systems and the danger resulting from operational voltage of more than 1,000 volts	Examination and assessment of evidence obtained from one or more of the following: .1 approved in-service experience .2 approved training ship experience .3 approved simulator training, where appropriate .4 approved laboratory equipment training	Operations are planned and carried out in accordance with operating manuals, established rules and procedures to ensure safety of operations

Table A-III/6 *(continued)*

Function: Electrical, electronic and control engineering at the operational level *(continued)*

Column 1	Column 2	Column 3	Column 4
Competence	**Knowledge, understanding and proficiency**	**Methods for demonstrating competence**	**Criteria for evaluating competence**
Operate computers and computer networks on ships	Understanding of: .1 main features of data processing .2 construction and use of computer networks on ships .3 bridge-based, engine-room-based and commercial computer use	Examination and assessment of evidence obtained from one or more of the following: .1 approved in-service experience .2 approved training ship experience .3 approved simulator training, where appropriate .4 approved laboratory equipment training	Computer networks and computers are correctly checked and handled
Use English in written and oral form	Adequate knowledge of the English language to enable the officer to use engineering publications and to perform the officer's duties	Examination and assessment of evidence obtained from practical instructions	English language publications relevant to the officer's duties are correctly interpreted Communications are clear and understood
Use internal communication systems	Operation of all internal communication systems on board	Examination and assessment of evidence obtained from one or more of the following: .1 approved in-service experience .2 approved training ship experience .3 approved simulator training, where appropriate .4 approved laboratory equipment training	Transmission and reception of messages are consistently successful Communication records are complete, accurate and comply with statutory requirements

Table A-III/6 *(continued)*

Function: Maintenance and repair at the operational level

Column 1	Column 2	Column 3	Column 4
Competence	**Knowledge, understanding and proficiency**	**Methods for demonstrating competence**	**Criteria for evaluating competence**
Maintenance and repair of electrical and electronic equipment	Safety requirements for working on shipboard electrical systems, including the safe isolation of electrical equipment required before personnel are permitted to work on such equipment Maintenance and repair of electrical system equipment, switchboards, electric motors, generators and DC electrical systems and equipment Detection of electric malfunction, location of faults and measures to prevent damage Construction and operation of electrical testing and measuring equipment Function and performance tests of the following equipment and their configuration: .1 monitoring systems .2 automatic control devices .3 protective devices The interpretation of electrical and electronic diagrams	Examination and assessment of evidence obtained from one or more of the following: .1 approved workshop skills training .2 approved practical experience and tests .3 approved in-service experience .4 approved training ship experience	Safety measures for working are appropriate Selection and use of hand tools, measuring instruments, and testing equipment are appropriate, and interpretation of results is accurate Dismantling, inspecting, repairing and reassembling equipment are in accordance with manuals and good practice Reassembling and performance testing is in accordance with manuals and good practice
Maintenance and repair of automation and control systems of main propulsion and auxiliary machinery	Appropriate electrical and mechanical knowledge and skills *Safety and emergency procedures* Safe isolation of equipment and associated systems required before personnel are permitted to work on such plant or equipment Practical knowledge for the testing, maintenance, fault finding and repair Test, detect faults and maintain and restore electrical and electronic control equipment to operating condition	Examination and assessment of evidence obtained from one or more of the following: .1 approved in-service experience .2 approved training ship experience .3 approved simulator training, where appropriate .4 approved laboratory equipment training	The effect of malfunctions on associated plant and systems is accurately identified, ship's technical drawings are correctly interpreted, measuring and calibrating instruments are correctly used and actions taken are justified Isolation, dismantling and reassembly of plant and equipment are in accordance with manufacturer's safety guidelines and shipboard instructions and legislative and safety specifications. Action taken leads to the restoration of automation and control systems by the method most suitable and appropriate to the prevailing circumstances and conditions

Table A-III/6 *(continued)*

Function: Maintenance and repair at the operational level *(continued)*

Column 1	Column 2	Column 3	Column 4
Competence	**Knowledge, understanding and proficiency**	**Methods for demonstrating competence**	**Criteria for evaluating competence**
Maintenance and repair of bridge navigation equipment and ship communication systems	Knowledge of the principles and maintenance procedures of navigation equipment, internal and external communication systems *Theoretical knowledge* Electrical and electronic systems operating in flammable areas *Practical knowledge* Carrying out safe maintenance and repair procedures Detection of machinery malfunction, location of faults and action to prevent damage		The effect of malfunctions on associated plant and systems is accurately identified, ship's technical drawings are correctly interpreted, measuring and calibrating instruments are correctly used and actions taken are justified Isolation, dismantling and re-assembly of plant and equipment are in accordance with manufacturer's safety guidelines and shipboard instructions, legislative and safety specifications. Action taken leads to the restoration of bridge navigation equipment and ship communication systems by the method most suitable and appropriate to the prevailing circumstances and conditions
Maintenance and repair of electrical, electronic and control systems of deck machinery and cargo-handling equipment	Appropriate electrical and mechanical knowledge and skills *Safety and emergency procedures* Safe isolation of equipment and associated systems required before personnel are permitted to work on such plant or equipment Practical knowledge for the testing, maintenance, fault finding and repair Test, detect faults and maintain and restore electrical and electronic control equipment to operating condition	Examination and assessment of evidence obtained from one or more of the following: .1 approved in-service experience .2 approved training ship experience .3 approved simulator training, where appropriate .4 approved laboratory equipment training	The effect of malfunctions on associated plant and systems is accurately identified, ship's technical drawings are correctly interpreted, measuring and calibrating instruments are correctly used and actions taken are justified Isolation, dismantling and re-assembly of plant and equipment are in accordance with manufacturer's safety guidelines and shipboard instructions, legislative and safety specifications. Action taken leads to the restoration of deck machinery and cargo-handling equipment by the method most suitable and appropriate to the prevailing circumstances and conditions

Table A-III/6 *(continued)*

Function: Maintenance and repair at the operational level *(continued)*

Column 1	Column 2	Column 3	Column 4
Competence	**Knowledge, understanding and proficiency**	**Methods for demonstrating competence**	**Criteria for evaluating competence**
Maintenance and repair of control and safety systems of hotel equipment	*Theoretical knowledge* Electrical and electronic systems operating in flammable areas *Practical knowledge* Carrying out safe maintenance and repair procedures Detection of machinery malfunction, location of faults and action to prevent damage		The effect of malfunctions on associated plant and systems is accurately identified, ship's technical drawings are correctly interpreted, measuring and calibrating instruments are correctly used and actions taken are justified Isolation, dismantling and re-assembly of plant and equipment are in accordance with manufacturer's safety guidelines and shipboard instructions, legislative and safety specifications. Action taken leads to the restoration of control and safety systems of hotel equipment by the method most suitable and appropriate to the prevailing circumstances and conditions

Table A-III/6 *(continued)*

Function: Controlling the operation of the ship and care for persons on board at the operational level

Column 1	Column 2	Column 3	Column 4
Competence	**Knowledge, understanding and proficiency**	**Methods for demonstrating competence**	**Criteria for evaluating competence**
Ensure compliance with pollution-prevention requirements	*Prevention of pollution of the marine environment* Knowledge of the precautions to be taken to prevent pollution of the marine environment Anti-pollution procedures and all associated equipment Importance of proactive measures to protect the marine environment	Examination and assessment of evidence obtained from one or more of the following: .1 approved in-service experience .2 approved training ship experience .3 approved training	Procedures for monitoring shipboard operations and ensuring compliance with pollution-prevention requirements are fully observed Actions to ensure that a positive environmental reputation is maintained
Prevent, control and fight fire on board	*Fire prevention and fire-fighting appliances* Ability to organize fire drills Knowledge of classes and chemistry of fire Knowledge of fire-fighting systems Action to be taken in the event of fire, including fires involving oil systems	Assessment of evidence obtained from approved fire-fighting training and experience as set out in section A-VI/3, paragraphs 1 to 3	The type and scale of the problem is promptly identified, and initial actions conform with the emergency procedure and contingency plans for the ship Evacuation, emergency shutdown and isolation procedures are appropriate to the nature of the emergency and are implemented promptly The order of priority, and the levels and time-scales of making reports and informing personnel on board, are relevant to the nature of the emergency and reflect the urgency of the problem
Operate life-saving appliances	*Life-saving* Ability to organize abandon ship drills and knowledge of the operation of survival craft and rescue boats, their launching appliances and arrangements, and their equipment, including radio life-saving appliances, satellite EPIRBs, SARTs, immersion suits and thermal protective aids	Assessment of evidence obtained from approved training and experience as set out in section A-VI/2, paragraphs 1 to 4	Actions in responding to abandon ship and survival situations are appropriate to the prevailing circumstances and conditions and comply with accepted safety practices and standards
Apply medical first aid on board ship	*Medical aid* Practical application of medical guides and advice by radio, including the ability to take effective action based on such knowledge in the case of accidents or illnesses that are likely to occur on board ship	Assessment of evidence obtained from approved training as set out in section A-VI/4, paragraphs 1 to 3	Identification of probable cause, nature and extent of injuries or conditions is prompt and treatment minimizes immediate threat to life

Table A-III/6 *(continued)*

Function: Controlling the operation of the ship and care for persons on board at the operational level *(continued)*

Column 1	Column 2	Column 3	Column 4
Competence	**Knowledge, understanding and proficiency**	**Methods for demonstrating competence**	**Criteria for evaluating competence**
Application of leadership and teamworking skills	Working knowledge of shipboard personnel management and training Ability to apply task and workload management, including: .1 planning and co-ordination .2 personnel assignment .3 time and resource constraints .4 prioritization Knowledge and ability to apply effective resource management: .1 allocation, assignment and prioritization of resources .2 effective communication on board and ashore .3 decisions reflect consideration of team experiences 4 assertiveness and leadership, including motivation .5 obtaining and maintaining situational awareness Knowledge and ability to apply decision-making techniques: .1 Situation and risk assessment .2 Identify and consider generated options .3 Selecting course of action .4 Evaluation of outcome effectiveness	Assessment of evidence obtained from one or more of the following: .1 approved training .2 approved in-service experience .3 practical demonstration	The crew are allocated duties and informed of expected standards of work and behaviour in a manner appropriate to the individuals concerned Training objectives and activities are based on assessment of current competence and capabilities and operational requirements Operations are planned and resources are allocated as needed in correct priority to perform necessary tasks Communication is clearly and unambiguously given and received Effective leadership behaviours are demonstrated Necessary team member(s) share accurate understanding of current and predicted vessel state and operational status and external environment Decisions are most effective for the situation
Contribute to the safety of personnel and ship	Knowledge of personal survival techniques Knowledge of fire prevention and ability to fight and extinguish fires Knowledge of elementary first aid Knowledge of personal safety and social responsibilities	Assessment of evidence obtained from approved training and experience as set out in section A-VI/1, paragraph 2	Appropriate safety and protective equipment is correctly used Procedures and safe working practices designed to safeguard personnel and the ship are observed at all times Procedures designed to safeguard the environment are observed at all times Initial and follow-up actions on becoming aware of an emergency conform with established emergency response procedures

Section A-III/7

Mandatory minimum requirements for certification of electro-technical rating

Standard of competence

1 Every electro-technical rating serving on a seagoing ship powered by main propulsion machinery of 750 kW propulsion power or more shall be required to demonstrate the competence to perform the functions at the support level, as specified in column 1 of table A-III/7.

2 The minimum knowledge, understanding and proficiency required of an electro-technical rating serving on a seagoing ship powered by main propulsion machinery of 750 kW propulsion power or more is listed in column 2 of table A-III/7.

3 Every candidate for certification shall be required to provide evidence of having achieved the required standard of competence in accordance with the methods for demonstrating competence and the criteria for evaluating competence specified in columns 3 and 4 of table A-III/7.

Table A-III/7

Specification of minimum standard of competence for electro-technical ratings

Function: Electrical, electronic and control engineering at the support level

Column 1	Column 2	Column 3	Column 4
Competence	**Knowledge, understanding and proficiency**	**Methods for demonstrating competence**	**Criteria for evaluating competence**
Safe use of electrical equipment	Safe use and operation of electrical equipment, including: .1 safety precautions before commencing work or repair .2 isolation procedures .3 emergency procedures .4 different voltages on board Knowledge of the causes of electric shock and precautions to be observed to prevent shock	Assessment of evidence obtained from one or more of the following: .1 approved in-service experience .2 practical training .3 examination .4 approved training ship experience	Understands and follows safety instructions of electrical equipment and machinery Recognizes and reports electrical hazards and unsafe equipment Understands safe voltages for hand-held equipment Understands risks associated with high-voltage equipment and onboard work
Contribute to monitoring the operation of electrical systems and machinery	Basic knowledge of the operation of mechanical engineering systems, including: .1 prime movers, including main propulsion plant .2 engine-room auxiliary machineries .3 steering systems .4 cargo-handling systems .5 deck machineries .6 hotel systems *Basic knowledge of:* .1 electro-technology and electrical machines theory .2 electrical power distribution boards and electrical equipment .3 fundamentals of automation, automatic control systems and technology .4 instrumentation, alarm and monitoring systems .5 electrical drives .6 electro-hydraulic and electro-pneumatic control systems .7 coupling, load sharing and changes in electrical configuration	Assessment of evidence obtained from one or more of the following: .1 approved in-service experience .2 practical training .3 examination .4 approved training ship experience	Knowledge that ensures: .1 operation of equipment and system is in accordance with operating manuals .2 performance levels are in accordance with technical specifications

Table A-III/7 *(continued)*

Function: Electrical, electronic and control engineering at the support level *(continued)*

Column 1	Column 2	Column 3	Column 4
Competence	**Knowledge, understanding and proficiency**	**Methods for demonstrating competence**	**Criteria for evaluating competence**
Use hand tools, electrical and electronic measurement equipment for fault finding, maintenance and repair operations	Safety requirements for working on shipboard electrical systems Application of safe working practices *Basic knowledge of*: .1 construction and operational characteristics of shipboard AC and DC systems and equipment .2 use of measuring instruments, machine tools, and hand and power tools	Assessment of evidence obtained from one or more of the following: .1 approved workshop skills training .2 approved practical experience and tests	Implementation of safety procedures is satisfactory Selection and use of test equipment is appropriate and interpretation of results is accurate Selection of procedures for the conduct of repair and maintenance is in accordance with manuals and good practice

Table A-III/7 *(continued)*

Function: Maintenance and repair at the support level

Column 1	Column 2	Column 3	Column 4
Competence	**Knowledge, understanding and proficiency**	**Methods for demonstrating competence**	**Criteria for evaluating competence**
Contribute to shipboard maintenance and repair	Ability to use lubrication and cleaning materials and equipment Knowledge of safe disposal of waste materials Ability to understand and execute routine maintenance and repair procedures Understanding manufacturer's safety guidelines and shipboard instructions	Assessment of evidence obtained from one or more of the following: .1 approved in-service experience .2 practical training .3 examination .4 approved training ship experience	Maintenance activities are carried out in accordance with technical, safety and procedural specifications Selection and use of equipment and tools is appropriate
Contribute to the maintenance and repair of electrical systems and machinery on board	*Safety and emergency procedures* Basic knowledge of electro-technical drawings and safe isolation of equipment and associated systems required before personnel are permitted to work on such plant or equipment Test, detect faults and maintain and restore electrical control equipment and machinery to operating condition Electrical and electronic equipment operating in flammable areas Basics of ship's fire-detection system Carrying out safe maintenance and repair procedures Detection of machinery malfunction, location of faults and action to prevent damage Maintenance and repair of lighting fixtures and supply systems	Examination and assessment of evidence obtained from one or more of the following: .1 approved in-service experience .2 approved training ship experience .3 approved simulator training, where appropriate .4 approved laboratory equipment training	The effect of malfunctions on associated plant and systems is accurately identified, ship's technical drawings are correctly interpreted, measuring and calibrating instruments are correctly used and actions taken are justified Isolation, dismantling and reassembly of plant and equipment is in accordance with manufacturer's safety guidelines and shipboard instructions

Table A-III/7 *(continued)*

Function: Controlling the operation of the ship and care for persons on board at the support level

Column 1	Column 2	Column 3	Column 4
Competence	**Knowledge, understanding and proficiency**	**Methods for demonstrating competence**	**Criteria for evaluating competence**
Contribute to the handling of stores	Knowledge of procedures for safe handling, stowage and securing of stores	Assessment of evidence obtained from one or more of the following: .1 approved in-service experience .2 practical training .3 examination .4 approved training ship experience	Stores stowage operations are carried out in accordance with established safety practices and equipment operating instructions The handling of dangerous, hazardous and harmful stores complies with established safety practices Communications within the operator's area of responsibility are consistently successful
Apply precautions and contribute to the prevention of pollution of the marine environment	Knowledge of the precautions to be taken to prevent pollution of the marine environment Knowledge of use and operation of anti-pollution equipment/agents Knowledge of approved methods for disposal of marine pollutants	Assessment of evidence obtained from one or more of the following: .1 approved in-service experience .2 practical training .3 examination .4 approved training ship experience	Procedures designed to safeguard the marine environment are observed at all times
Apply occupational health and safety procedures	Working knowledge of safe working practices and personal shipboard safety, including: .1 electrical safety .2 lockout/tag-out .3 mechanical safety .4 permit to work systems .5 working aloft .6 working in enclosed spaces .7 lifting techniques and methods of preventing back injury .8 chemical and biohazard safety .9 personal safety equipment	Assessment of evidence obtained from one or more of the following: .1 approved in-service experience .2 practical training .3 examination .4 approved training ship experience	Procedures designed to safeguard personnel and the ship are observed at all times Safe working practices are observed and appropriate safety and protective equipment is correctly used at all times

Chapter IV
Standards regarding radio operators

Section A-IV/1
Application

(No provisions)

Section A-IV/2
Mandatory minimum requirements for certification of GMDSS radio operators

Standard of competence

1 The minimum knowledge, understanding and proficiency required for certification of GMDSS radio operators shall be sufficient for radio operators to carry out their radio duties. The knowledge required for obtaining each type of certificate defined in the Radio Regulations shall be in accordance with those regulations. In addition, every candidate for certification of competency shall be required to demonstrate ability to undertake the tasks, duties and responsibilities listed in column 1 of table A-IV/2.

2 The knowledge, understanding and proficiency for endorsement under the Convention of certificates issued under the provisions of the Radio Regulations are listed in column 2 of table A-IV/2.

3 The level of knowledge of the subjects listed in column 2 of table A-IV/2 shall be sufficient for the candidate to carry out his duties.*

4 Every candidate shall provide evidence of having achieved the required standard of competence through:

.1 demonstration of competence to perform the tasks and duties and to assume responsibilities listed in column 1 of table A-IV/2, in accordance with the methods for demonstrating competence and the criteria for evaluating competence tabulated in columns 3 and 4 of that table; and

.2 examination or continuous assessment as part of an approved course of training based on the material set out in column 2 of table A-IV/2.

* The relevant IMO Model Course(s) may be of assistance in the preparation of courses.

Table A-IV/2

Specification of minimum standard of competence for GMDSS radio operators

Function: Radiocommunications at the operational level

Column 1	Column 2	Column 3	Column 4
Competence	**Knowledge, understanding and proficiency**	**Methods for demonstrating competence**	**Criteria for evaluating competence**
Transmit and receive information using GMDSS subsystems and equipment and fulfilling the functional requirements of GMDSS	In addition to the requirements of the Radio Regulations, a knowledge of: .1 search and rescue radiocommunications, including procedures in the International Aeronautical and Maritime Search and Rescue (IAMSAR) Manual .2 the means to prevent the transmission of false distress alerts and the procedures to mitigate the effects of such alerts .3 ship reporting systems .4 radio medical services .5 use of the International Code of Signals and the IMO Standard Marine Communication Phrases .6 the English language, both written and spoken, for the communication of information relevant to safety of life at sea **Note:** This requirement may be reduced in the case of the Restricted Radio Operator's Certificate	Examination and assessment of evidence obtained from practical demonstration of operational procedures, using: .1 approved equipment .2 GMDSS communication simulator, where appropriate* .3 radiocommunication laboratory equipment	Transmission and reception of communications comply with international regulations and procedures and are carried out efficiently and effectively English language messages relevant to the safety of the ship, security and persons on board and protection of the marine environment are correctly handled
Provide radio services in emergencies	The provision of radio services in emergencies such as: .1 abandon ship .2 fire on board ship .3 partial or full breakdown of radio installations Preventive measures for the safety of ship and personnel in connection with hazards related to radio equipment, including electrical and non-ionizing radiation hazards	Examination and assessment of evidence obtained from practical demonstration of operational procedures, using: .1 approved equipment .2 GMDSS communication simulator, where appropriate* .3 radiocommunication laboratory equipment	Response is carried out efficiently and effectively

* See paragraph 72 of section B-I/12 of this Code.

Chapter V
Standards regarding special training requirements for personnel on certain types of ships

Section A-V/1-1
Mandatory minimum requirements for the training and qualifications of masters, officers and ratings on oil and chemical tankers

Standard of competence

1 Every candidate for certification in basic training for oil and chemical tanker cargo operations shall be required to:

.1 demonstrate the competence to undertake the tasks, duties and responsibilities listed in column 1 of table A-V/1-1-1; and

.2 provide evidence of having achieved:

.2.1 the minimum knowledge, understanding and proficiency listed in column 2 of table A-V/1-1-1, and

.2.2 the required standard of competence in accordance with the methods for demonstrating competence and the criteria for evaluating competence tabulated in columns 3 and 4 of table A-V/1-1-1.

2 Every candidate for certification in advanced training for oil tanker cargo operations shall be required to:

.1 demonstrate the competence to undertake the tasks, duties and responsibilities listed in column 1 of table A-V/1-1-2; and

.2 provide evidence of having achieved:

.2.1 the minimum knowledge, understanding and proficiency listed in column 2 of table A-V/1-1-2, and

.2.2 the required standard of competence in accordance with the methods for demonstrating competence and the criteria for evaluating competence tabulated in columns 3 and 4 of table A-V/1-1-2.

3 Every candidate for certification in advanced training for chemical tanker cargo operations shall be required to:

.1 demonstrate the competence to undertake the tasks, duties and responsibilities listed in column 1 of table A-V/1-1-3; and

.2 provide evidence of having achieved:

.2.1 the minimum knowledge, understanding and proficiency listed in column 2 of table A-V/1-1-3, and

.2.2 the required standard of competence in accordance with the methods for demonstrating competence and the criteria for evaluating competence tabulated in columns 3 and 4 of table A-V/1-1-3.

Table A-V/1-1-1

Specification of minimum standard of competence in basic training for oil and chemical tanker cargo operations

Column 1	Column 2	Column 3	Column 4
Competence	**Knowledge, understanding and proficiency**	**Methods for demonstrating competence**	**Criteria for evaluating competence**
Contribute to the safe cargo operation of oil and chemical tankers	Basic knowledge of tankers: .1 types of oil and chemical tankers .2 general arrangement and construction Basic knowledge of cargo operations: .1 piping systems and valves .2 cargo pumps .3 loading and unloading .4 tank cleaning, purging, gas-freeing and inerting Basic knowledge of the physical properties of oil and chemicals: .1 pressure and temperature, including vapour pressure/temperature relationship .2 types of electrostatic charge generation .3 chemical symbols Knowledge and understanding of tanker safety culture and safety management	Examination and assessment of evidence obtained from one or more of the following: .1 approved in-service experience .2 approved training ship experience .3 approved simulator training .4 approved training programme	Communications within the area of responsibility are clear and effective Cargo operations are carried out in accordance with accepted principles and procedures to ensure safety of operations

Table A-V/1-1-1 *(continued)*

Column 1	Column 2	Column 3	Column 4
Competence	**Knowledge, understanding and proficiency**	**Methods for demonstrating competence**	**Criteria for evaluating competence**
Take precautions to prevent hazards	Basic knowledge of the hazards associated with tanker operations, including: .1 health hazards .2 environmental hazards .3 reactivity hazards .4 corrosion hazards .5 explosion and flammability hazards .6 sources of ignition, including electrostatic hazards .7 toxicity hazards .8 vapour leaks and clouds Basic knowledge of hazard controls: .1 inerting, water padding, drying agents and monitoring techniques .2 anti-static measures .3 ventilation .4 segregation .5 cargo inhibition .6 importance of cargo compatibility .7 atmospheric control .8 gas testing Understanding of information on a Material Safety Data Sheet (MSDS)	Examination and assessment of evidence obtained from one or more of the following: .1 approved in-service experience .2 approved training ship experience .3 approved simulator training .4 approved training programme	Correctly identifies, on an MSDS, relevant cargo-related hazards to the vessel and to personnel, and takes the appropriate actions in accordance with established procedures Identification and actions on becoming aware of a hazardous situation conform to established procedures in line with best practice

Table A-V/1-1-1 *(continued)*

Column 1	Column 2	Column 3	Column 4
Competence	**Knowledge, understanding and proficiency**	**Methods for demonstrating competence**	**Criteria for evaluating competence**
Apply occupational health and safety precautions and measures	Function and proper use of gas-measuring instruments and similar equipment Proper use of safety equipment and protective devices, including: .1 breathing apparatus and tank-evacuating equipment .2 protective clothing and equipment .3 resuscitators .4 rescue and escape equipment Basic knowledge of safe working practices and procedures in accordance with legislation and industry guidelines and personal shipboard safety relevant to oil and chemical tankers, including: .1 precautions to be taken when entering enclosed spaces .2 precautions to be taken before and during repair and maintenance work .3 safety measures for hot and cold work .4 electrical safety .5 ship/shore safety checklist Basic knowledge of first aid with reference to a Material Safety Data Sheet (MSDS)	Examination and assessment of evidence obtained from one or more of the following: .1 approved in-service experience .2 approved training ship experience .3 approved simulator training .4 approved training programme	Procedures for entry into enclosed spaces are observed Procedures and safe working practices designed to safeguard personnel and the ship are observed at all times Appropriate safety and protective equipment is correctly used First aid do's and don'ts

Table A-V/1-1-1 *(continued)*

Column 1	Column 2	Column 3	Column 4
Competence	**Knowledge, understanding and proficiency**	**Methods for demonstrating competence**	**Criteria for evaluating competence**
Carry out fire-fighting operations	Tanker fire response organization and action to be taken Fire hazards associated with cargo handling and transportation of hazardous and noxious liquids in bulk Fire-fighting agents used to extinguish oil and chemical fires Fixed fire-fighting foam system operations Portable fire-fighting foam operations Fixed dry chemical system operations Spill containment in relation to fire-fighting operations	Practical exercises and instruction conducted under approved and truly realistic training conditions (e.g., simulated shipboard conditions) and, whenever possible and practicable, in darkness	Initial actions and follow-up actions on becoming aware of fire on board conform with established practices and procedures Action taken on identifying muster signal is appropriate to the indicated emergency and complies with established procedures Clothing and equipment are appropriate to the nature of the fire-fighting operations The timing and sequence of individual actions are appropriate to the prevailing circumstances and conditions Extinguishment of fire is achieved using appropriate procedures, techniques and fire-fighting agents
Respond to emergencies	Basic knowledge of emergency procedures, including emergency shutdown	Examination and assessment of evidence obtained from one or more of the following: .1 approved in-service experience .2 approved training ship experience .3 approved simulator training .4 approved training programme	The type and impact of the emergency is promptly identified, and the response actions conform to the emergency procedures and contingency plans
Take precautions to prevent pollution of the environment from the release of oil or chemicals	Basic knowledge of the effects of oil and chemical pollution on human and marine life Basic knowledge of shipboard procedures to prevent pollution Basic knowledge of measures to be taken in the event of spillage, including the need to: .1 report relevant information to the responsible persons .2 assist in implementing shipboard spill-containment procedures	Examination and assessment of evidence obtained from one or more of the following: .1 approved in-service experience .2 approved training ship experience .3 approved simulator training .4 approved training programme	Procedures designed to safeguard the environment are observed at all times

Table A-V/1-1-2

Specification of minimum standard of competence in advanced training for oil tanker cargo operations

Column 1	Column 2	Column 3	Column 4
Competence	**Knowledge, understanding and proficiency**	**Methods for demonstrating competence**	**Criteria for evaluating competence**
Ability to safely perform and monitor all cargo operations	*Design and characteristics of an oil tanker* Knowledge of oil tanker design, systems and equipment, including: .1 general arrangement and construction .2 pumping arrangement and equipment .3 tank arrangement, pipeline system and tank venting arrangement .4 gauging systems and alarms .5 cargo heating systems .6 tank cleaning, gas-freeing and inerting systems .7 ballast system .8 cargo area venting and accommodation ventilation .9 slop arrangements .10 vapour recovery systems .11 cargo-related electrical and electronic control system .12 environmental protection equipment, including Oil Discharge Monitoring Equipment (ODME) .13 tank coating .14 tank temperature and pressure control systems .15 fire-fighting systems Knowledge of pump theory and characteristics, including types of cargo pumps and their safe operation Proficiency in tanker safety culture and implementation of safety-management system Knowledge and understanding of monitoring and safety systems, including the emergency shutdown	Examination and assessment of evidence obtained from one or more of the following: .1 approved in-service experience .2 approved training ship experience .3 approved simulator training .4 approved training programme	Communications are clear, understood and successful Cargo operations are carried out in a safe manner, taking into account oil tanker designs, systems and equipment Cargo operations are planned, risk is managed and carried out in accordance with accepted principles and procedures to ensure safety of operations and avoid pollution of the marine environment Potential non-compliance with cargo-operation-related procedures is promptly identified and rectified Proper loading, stowage and unloading of cargoes ensures that stability and stress conditions remain within safe limits at all times Actions taken and procedures followed are correctly applied and the appropriate shipboard cargo-related equipment is properly used Calibration and use of monitoring and gas-detection equipment comply with operational practices and procedures Procedures for monitoring and safety systems ensure that all alarms are detected promptly and acted upon in accordance with established emergency procedures

Table A-V/1-1-2 *(continued)*

Column 1	Column 2	Column 3	Column 4
Competence	**Knowledge, understanding and proficiency**	**Methods for demonstrating competence**	**Criteria for evaluating competence**
Ability to safely perform and monitor all cargo operations *(continued)*	*Loading, unloading, care and handling of cargo* Ability to perform cargo measurements and calculations Knowledge of the effect of bulk liquid cargoes on trim, stability and structural integrity Knowledge and understanding of oil cargo-related operations, including: .1 loading and unloading plans .2 ballasting and deballasting .3 tank cleaning operations .4 inerting .5 gas-freeing .6 ship-to-ship transfers .7 load on top .8 crude oil washing Development and application of cargo-related operation plans, procedures and checklists Ability to calibrate and use monitoring and gas-detection systems, instruments and equipment Ability to manage and supervise personnel with cargo-related responsibilities		Personnel are allocated duties and informed of procedures and standards of work to be followed, in a manner appropriate to the individuals concerned and in accordance with safe operational practices
Familiarity with physical and chemical properties of oil cargoes	Knowledge and understanding of the physical and chemical properties of oil cargoes Understanding the information contained in a Material Safety Data Sheet (MSDS)	Examination and assessment of evidence obtained from one or more of the following: .1 approved in-service experience .2 approved training ship experience .3 approved simulator training .4 approved training programme	Effective use is made of information resources for identification of properties and characteristics of oil cargoes and related gases, and their impact on safety, the environment and vessel operation

Table A-V/1-1-2 *(continued)*

Column 1	Column 2	Column 3	Column 4
Competence	**Knowledge, understanding and proficiency**	**Methods for demonstrating competence**	**Criteria for evaluating competence**
Take precautions to prevent hazards	Knowledge and understanding of the hazards and control measures associated with oil tanker cargo operations, including: .1 toxicity .2 flammability and explosion .3 health hazards .4 inert gas composition .5 electrostatic hazards Knowledge and understanding of dangers of non-compliance with relevant rules/regulations	Examination and assessment of evidence obtained from one or more of the following: .1 approved in-service experience .2 approved training ship experience .3 approved simulator training .4 approved training programme	Relevant cargo-related hazards to the vessel and to personnel associated with oil tanker cargo operations are correctly identified, and proper control measures are taken
Apply occupational health and safety precautions	Knowledge and understanding of safe working practices, including risk assessment and personal shipboard safety relevant to oil tankers: .1 precautions to be taken when entering enclosed spaces, including correct use of different types of breathing apparatus .2 precautions to be taken before and during repair and maintenance work .3 precautions for hot and cold work .4 precautions for electrical safety .5 use of appropriate Personal Protective Equipment (PPE)	Examination and assessment of evidence obtained from one or more of the following: .1 approved in-service experience .2 approved training ship experience .3 approved simulator training .4 approved training programme	Procedures designed to safeguard personnel and the ship are observed at all times Safe working practices are observed and appropriate safety and protective equipment is correctly used Working practices are in accordance with legislative requirements, codes of practice, permits to work and environmental concerns Correct use of breathing apparatus Procedures for entry into enclosed spaces are observed
Respond to emergencies	Knowledge and understanding of oil tanker emergency procedures, including: .1 ship emergency response plans .2 cargo operations emergency shutdown .3 actions to be taken in the event of failure of systems or services essential to cargo .4 fire fighting on oil tankers .5 enclosed space rescue .6 use of a Material Safety Data Sheet (MSDS) Actions to be taken following collision, grounding, or spillage	Examination and assessment of evidence obtained from one or more of the following: .1 approved in-service experience .2 approved training ship experience .3 approved simulator training .4 approved training programme	The type and impact of the emergency is promptly identified, and the response actions conform with established emergency procedures and contingency plans The order of priority, and the levels and time-scales of making reports and informing personnel on board, are relevant to the nature of the emergency and reflect the urgency of the problem Evacuation, emergency shutdown and isolation procedures are appropriate to the nature of the emergency and are implemented promptly

Table A-V/1-1-2 *(continued)*

Column 1	Column 2	Column 3	Column 4
Competence	**Knowledge, understanding and proficiency**	**Methods for demonstrating competence**	**Criteria for evaluating competence**
Respond to emergencies *(continued)*	Knowledge of medical first aid procedures on board oil tankers		The identification of and actions taken in a medical emergency conform to current recognized first aid practice and international guidelines
Take precautions to prevent pollution of the environment	Understanding of procedures to prevent pollution of the atmosphere and the environment	Examination and assessment of evidence obtained from one or more of the following: .1 approved in-service experience .2 approved training ship experience .3 approved simulator training .4 approved training programme	Operations are conducted in accordance with accepted principles and procedures to prevent pollution of the environment
Monitor and control compliance with legislative requirements	Knowledge and understanding of relevant provisions of the International Convention for the Prevention of Pollution from Ships (MARPOL), as amended, and other relevant IMO instruments, industry guidelines and port regulations as commonly applied	Examination and assessment of evidence obtained from one or more of the following: .1 approved in-service experience .2 approved training ship experience .3 approved simulator training .4 approved training programme	The handling of cargoes complies with relevant IMO instruments and established industrial standards and codes of safe working practice

Table A-V/1-1-3

Specification of minimum standard of competence in advanced training for chemical tanker cargo operations

Column 1	Column 2	Column 3	Column 4
Competence	**Knowledge, understanding and proficiency**	**Methods for demonstrating competence**	**Criteria for evaluating competence**
Ability to safely perform and monitor all cargo operations	*Design and characteristics of a chemical tanker* Knowledge of chemical tanker designs, systems and equipment, including: .1 general arrangement and construction .2 pumping arrangement and equipment .3 tank construction and arrangement .4 pipeline and drainage systems .5 tank and cargo pipeline pressure and temperature control systems and alarms .6 gauging control systems and alarms .7 gas-detecting systems .8 cargo heating and cooling systems .9 tank cleaning systems .10 cargo tank environmental control systems .11 ballast systems .12 cargo area venting and accommodation ventilation .13 vapour return/recovery systems .14 fire-fighting systems .15 tank, pipeline and fittings' material and coatings .16 slop management Knowledge of pump theory and characteristics, including types of cargo pumps and their safe operation Proficiency in tanker safety culture and implementation of safety management system	Examination and assessment of evidence obtained from one or more of the following: .1 approved in-service experience .2 approved training ship experience .3 approved simulator training .4 approved training programme	Communications are clear, understood and successful Cargo operations are carried out in a safe manner, taking into account chemical tanker designs, systems and equipment Cargo operations are planned, risk is managed and carried out in accordance with accepted principles and procedures to ensure safety of operations and avoid pollution of the marine environment
	Knowledge and understanding of monitoring and safety systems, including the emergency shutdown system		Procedures for monitoring and safety systems ensure that all alarms are detected promptly and acted upon in accordance with established procedures

Table A-V/1-1-3 *(continued)*

Column 1	Column 2	Column 3	Column 4
Competence	**Knowledge, understanding and proficiency**	**Methods for demonstrating competence**	**Criteria for evaluating competence**
Ability to safely perform and monitor all cargo operations *(continued)*	*Loading, unloading, care and handling of cargo* Ability to perform cargo measurements and calculations Knowledge of the effect of bulk liquid cargoes on trim and stability and structural integrity Knowledge and understanding of chemical cargo-related operations, including: .1 loading and unloading plans .2 ballasting and deballasting .3 tank cleaning operations .4 tank atmosphere control .5 inerting .6 gas-freeing .7 ship-to-ship transfers .8 inhibition and stabilization requirements .9 heating and cooling requirements and consequences to adjacent cargoes .10 cargo compatibility and segregation .11 high-viscosity cargoes .12 cargo residue operations .13 operational tank entry Development and application of cargo-related operation plans, procedures and checklists Ability to calibrate and use monitoring and gas-detection systems, instruments and equipment Ability to manage and supervise personnel with cargo-related responsibilities		Proper loading, stowage and unloading of cargoes ensures that stability and stress conditions remain within safe limits at all times Potential non-compliance with cargo-related procedures is promptly identified and rectified Actions taken and procedures followed are correctly identified, and appropriate shipboard cargo-related equipment is properly used Calibration and use of monitoring and gas-detection equipment are consistent with safe operational practices and procedures Personnel are allocated duties and informed of procedures and standards of work to be followed, in a manner appropriate to the individuals concerned and in accordance with safe operational practices

Table A-V/1-1-3 *(continued)*

Column 1	Column 2	Column 3	Column 4
Competence	**Knowledge, understanding and proficiency**	**Methods for demonstrating competence**	**Criteria for evaluating competence**
Familiarity with physical and chemical properties of chemical cargoes	Knowledge and understanding of the chemical and the physical properties of noxious liquid substances, including: .1 chemical cargoes categories (corrosive, toxic, flammable, explosive) .2 chemical groups and industrial usage .3 reactivity of cargoes Understanding the information contained in a Material Safety Data Sheet (MSDS)	Examination and assessment of evidence obtained from one or more of the following: .1 approved in-service experience .2 approved training ship experience .3 approved simulator training .4 approved training programme	Effective use is made of information resources for identification of properties and characteristics of noxious liquid substances and related gases, and their impact on safety, environmental protection and vessel operation
Take precautions to prevent hazards	Knowledge and understanding of the hazards and control measures associated with chemical tanker cargo operations, including: .1 flammability and explosion .2 toxicity .3 health hazards .4 inert gas composition .5 electrostatic hazards .6 reactivity .7 corrosivity .8 low-boiling-point cargoes .9 high-density cargoes .10 solidifying cargoes .11 polymerizing cargoes Knowledge and understanding of dangers of non-compliance with relevant rules/regulations	Examination and assessment of evidence obtained from one or more of the following: .1 approved in-service experience .2 approved training ship experience .3 approved simulator training .4 approved training programme	Relevant cargo-related hazards to the vessel and to personnel associated with chemical tanker cargo operations are correctly identified, and proper control measures are taken
Apply occupational health and safety precautions	Knowledge and understanding of safe working practices, including risk assessment and personal shipboard safety relevant to chemical tankers: .1 precautions to be taken when entering enclosed spaces, including correct use of different types of breathing apparatus .2 precautions to be taken before and during repair and maintenance work .3 precautions for hot and cold work .4 precautions for electrical safety .5 use of appropriate Personal Protective Equipment (PPE)	Examination and assessment of evidence obtained from one or more of the following: .1 approved in-service experience .2 approved training ship experience .3 approved simulator training .4 approved training programme	Procedures designed to safeguard personnel and the ship are observed at all times Safe working practices are observed and appropriate safety and protective equipment is correctly used Working practices are in accordance with legislative requirements, codes of practice, permits to work and environmental concerns Correct use of breathing apparatus Procedures for entry into enclosed spaces are observed

Table A-V/1-1-3 *(continued)*

Column 1	Column 2	Column 3	Column 4
Competence	**Knowledge, understanding and proficiency**	**Methods for demonstrating competence**	**Criteria for evaluating competence**
Respond to emergencies	Knowledge and understanding of chemical tanker emergency procedures, including: .1 ship emergency response plans .2 cargo operations emergency shutdown .3 actions to be taken in the event of failure of systems or services essential to cargo .4 fire fighting on chemical tankers .5 enclosed space rescue .6 cargo reactivity .7 jettisoning cargo .8 use of a Material Safety Data Sheet (MSDS) Actions to be taken following collision, grounding or spillage Knowledge of medical first aid procedures on board chemical tankers, with reference to the Medical First Aid Guide for Use in Accidents Involving Dangerous Goods (MFAG)	Examination and assessment of evidence obtained from one or more of the following: .1 approved in-service experience .2 approved training ship experience .3 approved simulator training .4 approved training programme	The type and impact of the emergency is promptly identified, and the response actions conform with established emergency procedures and contingency plans The order of priority, and the levels and time-scales of making reports and informing personnel on board, are relevant to the nature of the emergency and reflect the urgency of the problem Evacuation, emergency shutdown and isolation procedures are appropriate to the nature of the emergency and are implemented promptly The identification of and actions taken in a medical emergency conform to current recognized first aid practice and international guidelines
Take precautions to prevent pollution of the environment	Understanding of procedures to prevent pollution of the atmosphere and the environment	Examination and assessment of evidence obtained from one or more of the following: .1 approved in-service experience .2 approved training ship experience .3 approved simulator training .4 approved training programme	Operations are conducted in accordance with accepted principles and procedures to prevent pollution of the environment
Monitor and control compliance with legislative requirements	Knowledge and understanding of relevant provisions of the International Convention for the Prevention of Pollution from Ships (MARPOL) and other relevant IMO instruments, industry guidelines and port regulations as commonly applied Proficiency in the use of the IBC Code and related documents	Examination and assessment of evidence obtained from one or more of the following: .1 approved in-service experience .2 approved training ship experience .3 approved simulator training .4 approved training programme	The handling of cargoes complies with relevant IMO instruments and established industrial standards and codes of safe working practice

Section A-V/1-2

Mandatory minimum requirements for the training and qualifications of masters, officers and ratings on liquefied gas tankers

Standard of competence

1 Every candidate for certification in basic training for liquefied gas tanker cargo operations shall be required to:

- **.1** demonstrate the competence to undertake the tasks, duties and responsibilities listed in column 1 of table A-V/1-2-1; and
- **.2** provide evidence of having achieved:
  - **.2.1** the minimum knowledge, understanding and proficiency listed in column 2 of table A-V/1-2-1, and
  - **.2.2** the required standard of competence in accordance with the methods for demonstrating competence and the criteria for evaluating competence tabulated in columns 3 and 4 of table A-V/1-2-1.

2 Every candidate for certification in advanced training for liquefied gas tanker cargo operations shall be required to:

- **.1** demonstrate the competence to undertake the tasks, duties and responsibilities listed in column 1 of table A-V/1-2-2; and
- **.2** provide evidence of having achieved:
  - **.2.1** the minimum knowledge, understanding and proficiency listed in column 2 of table A-V/1-2-2, and
  - **.2.2** the required standard of competence in accordance with the methods for demonstrating competence and the criteria for evaluating competence tabulated in columns 3 and 4 of table A-V/1-2-2.

Table A-V/1-2-1

Specification of minimum standard of competence in basic training for liquefied gas tanker cargo operations

Column 1	Column 2	Column 3	Column 4
Competence	**Knowledge, understanding and proficiency**	**Methods for demonstrating competence**	**Criteria for evaluating competence**
Contribute to the safe operation of a liquefied gas tanker	*Design and operational characteristics of liquefied gas tankers* Basic knowledge of liquefied gas tankers .1 types of liquefied gas tankers .2 general arrangement and construction Basic knowledge of cargo operations: .1 piping systems and valves .2 cargo handling equipment .3 loading, unloading and care in transit .4 emergency shutdown (ESD) system .5 tank cleaning, purging, gas-freeing and inerting Basic knowledge of the physical properties of liquefied gases, including: .1 properties and characteristics .2 pressure and temperature, including vapour pressure/temperature relationship .3 types of electrostatic charge generation .4 chemical symbols Knowledge and understanding of tanker safety culture and safety management	Examination and assessment of evidence obtained from one or more of the following: .1 approved in-service experience .2 approved training ship experience .3 approved simulator training .4 approved training programme	Communications within the area of responsibility are clear and effective Cargo operations are carried out in accordance with accepted principles and procedures to ensure safety of operations

Table A-V/1-2-1 *(continued)*

Column 1	Column 2	Column 3	Column 4
Competence	**Knowledge, understanding and proficiency**	**Methods for demonstrating competence**	**Criteria for evaluating competence**
Take precautions to prevent hazards	Basic knowledge of the hazards associated with tanker operations, including: .1 health hazards .2 environmental hazards .3 reactivity hazards .4 corrosion hazards .5 explosion and flammability hazards .6 sources of ignition .7 electrostatic hazards .8 toxicity hazards .9 vapour leaks and clouds .10 extremely low temperatures .11 pressure hazards Basic knowledge of hazard controls: .1 inerting, drying and monitoring techniques .2 anti-static measures .3 ventilation .4 segregation .5 cargo inhibition .6 importance of cargo compatibility .7 atmospheric control .8 gas testing Understanding of information on a Material Safety Data Sheet (MSDS)	Examination and assessment of evidence obtained from one or more of the following: .1 approved in-service experience .2 approved training ship experience .3 approved simulator training .4 approved training programme	Correctly identifies, on an MSDS, relevant cargo-related hazards to the vessel and to personnel, and takes the appropriate actions in accordance with established procedures Identification and actions on becoming aware of a hazardous situation conform to established procedures in line with best practice

Table A-V/1-2-1 *(continued)*

Column 1	Column 2	Column 3	Column 4
Competence	**Knowledge, understanding and proficiency**	**Methods for demonstrating competence**	**Criteria for evaluating competence**
Apply occupational health and safety precautions and measures	Function and proper use of gas-measuring instruments and similar equipment Proper use of safety equipment and protective devices, including: .1 breathing apparatus and tank evacuating equipment .2 protective clothing and equipment .3 resuscitators .4 rescue and escape equipment Basic knowledge of safe working practices and procedures in accordance with legislation and industry guidelines and personal shipboard safety relevant to liquefied gas tankers, including: .1 precautions to be taken when entering enclosed spaces .2 precautions to be taken before and during repair and maintenance work .3 safety measures for hot and cold work .4 electrical safety .5 ship/shore safety checklist Basic knowledge of first aid with reference to a Material Safety Data Sheet (MSDS)	Examination and assessment of evidence obtained from one or more of the following: .1 approved in-service experience .2 approved training ship experience .3 approved simulator training .4 approved training programme	Procedures for entry into enclosed spaces are observed Procedures and safe working practices designed to safeguard personnel and the ship are observed at all times Appropriate safety and protective equipment is correctly used First aid do's and don'ts

Table A-V/1-2-1 *(continued)*

Column 1	Column 2	Column 3	Column 4
Competence	**Knowledge, understanding and proficiency**	**Methods for demonstrating competence**	**Criteria for evaluating competence**
Carry out fire-fighting operations	Tanker fire organization and action to be taken Special hazards associated with cargo handling and transportation of liquefied gases in bulk Fire-fighting agents used to extinguish gas fires Fixed fire-fighting foam system operations Portable fire-fighting foam operations Fixed dry chemical system operations Basic knowledge of spill containment in relation to fire-fighting operations	Practical exercises and instruction conducted under approved and truly realistic training conditions (e.g. simulated shipboard conditions) and, whenever possible and practicable, in darkness	Initial actions and follow-up actions on becoming aware of an emergency conform with established practices and procedures Action taken on identifying muster signals is appropriate to the indicated emergency and complies with established procedures Clothing and equipment are appropriate to the nature of the fire-fighting operations The timing and sequence of individual actions are appropriate to the prevailing circumstances and conditions Extinguishment of fire is achieved using appropriate procedures, techniques and fire-fighting agents
Respond to emergencies	Basic knowledge of emergency procedures, including emergency shutdown	Examination and assessment of evidence obtained from one or more of the following: .1 approved in-service experience .2 approved training ship experience .3 approved simulator training .4 approved training programme	The type and impact of the emergency is promptly identified and the response actions conform to the emergency procedures and contingency plans
Take precautions to prevent pollution of the environment from the release of liquefied gases	Basic knowledge of the effects of pollution on human and marine life Basic knowledge of shipboard procedures to prevent pollution Basic knowledge of measures to be taken in the event of spillage, including the need to: .1 report relevant information to the responsible persons .2 assist in implementing shipboard spill-containment procedures .3 prevent brittle fracture	Examination and assessment of evidence obtained from one or more of the following: .1 approved in-service experience .2 approved training ship experience .3 approved simulator training .4 approved training programme	Procedures designed to safeguard the environment are observed at all times

Table A-V/1-2-2

Specification of minimum standard of competence in advanced training for liquefied gas tanker cargo operations

Column 1	Column 2	Column 3	Column 4
Competence	**Knowledge, understanding and proficiency**	**Methods for demonstrating competence**	**Criteria for evaluating competence**
Ability to safely perform and monitor all cargo operations	*Design and characteristics of a liquefied gas tanker* Knowledge of liquefied gas tanker design, systems, and equipment, including: .1 types of liquefied gas tankers and cargo tanks construction .2 general arrangement and construction .3 cargo containment systems, including materials of construction and insulation .4 cargo-handling equipment and instrumentation, including: .4.1 cargo pumps and pumping arrangements .4.2 cargo pipelines and valves .4.3 expansion devices .4.4 flame screens .4.5 temperature monitoring systems .4.6 cargo tank level-gauging systems .4.7 tank pressure monitoring and control systems .5 cargo temperature maintenance system .6 tank atmosphere control systems (inert gas, nitrogen), including storage, generation and distribution systems .7 cofferdam heating systems .8 gas-detecting systems .9 ballast system .10 boil-off systems .11 reliquefaction systems .12 cargo Emergency Shut Down system (ESD) .13 custody transfer system Knowledge of pump theory and characteristics, including types of cargo pumps and their safe operation	Examination and assessment of evidence obtained from one or more of the following: .1 approved in-service experience .2 approved training ship experience .3 approved simulator training .4 approved training programme	Communications are clear, understood and successful Cargo operations are carried out in a safe manner, taking into account liquefied gas tanker designs, systems and equipment Pumping operations are carried out in accordance with accepted principles and procedures and are relevant to the type of cargo Cargo operations are planned, risk is managed and carried out in accordance with accepted principles and procedures to ensure safety of operations and avoid pollution of the marine environment

Table A-V/1-2-2 *(continued)*

Column 1	Column 2	Column 3	Column 4
Competence	**Knowledge, understanding and proficiency**	**Methods for demonstrating competence**	**Criteria for evaluating competence**
Ability to safely perform and monitor all cargo operations *(continued)*	*Loading, unloading, care and handling of cargo* Knowledge of the effect of bulk liquid cargoes on trim and stability and structural integrity Proficiency in tanker safety culture and implementation of safety management requirements Proficiency to apply safe preparations, procedures and checklists for all cargo operations, including: .1 post docking and loading: .1.1 tank inspection .1.2 inerting (Oxygen reduction, dewpoint reduction) .1.3 gassing-up .1.4 cooling down .1.5 loading .1.6 deballasting .1.7 sampling, including closed-loop sampling .2 sea passage: .2.1 cooling down .2.2 pressure maintenance .2.3 boil-off .2.4 inhibiting .3 unloading: .3.1 unloading .3.2 ballasting .3.3 stripping and cleaning systems .3.4 systems to make the tank liquid-free .4 pre-docking preparation: .4.1 warm-up .4.2 inerting .4.3 gas-freeing .5 ship-to-ship transfer		Proper loading, stowage and unloading of liquefied gas cargoes ensures that stability and stress conditions remain within safe limits at all times Potential non-compliance with cargo-related procedures is promptly identified and rectified Actions taken and procedures followed correctly identify and make full use of appropriate shipboard equipment Calibration and use of monitoring and gas-detection equipment is consistent with safe operational practices and procedures Procedures for monitoring and safety systems ensure that all alarms are detected promptly and acted upon in accordance with established procedures

Table A-V/1-2-2 *(continued)*

Column 1	Column 2	Column 3	Column 4
Competence	**Knowledge, understanding and proficiency**	**Methods for demonstrating competence**	**Criteria for evaluating competence**
Ability to safely perform and monitor all cargo operations *(continued)*	Proficiency to perform cargo measurements and calculations, including: .1 liquid phase .2 gas phase .3 On Board Quantity (OBQ) .4 Remain On Board (ROB) .5 boil-off cargo calculations		
	Proficiency to manage and supervise personnel with cargo-related responsibilities		Personnel are allocated duties and informed of procedures and standards of work to be followed, in a manner appropriate to the individuals concerned and in accordance with safe operational practices
Familiarity with physical and chemical properties of liquefied gas cargoes	Knowledge and understanding of basic chemistry and physics and the relevant definitions related to the safe carriage of liquefied gases in bulk in ships, including: .1 the chemical structure of gases .2 the properties and characteristics of liquefied gases (including CO_2) and their vapours, including: .2.1 simple gas laws .2.2 states of matter .2.3 liquid and vapour densities .2.4 diffusion and mixing of gases .2.5 compression of gases .2.6 reliquefaction and refrigeration of gases .2.7 critical temperature of gases and pressure .2.8 flashpoint, upper and lower explosive limits, auto-ignition temperature .2.9 compatibility, reactivity and positive segregation of gases .2.10 polymerization .2.11 saturated vapour pressure/reference temperature .2.12 dewpoint and bubble point .2.13 lubrication of compressors .2.14 hydrate formation	Examination and assessment of evidence obtained from one or more of the following: .1 approved in-service experience .2 approved training ship experience .3 approved simulator training .4 approved training programme	Effective use is made of information resources for identification of properties and characteristics of liquefied gases and their impact on safety, environmental protection and vessel operation

Table A-V/1-2-2 *(continued)*

Column 1	Column 2	Column 3	Column 4
Competence	**Knowledge, understanding and proficiency**	**Methods for demonstrating competence**	**Criteria for evaluating competence**
Familiarity with physical and chemical properties of liquefied gas cargoes (*continued*)	.3 the properties of single liquids .4 the nature and properties of solutions .5 thermodynamic units .6 basic thermodynamic laws and diagrams .7 properties of materials .8 effect of low temperature – brittle fracture Understanding the information contained in a Material Safety Data Sheet (MSDS)		
Take precautions to prevent hazards	Knowledge and understanding of the hazards and control measures associated with liquefied gas tanker cargo operations, including: .1 flammability .2 explosion .3 toxicity .4 reactivity .5 corrosivity .6 health hazards .7 inert gas composition .8 electrostatic hazards .9 polymerizing cargoes	Examination and assessment of evidence obtained from one or more of the following: .1 approved in-service experience .2 approved training ship experience .3 approved simulator training .4 approved training programme	Relevant cargo-related hazards to the vessel and to personnel associated with liquefied gas tanker cargo operations are correctly identified, and proper control measures are taken
	Proficiency to calibrate and use monitoring and gas-detection systems, instruments and equipment Knowledge and understanding of dangers of non-compliance with relevant rules/regulations		Use of gas-detection devices is in accordance with manuals and good practice
Apply occupational health and safety precautions	Knowledge and understanding of safe working practices, including risk assessment and personal shipboard safety relevant to liquefied gas tankers, including: .1 precautions to be taken when entering enclosed spaces (such as compressor rooms), including the correct use of different types of breathing apparatus .2 precautions to be taken before and during repair and maintenance work, including work affecting pumping, piping, electrical and control systems	Assessment of evidence obtained from one or more of the following: .1 approved in-service experience .2 approved training ship experience .3 approved simulator training .4 approved training programme	Procedures designed to safeguard personnel and the ship are observed at all times Safe working practices are observed and appropriate safety and protective equipment is correctly used Working practices are in accordance with legislative requirements, codes of practice, permits to work and environmental concerns Correct use of breathing apparatus

Table A-V/1-2-2 *(continued)*

Column 1	Column 2	Column 3	Column 4
Competence	**Knowledge, understanding and proficiency**	**Methods for demonstrating competence**	**Criteria for evaluating competence**
Apply occupational health and safety precautions *(continued)*	.3 precautions for hot and cold work .4 precautions for electrical safety .5 use of appropriate Personal Protective Equipment (PPE) .6 precautions for cold burn and frostbite .7 proper use of personal toxicity monitoring equipment		
Respond to emergencies	Knowledge and understanding of liquefied gas tanker emergency procedures, including: .1 ship emergency response plans .2 cargo operations emergency shutdown procedure .3 emergency cargo valve operations .4 actions to be taken in the event of failure of systems or services essential to cargo operations .5 fire fighting on liquefied gas tankers .6 jettisoning of cargo .7 enclosed space rescue Actions to be taken following collision, grounding or spillage and envelopment of the ship in toxic or flammable vapour Knowledge of medical first-aid procedures and antidotes on board liquefied gas tankers, with reference to the Medical First Aid Guide for Use in Accidents Involving Dangerous Goods (MFAG)	Assessment of evidence obtained from one or more of the following: .1 approved in-service experience .2 approved training ship experience .3 approved simulator training .4 approved training programme	The type and impact of emergency is promptly identified, and the response actions conform with established emergency procedures and contingency plans The order of priority and the levels and timescales of making reports and informing personnel on board are relevant to the nature of the emergency and reflect the urgency of the problem Evacuation, emergency shutdown and isolation are appropriate to the nature of the emergency and implemented promptly The identification of and actions taken in a medical emergency conform to current recognized first aid practice and international guidelines
Take precautions to prevent pollution of the environment	Understanding of procedures to prevent pollution of the environment	Assessment of evidence obtained from one or more of the following: .1 approved in-service experience .2 approved training ship experience .3 approved simulator training .4 approved training programme	Operations are conducted in accordance with accepted principles and procedures to prevent pollution of the environment

Table A-V/1-2-2 *(continued)*

Column 1	Column 2	Column 3	Column 4
Competence	**Knowledge, understanding and proficiency**	**Methods for demonstrating competence**	**Criteria for evaluating competence**
Monitor and control compliance with legislative requirements	Knowledge and understanding of relevant provisions of the International Convention for the Prevention of Pollution from Ships (MARPOL) and other relevant IMO instruments, industry guidelines and port regulations as commonly applied Proficiency in the use of the IBC and IGC Codes and related documents	Assessment of evidence obtained from one or more of the following: .1 approved in-service experience .2 approved training ship experience .3 approved simulator training .4 approved training programme	The handling of liquefied gas cargoes complies with relevant IMO instruments and established industrial standards and codes of safe working practices

Section A-V/2

Mandatory minimum requirements for the training and qualification of masters, officers, ratings and other personnel on passenger ships

Passenger ship emergency familiarization

1 Before being assigned to shipboard duties, all personnel serving on board passenger ships engaged on international voyages shall have attained the abilities that are appropriate to their duties and responsibilities as follows:

Contribute to the implementation of emergency plans, instructions and procedures

.1 Familiar with:

.1.1 general safety features aboard ship;

.1.2 location of essential safety and emergency equipment, including life-saving appliances;

.1.3 importance of personal conduct during an emergency; and

.1.4 restrictions on the use of elevators during emergencies.

Contribute to the effective communication with passengers during an emergency

.2 Ability to:

.2.1 communicate in the working language of the ship;

.2.2 non-verbally communicate safety information; and

.2.3 understand one of the languages in which emergency announcements may be broadcast on the ship during an emergency or drill.

Safety training for personnel providing direct service to passengers in passenger spaces

2 Before being assigned to shipboard duties, personnel providing direct service to passengers in passenger spaces shall receive the additional safety training required by regulation V/2, paragraph 6, that ensures at least the attainment of the abilities as follows:

Communication

.1 Ability to communicate with passengers during an emergency, taking into account:

.1.1 the language or languages appropriate to the principal nationalities of passengers carried on the particular route;

.1.2 the likelihood that an ability to use an elementary English vocabulary for basic instructions can provide a means of communicating with a passenger in need of assistance whether or not the passenger and crew member share a common language;

.1.3 the possible need to communicate during an emergency by some other means, such as by demonstration, or hand signals, or calling attention to the location of instructions, muster stations, life-saving devices or evacuation routes, when oral communication is impractical;

1.4 the extent to which complete safety instructions have been provided to passengers in their native language or languages; and

.1.5 the languages in which emergency announcements may be broadcast during an emergency or drill to convey critical guidance to passengers and to facilitate crew members in assisting passengers.

Loading and embarkation procedures

.1 Ability to apply properly the procedures established for the ship regarding:

.1.1 loading and discharging vehicles, rail cars and other cargo transport units, including related communications;

.1.2 lowering and hoisting ramps;

.1.3 setting up and stowing retractable vehicle decks; and

.1.4 embarking and disembarking passengers, with special attention to disabled persons and persons needing assistance.

Carriage of dangerous goods

.2 Ability to apply any special safeguards, procedures and requirements regarding the carriage of dangerous goods on board ro–ro passenger ships.

Securing cargoes

.3 Ability to:

.3.1 apply correctly the provisions of the Code of Safe Practice for Cargo Stowage and Securing to the vehicles, rail cars and other cargo transport units carried; and

.3.2 use properly the cargo-securing equipment and materials provided, taking into account their limitations.

Stability, trim and stress calculations

.4 Ability to:

.4.1 make proper use of the stability and stress information provided;

.4.2 calculate stability and trim for different conditions of loading, using the stability calculators or computer programs provided;

.4.3 calculate load factors for decks; and

.4.4 calculate the impact of ballast and fuel transfers on stability, trim and stress.

Life-saving appliances

.2 Ability to demonstrate to passengers the use of personal life-saving appliances.

Embarkation procedures

.3 Embarking and disembarking passengers, with special attention to disabled persons and persons needing assistance.

Passenger ship crowd management training

3 Before being assigned to shipboard duties, masters, officers, ratings qualified in accordance with chapters II, III and VII and personnel designated on the muster list to assist passengers in emergency situations shall:

.1 have successfully completed the crowd management training required by regulation V/2, paragraph 7, as set out in table A-V/2-1; and

.2 be required to provide evidence that the training has been completed in accordance with table A-V/2-1.

Crisis management and human behaviour training

4 Before being assigned to shipboard duties, masters, chief engineer officers, chief mates, second engineer officers and any person designated on the muster list as having responsibility for the safety of passengers in emergency situations shall:

.1 have successfully completed the approved crisis management and human behaviour training required by regulation V/2, paragraph 8, as set out in table A-V/2-2; and

.2 be required to provide evidence that the required standard of competence has been achieved in accordance with the methods and the criteria for evaluating competence tabulated in columns 3 and 4 of table A-V/2-2.

Passenger safety, cargo safety and hull integrity training

5 Before being assigned to shipboard duties, masters, chief engineer officers, chief mates, second engineer officers and every person assigned immediate responsibility for embarking and disembarking passengers, for loading, discharging or securing cargo, or for closing hull openings on board ro-ro passenger ships shall receive the passenger safety, cargo safety and hull integrity training required by regulation V/2, paragraph 9, that ensures at least attainment of the abilities that are appropriate to their duties and responsibilities as follows:

Opening, closing and securing hull openings

.5 Ability to:

.5.1 apply properly the procedures established for the ship regarding the opening, closing and securing of bow, stern and side doors and ramps and to correctly operate the associated systems; and

.5.2 conduct surveys on proper sealing.

Ro-ro deck atmosphere

.6 Ability to:

.6.1 use equipment, where carried, to monitor atmosphere in ro ro spaces; and

.6.2 apply properly the procedures established for the ship for ventilation of ro-ro spaces during loading and discharging of vehicles, while on voyage and in emergencies.

Table A-V/2-1

Specification of minimum standard of competence in passenger ship crowd management training

Column 1	Column 2	Column 3	Column 4
Competence	**Knowledge, understanding and proficiency**	**Methods for demonstrating competence**	**Criteria for evaluating competence**
Contribute to the implementation of shipboard emergency plans and procedures to muster and evacuate passengers	Knowledge of the shipboard emergency plans, instructions and procedures related to the management and evacuation of passengers Knowledge of applicable crowd management techniques and relevant equipment to be used to assist passengers in an emergency situation Knowledge of muster lists and emergency instructions	Assessment of evidence obtained from training and/or instruction	Actions taken in case of an emergency are appropriate and comply with established procedures
Assist passengers *en route* to muster and embarkation stations	Ability to give clear reassuring orders Ability to manage passengers in corridors, staircases and passageways Understanding the importance of and having the ability to maintain escape routes clear of obstructions Knowledge of methods available for evacuation of disabled persons and persons needing special assistance Knowledge of methods of searching passenger accommodation and public spaces Ability to disembark passengers, with special attention to disabled persons and persons needing assistance Importance of effective mustering procedures, including: .1 the importance of keeping order; .2 the ability to use procedures for reducing and avoiding panic; .3 the ability to use, where appropriate, passenger lists for evacuation counts; .4 the importance of passengers being suitably clothed as far as possible when mustering; and .5 the ability to check that the passengers have donned their life jackets correctly.	Assessment of evidence obtained from practical training and/or instruction	Actions taken conform with emergency plans, instructions and procedures Information given to individuals, emergency response teams and passengers is accurate, relevant and timely

Table A-V/2-2

Specification of minimum standard of competence in passenger ship crisis management and human behaviour

Column 1	Column 2	Column 3	Column 4
Competence	**Knowledge, understanding and proficiency**	**Methods for demonstrating competence**	**Criteria for evaluating competence**
Organize shipboard emergency procedures	Knowledge of: .1 the general design and layout of the ship .2 safety regulations .3 emergency plans and procedures The importance of the principles for the development of ship specific emergency procedures, including: .1 the need for pre-planning and drills of shipboard emergency procedures .2 the need for all personnel to be aware of and adhere to pre-planned emergency procedures as carefully as possible in the event of an emergency situation	Assessment of evidence obtained from approved training, exercises with one or more prepared emergency plans and practical demonstration	The shipboard emergency procedures ensure a state of readiness to respond to emergency situations
Optimize the use of resources	Ability to optimize the use of resources, taking into account: .1 the possibility that resources available in an emergency may be limited .2 the need to make full use of personnel and equipment immediately available and, if necessary, to improvise Ability to organize realistic drills to maintain a state of readiness, taking into account lessons learnt from previous accidents involving passenger ships; debriefing after drills	Assessment of evidence obtained from approved training, practical demonstration and shipboard training and drills of emergency procedures	Contingency plans optimize the use of available resources Allocation of tasks and responsibilities reflects the known competence of individuals Roles and responsibilities of teams and individuals are clearly defined

Table A-V/2-2 *(continued)*

Column 1	Column 2	Column 3	Column 4
Competence	**Knowledge, understanding and proficiency**	**Methods for demonstrating competence**	**Criteria for evaluating competence**
Control response to emergencies	Ability to make an initial assessment and provide an effective response to emergency situations in accordance with established emergency procedures *Leadership skills* Ability to lead and direct others in emergency situations, including the need: .1 to set an example during emergency situations .2 to focus decision making, given the need to act quickly in an emergency .3 to motivate, encourage and reassure passengers and other personnel *Stress handling* Ability to identify the development of symptoms of excessive personal stress and those of other members of the ship's emergency team Understanding that stress generated by emergency situations can affect the performance of individuals and their ability to act on instructions and follow procedures	Assessment of evidence obtained from approved training, practical demonstration and shipboard training and drills of emergency procedures	Procedures and actions are in accordance with established principles and plans for crisis management on board Objectives and strategy are appropriate to the nature of the emergency, take account of contingencies and make optimum use of available resources Actions of crew members contribute to maintaining order and control

Table A-V/2-2 *(continued)*

Column 1	Column 2	Column 3	Column 4
Competence	**Knowledge, understanding and proficiency**	**Methods for demonstrating competence**	**Criteria for evaluating competence**
Control passengers and other personnel during emergency situations	*Human behaviour and responses* Ability to control passengers and other personnel in emergency situations, including: .1 awareness of the general reaction patterns of passengers and other personnel in emergency situations, including the possibility that: .1.1 generally it takes some time before people accept the fact that there is an emergency situation .1.2 some people may panic and not behave with a normal level of rationality, that their ability to comprehend may be impaired and they may not be as responsive to instructions as in non-emergency situations .2 awareness that passengers and other personnel may, inter alia: .2.1 start looking for relatives, friends and/or their belongings as a first reaction when something goes wrong .2.2 seek safety in their cabins or in other places on board where they think that they can escape danger .2.3 tend to move to the upper side when the ship is listing .3 appreciation of the possible problem of panic resulting from separating families	Assessment of evidence obtained from approved training, practical demonstration and shipboard training and drills of emergency procedures	Actions of crew members contribute to maintaining order and control

Table A-V/2-2 *(continued)*

Column 1	Column 2	Column 3	Column 4
Competence	**Knowledge, understanding and proficiency**	**Methods for demonstrating competence**	**Criteria for evaluating competence**
Establish and maintain effective communications	Ability to establish and maintain effective communications, including: .1 the importance of clear and concise instructions and reports .2 the need to encourage an exchange of information with, and feedback from, passengers and other personnel Ability to provide relevant information to passengers and other personnel during an emergency situation, to keep them apprised of the overall situation and to communicate any action required of them, taking into account: .1 the language or languages appropriate to the principal nationalities of passengers and other personnel carried on the particular route .2 the possible need to communicate during an emergency by some other means, such as by demonstration, or by hand signals or calling attention to the location of instructions, muster stations, life-saving devices or evacuation routes, when oral communication is impractical .3 the language in which emergency announcements may be broadcast during an emergency or drill to convey critical guidance to passengers and to facilitate crew members in assisting passengers	Assessment of evidence obtained from approved training, exercises and practical demonstration	Information from all available sources is obtained, evaluated and confirmed as quickly as possible and reviewed throughout the emergency Information given to individuals, emergency response teams and passengers is accurate, relevant and timely Information keeps passengers informed as to the nature of the emergency and the actions required of them

Section A-V/3

Mandatory minimum requirements for the training and qualification of masters, officers, ratings and other personnel on ships subject to the IGF Code

Basic training for ships subject to the IGF Code

1 Every candidate for a certificate in basic training for service on ships subject to the IGF Code shall:

.1.1 have successfully completed the approved basic training required by regulation V/3, paragraph 5, in accordance with their capacity, duties and responsibilities as set out in table A-V/3-1; and

.1.2 be required to provide evidence that the required standard of competence has been achieved in accordance with the methods and the criteria for evaluating competence tabulated in columns 3 and 4 of table A-V/3-1; or

.2 have received appropriate training and certification according to the requirements for service on liquefied gas tankers as set out in regulation V/3, paragraph 6.

Advanced training for ships subject to the IGF Code

2 Every candidate for a certificate in advanced training for service on ships subject to the IGF Code shall:

.1.1 have successfully completed the approved advanced training required by regulation V/3, paragraph 8 in accordance with their capacity, duties and responsibilities as set out in table A-V/3-2; and

.1.2 provide evidence that the required standard of competence has been achieved in accordance with the methods and the criteria for evaluating competence tabulated in columns 3 and 4 of table A-V/3-2; or

.2 have received appropriate training and certification according to the requirements for service on liquefied gas tankers as set out in regulation V/3, paragraph 9.

Exemptions

3 The Administration may, in respect of ships of less than 500 gross tonnage, except for passenger ships, if it considers that a ship's size and the length or character of its voyage are such as to render the application of the full requirements of this section unreasonable or impracticable, exempt the seafarers on such a ship or class of ships from some of the requirements, bearing in mind the safety of people on board, the ship and property and the protection of the marine environment.

STCW CODE

A

V

Table A-V/3-1

Specification of minimum standard of competence in basic training for ships subject to the IGF Code

Column 1	Column 2	Column 3	Column 4
Competence	**Knowledge, understanding and proficiency**	**Methods for demonstrating competence**	**Criteria for evaluating competence**
Contribute to the safe operation of a ship subject to the IGF Code	Design and operational characteristics of ships subject to the IGF Code Basic knowledge of ships subject to the IGF Code, their fuel systems and fuel storage systems: .1 fuels addressed by the IGF Code .2 types of fuel systems subject to the IGF Code .3 atmospheric, cryogenic or compressed storage of fuels on board ships subject to the IGF Code .4 general arrangement of fuel storage systems on board ships subject to the IGF Code .5 hazard zones and areas .6 typical fire safety plan .7 monitoring, control and safety systems aboard ships subject to the IGF Code Basic knowledge of fuels and fuel storage systems' operations on board ships subject to the IGF Code: .1 piping systems and valves .2 atmospheric, compressed or cryogenic storage .3 relief systems and protection screens .4 basic bunkering operations and bunkering systems .5 protection against cryogenic accidents .6 fuel leak monitoring and detection Basic knowledge of the physical properties of fuels on board ships subject to the IGF Code, including: .1 properties and characteristics .2 pressure and temperature, including vapour pressure/temperature relationship Knowledge and understanding of safety requirements and safety management on board ships subject to the IGF Code	Examination and assessment of evidence obtained from one or more of the following: .1 approved in-service experience .2 approved training ship experience .3 approved simulator training .4 approved training programme	Communications within the area of responsibility are clear and effective Operations related to ships subject to the IGF Code are carried out in accordance with accepted principles and procedures to ensure safety of operations

Table A-V/3-1 *(continued)*

Column 1	Column 2	Column 3	Column 4
Competence	**Knowledge, understanding and proficiency**	**Methods for demonstrating competence**	**Criteria for evaluating competence**
Take precautions to prevent hazards on a ship subject to the IGF Code	Basic knowledge of the hazards associated with operations on ships subject to the IGF Code, including: .1 health hazards .2 environmental hazards .3 reactivity hazards .4 corrosion hazards .5 ignition, explosion and flammability hazards .6 sources of ignition .7 electrostatic hazards .8 toxicity hazards .9 vapour leaks and clouds .10 extremely low temperatures .11 pressure hazards .12 fuel batch differences Basic knowledge of hazard controls: .1 emptying, inerting, drying and monitoring techniques .2 anti-static measures .3 ventilation .4 segregation .5 inhibition .6 measures to prevent ignition, fire and explosion .7 atmospheric control .8 gas testing .9 protection against cryogenic damages (LNG) Understanding of fuel characteristics on ships subject to the IGF Code as found on a Safety Data Sheet (SDS)	Examination and assessment of evidence obtained from one or more of the following: .1 approved in-service experience .2 approved training ship experience .3 approved simulator training .4 approved training programme	Correctly identifies, on a Safety Data Sheet (SDS), relevant hazards to the ship and to personnel, and takes the appropriate actions in accordance with established procedures Identification and actions on becoming aware of a hazardous situation conform to established procedures in line with best practice

Table A-V/3-1 *(continued)*

<table>
<tr><th>Column 1</th><th>Column 2</th><th>Column 3</th><th>Column 4</th></tr>
<tr><th>Competence</th><th>Knowledge, understanding and proficiency</th><th>Methods for demonstrating competence</th><th>Criteria for evaluating competence</th></tr>
<tr><td>Apply occupational health and safety precautions and measures</td><td>Awareness of function of gas-measuring instruments and similar equipment:
.1 gas testing

Proper use of specialized safety equipment and protective devices, including:
.1 breathing apparatus
.2 protective clothing
.3 resuscitators
.4 rescue and escape equipment

Basic knowledge of safe working practices and procedures in accordance with legislation and industry guidelines and personal shipboard safety relevant to ships subject to the IGF Code, including:
.1 precautions to be taken before entering hazardous spaces and zones
.2 precautions to be taken before and during repair and maintenance work
.3 safety measures for hot and cold work

Basic knowledge of first aid with reference to a Safety Data Sheet (SDS)</td><td>Examination and assessment of evidence obtained from one or more of the following:
.1 approved in-service experience
.2 approved training ship experience
.3 approved simulator training
.4 approved training programme</td><td>Procedures and safe working practices designed to safeguard personnel and the ship are observed at all times

Appropriate safety and protective equipment is correctly used

First aid do's and don'ts</td></tr>
<tr><td>Carry out fire-fighting operations on a ship subject to the IGF Code</td><td>Fire organization and action to be taken on ships subject to the IGF Code

Special hazards associated with fuel systems and fuel handling on ships subject to the IGF Code

Fire-fighting agents and methods used to control and extinguish fires in conjunction with the different fuels found on board ships subject to the IGF Code

Fire-fighting system operations</td><td>Practical exercises and instruction conducted under approved and truly realistic training conditions (e.g. Simulated shipboard conditions) and, whenever possible and practicable, in darkness</td><td>Initial actions and follow-up actions on becoming aware of an emergency conform with established practices and procedures

Action taken on identifying muster signals is appropriate to the indicated emergency and complies with established procedures

Clothing and equipment are appropriate to the nature of the fire-fighting operations

The timing and sequence of individual actions are appropriate to the prevailing circumstances and conditions

Extinguishment of fire is achieved using appropriate procedures techniques and fire-fighting agents</td></tr>
</table>

Table A-V/3-1 *(continued)*

Column 1	Column 2	Column 3	Column 4
Competence	**Knowledge, understanding and proficiency**	**Methods for demonstrating competence**	**Criteria for evaluating competence**
Respond to emergencies	Basic knowledge of emergency procedures, including emergency shutdown	Examination and assessment of evidence obtained from one or more of the following: .1 approved in-service experience .2 approved training ship experience .3 approved simulator training .4 approved training programme	The type and impact of the emergency is promptly identified, and the response actions conform to the emergency procedures and contingency plans
Take precautions to prevent pollution of the environment from the release of fuels found on ships subject to the IGF Code	Basic knowledge of measures to be taken in the event of leakage/spillage/venting of fuels from ships subject to the IGF Code, including the need to: .1 report relevant information to the responsible persons .2 awareness of shipboard spill/leakage/venting response procedures .3 awareness of appropriate personal protection when responding to a spill/ leakage of fuels addressed by the IGF Code	Examination or assessment of evidence obtained from one or more of the following: .1 approved in-service experience .2 approved training ship experience .3 approved simulator training .4 approved training programme	Procedures designed to safeguard the environment are observed at all times

Table A-V/3-2

Specification of minimum standard of competence of advanced training for ships subject to the IGF Code

Column 1	Column 2	Column 3	Column 4
Competence	**Knowledge, understanding and proficiency**	**Methods for demonstrating competence**	**Criteria for evaluating competence**
Familiarity with physical and chemical properties of fuels aboard ships subject to the IGF Code	Basic knowledge and understanding of simple chemistry and physics and the relevant definitions related to safe bunkering and use of fuels used on board ships subject to the IGF Code, including: .1 the chemical structure of different fuels used on board ships subject to the IGF Code .2 the properties and characteristics of fuels used on board ships subject to the IGF Code, including: .2.1 simple physical laws .2.2 states of matter .2.3 liquid and vapour densities .2.4 boil-off and weathering of cryogenic fuels .2.5 compression and expansion of gases .2.6 critical pressure and temperature of gases .2.7 flashpoint, upper and lower flammable limits, auto-ignition temperature .2.8 saturated vapour pressure/reference temperature .2.9 dewpoint and bubble point .2.10 hydrate formation .2.11 combustion properties: heating values .2.12 methane number/knocking .2.13 pollutant characteristics of fuels addressed by the IGF Code .3 the properties of single liquids .4 the nature and properties of solutions	Examination and assessment of evidence obtained from one or more of the following: .1 approved in-service experience .2 approved training ship experience .3 approved simulator training .4 approved training programme	Effective use is made of information resources for identification of properties and characteristics of fuels addressed by the IGF Code and their impact on safety, environmental protection and ship operation

Table A-V/3-2 *(continued)*

Column 1	Column 2	Column 3	Column 4
Competence	**Knowledge, understanding and proficiency**	**Methods for demonstrating competence**	**Criteria for evaluating competence**
Familiarity with physical and chemical properties of fuels aboard ships subject to the IGF Code *(continued)*	.5 thermodynamic units .6 basic thermodynamic laws and diagrams .7 properties of materials .8 effect of low temperature, including brittle fracture, for liquid cryogenic fuels Understanding the information contained in a Safety Data Sheet (SDS) about fuels addressed by the IGF Code		
Operate controls of fuel related to propulsion plant and engineering systems and services and safety devices on ships subject to the IGF Code	Operating principles of marine power plants Ships' auxiliary machinery Knowledge of marine engineering terms	Examination and assessment of evidence obtained from one or more of the following: .1 approved in-service experience .2 approved training ship experience .3 approved simulator training .4 approved training programme	Plant, auxiliary machinery and equipment is operated in accordance with technical specifications and within safe operating limits at all times

Table A-V/3-2 *(continued)*

Column 1	Column 2	Column 3	Column 4
Competence	**Knowledge, understanding and proficiency**	**Methods for demonstrating competence**	**Criteria for evaluating competence**
Ability to safely perform and monitor all operations related to the fuels used on board ships subject to the IGF Code	Design and characteristics of ships subject to the IGF Code Knowledge of ship design, systems, and equipment found on ships subject to the IGF Code, including: .1 fuel systems for different propulsion engines .2 general arrangement and construction .3 fuel storage systems on board ships subject to the IGF Code, including materials of construction and insulation .4 fuel-handling equipment and instrumentations on board ships: .4.1 fuel pumps and pumping arrangements .4.2 fuel pipelines .4.3 expansion devices .4.4 flame screens .4.5 temperature monitoring systems .4.6 fuel tank level gauging systems .4.7 tank pressure monitoring and control systems .5 cryogenic fuel tanks temperature and pressure maintenance .6 fuel system atmosphere control systems (inert gas, nitrogen), including storage, generation and distribution .7 toxic and flammable gas-detecting systems .8 fuel Emergency Shut Down system (ESD)	Examination and assessment of evidence obtained from one or more of the following: .1 approved in-service experience .2 approved training ship experience .3 approved simulator training .4 approved training programme	Communications are clear and understood Successful ship operations using fuels addressed by the IGF Code are carried out in a safe manner, taking into account ship designs, systems and equipment Pumping operations are carried out in accordance with accepted principles and procedures and are relevant to the type of fuel Operations are planned, risk is managed and carried out in accordance with accepted principles and procedures to ensure safety of operations and to avoid pollution of the marine environment

Table A-V/3-2 *(continued)*

Column 1	Column 2	Column 3	Column 4
Competence	**Knowledge, understanding and proficiency**	**Methods for demonstrating competence**	**Criteria for evaluating competence**
Ability to safely perform and monitor all operations related to the fuels used on board ships subject to the IGF Code *(continued)*	Knowledge of fuel system theory and characteristics, including types of fuel system pumps and their safe operation on board ships subject to the IGF Code .1 low pressure pumps .2 high pressure pumps .3 vaporizers .4 heaters .5 pressure build up units Knowledge of safe procedures and checklists for taking fuel tanks in and out of service, including: .1 inerting .2 cooling down .3 initial loading .4 pressure control .5 heating of fuel .6 emptying systems		

Table A-V/3-2 *(continued)*

Column 1	Column 2	Column 3	Column 4
Competence	**Knowledge, understanding and proficiency**	**Methods for demonstrating competence**	**Criteria for evaluating competence**
Plan and monitor safe bunkering, stowage and securing of the fuel on board ships subject to the IGF Code	General knowledge of ships subject to the IGF Code Ability to use all data available on board related to bunkering, storage and securing of fuels addressed by the IGF Code Ability to establish clear and concise communications and between the ship and the terminal, truck or the bunker-supply ship Knowledge of safety and emergency procedures for operation of machinery, fuel- and control systems for ships subject to the IGF Code Proficiency in the operation of bunkering systems on board ships subject to the IGF Code including: .1 bunkering procedures .2 emergency procedures .3 ship-shore/ship-ship interface .4 prevention of rollover Proficiency to perform fuel system measurements and calculations, including: .1 maximum fill quantity .2 On Board Quantity (OBQ) .3 Minimum Remain On Board (ROB) .4 fuel consumption calculations Ability to ensure the safe management of bunkering and other IGF Code fuel related operations concurrent with other onboard operations, both in port and at sea	Examination and assessment of evidence obtained from one or more of the following: .1 approved in-service experience .2 approved simulator training .3 approved training programme .4 approved laboratory equipment training or witnessing bunker operation	Fuel quality and quantity is determined taking into account the current conditions and necessary corrective safe measures are taken Procedures for monitoring safety systems to ensure that all alarms are detected promptly and acted upon in accordance with established procedures Operations are planned and carried out in accordance with fuel transfer manuals and procedures to ensure safety of operations and avoid spill damages and pollution of the environment Personnel are allocated duties and informed of procedures and standards of work to be followed, in a manner appropriate to the individuals concerned and in accordance with safe working procedures

Table A-V/3-2 *(continued)*

Column 1	Column 2	Column 3	Column 4
Competence	**Knowledge, understanding and proficiency**	**Methods for demonstrating competence**	**Criteria for evaluating competence**
Take precautions to prevent pollution of the environment from the release of fuels from ships subject to the IGF Code	Knowledge of the effects of pollution on human and environment Knowledge of measures to be taken in the event of spillage/ leakage/ venting	Examination and assessment of evidence obtained from one or more of the following: .1 approved in-service experience .2 approved training ship experience .3 approved simulator training .4 approved training programme	Procedures designed to safeguard the environment are observed at all times
Monitor and control compliance with legislative requirements	Knowledge and understanding of relevant provisions of the International Convention for the Prevention of Pollution from Ships (MARPOL), as amended and other relevant IMO instruments, industry guidelines and port regulations as commonly applied Proficiency in the use of the IGF Code and related documents	Assessment of evidence obtained from one or more of the following: .1 approved in-service experience .2 approved training ship experience .3 approved simulator training .4 approved training programme	The handling of fuels on board ships subject to the IGF Code complies with relevant IMO instruments and established industrial standards and codes of safe working practices Operations are planned and performed in conformity with approved procedures and legislative requirements

Table A-V/3-2 *(continued)*

Column 1	Column 2	Column 3	Column 4
Competence	**Knowledge, understanding and proficiency**	**Methods for demonstrating competence**	**Criteria for evaluating competence**
Take precautions to prevent hazards	Knowledge and understanding of the hazards and control measures associated with fuel system operations on board ships subject to the IGF Code, including: .1 flammability .2 explosion .3 toxicity .4 reactivity .5 corrosivity .6 health hazards .7 inert gas composition .8 electrostatic hazards .9 pressurized gases .10 low temperature Proficiency to calibrate and use monitoring and fuel detection systems, instruments and equipment on board ships subject to the IGF Code Knowledge and understanding of dangers of non-compliance with relevant rules/regulations Knowledge and understanding of risks assessment method analysis on board ships subject to the IGF Code Ability to elaborate and develop risks analysis related to risks on board ships subject to the IGF Code Ability to elaborate and develop safety plans and safety instructions for ships subject to the IGF Code Knowledge of hot work, enclosed spaces and tank entry including permitting procedures	Examination and assessment of evidence obtained from one or more of the following: .1 approved in-service experience .2 approved training ship experience .3 approved simulator training .4 approved training programme	Relevant hazards to the ship and to personnel associated with operations on board ships subject to the IGF Code are correctly identified and proper control measures are taken Use of flammable and toxic gas detection devices are in accordance with manuals and good practice

Table A-V/3-2 *(continued)*

Column 1	Column 2	Column 3	Column 4
Competence	**Knowledge, understanding and proficiency**	**Methods for demonstrating competence**	**Criteria for evaluating competence**
Apply occupational health and safety precautions and measures on board a ship subject to the IGF Code	Proper use of safety equipment and protective devices, including: .1 breathing apparatus and evacuating equipment .2 protective clothing and equipment .3 resuscitators .4 rescue and escape equipment Knowledge of safe working practices and procedures in accordance with legislation and industry guidelines and personal shipboard safety including: .1 precautions to be taken before, during and after repair and maintenance work on fuel systems addressed in the IGF Code .2 electrical safety (reference to IEC 60079-17) .3 ship/shore safety checklist Basic knowledge of first aid with reference to a Safety Data Sheets (SDS) for fuels addressed by the IGF Code	Examination and assessment of evidence obtained from one or more of the following: .1 approved in-service experience .2 approved training ship experience .3 approved simulator training .4 approved training programme	Appropriate safety and protective equipment is correctly used Procedures designed to safeguard personnel and the ship are observed at all times Working practices are in accordance with legislative requirements, codes of practice, permits to work and environmental concerns First aid do's and don'ts
Knowledge of the prevention, control and fire fighting and extinguishing systems on board ships subject to the IGF Code	Knowledge of the methods and fire-fighting appliances to detect, control and extinguish fires of fuels addressed by the IGF Code	Examination and assessment of evidence obtained from one or more of the following: .1 approved in-service experience .2 approved training ship experience .3 approved simulator training .4 approved training programme	The type and scale of the problem is promptly identified, and initial actions conform with the emergency procedures for fuels addressed by the IGF Code Evacuation, emergency shutdown and isolation procedures are appropriate to the fuels addressed by the IGF Code

Section A-V/4

Mandatory minimum requirements for the training and qualification of masters and deck officers on ships operating in polar waters

Standard of competence

1 Every candidate for certification in basic training for ships operating in polar waters shall be required to:

.1 demonstrate the competence to undertake the tasks, duties and responsibilities listed in column 1 of table A-V/4-1; and

.2 provide evidence of having achieved:

.1 the minimum knowledge, understanding and proficiency listed in column 2 of table A-V/4-1; and

.2 the required standard of competence in accordance with the methods for demonstrating competence and the criteria for evaluating competence tabulated in columns 3 and 4 of table A-V/4-1.

2 Every candidate for certification in advanced training for ships operating in polar waters shall be required to:

.1 demonstrate the competence to undertake the tasks, duties and responsibilities listed in column 1 of table A-V/4-2; and

.2 provide evidence of having achieved:

.1 the minimum knowledge, understanding and proficiency listed in column 2 of table A-V/4-2; and

.2 the required standard of competence in accordance with the methods for demonstrating competence and the criteria for evaluating competence tabulated in columns 3 and 4 of table A-V/4-2.

Table A-V/4-1

Specification of minimum standard of competence in basic training for ships operating in polar waters

Column 1	Column 2	Column 3	Column 4
Competence	**Knowledge, understanding and proficiency**	**Methods for demonstrating competence**	**Criteria for evaluating competence**
Contribute to safe operation of vessels operating in polar waters	*Basic knowledge of ice characteristics and areas where different types of ice can be expected in the area of operation:* .1 ice physics, terms, formation, growth, ageing and stage of melt .2 ice types and concentrations .3 ice pressure and distribution .4 friction from snow covered ice .5 implications of spray icing; danger of icing up; precautions to avoid icing up and options during icing up .6 ice regimes in different regions; significant differences between the Arctic and the Antarctic, first year and multiyear ice, sea ice and land ice .7 use of ice imagery to recognize consequences of rapid change in ice and weather conditions .8 knowledge of ice blink and water sky .9 knowledge of differential movement of icebergs and pack ice .10 knowledge of tides and currents in ice .11 knowledge of effect of wind and current on ice	Examination and assessment of evidence obtained from one or more of the following: .1 approved in service experience .2 approved training ship experience .3 approved simulator training, where appropriate .4 approved training programme	Identification of ice properties and their characteristics of relevance for safe vessel operation Information obtained from ice information and publications is interpreted correctly and properly applied Use of visible and infrared satellite images Use of egg charts Coordination of meteorological and oceanographic data with ice data Measurements and observations of weather and ice conditions are accurate and appropriate for safe passage planning

Table A-V/4-1 *(continued)*

Column 1	Column 2	Column 3	Column 4
Competence	**Knowledge, understanding and proficiency**	**Methods for demonstrating competence**	**Criteria for evaluating competence**
Contribute to safe operation of vessels operating in polar waters *(continued)*	*Basic knowledge of vessel performance in ice and low air temperature:* .1 vessel characteristics .2 vessel types, hull designs .3 engineering requirements for operating in ice .4 Ice strengthening requirements .5 limitations of ice-classes .6 winterization and preparedness of vessel, including deck and engine .7 low-temperature system performance .8 equipment and machinery limitation in ice condition and low air temperature .9 monitoring of ice pressure on hull .10 sea suction, water intake, superstructure insulation and special systems	Examination and assessment of evidence obtained from one or more of the following: .1 approved in-service experience .2 approved training ship experience .3 approved simulator training, where appropriate .4 approved training programme	Identification of vessel characteristics and limitations under different ice conditions and cold environmental impact Procedures are made for risk assessment before entering ice Awareness of fresh water ballast freezing in ballast tanks Actions are carried out in accordance with accepted principles and procedures to prepare the vessel and the crew for operations in ice and low air temperature Communications are clear, concise and effective at all times in a seamanlike manner
	Basic knowledge and ability to operate and manoeuvre a vessel in ice: .1 safe speed in the presence of ice and icebergs .2 ballast tank monitoring .3 cargo operations in polar waters .4 awareness of engine loads and cooling problems .5 safety procedures during ice transit	Examination and assessment of evidence obtained from one or more of the following: .1 approved in service experience .2 approved training ship experience .3 approved simulator training, where appropriate .4 approved training programme	Use Polar Code and Polar Water Operations Manual to correctly determine the recommended procedures to load/unload cargo and/or embark/disembark passengers in low temperatures, monitor ballast water for icing, monitor engine temperatures, anchor watch concerns in ice, and transit near ice Interpretation and analysis of information from radar is in accordance with lookout procedures with special caution regarding identification of dangerous ice features Information obtained from navigational charts, including electronic charts, and publications is relevant, assessed, interpreted correctly and properly applied The primary method of position fixing is frequent and the most appropriate for the prevailing conditions and routing through ice Performance checks and tests of navigation and communication systems comply with recommendations for high latitude and low air temperature operation

Table A-V/4-1 *(continued)*

Column 1	Column 2	Column 3	Column 4
Competence	**Knowledge, understanding and proficiency**	**Methods for demonstrating competence**	**Criteria for evaluating competence**
Monitor and ensure compliance with legislative requirements	*Basic knowledge of regulatory considerations:* .1 Antarctic Treaty and the Polar Code .2 accident reports concerning vessels in polar waters .3 IMO standards for operation in remote areas	Examination and assessment of evidence obtained from one or more of the following: .1 approved in-service experience .2 approved training ship experience .3 approved simulator training, where appropriate .4 approved training programme	Locate and apply relevant parts of the Polar Water Operations Manual Communication is in accordance with local/regional and international standard procedures Legislative requirements related to relevant regulations, codes and practices are identified

Table A-V/4-1 *(continued)*

Column 1	Column 2	Column 3	Column 4
Competence	**Knowledge, understanding and proficiency**	**Methods for demonstrating competence**	**Criteria for evaluating competence**
Apply safe working practices, respond to emergencies	Basic knowledge of crew preparation, working conditions and safety: .1 recognize limitations of search and rescue readiness and responsibility, including sea area A4 and its SAR communication facility limitation .2 awareness of contingency planning .3 how to establish and implement safe working procedures for crew specific to polar environments such as low temperatures, ice covered surfaces, personal protective equipment, use of buddy system, and working time limitations .4 recognize dangers when crews are exposed to low temperatures .5 human factors including cold fatigue, medical-first aid aspects, crew welfare .6 survival requirements including the use of personal survival equipment and group survival equipment .7 awareness of the most common hull and equipment damages and how to avoid these .8 superstructure deck icing, including effect on stability and trim .9 prevention and removal of ice including the factors of accretion .10 recognize fatigue problems due to noise and vibrations .11 identify need for extra resources, such as bunker, food and extra clothing	Examination and assessment of evidence obtained from one or more of the following: .1 approved in-service experience .2 approved training ship experience .3 approved simulator training, where appropriate .4 approved training programme	Identification and initial actions on becoming aware of hazardous situations for vessel and individual crew members Actions are carried out in accordance with Polar Water Operations Manual, accepted principles and procedures to ensure safety of operations and to avoid pollution of the marine environment Safe working practices are observed and appropriate safety and protective equipment is correctly used at all times Response actions are in accordance with established plans and are appropriate to the situation and nature of the emergency Correctly identifies and applies legislative requirements related to relevant regulations, codes and practices Appropriate safety and protective equipment is correctly used Defects and damages are detected and properly reported

Table A-V/4-1 *(continued)*

Column 1	Column 2	Column 3	Column 4
Competence	**Knowledge, understanding and proficiency**	**Methods for demonstrating competence**	**Criteria for evaluating competence**
Ensure compliance with pollution-prevention requirements and prevent environmental hazards	*Basic knowledge of environmental factors and regulations:* *.1* identify particularly sensitive sea areas regarding discharge .2 identify areas where shipping is prohibited or should be avoided .3 special areas defined in MARPOL .4 recognize limitations of oil-spill equipment .5 plan for coping with increased volumes of garbage, bilge water, sewage, etc. .6 lack of infrastructure .7 oil spill and pollution in ice, including *consequences*	Examination and assessment of evidence obtained from one or more of the following: .1 approved in-service experience .2 approved training ship experience .3 approved simulator training, where appropriate .4 approved training programme	Legislative requirements related to relevant regulations, codes and practices are identified Correctly identify/select the limitations on vessel discharges contained in the Polar Code Correctly apply Polar Water Operations Manual/Waste Management Plan to determine limitations on vessel discharges and plans for storing waste Identify references that provide details of areas to be avoided, such as wildlife refuges, ecological heritage parks, migratory pathways, etc. (MARPOL, Antarctic Treaty, etc.) Identify factors that must be considered to manage waste stream during polar voyages

Table A-V/4-2

Specification of minimum standard of competence in advanced training for ships operating in polar waters

Column 1	Column 2	Column 3	Column 4
Competence	**Knowledge, understanding and proficiency**	**Methods for demonstrating competence**	**Criteria for evaluating competence**
Plan and conduct a voyage in polar waters	*Knowledge of voyage planning and reporting:* .1 information sources .2 reporting regimes in polar waters .3 development of safe routeing and passage planning to avoid ice where possible .4 ability to recognize the limitations of hydrographic information and charts in polar regions and whether the information is suitable for safe navigation .5 passage planning deviation and modification for dynamic ice conditions *Knowledge of equipment limitations:* .1 understand and identify hazards associated with limited terrestrial navigational aids in polar regions .2 understand and recognize high latitude errors on compasses .3 understand and identify limitations in discrimination of radar targets and ice features in ice clutter .4 understand and recognize limitations of electronic positioning systems at high latitude .5 understand and recognize limitations in nautical charts and pilot descriptions .6 understand and recognize limitations in communication systems	Examination and assessment of evidence obtained from one or more of the following: .1 approved in-service experience .2 approved training ship experience .3 approved simulator training, where appropriate .4 approved training programme	The equipment, charts and nautical publications required for the voyage are enumerated and appropriate to the safe conduct of the voyage The reasons for the planned route are supported by facts obtained from relevant sources and publications, statistical data and limitations of communication and navigational systems Voyage plan correctly identified relevant polar regulatory regimes and need for ice pilotage and/or icebreaker assistance All potential navigational hazards are accurately identified Positions, courses, distances and time calculations are correct within accepted accuracy standards for navigational equipment

Table A-V/4-2 *(continued)*

Column 1	Column 2	Column 3	Column 4
Competence	**Knowledge, understanding and proficiency**	**Methods for demonstrating competence**	**Criteria for evaluating competence**
Manage the safe operation of vessels operating in polar waters	*Knowledge and ability to operate and manoeuvre a vessel in ice:* .1 preparation and risk assessment before approaching ice, including presence of icebergs, and taking into account wind, darkness, swell, fog and pressure ice .2 conduct communications with an icebreaker and other vessels in the area and with Rescue Coordination Centres .3 understand and describe the conditions for the safe entry and exit to and from ice or open water, such as leads or cracks, avoiding icebergs and dangerous ice conditions and maintaining safe distance to icebergs .4 understand and describe ice ramming procedures including double and single ramming passage .5 recognize and determine the need for bridge watch team augmentation based upon environmental conditions, vessel equipment and vessel ice class .6 recognize the presentations of the various ice conditions as they appear on radar .7 understand icebreaker convoy terminology, and communications, and take icebreaker direction and move in convoy .8 understand methods to avoid besetment and to free beset vessel, and consequences of besetment .9 understand towing and rescue in ice, including risks associated with operation .10 handling ship in various ice concentration and coverage, including risks associated with navigation in ice, e.g. avoid turning and backing simultaneously	Examination and assessment of evidence obtained from one or more of the following: .1 approved in-service experience .2 approved training ship experience .3 approved simulator training, where appropriate .4 approved training programme	All decisions concerning navigating in ice are based on a proper assessment of the ship's manoeuvring and engine characteristics and the forces to be expected while navigating within polar waters Demonstrate communication skills, request ice routeing, plot and commence voyage through ice All potential ice hazards are correctly identified All decisions concerning berthing anchoring, cargo and ballast operations are based on a proper assessment of the ship's manoeuvring and engine characteristics and the forces to be expected and in accordance with the Polar Code guidelines and applicable international agreements Safely demonstrate progression of a vessel through ice, manoeuvring vessel through moderate ice concentration (range of 1/10 to 5/10) Safely demonstrate progression of a vessel through ice, manoeuvring vessel through dense ice concentration (range of 6/10 to 10/10) Operations are planned and carried out in accordance with established rules and procedures to ensure safety of operation and to avoid pollution of the marine environment Safety of navigation is maintained through navigation strategy and adjustment of ship's speed and heading through different types of ice Actions are understood to permit use of anchoring system in cold temperatures

Table A-V/4-2 *(continued)*

Column 1	Column 2	Column 3	Column 4
Competence	**Knowledge, understanding and proficiency**	**Methods for demonstrating competence**	**Criteria for evaluating competence**
Manage the safe operation of vessels operating in polar waters *(continued)*	.11 use of different type of propulsion and rudder systems, including limitations to avoid damage when operating in ice .12 use of heeling and trim systems, hazards in connection with ballast and trim in relation with ice .13 docking and undocking in ice covered waters, including hazards associated with operation and the various techniques to safely dock and undock in ice covered waters .14 anchoring in ice, including the dangers to anchoring system – ice accretion to hawse pipe and ground tackle .15 recognize conditions which impact polar visibility and may give indication of local ice and water conditions, including sea smoke, water sky, ice blink and refraction		Actions are carried out in accordance with accepted principles and procedures to prepare for icebreaker towing, including notch towing
Maintain safety of the ship's crew and passengers and the operational condition of life saving, fire fighting and other safety systems	Knowledge of safety: .1 understand the procedures and techniques for abandoning the ship and survival on ice and in ice covered waters .2 recognize limitations of fire-fighting systems and life-saving appliances due to low air temperatures .3 understand unique concerns in conducting emergency drills in ice and low temperatures .4 understand unique concerns in conducting emergency response in ice and low air and water temperatures	Examination and assessment of evidence obtained from one or more of the following: .1 approved in-service experience .2 approved training ship experience .3 approved simulator training, where appropriate .4 approved training programme	Response measures are in accordance with established plans and procedures, and are appropriate to the situation and nature of the emergency

Chapter VI
Standards regarding emergency, occupational safety, security, medical care and survival functions

Section A-VI/1
Mandatory minimum requirements for safety familiarization, basic training and instruction for all seafarers

Safety familiarization training

1 Before being assigned to shipboard duties, all persons employed or engaged on a seagoing ship, other than passengers, shall receive approved familiarization training in personal survival techniques or receive sufficient information and instruction, taking account of the guidance given in part B, to be able to:

.1 communicate with other persons on board on elementary safety matters and understand safety information symbols, signs and alarm signals;

.2 know what to do if:

.2.1 a person falls overboard,

.2.2 fire or smoke is detected, or

.2.3 the fire or abandon ship alarm is sounded;

.3 identify muster and embarkation stations and emergency escape routes;

.4 locate and don lifejackets;

.5 raise the alarm and have basic knowledge of the use of portable fire extinguishers;

.6 take immediate action upon encountering an accident or other medical emergency before seeking further medical assistance on board; and

.7 close and open the fire, weathertight and watertight doors fitted in the particular ship other than those for hull openings.

Basic training*

2 Seafarers employed or engaged in any capacity on board ship on the business of that ship as part of the ship's complement with designated safety or pollution-prevention duties in the operation of the ship shall, before being assigned to any shipboard duties:

.1 receive appropriate approved basic training or instruction in:

.1.1 personal survival techniques as set out in table A-VI/1-1,

.1.2 fire prevention and fire fighting as set out in table A-VI/1-2,

.1.3 elementary first aid as set out in table A-VI/1-3, and

.1.4 personal safety and social responsibilities as set out in table A-VI/1-4;

.2 be required to provide evidence of having achieved the required standard of competence to undertake the tasks, duties and responsibilities listed in column 1 of tables A-VI/1-1, A-VI/1-2, A-VI/1-3 and A-VI/1-4 through:

* The relevant IMO Model Course(s) may assist in the preparation of courses.

.2.1 demonstration of competence, in accordance with the methods and the criteria for evaluating competence tabulated in columns 3 and 4 of those tables, and

.2.2 examination or continuous assessment as part of an approved training programme in the subjects listed in column 2 of those tables.

3 Seafarers qualified in accordance with paragraph 2 in basic training shall be required, every five years, to provide evidence of having maintained the required standard of competence, to undertake the tasks, duties and responsibilities listed in column 1 of tables A-VI/1-1 and A-VI/1-2.

4 Parties may accept onboard training and experience for maintaining the required standard of competence in the following areas:

.1 personal survival techniques as set out in table A-VI/1-1:

.1.1 don a lifejacket;

.1.2 board a survival craft from the ship, while wearing a lifejacket;

.1.3 take initial actions on boarding a lifeboat to enhance chance of survival;

.1.4 stream a lifeboat drogue or sea-anchor;

.1.5 operate survival craft equipment; and

.1.6 operate location devices, including radio equipment;

.2 fire prevention and fire fighting as set out in table A-VI/1-2:

.2.1 use self-contained breathing apparatus; and

.2.2 effect a rescue in a smoke-filled space, using an approved smoke-generating device aboard, while wearing a breathing apparatus.

Exemptions

5 The Administration may, in respect of ships other than passenger ships of more than 500 gross tonnage engaged on international voyages and tankers, if it considers that a ship's size and the length or character of its voyage are such as to render the application of the full requirements of this section unreasonable or impracticable, exempt to that extent the seafarers on such a ship or class of ships from some of the requirements, bearing in mind the safety of people on board, the ship and property and the protection of the marine environment.

Table A-VI/1-1

Specification of minimum standard of competence in personal survival techniques

Column 1	Column 2	Column 3	Column 4
Competence	**Knowledge, understanding and proficiency**	**Methods for demonstrating competence**	**Criteria for evaluating competence**
Survive at sea in the event of ship abandonment	Types of emergency situations which may occur, such as collision, fire, foundering Types of life-saving appliances normally carried on ships Equipment in survival craft Location of personal life-saving appliances Principles concerning survival, including: .1 value of training and drills .2 personal protective clothing and equipment .3 need to be ready for any emergency .4 actions to be taken when called to survival craft stations .5 actions to be taken when required to abandon ship .6 actions to be taken when in the water .7 actions to be taken when aboard a survival craft .8 main dangers to survivors	Assessment of evidence obtained from approved instruction or during attendance at an approved course or approved in-service experience and examination, including practical demonstration of competence to: .1 don a lifejacket .2 don and use an immersion suit .3 safely jump from a height into the water .4 right an inverted liferaft while wearing a lifejacket .5 swim while wearing a lifejacket .6 keep afloat without a lifejacket .7 board a survival craft from the ship and water while wearing a lifejacket .8 take initial actions on boarding survival craft to enhance chance of survival .9 stream a drogue or sea-anchor .10 operate survival craft equipment .11 operate location devices, including radio equipment	Action taken on identifying muster signals is appropriate to the indicated emergency and complies with established procedures The timing and sequence of individual actions are appropriate to the prevailing circumstance and conditions and minimize potential dangers and threats to survival Method of boarding survival craft is appropriate and avoids dangers to other survivors Initial actions after leaving the ship and procedures and actions in water minimize threats to survival

STCW CODE

A

Table A-VI/1-2

Specification of minimum standard of competence in fire prevention and fire fighting

Column 1	Column 2	Column 3	Column 4
Competence	**Knowledge, understanding and proficiency**	**Methods for demonstrating competence**	**Criteria for evaluating competence**
Minimize the risk of fire and maintain a state of readiness to respond to emergency situations involving fire	Shipboard fire-fighting organization Location of fire-fighting appliances and emergency escape routes The elements of fire and explosion (the fire triangle) Types and sources of ignition Flammable materials, fire hazards and spread of fire The need for constant vigilance Actions to be taken on board ship Fire and smoke detection and automatic alarm systems Classification of fire and applicable extinguishing agents	Assessment of evidence obtained from approved instruction or attendance at an approved course	Initial actions on becoming aware of an emergency conform with accepted practices and procedures Action taken on identifying muster signals is appropriate to the indicated emergency and complies with established procedures

VI

Table A-VI/1-2 *(continued)*

Column 1	Column 2	Column 3	Column 4
Competence	**Knowledge, understanding and proficiency**	**Methods for demonstrating competence**	**Criteria for evaluating competence**
Fight and extinguish fires	Fire-fighting equipment and its location on board Instruction in: .1 fixed installations .2 fire-fighter's outfits .3 personal equipment .4 fire-fighting appliances and equipment .5 fire-fighting methods .6 fire-fighting agents .7 fire-fighting procedures .8 use of breathing apparatus for fighting fires and effecting rescues	Assessment of evidence obtained from approved instruction or during attendance at an approved course, including practical demonstration in spaces which provide truly realistic training conditions (e.g., simulated shipboard conditions) and, whenever possible and practical, in darkness, of the ability to: .1 use various types of portable fire extinguishers .2 use self-contained breathing apparatus .3 extinguish smaller fires, e.g., electrical fires, oil fires, propane fires .4 extinguish extensive fires with water, using jet and spray nozzles .5 extinguish fires with foam, powder or any other suitable chemical agent .6 enter and pass through, with lifeline but without breathing apparatus, a compartment into which high-expansion foam has been injected .7 fight fire in smoke-filled enclosed spaces wearing self-contained breathing apparatus .8 extinguish fire with water fog or any other suitable fire-fighting agent in an accommodation room or simulated engine-room with fire and heavy smoke .9 extinguish oil fire with fog applicator and spray nozzles, dry chemical powder or foam applicators .10 effect a rescue in a smoke-filled space wearing breathing apparatus	Clothing and equipment are appropriate to the nature of the fire-fighting operations The timing and sequence of individual actions are appropriate to the prevailing circumstances and conditions Extinguishment of fire is achieved using appropriate procedures, techniques and fire-fighting agents Breathing apparatus procedures and techniques comply with accepted practices and procedures

Table A-VI/1-3

Specification of minimum standard of competence in elementary first aid

Column 1	Column 2	Column 3	Column 4
Competence	**Knowledge, understanding and proficiency**	**Methods for demonstrating competence**	**Criteria for evaluating competence**
Take immediate action upon encountering an accident or other medical emergency	Assessment of needs of casualties and threats to own safety Appreciation of body structure and functions Understanding of immediate measures to be taken in cases of emergency, including the ability to: .1 position casualty .2 apply resuscitation techniques .3 control bleeding .4 apply appropriate measures of basic shock management .5 apply appropriate measures in event of burns and scalds, including accidents caused by electric current .6 rescue and transport a casualty .7 improvise bandages and use materials in the emergency kit	Assessment of evidence obtained from approved instruction or during attendance at an approved course	The manner and timing of raising the alarm is appropriate to the circumstances of the accident or medical emergency The identification of probable cause, nature and extent of injuries is prompt and complete, and the priority and sequence of actions is proportional to any potential threat to life Risk of further harm to self and casualty is minimized at all times

Table A-VI/1-4

Specification of minimum standard of competence in personal safety and social responsibilities

Column 1	Column 2	Column 3	Column 4
Competence	**Knowledge, understanding and proficiency**	**Methods for demonstrating competence**	**Criteria for evaluating competence**
Comply with emergency procedures	Types of emergency which may occur, such as collision, fire, foundering Knowledge of shipboard contingency plans for response to emergencies Emergency signals and specific duties allocated to crew members in the muster list; muster stations; correct use of personal safety equipment Action to take on discovering potential emergency, including fire, collision, foundering and ingress of water into the ship Action to take on hearing emergency alarm signals Value of training and drills Knowledge of escape routes and internal communication and alarm systems	Assessment of evidence obtained from approved instruction or during attendance at an approved course	Initial action on becoming aware of an emergency conforms to established emergency response procedures Information given on raising alarm is prompt, accurate, complete and clear
Take precautions to prevent pollution of the marine environment	Basic knowledge of the impact of shipping on the marine environment and the effects of operational or accidental pollution on it Basic environmental protection procedures Basic knowledge of complexity and diversity of the marine environment	Assessment of evidence obtained from approved instruction or during attendance at an approved course	Organizational procedures designed to safeguard the marine environment are observed at all times
Observe safe working practices	Importance of adhering to safe working practices at all times Safety and protective devices available to protect against potential hazards aboard ship Precautions to be taken prior to entering enclosed spaces Familiarization with international measures concerning accident prevention and occupational health*	Assessment of evidence obtained from approved instruction or during attendance at an approved course	Safe working practices are observed, and appropriate safety and protective equipment is correctly used at all times

* The ILO Code of Practice on Accident prevention on board ship at sea and in port may be of assistance in the preparation of courses.

Table A-VI/1-4 *(continued)*

Column 1	Column 2	Column 3	Column 4
Competence	**Knowledge, understanding and proficiency**	**Methods for demonstrating competence**	**Criteria for evaluating competence**
Contribute to effective communications on board ship	Understand the principles of, and barriers to, effective communication between individuals and teams within the ship Ability to establish and maintain effective communications	Assessment of evidence obtained from approved instruction or during attendance at an approved course	Communications are clear and effective at all times
Contribute to effective human relationships on board ship	Importance of maintaining good human and working relationships aboard ship Basic teamworking principles and practice, including conflict resolution Social responsibilities; employment conditions; individual rights and obligations; dangers of drug and alcohol abuse	Assessment of evidence obtained from approved instruction or during attendance at an approved course	Expected standards of work and behaviour are observed at all times
Understand and take necessary actions to control fatigue	Importance of obtaining the necessary rest Effects of sleep, schedules, and the circadian rhythm on fatigue Effects of physical stressors on seafarers Effects of environmental stressors in and outside the ship and their impact on seafarers Effects of schedule changes on seafarer fatigue	Assessment of evidence obtained from approved instruction or during attendance at an approved course	Fatigue management practices are observed and appropriate actions are used at all times

Section A-VI/2

Mandatory minimum requirements for the issue of certificates of proficiency in survival craft, rescue boats and fast rescue boats

Proficiency in survival craft and rescue boats other than fast rescue boats

Standard of competence

1 Every candidate for a certificate of proficiency in survival craft and rescue boats other than fast rescue boats shall be required to demonstrate competence to undertake the tasks, duties and responsibilities listed in column 1 of table A-VI/2-1.

2 The level of knowledge of the subjects listed in column 2 of table A-VI/2-1 shall be sufficient to enable the candidate to launch and take charge of a survival craft or rescue boat in emergency situations.*

3 Training and experience to achieve the necessary level of theoretical knowledge, understanding and proficiency shall take account of the guidance given in part B of this Code.

4 Every candidate for certification shall be required to provide evidence of having achieved the required standard of competence through:

- **.1** demonstration of competence to undertake the tasks, duties and responsibilities listed in column 1 of table A-VI/2-1, in accordance with the methods for demonstrating competence and the criteria for evaluating competence tabulated in columns 3 and 4 of that table; and
- **.2** examination or continuous assessment as part of an approved training programme covering the material set out in column 2 of table A-VI/2-1.

5 Seafarers qualified in accordance with paragraph 4 in survival craft and rescue boats other than fast rescue boats shall be required, every five years, to provide evidence of having maintained the required standards of competence to undertake the tasks, duties and responsibilities listed in column 1 of table A-VI/2-1.

6 Parties may accept onboard training and experience for maintaining the required standard of competence of table A-VI/2-1 in the following areas:

- **.1** take charge of a survival craft or rescue boat during and after launch:
  - **.1.1** interpret the markings on survival craft as to the number of persons they are intended to carry;
  - **.1.2** give correct commands for launching and boarding survival craft, clearing the ship and handling and disembarking persons from survival craft;
  - **.1.3** prepare and safely launch survival craft and clear the ship's side quickly; and
  - **.1.4** safely recover survival craft and rescue boats;
- **.2** manage survivors and survival craft after abandoning ship:
  - **.2.1** row and steer a boat and steer by compass;
  - **.2.2** use individual items of equipment of survival crafts, except for pyrotechnics; and
  - **.2.3** rig devices to aid location;
- **.3** use locating devices, including communication and signalling apparatus:
  - **.3.1** use of portable radio equipment for survival craft; and
- **.4** apply first aid to survivors.

* The relevant IMO Model Course(s) may be of assistance in the preparation of courses.

Proficiency in fast rescue boats

Standard of competence

7 Every candidate for a certificate of proficiency in fast rescue boats shall be required to demonstrate competence to undertake the tasks, duties and responsibilities listed in column 1 of table A-VI/2-2.

8 The level of knowledge of the subjects listed in column 2 of table A-VI/2-2 shall be sufficient to enable the candidate to launch and take charge of a fast rescue boat in emergency situations.*

9 Training and experience to achieve the necessary level of theoretical knowledge, understanding and proficiency shall take account of the guidance given in part B of this Code.

10 Every candidate for certification shall be required to provide evidence of having achieved the required standard of competence through:

- **.1** demonstration of competence to undertake the tasks, duties and responsibilities listed in column 1 of table A-VI/2-2, in accordance with the methods for demonstrating competence and the criteria for evaluating competence tabulated in columns 3 and 4 of that table; and
- **.2** examination or continuous assessment as part of an approved training programme covering the material set out in column 2 of table A-VI/2-2.

11 Seafarers qualified in accordance with paragraph 10 in fast rescue boats shall be required, every five years, to provide evidence of having maintained the required standards of competence to undertake the tasks, duties and responsibilities listed in column 1 of table A-VI/2-2.

12 Parties may accept onboard training and experience for maintaining the required standard of competence of table A-VI/2-2, in the following areas:

- **.1** Take charge of a fast rescue boat during and after launch:
  - **.1.1** control safe launching and recovery of a fast rescue boat;
  - **.1.2** handle a fast rescue boat in prevailing weather and sea conditions;
  - **.1.3** use communications and signalling equipment between the fast rescue boat and a helicopter and a ship;
  - **.1.4** use the emergency equipment carried; and
  - **.1.5** carry out search patterns, taking account of environmental factors.

* The relevant IMO Model Course(s) may be of assistance in the preparation of courses.

Table A-VI/2-1

Specification of minimum standard of competence in survival craft and rescue boats other than fast rescue boats

Column 1	Column 2	Column 3	Column 4
Competence	**Knowledge, understanding and proficiency**	**Methods for demonstrating competence**	**Criteria for evaluating competence**
Take charge of a survival craft or rescue boat during and after launch	Construction and outfit of survival craft and rescue boats and individual items of their equipment Particular characteristics and facilities of survival craft and rescue boats Various types of device used for launching survival craft and rescue boats Methods of launching survival craft into a rough sea Methods of recovering survival craft Action to be taken after leaving the ship Methods of launching and recovering rescue boats in a rough sea Dangers associated with use of on-load release devices Knowledge of maintenance procedures	Assessment of evidence obtained from practical demonstration of ability to: .1 right an inverted liferaft while wearing a lifejacket .2 interpret the markings on survival craft as to the number of persons they are intended to carry .3 give correct commands for launching and boarding survival craft, clearing the ship and handling and disembarking persons from survival craft .4 prepare and safely launch survival craft and clear the ship's side quickly and operate off-load and on-load release devices .5 safely recover survival craft and rescue boats, including the proper resetting of both off-load and on-load release devices using: inflatable liferaft and open or enclosed lifeboat with inboard engine or approved simulator training, where appropriate	Preparation, boarding and launching of survival craft are within equipment limitations and enable survival craft to clear the ship safely Initial actions on leaving the ship minimize threat to survival Recovery of survival craft and rescue boats is within equipment limitations Equipment is operated in accordance with manufacturers' instructions for release and resetting
Operate a survival craft engine	Methods of starting and operating a survival craft engine and its accessories together with the use of the fire extinguisher provided	Assessment of evidence obtained from practical demonstration of ability to start and operate an inboard engine fitted in an open or enclosed lifeboat	Propulsion is available and maintained as required for manoeuvring

Table A-VI/2-1 *(continued)*

Column 1	Column 2	Column 3	Column 4
Competence	**Knowledge, understanding and proficiency**	**Methods for demonstrating competence**	**Criteria for evaluating competence**
Manage survivors and survival craft after abandoning ship	Handling survival craft in rough weather Use of painter, sea-anchor and all other equipment Apportionment of food and water in survival craft Action taken to maximize detectability and location of survival craft Method of helicopter rescue Effects of hypothermia and its prevention; use of protective covers and garments, including immersion suits and thermal protective aids Use of rescue boats and motor lifeboats for marshalling liferafts and rescue of survivors and persons in the sea Beaching survival craft	Assessment of evidence obtained from practical demonstration of ability to: .1 row and steer a boat and steer by compass .2 use individual items of equipment of survival craft .3 rig devices to aid location	Survival management is appropriate to prevailing circumstances and conditions
Use locating devices, including communication and signalling apparatus and pyrotechnics	Radio life-saving appliances carried in survival craft, including satellite EPIRBs and SARTs Pyrotechnic distress signals	Assessment of evidence obtained from practical demonstration of ability to: .1 use portable radio equipment for survival craft .2 use signalling equipment, including pyrotechnics	Use and choice of communication and signalling apparatus is appropriate to prevailing circumstances and conditions
Apply first aid to survivors	Use of the first-aid kit and resuscitation techniques Management of injured persons, including control of bleeding and shock	Assessment of evidence obtained from practical demonstration of ability to deal with injured persons both during and after abandonment, using first-aid kit and resuscitation techniques	Identification of the probable cause, nature and extent of injuries or condition is prompt and accurate Priority and sequence of treatment minimizes any threat to life

Table A-VI/2-2

Specification of minimum standard of competence in fast rescue boats

Column 1	Column 2	Column 3	Column 4
Competence	**Knowledge, understanding and proficiency**	**Methods for demonstrating competence**	**Criteria for evaluating competence**
Understand the construction, maintenance, repair and outfitting of fast rescue boats	Construction and outfitting of fast rescue boats and individual items of their equipment Knowledge of the maintenance and emergency repairs of fast rescue boats and the normal inflation and deflation of buoyancy compartments of inflated fast rescue boats	Assessment of evidence obtained from practical instruction	The method of carrying out routine maintenance and emergency repairs Identify components and required equipment for fast rescue boats
Take charge of the launching equipment and appliance as commonly fitted, during launching and recovery	Assessment of the readiness of launching equipment and launching appliance of fast rescue boats for immediate launching and operation Understand the operation and limitations of the winch, brakes, falls, painters, motion-compensation and other equipment as commonly fitted Safety precautions during launching and recovery of a fast rescue boat Launching and recovery of a fast rescue boat in prevailing and adverse weather and sea conditions	Assessment of evidence obtained from practical demonstration of ability to control safe launching and recovery of a fast rescue boat, with equipment as fitted	Ability to prepare and take charge of the launching equipment and appliance during launching and recovery of a fast rescue boat
Take charge of a fast rescue boat as commonly fitted, during launching and recovery	Assessment of the readiness of fast rescue boats and related equipment for immediate launching and operation Safety precautions during launching and recovery of a fast rescue boat Launching and recovery of a fast rescue boat in prevailing and adverse weather and sea conditions	Assessment of evidence obtained from practical demonstration of ability to conduct safe launching and recovery of a fast rescue boat, with equipment as fitted	Ability to take charge of a fast rescue boat during launching and recovery

Table A-VI/2-2 *(continued)*

Column 1	Column 2	Column 3	Column 4
Competence	**Knowledge, understanding and proficiency**	**Methods for demonstrating competence**	**Criteria for evaluating competence**
Take charge of a fast rescue boat after launching	Particular characteristics, facilities and limitations of fast rescue boats Procedures for the righting of a capsized fast rescue boat How to handle a fast rescue boat in prevailing and adverse weather and sea conditions Navigational and safety equipment available in a fast rescue boat Search patterns and environmental factors affecting their execution	Assessment of evidence obtained from practical demonstration of ability to: .1 right a capsized fast rescue boat .2 handle a fast rescue boat in prevailing weather and sea conditions .3 swim in special equipment .4 use communications and signalling equipment between the fast rescue boat and a helicopter and a ship .5 use the emergency equipment carried .6 recover a casualty from the water and transfer a casualty to a rescue helicopter or to a ship or to a place of safety .7 carry out search patterns, taking account of environmental factors	Demonstration of operation of fast rescue boats within equipment limitations in prevailing weather conditions
Operate a fast rescue boat engine	Methods of starting and operating a fast rescue boat engine and its accessories	Assessment of evidence obtained from practical demonstration of ability to start and operate a fast rescue boat engine	Engine is started and operated as required for manoeuvring

Section A-VI/3

Mandatory minimum requirements for training in advanced fire fighting

Standard of competence

1 Seafarers designated to control fire-fighting operations shall have successfully completed advanced training in techniques for fighting fire, with particular emphasis on organization, tactics and command, and shall be required to demonstrate competence to undertake the tasks, duties and responsibilities listed in column 1 of table A-VI/3.

2 The level of knowledge and understanding of the subjects listed in column 2 of table A-VI/3 shall be sufficient for the effective control of fire-fighting operations on board ship.*

3 Training and experience to achieve the necessary level of theoretical knowledge, understanding and proficiency shall take account of the guidance given in part B of this Code.

4 Every candidate for certification shall be required to provide evidence of having achieved the required standard of competence, in accordance with the methods for demonstrating competence and the criteria for evaluating competence tabulated in columns 3 and 4 of table A-VI/3.

5 Seafarers qualified in accordance with paragraph 4 in advanced fire fighting shall be required, every five years, to provide evidence of having maintained the required standards of competence to undertake the tasks, duties and responsibilities listed in column 1 of table A-VI/3.

6 Parties may accept onboard training and experience for maintaining the required standard of competence of table A-VI/3, in the following areas:

- **.1** Control fire-fighting operations aboard ships;
  - **.1.1** fire-fighting procedures at sea and in port, with particular emphasis on organization, tactics and command;
  - **.1.2** communication and coordination during fire-fighting operations;
  - **.1.3** ventilation control, including smoke extraction;
  - **.1.4** control of fuel and electrical systems;
  - **.1.5** fire-fighting process hazards (dry distillation, chemical reactions, boiler uptake, fires);
  - **.1.6** fire precautions and hazards associated with the storage and handling of materials;
  - **.1.7** management and control of injured persons; and
  - **.1.8** procedures for coordination with shore-based fire fighters.

* The relevant IMO Model Course(s) may be of assistance in the preparation of courses.

Table A-VI/3

Specification of minimum standard of competence in advanced fire fighting

Column 1	Column 2	Column 3	Column 4
Competence	**Knowledge, understanding and proficiency**	**Methods for demonstrating competence**	**Criteria for evaluating competence**
Control fire-fighting operations aboard ships	Fire-fighting procedures at sea and in port, with particular emphasis on organization, tactics and command Use of water for fire extinguishing, the effect on ship stability, precautions and corrective procedures Communication and coordination during fire-fighting operations Ventilation control, including smoke extraction Control of fuel and electrical systems Fire-fighting process hazards (dry distillation, chemical reactions, boiler uptake fires, etc.) Fire fighting involving dangerous goods Fire precautions and hazards associated with the storage and handling of materials (paints, etc.) Management and control of injured persons Procedures for coordination with shore-based fire fighters	Practical exercises and instruction conducted under approved and truly realistic training conditions (e.g., simulated shipboard conditions) and, whenever possible and practicable, in darkness	Actions taken to control fires are based on a full and accurate assessment of the incident, using all available sources of information The order of priority, timing and sequence of actions are appropriate to the overall requirements of the incident and to minimize damage and potential damage to the ship, injuries to personnel and impairment of the operational effectiveness of the ship Transmission of information is prompt, accurate, complete and clear Personal safety during fire control activities is safeguarded at all times
Organize and train fire parties	Preparation of contingency plans Composition and allocation of personnel to fire parties Strategies and tactics for control of fires in various parts of the ship	Practical exercises and instruction conducted under approved and truly realistic training conditions, e.g., simulated shipboard conditions	Composition and organization of fire control parties ensure the prompt and effective implementation of emergency plans and procedures
Inspect and service fire-detection and fire-extinguishing systems and equipment	Fire-detection systems; fixed fire-extinguishing systems; portable and mobile fire-extinguishing equipment, including appliances, pumps and rescue, salvage, life-support, personal protective and communication equipment Requirements for statutory and classification surveys	Practical exercises, using approved equipment and systems in a realistic training environment	Operational effectiveness of all fire-detection and fire-extinguishing systems and equipment is maintained at all times in accordance with performance specifications and legislative requirements
Investigate and compile reports on incidents involving fire	Assessment of cause of incidents involving fire	Practical exercises in a realistic training environment	Causes of fire are identified and the effectiveness of countermeasures is evaluated

Section A-VI/4

Mandatory minimum requirements related to medical first aid and medical care

Standard of competence for seafarers designated to provide medical first aid on board ship

1 Every seafarer who is designated to provide medical first aid on board ship shall be required to demonstrate the competence to undertake the tasks, duties and responsibilities listed in column 1 of table A-VI/4-1.

2 The level of knowledge of the subjects listed in column 2 of table A-VI/4-1 shall be sufficient to enable the designated seafarer to take immediate effective action in the case of accidents or illness likely to occur on board ship.*

3 Every candidate for certification under the provisions of regulation VI/4, paragraph 1, shall be required to provide evidence that the required standard of competence has been achieved in accordance with the methods for demonstrating competence and the criteria for evaluating competence tabulated in columns 3 and 4 of table A-VI/4-1.

Standard of competence for seafarers designated to take charge of medical care on board ship

4 Every seafarer who is designated to take charge of medical care on board ship shall be required to demonstrate the competence to undertake the tasks, duties and responsibilities listed in column 1 of table A-VI/4-2.

5 The level of knowledge of the subjects listed in column 2 of table A-VI/4-2 shall be sufficient to enable the designated seafarer to take immediate effective action in the case of accidents or illness likely to occur on board ship.*

6 Every candidate for certification under the provisions of regulation VI/4, paragraph 2, shall be required to provide evidence that the required standard of competence has been achieved in accordance with the methods for demonstrating competence and the criteria for evaluating competence tabulated in columns 3 and 4 of table A-VI/4-2.

* The relevant IMO Model Course(s) may assist in the preparation of courses.

Table A-VI/4-1
Specification of minimum standard of competence in medical first aid

Column 1	Column 2	Column 3	Column 4
Competence	**Knowledge, understanding and proficiency**	**Methods for demonstrating competence**	**Criteria for evaluating competence**
Apply immediate first aid in the event of accident or illness on board	First-aid kit Body structure and function Toxicological hazards on board, including use of the Medical First Aid Guide for Use in Accidents Involving Dangerous Goods (MFAG) or its national equivalent Examination of casualty or patient Spinal injuries Burns, scalds and effects of heat and cold Fractures, dislocations and muscular injuries Medical care of rescued persons Radio medical advice Pharmacology Sterilization Cardiac arrest, drowning and asphyxia	Assessment of evidence obtained from practical instruction	The identification of probable cause, nature and extent of injuries is prompt, complete and conforms to current first-aid practice Risk of harm to self and to others is minimized at all times Treatment of injuries and the patient's condition is appropriate and conforms to recognized first-aid practice and international guidelines

Table A-VI/4-2

Specification of minimum standard of competence in medical care

Column 1	Column 2	Column 3	Column 4
Competence	**Knowledge, understanding and proficiency**	**Methods for demonstrating competence**	**Criteria for evaluating competence**
Provide medical care to the sick and injured while they remain on board	Care of casualty involving: .1 head and spinal injuries .2 injuries of ear, nose, throat and eyes .3 external and internal bleeding .4 burns, scalds and frostbite .5 fractures, dislocations and muscular injuries .6 wounds, wound healing and infection .7 pain relief .8 techniques of sewing and clamping .9 management of acute abdominal conditions .10 minor surgical treatment .11 dressing and bandaging Aspects of nursing: .1 general principles .2 nursing care Diseases, including: .1 medical conditions and emergencies .2 sexually transmitted diseases .3 tropical and infectious diseases Alcohol and drug abuse Dental care Gynaecology, pregnancy and childbirth Medical care of rescued persons Death at sea Hygiene Disease prevention, including: .1 disinfection, disinfestation, de-ratting .2 vaccinations Keeping records and copies of applicable regulations: .1 keeping medical records .2 international and national maritime medical regulations	Assessment of evidence obtained from practical instruction and demonstration Where practicable, approved practical experience at a hospital or similar establishment	Identification of symptoms is based on the concepts of clinical examination and medical history Protection against infection and spread of diseases is complete and effective Personal attitude is calm, confident and reassuring Treatment of injury or condition is appropriate and conforms to accepted medical practice and relevant national and international medical guides The dosage and application of drugs and medication complies with manufacturers' recommendations and accepted medical practice The significance of changes in patient's condition is promptly recognized

Table A-VI/4-2 *(continued)*

Column 1	Column 2	Column 3	Column 4
Competence	**Knowledge, understanding and proficiency**	**Methods for demonstrating competence**	**Criteria for evaluating competence**
Participate in coordinated schemes for medical assistance to ships	External assistance, including: .1 radio medical advice .2 transportation of the ill and injured, including helicopter evacuation .3 medical care of sick seafarers involving co-operation with port health authorities or out-patient wards in port		Clinical examination procedures are complete and comply with instructions received The method and preparation for evacuation is in accordance with recognized procedures and is designed to maximize the welfare of the patient Procedures for seeking radio medical advice conform to established practice and recommendations

Section A-VI/5

Mandatory minimum requirements for the issue of certificates of proficiency for ship security officers

Standard of competence

1 Every candidate for a certificate of proficiency as a ship security officer shall be required to demonstrate competence to undertake the tasks, duties and responsibilities listed in column 1 of table A-VI/5.

2 The level of knowledge of the subjects listed in column 2 of table A-VI/5 shall be sufficient to enable the candidate to act as the designated ship security officer.

3 Training and experience to achieve the necessary level of theoretical knowledge, understanding and proficiency shall take into account the guidance in section B-VI/5 of this Code.

4 Every candidate for certification shall be required to provide evidence of having achieved the required standard of competence in accordance with the methods for demonstrating competence and the criteria for evaluating competence tabulated in columns 3 and 4 of table A-VI/5.

Table A-VI/5

Specification of minimum standard of competence for ship security officers

Column 1	Column 2	Column 3	Column 4
Competence	**Knowledge, understanding and proficiency**	**Methods for demonstrating competence**	**Criteria for evaluating competence**
Maintain and supervise the implementation of a ship security plan	Knowledge of international maritime security policy and responsibilities of Governments, companies and designated persons, including elements that may relate to piracy and armed robbery Knowledge of the purpose for and the elements that make up a ship security plan, related procedures and maintenance of records, including those that may relate to piracy and armed robbery Knowledge of procedures to be employed in implementing a ship security plan and reporting of security incidents Knowledge of maritime security levels and the consequential security measures and procedures aboard ship and in the port facility environment Knowledge of the requirements and procedures for conducting internal audits, on-scene inspections, control and monitoring of security activities specified in a ship security plan Knowledge of the requirements and procedures for reporting to the company security officer any deficiencies and non-conformities identified during internal audits, periodic reviews and security inspections Knowledge of the methods and procedures used to modify the ship security plan Knowledge of security-related contingency plans and the procedures for responding to security threats or breaches of security, including provisions for maintaining critical operations of the ship/port interface, including also elements that may relate to piracy and armed robbery Working knowledge of maritime security terms and definitions, including elements that may relate to piracy and armed robbery	Assessment of evidence obtained from approved training or examination	Procedures and actions are in accordance with the principles established by the ISPS Code and SOLAS, 1974, as amended Legislative requirements relating to security are correctly identified Procedures achieve a state of readiness to respond to changes in maritime security levels Communications within the ship security officer's area of responsibility are clear and understood

Table A-VI/5 *(continued)*

Column 1	Column 2	Column 3	Column 4
Competence	**Knowledge, understanding and proficiency**	**Methods for demonstrating competence**	**Criteria for evaluating competence**
Assess security risk, threat and vulnerability	Knowledge of risk assessment and assessment tools Knowledge of security assessment documentation, including the Declaration of Security Knowledge of techniques used to circumvent security measures, including those used by pirates and armed robbers Knowledge enabling recognition, on a non-discriminatory basis, of persons posing potential security risks Knowledge enabling recognition of weapons, dangerous substances and devices and awareness of the damage they can cause Knowledge of crowd management and control techniques, where appropriate Knowledge in handling sensitive security-related information and security-related communications Knowledge of implementing and coordinating searches Knowledge of the methods for physical searches and non-intrusive inspections	Assessment of evidence obtained from approved training, or approved experience and examination, including practical demonstration of competence to: .1 conduct physical searches .2 conduct non-intrusive inspections	Procedures and actions are in accordance with the principles established by the ISPS Code and SOLAS, 1974, as amended Procedures achieve a state of readiness to respond to changes in the maritime security levels Communications within the ship security officer's area of responsibility are clear and understood
Undertake regular inspections of the ship to ensure that appropriate security measures are implemented and maintained	Knowledge of the requirements for designating and monitoring restricted areas Knowledge of controlling access to the ship and to restricted areas on board ship Knowledge of methods for effective monitoring of deck areas and areas surrounding the ship Knowledge of security aspects relating to the handling of cargo and ship's stores with other shipboard personnel and relevant port facility security officers Knowledge of methods for controlling the embarkation, disembarkation and access while on board of persons and their effects	Assessment of evidence obtained from approved training or examination	Procedures and actions are in accordance with the principles established by the ISPS Code and SOLAS, 1974, as amended Procedures achieve a state of readiness to respond to changes in the maritime security levels Communications within the ship security officer's area of responsibility are clear and understood

Table A-VI/5 *(continued)*

Column 1	Column 2	Column 3	Column 4
Competence	**Knowledge, understanding and proficiency**	**Methods for demonstrating competence**	**Criteria for evaluating competence**
Ensure that security equipment and systems, if any, are properly operated, tested and calibrated	Knowledge of the various types of security equipment and systems and their limitations, including those that could be used in case of attacks by pirates and armed robbers Knowledge of the procedures, instructions and guidance on the use of ship security alert systems Knowledge of the methods for testing, calibrating and maintaining security systems and equipment, particularly whilst at sea	Assessment of evidence obtained from approved training or examination	Procedures and actions are in accordance with the principles established by the ISPS Code and SOLAS, 1974, as amended
Encourage security awareness and vigilance	Knowledge of training, drill and exercise requirements under relevant conventions, codes and IMO circulars, including those relevant to anti-piracy and anti-armed robbery Knowledge of the methods for enhancing security awareness and vigilance on board Knowledge of the methods for assessing the effectiveness of drills and exercises	Assessment of evidence obtained from approved training or examination	Procedures and actions are in accordance with the principles established by the ISPS Code and SOLAS, 1974, as amended Communications within the ship security officer's area of responsibility are clear and understood

Section A-VI/6

Mandatory minimum requirements for security-related training and instruction for all seafarers

Standard of competence for security-related familiarization training

1 Before being assigned to shipboard duties, all persons employed or engaged on a seagoing ship which is required to comply with the provisions of the ISPS Code, other than passengers, shall receive approved security-related familiarization training, taking account of the guidance given in part B, to be able to:

- **.1** report a security incident, including a piracy or armed robbery threat or attack;
- **.2** know the procedures to follow when they recognize a security threat; and
- **.3** take part in security-related emergency and contingency procedures.

2 Seafarers with designated security duties engaged or employed on a seagoing ship shall, before being assigned such duties, receive security-related familiarization training in their assigned duties and responsibilities, taking into account the guidance given in part B.

3 The security-related familiarization training shall be conducted by the ship security officer or an equally qualified person.

Standard of competence for security-awareness training

4 Seafarers employed or engaged in any capacity on board a ship which is required to comply with the provisions of the ISPS Code on the business of that ship as part of the ship's complement without designated security duties shall, before being assigned to any shipboard duties:

- **.1** receive appropriate approved training or instruction in security awareness as set out in table A-VI/6-1;
- **.2** be required to provide evidence of having achieved the required standard of competence to undertake the tasks, duties and responsibilities listed in column 1 of table A-VI/6-1:
  - **.2.1** by demonstration of competence, in accordance with the methods and the criteria for evaluating competence tabulated in columns 3 and 4 of table A-VI/6-1; and
  - **.2.2** by examination or continuous assessment as part of an approved training programme in the subjects listed in column 2 of table A-VI/6-1.

Transitional provisions

5 Until 1 January 2014, seafarers who commenced an approved seagoing service prior to the date of entry into force of this section shall be able to establish that they meet the requirements of paragraph 4 by:

- **.1** approved seagoing service as shipboard personnel, for a period of at least six months in total during the preceding three years; or
- **.2** having performed security functions considered to be equivalent to the seagoing service required in paragraph 5.1; or
- **.3** passing an approved test; or
- **.4** successfully completing approved training.

Standard of competence for seafarers with designated security duties

6 Every seafarer who is designated to perform security duties, including anti-piracy and anti-armed-robbery-related activities, shall be required to demonstrate competence to undertake the tasks, duties and responsibilities listed in column 1 of table A-VI/6-2.

7 The level of knowledge of the subjects in column 2 of table A-VI/6-2 shall be sufficient to enable every candidate to perform on board designated security duties, including anti-piracy and anti-armed-robbery-related activities.

8 Every candidate for certification shall be required to provide evidence of having achieved the required standard of competence through:

.1 demonstration of competence to undertake the tasks, duties and responsibilities listed in column 1 of table A-VI/6-2, in accordance with the methods for demonstrating competence and the criteria for evaluating competence tabulated in columns 3 and 4 of that table; and

.2 examination or continuous assessment as part of an approved training programme covering the material set out in column 2 of table A-VI/6-2.

Transitional provisions

9 Until 1 January 2014, seafarers with designated security duties who commenced an approved seagoing service prior to the date of entry into force of this section shall be able to demonstrate competence to undertake the tasks, duties and responsibilities listed in column 1 of table A-VI/6-2 by:

.1 approved seagoing service as shipboard personnel with designated security duties, for a period of at least six months in total during the preceding three years; or

.2 having performed security functions considered to be equivalent to the seagoing service required in paragraph 9.1; or

.3 passing an approved test; or

.4 successfully completing approved training.

Table A-VI/6-1

Specification of minimum standard of competence in security awareness

Column 1	Column 2	Column 3	Column 4
Competence	**Knowledge, understanding and proficiency**	**Methods for demonstrating competence**	**Criteria for evaluating competence**
Contribute to the enhancement of maritime security through heightened awareness	Basic working knowledge of maritime security terms and definitions, including elements that may relate to piracy and armed robbery Basic knowledge of international maritime security policy and responsibilities of Governments, companies and persons Basic knowledge of maritime security levels and their impact on security measures and procedures aboard ship and in port facilities Basic knowledge of security reporting procedures Basic knowledge of security-related contingency plans	Assessment of evidence obtained from approved instruction or during attendance at an approved course	Requirements relating to enhanced maritime security are correctly identified
Recognition of security threats	Basic knowledge of techniques used to circumvent security measures Basic knowledge enabling recognition of potential security threats, including elements that may relate to piracy and armed robbery Basic knowledge enabling recognition of weapons, dangerous substances and devices and awareness of the damage they can cause Basic knowledge in handling security-related information and security-related communications	Assessment of evidence obtained from approved instruction or during attendance at an approved course	Maritime security threats are correctly identified
Understanding of the need for and methods of maintaining security awareness and vigilance	Basic knowledge of training, drill and exercise requirements under relevant conventions, codes and IMO circulars, including those relevant for anti-piracy and anti-armed robbery	Assessment of evidence obtained from approved instruction or during attendance at an approved course	Requirements relating to enhanced maritime security are correctly identified

Table A-VI/6-2

Specification of minimum standard of competence for seafarers with designated security duties

Column 1	Column 2	Column 3	Column 4
Competence	**Knowledge, understanding and proficiency**	**Methods for demonstrating competence**	**Criteria for evaluating competence**
Maintain the conditions set out in a ship security plan	Working knowledge of maritime security terms and definitions, including elements that may relate to piracy and armed robbery Knowledge of international maritime security policy and responsibilities of Governments, companies and persons, including working knowledge of elements that may relate to piracy and armed robbery Knowledge of maritime security levels and their impact on security measures and procedures aboard ship and in the port facilities Knowledge of security reporting procedures Knowledge of procedures and requirements for drills and exercises under relevant conventions, codes and IMO circulars, including working knowledge of those that may relate to piracy and armed robbery Knowledge of the procedures for conducting inspections and surveys and for the control and monitoring of security activities specified in a ship security plan Knowledge of security-related contingency plans and the procedures for responding to security threats or breaches of security, including provisions for maintaining critical operations of the ship/port interface, and including also working knowledge of those that may relate to piracy and armed robbery	Assessment of evidence obtained from approved instruction or during attendance at an approved course	Procedures and actions are in accordance with the principles established by the ISPS Code and SOLAS, 1974, as amended Legislative requirements relating to security are correctly identified Communications within the area of responsibility are clear and understood

Table A-VI/6-2 *(continued)*

Column 1	Column 2	Column 3	Column 4
Competence	**Knowledge, understanding and proficiency**	**Methods for demonstrating competence**	**Criteria for evaluating competence**
Recognition of security risks and threats	Knowledge of security documentation, including the Declaration of Security Knowledge of techniques used to circumvent security measures, including those used by pirates and armed robbers Knowledge enabling recognition of potential security threats Knowledge enabling recognition of weapons, dangerous substances and devices and awareness of the damage they can cause Knowledge of crowd management and control techniques, where appropriate Knowledge in handling security-related information and security-related communications Knowledge of the methods for physical searches and non-intrusive inspections	Assessment of evidence obtained from approved instruction or during attendance at an approved course	Procedures and actions are in accordance with the principles established by the ISPS Code and SOLAS, 1974, as amended
Undertake regular security inspections of the ship	Knowledge of the techniques for monitoring restricted areas Knowledge of controlling access to the ship and to restricted areas on board ship Knowledge of methods for effective monitoring of deck areas and areas surrounding the ship Knowledge of inspection methods relating to the cargo and ship's stores Knowledge of methods for controlling the embarkation, disembarkation and access while on board of persons and their effects	Assessment of evidence obtained from approved instruction or during attendance at an approved course	Procedures and actions are in accordance with the principles established by the ISPS Code and SOLAS, 1974, as amended
Proper usage of security equipment and systems, if any	General knowledge of various types of security equipment and systems, including those that could be used in case of attacks by pirates and armed robbers, including their limitations Knowledge of the need for testing, calibrating, and maintaining security systems and equipment, particularly whilst at sea	Assessment of evidence obtained from approved instruction or during attendance at an approved course	Equipment and systems operations are carried out in accordance with established equipment operating instructions and taking into account the limitations of the equipment and systems Procedures and actions are in accordance with the principles established by the ISPS Code and SOLAS, 1974, as amended

Chapter VII
Standards regarding alternative certification

Section A-VII/1
Issue of alternative certificates

1 Every candidate for certification at the operational level under the provisions of chapter VII of the annex to the Convention shall be required to complete relevant education and training and meet the standard of competence for all the functions prescribed in either table A-II/1 or table A-III/1. Functions specified in table A-II/1 or A-III/1 respectively may be added provided the candidate completes, as appropriate, additional relevant education and training and meets the standards of competence prescribed in those tables for the functions concerned.

2 Every candidate for certification at the management level as the person having command of a ship of 500 gross tonnage or more, or the person upon whom the command of such a ship will fall in the event of the incapacity of the person in command, shall be required, in addition to compliance with the standard of competence specified in table A-II/1, to complete relevant education and training and meet the standard of competence for all of the functions prescribed in table A-II/2. Functions specified in the tables of chapter III of this part may be added provided the candidate completes, as appropriate, additional relevant education and training and meets the standards of competence prescribed in those tables for the functions concerned.

3 Every candidate for certification at the management level as the person responsible for the mechanical propulsion of a ship powered by main propulsion machinery of 750 kW or more, or the person upon whom such responsibility will fall in the event of the incapacity of the person responsible for the mechanical propulsion of the ship, shall be required, in addition to compliance with the standard of competence specified in table A-III/1, to complete relevant education and training and meet the standard of competence for all of the functions prescribed in table A-III/2, as appropriate. Functions specified in the tables of chapter II of this part may be added provided the candidate completes, as appropriate, additional relevant education and training and meets the standards of competence prescribed in those tables for the functions concerned.

4 Every candidate for certification at the support level:

.1 in navigation or marine engineering shall be required to complete relevant training and meet the standard of competence for the function prescribed in either table A-II/4 or table A-III/4. Functions specified in table A-III/4 or A-II/4 respectively may be added provided the candidate completes, as appropriate, additional relevant training and meets the standards of competence prescribed in those tables for the function concerned;

.2 as able seafarer deck shall be required, in addition to compliance with the standard of competence specified in table A-II/4, to complete relevant training and meet the standard of competence for all of the functions prescribed in table A-II/5. Functions specified in table A-III/4 or A-III/5 may be added provided the candidate completes, as appropriate, additional relevant training and meets the standard of competence prescribed in that (those) table(s) for the function(s) concerned; and

.3 as able seafarer engine shall be required, in addition to compliance with the standard of competence specified in table A-III/4, to complete relevant training and meet the standard of competence for all of the functions prescribed in table A-III/5. Functions specified in table A-II/4 or A-II/5 may be added provided the candidate completes, as appropriate, additional relevant training and meets the standards of competence prescribed in that (those) table(s) for the function(s) concerned.

Section A-VII/2
Certification of seafarers

1 In accordance with the requirements of regulation VII/1, paragraph 1.3, every candidate for certification under the provisions of chapter VII at the operational level in functions specified in tables A-II/1 and A-III/1 shall:

.1 have approved seagoing service of not less than 12 months, which service shall include a period of at least six months performing engine-room duties under the supervision of a qualified engineer officer and, where the function of navigation is required, a period of at least six months performing bridge watchkeeping duties under the supervision of a qualified bridge watchkeeping officer; and

.2 have completed, during this service, onboard training programmes approved as meeting the relevant requirements of sections A-II/1 and A-III/1 and documented in an approved training record book.

2 Every candidate for certification under the provisions of chapter VII at the management level in a combination of functions specified in tables A-II/2 and A-III/2 shall have approved seagoing service related to the functions to be shown in the endorsement to the certificate as follows:

.1 *for persons other than those having command or responsibility for the mechanical propulsion of a ship* – 12 months performing duties at the operational level related to regulation III/2 or III/3 as appropriate and, where the function of navigation at the management level is required, at least 12 months performing bridge watchkeeping duties at the operational level;

.2 *for those having command or the responsibility for the mechanical propulsion of a ship* – not less than 48 months, including the provisions in paragraph 2.1 of this section, performing, as a certificated officer, duties related to the functions to be shown in the endorsement to the certificate, of which 24 months shall be served performing functions set out in table A-II/1 and 24 months shall be served performing functions set out in tables A-III/1 and A-III/2.

3 In accordance with the requirements of regulation VII/1, paragraph 1.3, every candidate for certification under the provisions of chapter VII at support level in functions specified in tables A-II/4 and A-III/4 shall have completed:

.1 approved seagoing service including not less than 12 months experience, made up of:

.1.1 not less than 6 months associated with navigational watchkeeping duties; and

.1.2 not less than 6 months associated with engine-room duties; or

.2 special training, either pre-sea or on board ship, including an approved period of seagoing service which shall not be less than 4 months, made up of:

.2.1 not less than 2 months associated with navigational watchkeeping duties; and

.2.2 not less than 2 months associated with engine-room duties;

.3 the seagoing service, training and experience required by paragraph 3.1 or 3.2 shall be carried out under the direct supervision of an appropriately qualified officer or rating.

4 In accordance with the requirements of regulation VII/1, paragraph 1.3, every candidate for certification under the provisions of chapter VII at the support level in functions specified in tables A-II/5 and A-III/5 shall, while qualified to serve as a rating forming part of a navigational and engine-room watch, meet the standards of competence specified in sections A-II/5 and A-III/5 of the STCW Code and have completed:

.1 approved seagoing service of not less than 30 months, made up of:

.1.1 not less than 18 months associated with able seafarer deck duties, and

.1.2 not less than 12 months associated with able seafarer engine duties; or

.2 an approved training programme and not less than 18 months of approved seagoing service, made up of:

.2.1 not less than 12 months associated with able seafarer deck duties; and

.2.2 not less than 6 months associated with able seafarer engine duties; or

.3 an approved special integrated deck and engine training programme, including not less than 12 months' approved seagoing service in an integrated deck and engine department, made up of:

.3.1 not less than 6 months associated with able seafarer deck duties; and

.3.2 not less than 6 months associated with able seafarer engine duties.

Section A-VII/3

Principles governing the issue of alternative certificates

(No provisions)

Chapter VIII
Standards regarding watchkeeping

Section A-VIII/1
Fitness for duty

1 Administrations shall take account of the danger posed by fatigue of seafarers, especially those whose duties involve the safe and secure operation of a ship.

2 All persons who are assigned duty as officer in charge of a watch or as a rating forming part of a watch and those whose duties involve designated safety, prevention of pollution and security duties shall be provided with a rest period of not less than:

.1 a minimum of 10 hours of rest in any 24-hour period; and

.2 77 hours in any 7-day period.

3 The hours of rest may be divided into no more than two periods, one of which shall be at least 6 hours in length, and the intervals between consecutive periods of rest shall not exceed 14 hours.

4 The requirements for rest periods laid down in paragraphs 2 and 3 need not be maintained in the case of an emergency or in other overriding operational conditions. Musters, fire-fighting and lifeboat drills, and drills prescribed by national laws and regulations and by international instruments, shall be conducted in a manner that minimizes the disturbance of rest periods and does not induce fatigue.

5 Administrations shall require that watch schedules be posted where they are easily accessible. The schedules shall be established in a standardized format* in the working language or languages of the ship and in English.

6 When a seafarer is on call, such as when a machinery space is unattended, the seafarer shall have an adequate compensatory rest period if the normal period of rest is disturbed by call-outs to work.

7 Administrations shall require that records of daily hours of rest of seafarers be maintained in a standardized format,* in the working language or languages of the ship and in English, to allow monitoring and verification of compliance with the provisions of this section. The seafarers shall receive a copy of the records pertaining to them, which shall be endorsed by the master or by a person authorized by the master and by the seafarers.

8 Nothing in this section shall be deemed to impair the right of the master of a ship to require a seafarer to perform any hours of work necessary for the immediate safety of the ship, persons on board or cargo, or for the purpose of giving assistance to other ships or persons in distress at sea. Accordingly, the master may suspend the schedule of hours of rest and require a seafarer to perform any hours of work necessary until the normal situation has been restored. As soon as practicable after the normal situation has been restored, the master shall ensure that any seafarers who have performed work in a scheduled rest period are provided with an adequate period of rest.

9 Parties may allow exceptions from the required hours of rest in paragraphs 2.2 and 3 above provided that the rest period is not less than 70 hours in any 7-day period.

---

* The IMO/ILO Guidelines for the development of tables of seafarers' shipboard working arrangements and formats of records of seafarers' hours of work or hours of rest may be used.

Exceptions from the weekly rest period provided for in paragraph 2.2 shall not be allowed for more than two consecutive weeks. The intervals between two periods of exceptions on board shall not be less than twice the duration of the exception.

The hours of rest provided for in paragraph 2.1 may be divided into no more than three periods, one of which shall be at least 6 hours in length, and neither of the other two periods shall be less than one hour in length. The intervals between consecutive periods of rest shall not exceed 14 hours. Exceptions shall not extend beyond two 24-hour periods in any 7-day period.

Exceptions shall, as far as possible, take into account the guidance regarding prevention of fatigue in section B-VIII/1.

10 Each Administration shall establish, for the purpose of preventing alcohol abuse, a limit of not greater than 0.05% blood alcohol level (BAC) or 0.25 mg/*l* alcohol in the breath or a quantity of alcohol leading to such alcohol concentration for masters, officers and other seafarers while performing designated safety, security and marine environmental duties.

Section A-VIII/2

Watchkeeping arrangements and principles to be observed

Part 1 – Certification

1 The officer in charge of the navigational or deck watch shall be duly qualified in accordance with the provisions of chapter II or chapter VII appropriate to the duties related to navigational or deck watchkeeping.

2 The officer in charge of the engineering watch shall be duly qualified in accordance with the provisions of chapter III or chapter VII appropriate to the duties related to engineering watchkeeping.

Part 2 – Voyage planning

General requirements

3 The intended voyage shall be planned in advance, taking into consideration all pertinent information, and any course laid down shall be checked before the voyage commences.

4 The chief engineer officer shall, in consultation with the master, determine in advance the needs of the intended voyage, taking into consideration the requirements for fuel, water, lubricants, chemicals, expendable and other spare parts, tools, supplies and any other requirements.

Planning prior to each voyage

5 Prior to each voyage, the master of every ship shall ensure that the intended route from the port of departure to the first port of call is planned using adequate and appropriate charts and other nautical publications necessary for the intended voyage, containing accurate, complete and up-to-date information regarding those navigational limitations and hazards which are of a permanent or predictable nature and which are relevant to the safe navigation of the ship.

Verification and display of planned route

6 When the route planning is verified, taking into consideration all pertinent information, the planned route shall be clearly displayed on appropriate charts and shall be continuously available to the officer in charge of the watch, who shall verify each course to be followed prior to using it during the voyage.

Performing the engineering watch

59 The officer in charge of the engineering watch shall ensure that the established watchkeeping arrangements are maintained and that, under direction, engine-room ratings, if forming part of the engineering watch, assist in the safe and efficient operation of the propulsion machinery and auxiliary equipment.

60 The officer in charge of the engineering watch shall continue to be responsible for machinery-space operations, despite the presence of the chief engineer officer in the machinery spaces, until specifically informed that the chief engineer officer has assumed that responsibility and this is mutually understood.

61 All members of the engineering watch shall be familiar with their assigned watchkeeping duties. In addition, every member shall, with respect to the ship they are serving in, have knowledge of:

- **.1** the use of appropriate internal communication systems;
- **.2** the escape routes from machinery spaces;
- **.3** the engine-room alarm systems and be able to distinguish between the various alarms, with special reference to the fire-extinguishing media alarm; and
- **.4** the number, location and types of fire-fighting equipment and damage-control gear in the machinery spaces, together with their use and the various safety precautions to be observed.

62 Any machinery not functioning properly, expected to malfunction or requiring special service shall be noted along with any action already taken. Plans shall be made for any further action if required.

63 When the machinery spaces are in the manned condition, the officer in charge of the engineering watch shall at all times be readily capable of operating the propulsion equipment in response to needs for changes in direction or speed.

64 When the machinery spaces are in the periodic unmanned condition, the designated duty officer in charge of the engineering watch shall be immediately available and on call to attend the machinery spaces.

65 All bridge orders shall be promptly executed. Changes in direction or speed of the main propulsion units shall be recorded, except where an Administration has determined that the size or characteristics of a particular ship make such recording impracticable. The officer in charge of the engineering watch shall ensure that the main propulsion unit controls, when in the manual mode of operation, are continuously attended under stand-by or manoeuvring conditions.

66 Due attention shall be paid to the ongoing maintenance and support of all machinery, including mechanical, electrical, electronic, hydraulic and pneumatic systems, their control apparatus and associated safety equipment, all accommodation service systems equipment and the recording of stores and spare gear usage.

67 The chief engineer officer shall ensure that the officer in charge of the engineering watch is informed of all preventive maintenance, damage control, or repair operations to be performed during the engineering watch. The officer in charge of the engineering watch shall be responsible for the isolation, bypassing and adjustment of all machinery under the responsibility of the engineering watch that is to be worked on, and shall record all work carried out.

68 When the engine-room is put in a stand-by condition, the officer in charge of the engineering watch shall ensure that all machinery and equipment which may be used during manoeuvring is in a state of immediate readiness and that an adequate reserve of power is available for steering gear and other requirements.

69 Officers in charge of an engineering watch shall not be assigned or undertake any duties which would interfere with their supervisory duties in respect of the main propulsion system and ancillary equipment. They shall keep the main propulsion plant and auxiliary systems under constant supervision until properly relieved, and shall periodically inspect the machinery in their charge. They shall also ensure that adequate rounds of the machinery and steering-gear spaces are made for the purpose of observing and reporting equipment malfunctions or breakdowns, performing or directing routine adjustments, required upkeep and any other necessary tasks.

70 Officers in charge of an engineering watch shall direct any other member of the engineering watch to inform them of potentially hazardous conditions which may adversely affect the machinery or jeopardize the safety of life or of the ship.

71 The officer in charge of the engineering watch shall ensure that the machinery space watch is supervised, and shall arrange for substitute personnel in the event of the incapacity of any engineering watch personnel. The engineering watch shall not leave the machinery spaces unsupervised in a manner that would prevent the manual operation of the engine-room plant or throttles.

72 The officer in charge of the engineering watch shall take the action necessary to contain the effects of damage resulting from equipment breakdown, fire, flooding, rupture, collision, stranding or other cause.

73 Before going off duty, the officer in charge of the engineering watch shall ensure that all events related to the main and auxiliary machinery which have occurred during the engineering watch are suitably recorded.

74 The officer in charge of the engineering watch shall co-operate with any engineer in charge of maintenance work during all preventive maintenance, damage control or repairs. This shall include, but not necessarily be limited to:

- **.1** isolating and bypassing machinery to be worked on;
- **.2** adjusting the remaining plant to function adequately and safely during the maintenance period;
- **.3** recording, in the engine-room log or other suitable document, the equipment worked on and the personnel involved, and which safety steps have been taken and by whom, for the benefit of relieving officers and for record purposes; and
- **.4** testing and putting into service, when necessary, the repaired machinery or equipment.

75 The officer in charge of the engineering watch shall ensure that any engine-room ratings who perform maintenance duties are available to assist in the manual operation of machinery in the event of automatic equipment failure.

76 The officer in charge of the engineering watch shall bear in mind that changes in speed, resulting from machinery malfunction, or any loss of steering may imperil the safety of the ship and life at sea. The bridge shall be immediately notified in the event of fire and of any impending action in machinery spaces that may cause reduction in the ship's speed, imminent steering failure, stoppage of the ship's propulsion system or any alteration in the generation of electric power or similar threat to safety. This notification, where possible, shall be accomplished before changes are made, in order to afford the bridge the maximum available time to take whatever action is possible to avoid a potential marine casualty.

77 The officer in charge of the engineering watch shall notify the chief engineer officer without delay:

- **.1** when engine damage or a malfunction occurs which may be such as to endanger the safe operation of the ship;
- **.2** when any malfunction occurs which, it is believed, may cause damage or breakdown of propulsion machinery, auxiliary machinery or monitoring and governing systems; and
- **.3** in any emergency or if in any doubt as to what decision or measures to take.

78 Despite the requirement to notify the chief engineer officer in the foregoing circumstances, the officer in charge of the engineering watch shall not hesitate to take immediate action for the safety of the ship, its machinery and crew where circumstances require.

79 The officer in charge of the engineering watch shall give the watchkeeping personnel all appropriate instructions and information which will ensure the keeping of a safe engineering watch. Routine machinery upkeep, performed as incidental tasks as a part of keeping a safe watch, shall be set up as an integral part of the watch routine. Detailed repair maintenance involving repairs to electrical, mechanical, hydraulic, pneumatic or applicable electronic equipment throughout the ship shall be performed with the cognizance of the officer in charge of the engineering watch and chief engineer officer. These repairs shall be recorded.

Engineering watchkeeping under different conditions and in different areas

Restricted visibility

80 The officer in charge of the engineering watch shall ensure that permanent air or steam pressure is available for sound signals and that at all times bridge orders relating to changes in speed or direction of operation are immediately implemented and, in addition, that auxiliary machinery used for manoeuvring is readily available.

Coastal and congested waters

81 The officer in charge of the engineering watch shall ensure that all machinery involved with the manoeuvring of the ship can immediately be placed in the manual mode of operation when notified that the ship is in congested waters. The officer in charge of the engineering watch shall also ensure that an adequate reserve of power is available for steering and other manoeuvring requirements. Emergency steering and other auxiliary equipment shall be ready for immediate operation.

Ship at anchor

82 At an unsheltered anchorage the chief engineer officer shall consult with the master whether or not to maintain the same engineering watch as when under way.

83 When a ship is at anchor in an open roadstead or any other virtually "at-sea" condition, the engineer officer in charge of the engineering watch shall ensure that:

.1 an efficient engineering watch is kept;

.2 periodic inspection is made of all operating and stand-by machinery;

.3 main and auxiliary machinery is maintained in a state of readiness in accordance with orders from the bridge;

.4 measures are taken to protect the environment from pollution by the ship, and that applicable pollution-prevention regulations are complied with; and

.5 all damage-control and fire-fighting systems are in readiness.

Part 4-3 – Principles to be observed in keeping a radio watch

General provisions

84 Administrations shall direct the attention of companies, masters and radio watchkeeping personnel to comply with the following provisions to ensure that an adequate safety radio watch is maintained while a ship is at sea. In complying with this Code, account shall be taken of the Radio Regulations.

Watch arrangements

85 In deciding the arrangements for the radio watch, the master of every seagoing ship shall:

.1 ensure that the radio watch is maintained in accordance with the relevant provisions of the Radio Regulations and the SOLAS Convention;

.2 ensure that the primary duties for radio watchkeeping are not adversely affected by attending to radio traffic not relevant to the safe movement of the ship and safety of navigation; and

.3 take into account the radio equipment fitted on board and its operational status.

Performing the radio watch

86 The radio operator performing radio watchkeeping duties shall:

.1 ensure that watch is maintained on the frequencies specified in the Radio Regulations and the SOLAS Convention; and

.2 while on duty, regularly check the operation of the radio equipment and its sources of energy and report to the master any observed failure of this equipment.

87 The requirements of the Radio Regulations and the SOLAS Convention on keeping a radiotelegraph or radio log, as appropriate, shall be complied with.

88 The maintenance of radio records, in compliance with the requirements of the Radio Regulations and the SOLAS Convention, is the responsibility of the radio operator designated as having primary responsibility for radiocommunications during distress incidents. The following shall be recorded, together with the times at which they occur:

.1 a summary of distress, urgency and safety radiocommunications;

.2 important incidents relating to the radio service;

.3 where appropriate, the position of the ship at least once per day; and

.4 a summary of the condition of the radio equipment, including its sources of energy.

89 The radio records shall be kept at the distress communications operating position, and shall be made available:

.1 for inspection by the master; and

.2 for inspection by any authorized official of the Administration and by any duly authorized officer exercising control under article X of the Convention.

Part 5 – Watchkeeping in port

Principles applying to all watchkeeping

General

90 On any ship safely moored or safely at anchor under normal circumstances in port, the master shall arrange for an appropriate and effective watch to be maintained for the purpose of safety. Special requirements may be necessary for special types of ships' propulsion systems or ancillary equipment and for ships carrying hazardous, dangerous, toxic or highly flammable materials or other special types of cargo.

Watch arrangements

91 Arrangements for keeping a deck watch when the ship is in port shall at all times be adequate to:

.1 ensure the safety of life, of the ship, the port and the environment, and the safe operation of all machinery related to cargo operation;

.2 observe international, national and local rules; and

.3 maintain order and the normal routine of the ship.

92 The master shall decide the composition and duration of the deck watch depending on the conditions of mooring, type of the ship and character of duties.

93 If the master considers it necessary, a qualified officer shall be in charge of the deck watch.

94 The necessary equipment shall be so arranged as to provide for efficient watchkeeping.

95 The chief engineer officer, in consultation with the master, shall ensure that engineering watchkeeping arrangements are adequate to maintain a safe engineering watch while in port. When deciding the composition of the engineering watch, which may include appropriate engine-room ratings, the following points are among those to be taken into account:

- **.1** on all ships of 3,000 kW propulsion power and over there shall always be an officer in charge of the engineering watch;
- **.2** on ships of less than 3,000 kW propulsion power there may be, at the master's discretion and in consultation with the chief engineer officer, no officer in charge of the engineering watch; and
- **.3** officers, while in charge of an engineering watch, shall not be assigned or undertake any task or duty which would interfere with their supervisory duty in respect of the ship's machinery system.

Taking over the watch

96 Officers in charge of the deck or engineering watch shall not hand over the watch to their relieving officer if they have any reason to believe that the latter is obviously not capable of carrying out watchkeeping duties effectively, in which case the master or chief engineer shall be notified accordingly. Relieving officers of the deck or engineering watch shall ensure that all members of their watch are apparently fully capable of performing their duties effectively.

97 If, at the moment of handing over the deck or engineering watch, an important operation is being performed, it shall be concluded by the officer being relieved, except when ordered otherwise by the master or chief engineer officer.

Part 5-1 – Taking over the deck watch

98 Prior to taking over the deck watch, the relieving officer shall be informed by the officer in charge of the deck watch as to the following:

- **.1** the depth of the water at the berth, the ship's draught, the level and time of high and low waters; the securing of the moorings, the arrangement of anchors and the scope of the anchor chain, and other mooring features important to the safety of the ship; the state of main engines and their availability for emergency use;
- **.2** all work to be performed on board the ship; the nature, amount and disposition of cargo loaded or remaining, and any residue on board after unloading the ship;
- **.3** the level of water in bilges and ballast tanks;
- **.4** the signals or lights being exhibited or sounded;
- **.5** the number of crew members required to be on board and the presence of any other persons on board;
- **.6** the state of fire-fighting appliances;
- **.7** any special port regulations;
- **.8** the master's standing and special orders;
- **.9** the lines of communication available between the ship and shore personnel, including port authorities, in the event of an emergency arising or assistance being required;
- **.10** any other circumstances of importance to the safety of the ship, its crew, cargo or protection of the environment from pollution; and
- **.11** the procedures for notifying the appropriate authority of any environmental pollution resulting from ship activities.

99 Relieving officers, before assuming charge of the deck watch, shall verify that:

.1 the securing of moorings and anchor chain is adequate;

.2 the appropriate signals or lights are properly exhibited or sounded;

.3 safety measures and fire-protection regulations are being maintained;

.4 they are aware of the nature of any hazardous or dangerous cargo being loaded or discharged and the appropriate action to be taken in the event of any spillage or fire; and

.5 no external conditions or circumstances imperil the ship and that it does not imperil others.

Part 5-2 – Taking over the engineering watch

100 Prior to taking over the engineering watch, the relieving officer shall be informed by the officer in charge of the engineering watch as to:

.1 the standing orders of the day, any special orders relating to the ship operations, maintenance functions, repairs to the ship's machinery or control equipment;

.2 the nature of all work being performed on machinery and systems on board ship, personnel involved and potential hazards;

.3 the level and condition, where applicable, of water or residue in bilges, ballast tanks, slop tanks, sewage tanks, reserve tanks and special requirements for the use or disposal of the contents thereof;

.4 any special requirements relating to sanitary system disposals;

.5 the condition and state of readiness of portable fire-extinguishing equipment and fixed fire-extinguishing installations and fire-detection systems;

.6 authorized repair personnel on board engaged in engineering activities, their work locations and repair functions and other authorized persons on board and the required crew;

.7 any port regulations pertaining to ship effluents, fire-fighting requirements and ship readiness, particularly during potential bad weather conditions;

.8 the lines of communication available between the ship and shore personnel, including port authorities, in the event of an emergency arising or assistance being required;

.9 any other circumstance of importance to the safety of the ship, its crew, cargo or the protection of the environment from pollution; and

.10 the procedures for notifying the appropriate authority of environmental pollution resulting from engineering activities.

101 Relieving officers, before assuming charge of the engineering watch, shall satisfy themselves that they are fully informed by the officer being relieved, as outlined above; and:

.1 be familiar with existing and potential sources of power, heat and lighting and their distribution;

.2 know the availability and condition of ship's fuel, lubricants and all water supplies; and

.3 be ready to prepare the ship and its machinery, as far as is possible, for stand-by or emergency conditions as required.

Part 5-3 – Performing the deck watch

102 The officer in charge of the deck watch shall:

.1 make rounds to inspect the ship at appropriate intervals;

.2 pay particular attention to:

.2.1 the condition and securing of the gangway, anchor chain and moorings, especially at the turn of the tide and in berths with a large rise and fall, if necessary, taking measures to ensure that they are in normal working condition;

.2.2 the draught, under-keel clearance and the general state of the ship, to avoid dangerous listing or trim during cargo handling or ballasting;

.2.3 the weather and sea state;

.2.4 the observance of all regulations concerning safety and fire protection;

.2.5 the water level in bilges and tanks;

.2.6 all persons on board and their location, especially those in remote or enclosed spaces; and

.2.7 the exhibition and sounding, where appropriate, of lights and signals;

.3 in bad weather, or on receiving a storm warning, take the necessary measures to protect the ship, persons on board and cargo;

.4 take every precaution to prevent pollution of the environment by the ship;

.5 in an emergency threatening the safety of the ship, raise the alarm, inform the master, take all possible measures to prevent any damage to the ship, its cargo and persons on board and, if necessary, request assistance from the shore authorities or neighbouring ships;

.6 be aware of the ship's stability condition so that, in the event of fire, the shore fire-fighting authority may be advised of the approximate quantity of water that can be pumped on board without endangering the ship;

.7 offer assistance to ships or persons in distress;

.8 take necessary precautions to prevent accidents or damage when propellers are to be turned; and

.9 enter, in the appropriate log-book, all important events affecting the ship.

Part 5-4 – Performing the engineering watch

103 Officers in charge of the engineering watch shall pay particular attention to:

.1 the observance of all orders, special operating procedures and regulations concerning hazardous conditions and their prevention in all areas in their charge;

.2 the instrumentation and control systems, monitoring of all power supplies, components and systems in operation;

.3 the techniques, methods and procedures necessary to prevent violation of the pollution regulations of the local authorities; and

.4 the state of the bilges.

104 Officers in charge of the engineering watch shall:

.1 in emergencies, raise the alarm when, in their opinion, the situation so demands, and take all possible measures to prevent damage to the ship, persons on board and cargo;

.2 be aware of the deck officer's needs relating to the equipment required in the loading or unloading of the cargo and the additional requirements of the ballast and other ship stability control systems;

.3 make frequent rounds of inspection to determine possible equipment malfunction or failure, and take immediate remedial action to ensure the safety of the ship, of cargo operations, of the port and the environment;

.4 ensure that the necessary precautions are taken, within their area of responsibility, to prevent accidents or damage to the various electrical, electronic, hydraulic, pneumatic and mechanical systems of the ship; and

.5 ensure that all important events affecting the operation, adjustment or repair of the ship's machinery are satisfactorily recorded.

Part 5-5 – Watch in port on ships carrying hazardous cargo

General

105 The master of every ship carrying cargo that is hazardous, whether explosive, flammable, toxic, health-threatening or environment-polluting, shall ensure that safe watchkeeping arrangements are maintained. On ships carrying hazardous cargo in bulk, this will be achieved by the ready availability on board of a duly qualified officer or officers, and ratings where appropriate, even when the ship is safely moored or safely at anchor in port.

106 On ships carrying hazardous cargo other than in bulk, the master shall take full account of the nature, quantity, packing and stowage of the hazardous cargo and of any special conditions on board, afloat and ashore.

Part 5-6 – Cargo watch

107 Officers with responsibility for the planning and conduct of cargo operations shall ensure that such operations are conducted safely through the control of the specific risks, including when non-ship's personnel are involved.

Part B

Recommended guidance regarding provisions of the STCW Convention and its annex

Introduction

1 This part of the STCW Code contains recommended guidance intended to assist Parties to the STCW Convention and those involved in implementing, applying or enforcing its measures to give the Convention full and complete effect in a uniform manner.

2 The measures suggested are not mandatory, and the examples given are only intended to illustrate how certain Convention requirements may be complied with. However, the recommendations in general represent an approach to the matters concerned which has been harmonized through discussion within IMO involving, where appropriate, consultation with the International Labour Organization, the International Telecommunication Union and the World Health Organization.

3 Observance of the recommendations contained in this part will assist the Organization in achieving its goal of maintaining the highest practicable standards of competence in respect of crews of all nationalities and ships of all flags.

4 Guidance is provided in this part in respect of certain articles of the Convention, in addition to guidance on certain regulations in its annex. The numbering of the sections of this part therefore corresponds with that of the articles and the regulations of the Convention. As in part A, the text of each section may be divided into numbered parts and paragraphs, but such numbering is unique to that text alone.

Guidance regarding provisions of the articles

Section B-I
Guidance regarding general obligations under the Convention

(No provisions)

Section B-II
Guidance regarding definitions and clarifications

1 The definitions contained in article II of the Convention, and the definitions and clarifications contained in regulation I/1 of its annex, apply equally to the terms used in parts A and B of this Code. Supplementary definitions which apply only to the provisions of this Code are contained in section A-I/1.

2 The definition of *certificate* appearing in article II (c) provides for three possibilities:

.1 the Administration may issue the certificate;

.2 the Administration may have the certificate issued under its authority; or

.3 the Administration may recognize a certificate issued by another Party, as provided for in regulation I/10.

Section B-III
Guidance regarding the application of the Convention

1 While the definition of *fishing vessel* contained in article II, paragraph (h) excludes vessels used for catching fish, whales, seals, walrus or other living resources of the sea from application of the Convention, vessels not engaged in the catching activity cannot enjoy such exclusion.

2 The Convention excludes all wooden ships of primitive build, including junks.

Section B-IV
Guidance regarding the communication of information

1 In paragraph (1)(b) of article IV, the words "where appropriate" are intended to include:

.1 the recognition of a certificate issued by another Party; or

.2 the issue of the Administration's own certificate, where applicable, on the basis of recognition of a certificate issued by another Party.

Section B-V
Guidance regarding other treaties and interpretation

The word "arrangements" in paragraph (1) of article V is intended to include provisions previously established between States for the reciprocal recognition of certificates.

Section B-VI

Guidance regarding certificates

See the guidance given in sections B-I/2 and B-II.

A policy statement and an outline of the procedures to be followed should be published for the information of companies operating ships under the flag of the Administration.

Section B-VII

Guidance regarding transitional provisions

Certificates issued for service in one capacity which are currently recognized by a Party as an adequate qualification for service in another capacity, e.g., chief mate certificates recognized for service as master, should continue to be accepted as valid for such service under article VII. This acceptance also applies to such certificates issued under the provisions of paragraph (2) of article VII.

Section B-VIII

Guidance regarding dispensations

A policy statement and an outline of the procedures to be followed should be published for the information of companies operating ships under the flag of the Administration. Guidance should be provided to those officials authorized by the Administration to issue dispensations. Information on action taken should be summarized in the initial report communicated to the Secretary-General in accordance with the requirements of section A-I/7.

Section B-IX

Guidance regarding equivalents

Naval certificates may continue to be accepted and certificates of service may continue to be issued to naval officers as equivalents under article IX, provided that the requirements of the Convention are met.

Section B-X

Guidance regarding control

(No provisions – see section B-I/4.)

Section B-XI

Guidance regarding the promotion of technical co-operation

1 Governments should provide, or arrange to provide, in collaboration with IMO, assistance to States which have difficulty in meeting the requirements of the Convention and which request such assistance.

2 The importance of adequate training for masters and other personnel serving on board oil, chemical and liquefied gas tankers and ro–ro passenger ships is stressed, and it is recognized that in some cases there may be limited facilities for obtaining the required experience and providing specialized training programmes, particularly in developing countries.

Examination database

3 Parties with maritime training academies or examination centres serving several countries and wishing to establish a database of examination questions and answers are encouraged to do so, on the basis of bilateral co-operation with a country or countries which already have such a database.

Availability of maritime training simulators

4 The IMO Secretariat maintains a list of maritime training simulators, as a source of information for Parties and others on the availability of different types of simulators for training seafarers, in particular where such training facilities may not be available to them nationally.

5 Parties are urged* to provide information on their national maritime training simulators to the IMO Secretariat and to update the information whenever any change or addition is made to their maritime training simulator facilities.

Information on technical co-operation

6 Information on technical advisory services, access to international training institutions affiliated with IMO, and information on fellowships and other technical co-operation which may be provided by or through IMO may be obtained by contacting the Secretary-General at 4 Albert Embankment, London SE1 7SR, United Kingdom.

(No guidance is provided regarding articles XII to XVII.)

* See MSC.1/Circ.1209 on simulators available for maritime training.

Guidance regarding provisions of the annex to the STCW Convention

Chapter I
Guidance regarding general provisions

Section B-I/1
Guidance regarding definitions and clarifications

1 The definitions contained in article II of the Convention, and the definitions and interpretations contained in regulation I/1 of its annex, apply equally to the terms used in parts A and B of this Code. Supplementary definitions which apply only to the provisions of this Code are contained in section A-I/1.

2 Officers with capacities covered under the provisions of chapter VII may be designated as "polyvalent officer", "dual-purpose officer" or other designations as approved by the Administration, in accordance with the terminology used in the applicable safe manning requirements.

3 Ratings qualified to serve in capacities covered under the provisions of chapter VII may be designated as "polyvalent ratings" or other designations as approved by the Administration, in accordance with the terminology used in the applicable safe manning requirements.

Section B-I/2
Guidance regarding certificates and endorsements

1 Where an endorsement is integrated in the format of a certificate as provided by section A-I/2, paragraph 1, the relevant information should be inserted in the certificate in the manner explained hereunder, except for the omission of the space numbered .2. Otherwise, in preparing endorsements attesting the issue of a certificate, the spaces numbered .1 to .17 in the form which follows the text hereunder should be completed as follows:

- **.1** Enter the name of the issuing State.
- **.2** Enter the number assigned to the certificate by the Administration.
- **.3** Enter the full name of the seafarer to whom the certificate is issued. The name should be the same as that appearing in the seafarer's passport, seafarer's identity certificate and other official documents issued by the Administration.
- **.4** The number or numbers of the STCW Convention regulation or regulations under which the seafarer has been found qualified should be entered here, for example:
  - **.4.1** "Regulation II/1", if the seafarer has been found qualified to fill the capacity of officer in charge of a navigational watch;
  - **.4.2** "Regulation III/1", if the seafarer has been found qualified to act as engineer officer in charge of a watch in a manned engine-room, or as designated duty engineer officer in a periodically unmanned engine-room;
  - **.4.3** "Regulation IV/2", if the seafarer has been found qualified to fill the capacity of radio operator;

.4.4 "Regulation VII/1", if the certificate is a functional certificate and the seafarer has been found qualified to perform functions specified in part A of the Code, for example, the function of marine engineering at the management level; and

.4.5 "Regulations III/1 and V/1", if found qualified to act as the engineer officer in charge of a watch in a manned engine-room, or as designated duty engineer officer in a periodically unmanned engine-room in tankers. (See limitations in paragraphs .8 and .10 below.)

.5 Enter the date of expiry of the endorsement. This date should not be later than the date of expiry, if any, of the certificate in respect of which the endorsement is issued, nor later than five years after the date of issue of the endorsement.

.6 In this column should be entered each of the functions specified in part A of the Code which the seafarer is qualified to perform. Functions and their associated levels of responsibility are specified in the tables of competence set out in chapters II, III and IV of part A of the Code, and are also listed for convenient reference in the introduction to part A. When reference is made under .4 above to regulations in chapter II, III or IV, it is not necessary to list specific functions.

.7 In this column should be entered the levels of responsibility at which the seafarer is qualified to perform each of the functions entered in column .6. These levels are specified in the tables of competence set out in chapters II, III and IV of part A of the Code, and are also listed, for convenient reference, in the introduction to part A.

.8 A general limitation, such as the requirement to wear corrective lenses when performing duties, should be entered prominently at the top of this limitations column. Limitations applying to the functions listed in column .6 should be entered on the appropriate line against the function concerned, for example:

.8.1 "Not valid for service in tankers" – if not qualified under chapter V;

.8.2 "Not valid for service in tankers other than oil tankers" – if qualified under chapter V for service only in oil tankers;

.8.3 "Not valid for service in ships in which steam boilers form part of the ship's machinery" – if the related knowledge has been omitted in accordance with STCW Code provisions; and

.8.4 "Valid only on near-coastal voyages" – if the related knowledge has been omitted in accordance with STCW Code provisions.

Note: Tonnage and power limitations need not be shown here if they are already indicated in the title of the certificate and in the capacity entered in column .9.

.9 The capacity or capacities entered in this column should be those specified in the title to the STCW regulation or regulations concerned in the case of certificates issued under chapter II or III, or should be as specified in the applicable safe manning requirements of the Administration, as appropriate.

.10 A general limitation, such as the requirement to wear corrective lenses when performing duties, should be entered prominently at the top of this limitations column also. The limitations entered in column .10 should be the same as those shown in column .8 for the functions performed in each capacity entered.

.11 The number entered in this space should be that of the certificate, so that both certificate and endorsement have the same unique number for reference and for location in the register of certificates and/or endorsements, etc.

.12 The date of original issue of the endorsement should be entered here; it may be the same as, or differ from, the date of issue of the certificate, in accordance with the circumstances.

.13 The name of the official authorized to issue the endorsement should be shown here in block letters below the official's signature.

.14 The date of birth shown should be the date confirmed from Administration records or as otherwise verified.

.15 The endorsement should be signed by the seafarer in the presence of an official, or may be incorporated from the seafarer's application form duly completed and verified.

.16 The photograph should be a standard black and white or colour passport-type head and shoulders photograph, supplied in duplicate by the seafarer so that one may be kept in or associated with the register of certificates.

.17 If the blocks for revalidation are shown as part of the endorsement form (see section A-I/2, paragraph 1), the Administration may revalidate the endorsement by completing the block after the seafarer has demonstrated continuing proficiency as required by regulation I/11.

(Official Seal)

(COUNTRY)

ENDORSEMENT ATTESTING THE ISSUE OF A CERTIFICATE UNDER THE PROVISIONS OF THE INTERNATIONAL CONVENTION ON STANDARDS OF TRAINING, CERTIFICATION AND WATCHKEEPING FOR SEAFARERS, 1978, AS AMENDED

The Government of . . . . .1 . . . . certifies that Certificate No. . . . . .2 . . . . has been issued to . . . . .3 . . . . who has been found duly qualified in accordance with the provisions of regulation . . . . .4 . . . . of the above Convention, as amended, and has been found competent to perform the following functions, at the levels specified, subject to any limitations indicated until . . . . .5 . . . . or until the date of expiry of any extension of the validity of this endorsement as may be shown overleaf:

.6 FUNCTION	.7 LEVEL	.8 LIMITATIONS APPLYING (IF ANY)

The lawful holder of this endorsement may serve in the following capacity or capacities specified in the applicable safe manning requirements of the Administration:

.9 CAPACITY	.10 LIMITATIONS APPLYING (IF ANY)

Endorsement No . . . . .11 . . . . issued on . . . . .12 . . . .

(Official Seal)

. . . .
Signature of duly authorized official

. . . . .13 . . . .
Name of duly authorized official

The original of this endorsement must be kept available in accordance with regulation I/2, paragraph 11, of the Convention while its holder is serving on a ship.

Date of birth of the holder of the certificate . . . . .14 . . . .

Signature of the holder of the certificate . . . . .15 . . . .

Photograph of the holder of the certificate

.16

The validity of this endorsement is hereby extended until	
(Official Seal)	.... *Signature of duly authorized official*
Date of revalidation .... .17	.... *Name of duly authorized official*
The validity of this endorsement is hereby extended until	
(Official Seal)	.... *Signature of the authorized official*
Date of revalidation .... .17	.... *Name of duly authorized official*

2 An endorsement attesting the recognition of a certificate may be attached to and form part of the certificate endorsed, or may be issued as a separate document (see STCW regulation I/2, paragraph 8). All entries made in the form are required to be in Roman characters and Arabic figures (see STCW regulation I/2, paragraph 10). The spaces numbered .1 to .17 in the form which follows the text hereunder are intended to be completed as indicated in paragraph 1 above, except in respect of the following spaces:

- **.2** where the number assigned by the Party which issued the certificate being recognized should be entered;
- **.3** where the name entered should be the same as that appearing in the certificate being recognized;
- **.4** where the name of the Party which issued the certificate being recognized should be entered;
- **.9** where the capacity or capacities entered should be selected, as appropriate, from those specified in the safe applicable manning requirements of the Administration which is recognizing the certificate;
- **.11** where the number entered should be unique to the endorsement both for reference and for location in the register of endorsements; and
- **.12** where the date of original issue of the endorsement should be entered.

(Official Seal)

(COUNTRY)

ENDORSEMENT ATTESTING THE RECOGNITION OF A CERTIFICATE UNDER THE PROVISIONS OF THE INTERNATIONAL CONVENTION ON STANDARDS OF TRAINING, CERTIFICATION AND WATCHKEEPING FOR SEAFARERS, 1978, AS AMENDED

The Government of .... .1 .... certifies that Certificate No. .... .2 .... issued to .... .3 .... by or on behalf of the Government of .... .4 .... is duly recognized in accordance with the provisions of regulation I/10 of the above Convention, as amended, and the lawful holder is authorized to perform the following functions, at the levels specified, subject to any limitations indicated until .... .5 .... or until the date of expiry of any extension of the validity of this endorsement as may be shown overleaf:

.6 FUNCTION	.7 LEVEL	.8 LIMITATIONS APPLYING (IF ANY)

The lawful holder of this endorsement may serve in the following capacity or capacities specified in the applicable safe manning requirements of the Administration:

.9 CAPACITY	.10 LIMITATIONS APPLYING (IF ANY)

Endorsement No .... .11 .... issued on .... .12 ....

(Official Seal)

....
Signature of duly authorized official

.... .13 ....
Name of duly authorized official

The original of this endorsement must be kept available in accordance with regulation I/2, paragraph 11, of the Convention while its holder is serving on a ship.

Date of birth of the holder of the certificate .... .14 ....

Signature of the holder of the certificate .... .15 ....

Photograph of the holder of the certificate

.16

The validity of this endorsement is hereby extended until	
(Official Seal)	.... *Signature of duly authorized official*
Date of revalidation .... .17	.... *Name of duly authorized official*
The validity of this endorsement is hereby extended until	
(Official Seal)	.... *Signature of duly authorized official*
Date of revalidation .... .17	.... *Name of duly authorized official*

3 When replacing a certificate or endorsement which has been lost or destroyed, Parties should issue the replacement under a new number to avoid confusion with the document to be replaced.

4 If an application for revalidation is made within six months before the expiry of an endorsement, the endorsement referred to in paragraphs 5, 6 and 7 of regulation I/2 may be revalidated until:

- **.1** the fifth anniversary of the date of validity, or extension of the validity, of the endorsement; or
- **.2** the date the certificate endorsed expires, whichever is earlier.

5 Where a Certificate of Proficiency is issued, it should contain at least the following information:

- **.1** names of the issuing Party and authority;
- **.2** number assigned to the certificate by the issuing authority;
- **.3** full name and date of birth of the seafarer to whom the certificate is issued. The name and birthdate should be the same as that appearing in the seafarer's passport or seafarer's identification document;
- **.4** title of the certificate. For example, if the certificate is issued in relation to regulation VI/3, paragraph 2, the title used should be "advanced fire fighting" and if it is issued in relation to regulation VI/5, paragraph 1, the title used should be "ship security officer";
- **.5** number, or numbers, of the Convention regulation(s) or of the STCW Code section under which the seafarer has been found qualified;
- **.6** dates of issue and expiry of the certificate. If the validity of the certificate is unlimited, then, for the benefit of clarification, the "unlimited" term should be entered in front of the date of expiry;
- **.7** if applicable, limitations, either general limitation (such as the requirement to wear corrective lenses), ship's type limitation (such as "valid only for service on ships of GT<500") or, voyage limitation (such as "valid only on near-coastal voyages");
- **.8** name and signature of the authorized person who issues the certificate;

.9 photograph of the seafarer. The photograph should be a standard black and white or colour passport-type head and shoulders photograph;

.10 if the certificate is intended to be revalidated, then the date of revalidation, extension of the validity, name and signature of the authorized person; and

.11 the contact details of the issuing Authority.

Table B-I/2

List of certificates or documentary evidence required under the STCW Convention

The list below identifies all certificates or documentary evidence described in the Convention which authorize the holder to serve in certain functions on board ships. The certificates are subject to the requirements of regulation I/2 regarding language and their availability in original form.

The list also references the relevant regulations and the requirements for endorsement, registration and revalidation.

Regulations	Type of certificate and brief description	Endorsement attesting recognition of a certificate[1]	Registration required[2]	Revalidation of certificate[3]
II/1, II/2, II/3, III/1, III/2, III/3, III/6, IV/2, VII/2	Certificate of Competency – For masters, officers and GMDSS radio operators	Yes	Yes	Yes
II/4, III/4, VII/2	Certificate of Proficiency – For ratings duly certified to be a part of a navigational or engine-room watch	No	Yes	No
II/5, III/5, III/7, VII/2	Certificate of Proficiency – For ratings duly certified as able seafarer deck, able seafarer engine or electro-technical rating	No	Yes	No
V/1-1, V/1-2	Certificate of Proficiency or endorsement to a Certificate of Competency – For masters and officers on oil, chemical or liquefied gas tankers	Yes	Yes	Yes
V/1-1, V/1-2	Certificate of Proficiency – For ratings on oil, chemical or liquefied gas tankers	No	Yes	No
V/2	Documentary evidence – Training for masters, officers, ratings and other personnel serving on passenger ships	No	No	No[4]
V/3	Certificate of Proficiency – training for masters, officers, ratings and other personnel on ships subject to the IGF Code	No	Yes	Yes[8]
V/4	Certificate of Proficiency – for masters and officers on ships operating in polar waters	No	Yes	Yes
VI/1	Certificate of Proficiency[5] – Basic training	No	Yes	Yes[6]
VI/2	Certificate of Proficiency[5] – Survival craft, rescue boats and fast rescue boats	No	Yes	Yes[6]
VI/3	Certificate of Proficiency[5] – Advanced fire fighting	No	Yes	Yes[6]
VI/4	Certificate of Proficiency[5] – Medical first aid and medical care	No	Yes	No
VI/5	Certificate of Proficiency – Ship security officer	No	Yes	No
VI/6	Certificate of Proficiency[7] – Security awareness training or security training for seafarers with designated security duties	No	Yes	No

Table B-I/2 *(continued)*

Notes:

[1] *Endorsement attesting recognition of a certificate* means endorsement in accordance with regulation I/2, paragraph 7.

[2] *Registration required* means as part of register or registers in accordance with regulation I/2, paragraph 14.

[3] *Revalidation of a certificate* means establishing continued professional competence in accordance with regulation I/11 or maintaining the required standards of competence in accordance with sections A-V/3 and A-VI/1 to A-VI/3, as applicable.

[4] As required by regulation V/2, paragraph 4, seafarers who have completed training in "crowd management", "crisis management and human behaviour" or "passenger safety, cargo safety and hull integrity" shall, at intervals not exceeding five years, undertake appropriate refresher training or to provide evidence of having achieved the required standards of competence within the previous five years.

[5] The certificates of competency issued in accordance with regulations II/1, II/2, II/3, III/1, III/2, III/3, III/6 and VII/2 include the proficiency requirements in "basic training", "survival craft and rescue boats other than fast rescue boats", "advanced fire fighting" and "medical first aid"; therefore, holders of mentioned certificates of competency are not required to carry Certificates of Proficiency in respect of those competences of chapter VI.

[6] In accordance with sections A-VI/1, A-VI/2 and A-VI/3, seafarers shall provide evidence of having maintained the required standards of competence every five years.

[7] Where security awareness training or training in designated security duties is not included in the qualification for the certificate to be issued.

[8] In accordance with regulation V/3, seafarers shall, at intervals not exceeding five years, undertake appropriate refresher training or be required to provide evidence of having achieved the required standard of competence within the previous five years.

Section B-I/3
Guidance regarding near-coastal voyages

Coastal States may adopt regional "near-coastal voyage limits" through bilateral or multilateral arrangements. Details of such arrangements shall be reported to the Secretary-General, who shall circulate such particulars to all Parties.

Section B-I/4
Guidance regarding control procedures[*]

Introduction

1 The purpose of the control procedures of regulation I/4 is to enable officers duly authorized by port States to ensure that the seafarers on board have sufficient competence to ensure safe, secure and pollution-free operation of the ship.

2 This provision is no different in principle from the need to make checks on ships' structures and equipment. Indeed, it builds on these inspections to make an appraisal of the total system of onboard safety, security and pollution prevention.

Assessment

3 By restricting assessment as indicated in section A-I/4, the subjectivity which is an unavoidable element in all control procedures is reduced to a minimum, no more than would be evident in other types of control inspection.

4 The clear grounds given in regulation I/4, paragraph 1.3, will usually be sufficient to direct the inspector's attention to specific areas of competency, which could then be followed up by seeking evidence of training in the skills in question. If this evidence is inadequate or unconvincing, the authorized officer may ask to observe a demonstration of the relevant skill.

[*] The relevant IMO Model Course(s) may be of assistance in the preparation of courses.

5 It will be a matter for the professional judgement of the inspector when on board, either following an incident* as outlined in regulation I/4 or for the purposes of a routine inspection, whether the ship is operated in a manner likely to pose a danger to persons, property or the environment.*

Section B-I/5

Guidance regarding national provisions

(No provisions)

Section B-I/6

Guidance regarding training and assessment

Qualifications of instructors and assessors

1 Each Party should ensure that instructors and assessors are appropriately qualified and experienced for the particular types and levels of training or assessment of competence of seafarers, as required under the Convention, in accordance with the guidelines in this section.

In-service training and assessment

2 Any person, on board or ashore, conducting in-service training of a seafarer intended to be used in qualifying for certification under the Convention should have received appropriate guidance in instructional techniques.†

3 Any person responsible for the supervision of in-service training of a seafarer intended to be used in qualifying for certification under the Convention should have appropriate knowledge of instructional techniques and of training methods and practice.

4 Any person, on board or ashore, conducting an in-service assessment of the competence of a seafarer intended to be used in qualifying for certification under the Convention should have:

.1 received appropriate guidance in assessment methods and practice;* and

.2 gained practical assessment experience under the supervision and to the satisfaction of an experienced assessor.

5 Any person responsible for the supervision of the in-service assessment of competence of a seafarer intended to be used in qualifying for certification under the Convention should have a full understanding of the assessment system, assessment methods and practice.*

Use of distance learning and e-learning

6 Parties may allow the training of seafarers by distance learning and e-learning in accordance with the standards of training and assessment set out in section A-I/6 and the guidance given below.

Guidance for training by distance learning and e-learning

7 Each Party should ensure that any distance learning and e-learning programme:

.1 is provided by an entity that is approved by the Party;

* See the *Code of International Standards and Recommended Practices for a Safety Investigation into a Marine Casualty or Marine Incident* (Casualty Investigation Code)

† The relevant IMO Model Course(s) may be of assistance in the preparation of courses.

.2 is suitable for the selected objectives and training tasks to meet the competence level for the subject covered;

.3 has clear and unambiguous instructions for the trainees to understand how the programme operates;

.4 provides learning outcomes that meet all the requirements to provide the underpinning knowledge and proficiency of the subject;

.5 is structured in a way that enables the trainee to systematically reflect on what has been learnt through both self assessment and tutor-marked assignments; and

.6 provides professional tutorial support through telephone, facsimile or e-mail communications.

8 Companies should ensure that a safe learning environment is provided and that there has been sufficient time provided to enable the trainee to study.

9 Where e-learning is provided, common information formats such as XML (Extensible Markup Language), which is a flexible way to share both the format and the data on the World Wide Web, intranets and elsewhere, should be used.

10 The e-learning system should be secured from tampering and attempts to hack into the system.

Guidance for assessing a trainee's progress and achievements by training by distance learning and e-learning

11 Each Party should ensure that approved assessment procedures are provided for any distance learning and e-learning programme, including:

.1 clear information to the trainees on the way that tests and examinations are conducted and how the results are communicated;

.2 have test questions that are comprehensive and will adequately assess a trainee's competence and are appropriate to the level being examined;

.3 procedures in place to ensure questions are kept up to date;

.4 the conditions where the examinations can take place and the procedures for invigilation to be conducted;

.5 secure procedures for the examination system so that it will prevent cheating; and

.6 secure validation procedures to record results for the benefit of the Party.

Register of approved training providers, courses and programmes

12 Each Party should ensure that a register or registers of approved training providers, courses and programmes are maintained and made available to companies and other Parties on request.

Section B-I/7

Guidance regarding communication of information

Reports of difficulties encountered

1 Parties are encouraged, when communicating information in accordance with article IV and regulation I/7 of the Convention, to include an index specifically locating the required information as follows:

Index of materials submitted in accordance with article IV and regulation I/7 of the STCW Convention

Article IV of the STCW Convention		Location
1	Text of laws, decrees, orders, regulations and instruments (article IV(1)(a))	
2	Details on study courses (article IV(1)(b))	
3	National examination and other requirements (article IV(1)(b))	
4	Specimen certificates (article IV(1)(c))	

Section A-I/7, part 1, of the STCW Code		Location
5	Information on Governmental organization (section A-I/7, paragraph 2.1)	
6	Explanation of legal and administrative measures (section A-I/7, paragraph 2.2)	
7	Statement of the education, training, examination, assessment and certification policies (section A-I/7, paragraph 2.3)	
8	Summary of the courses, training programmes, examinations and assessments by certificate (section A-I/7, paragraph 2.4)	
9	Outline of the procedures and conditions for authorizations, accreditations and approvals (section A-I/7, paragraph 2.5)	
10	List of authorizations, accreditations and approvals granted (section A-I/7, paragraph 2.5)	
11	Summary of procedures for dispensations (section A-I/7, paragraph 2.6)	
12	Comparison carried out pursuant to regulation I/11 (section A-I/7, paragraph 2.7)	
13	Outline of refresher and upgrading training mandated (section A-I/7, paragraph 2.7)	

Section A-I/7, part 2, paragraph 3, of the STCW Code		Location
14	Description of equivalency arrangements adopted pursuant to article IX (section A-I/7, paragraph 3.1)	
15	Summary of measures taken to ensure compliance with regulation I/10 (section A-I/7, paragraph 3.2)	
16	Specimen copy of safe manning documents issued to ships employing seafarers holding alternative certificates under regulation VII/1 (section A-I/7, paragraph 3.3)	

Section A-I/7, part 2, paragraph 4, of the STCW Code		Location
17	Report of results of independent evaluations carried out pursuant to regulation I/8 covering: .1 Terms of reference of evaluators for the independent evaluation .2 Qualifications and experience of evaluators .3 Date and scope of evaluation	

.4 Non-conformities found

.5 Corrective measures recommended

.6 Corrective measures carried out

.7 List of training institutions/centres covered by the independent evaluation

Section A-I/7, part 2, paragraph 6, of the STCW Code		Location
18	Explanation of legal and administrative measures (section A-I/7, paragraph 6.1)	
19	Statement of the education, training, examination, assessment and certification policies (section A-I/7, paragraph 6.2)	

Section A-I/7, part 2, paragraph 6, of the STCW Code *(continued)*		Location
20	Summary of the courses, training programmes, examinations and assessments by certificate (section A-I/7, paragraph 6.3)	
21	Outline of refresher and upgrading training mandated (section A-I/7, paragraph 6.4)	
22	Comparison carried out pursuant to regulation I/11 (section A-I/7, paragraph 6.5)	

2 Parties are requested to include, in the reports required by regulation I/7, an indication of any relevant guidance contained in part B of this Code, the observance of which has been found to be impracticable.

Section B-I/8
Guidance regarding quality standards

1 In applying quality standards under the provisions of regulation I/8 and section A-I/8 to the administration of its certification system, each Party should take account of existing national or international models, and incorporate the following key elements:

.1 an expressed policy regarding quality and the means by which such policy is to be implemented;

.2 a quality system incorporating the organizational structure, responsibilities, procedures, processes and resources necessary for quality management;

.3 the operational techniques and activities to ensure quality control;

.4 systematic monitoring arrangements, including internal quality-assurance evaluations, to ensure that all defined objectives are being achieved; and

.5 arrangements for periodic external quality evaluations as described in the following paragraphs.

2 In establishing such quality standards for the administration of their national certification system, Administrations should seek to ensure that the arrangements adopted:

.1 are sufficiently flexible to enable the certification system to take account of the varying needs of the industry, and that they facilitate and encourage the application of new technology;

.2 cover all the administrative matters that give effect to the various provisions of the Convention, in particular regulations I/2 to I/15 and other provisions which enable the Administration to grant certificates of service and dispensations and to withdraw, cancel and suspend certificates;

.3 encompass the Administration's responsibilities for approving training and assessment at all levels, from undergraduate-type courses and updating courses for certificates of competency to short courses of vocational training; and

.4 incorporate arrangements for the internal quality-assurance reviews under paragraph 1.4 involving a comprehensive self-study of the administrative procedures, at all levels, in order to measure achievement of defined objectives and to provide the basis for the independent external evaluation required under section A-I/8, paragraph 3.

Quality standards model for assessment of knowledge, understanding, skills and competence

3 The quality standards model for assessment of knowledge, understanding, skills and competence should incorporate the recommendations of this section within the general framework of either:

.1 a national scheme for education and training accreditation or quality standards; or

.2 an alternative quality-standards model acceptable to the Organization.

4 The above quality-standards model should incorporate:

.1 a quality policy, including a commitment by the training institution or unit to the achievement of its stated aims and objectives and to the consequential recognition by the relevant accrediting or quality-standards authority;

.2 those quality-management functions that determine and implement the quality policy, relating to aspects of the work which impinge on the quality of what is provided, including provisions for determining progression within a course or programme;

.3 quality system coverage, where appropriate, of the academic and administrative organizational structure, responsibilities, procedures, processes and the resources of staff and equipment;

.4 the quality-control functions to be applied at all levels to the teaching, training, examination and assessment activities, and to their organization and implementation, in order to ensure their fitness for their purpose and the achievement of their defined objectives;

.5 the internal quality-assurance processes and reviews which monitor the extent to which the institution, or training unit, is achieving the objectives of the programmes it delivers, and is effectively monitoring the quality-control procedures which it employs; and

.6 the arrangements made for periodic external quality evaluations required under regulation I/8, paragraph 2, and described in the following paragraphs, for which the outcome of the quality-assurance reviews forms the basis and starting point.

5 In establishing quality standards for education, training and assessment programmes, the organizations responsible for implementing these programmes should take account of the following:

.1 Where provisions exist for established national accreditation, or education quality standards, such provisions should be utilized for courses incorporating the knowledge and understanding requirements of the Convention. The quality standards should be applied to both management and operational levels of the activity, and should take account of how it is managed, organized, undertaken and evaluated, in order to ensure that the identified goals are achieved.

.2 Where acquisition of a particular skill or accomplishment of a designated task is the primary objective, the quality standards should take account of whether real or simulated equipment is utilized for this purpose, and of the appropriateness of the qualifications and experience of the assessors, in order to ensure achievement of the set standards.

.3 The internal quality-assurance evaluations should involve a comprehensive self-study of the programme, at all levels, to monitor achievement of defined objectives through the application of quality standards. These quality-assurance reviews should address the planning, design, presentation and evaluation of programmes as well as the teaching, learning and communication activities. The outcome provides the basis for the independent evaluation required under section A-I/8, paragraph 3.

The independent evaluation

6 Each independent evaluation should include a systematic and independent examination of all quality activities, but should not evaluate the validity of the defined objectives. The evaluation team should:

.1 carry out the evaluation in accordance with documented procedures;

.2 ensure that the results of each evaluation are documented and brought to the attention of those responsible for the area evaluated; and

.3 check that timely action is taken to correct any deficiencies.

7 The purpose of the evaluation is to provide an independent assessment of the effectiveness of the quality-standard arrangements at all levels. In the case of an education or training establishment, a recognized academic accreditation or quality-standards body or Government agency should be used. The evaluation team should be provided with sufficient advance information to give an overview of the tasks in hand. In the case of a major training institution or programme, the following items are indicative of the information to be provided:

.1 the mission statement of the institution;

.2 details of academic and training strategies in use;

.3 an organization chart and information on the composition of committees and advisory bodies;

.4 staff and student information;

.5 a description of training facilities and equipment; and

.6 an outline of the policies and procedures on:

.6.1 student admission;

.6.2 the development of new courses and review of existing courses;

.6.3 the examination system, including appeals and resits;

.6.4 staff recruitment, training, development, appraisal and promotion;

.6.5 feedback from students and from industry; and

.6.6 staff involvement in research and development.

The report

8 Before submitting a final report, the evaluation team should forward an interim report to the management, seeking their comments on their findings. Upon receiving their comments, the evaluators should submit their final report, which should:

.1 include brief background information about the institution or training programme;

.2 be full, fair and accurate;

.3 highlight the strengths and weaknesses of the institution;

.4 describe the evaluation procedure followed;

.5 cover the various elements identified in paragraph 4;

.6 indicate the extent of compliance or non-compliance with the requirements of the Convention and the effectiveness of the quality standards in ensuring achievement of defined aims and objectives; and

.7 spell out clearly the areas found to be deficient, offer suggestions for improvement and provide any other comments the evaluators consider relevant.

Section B-I/9
Guidance regarding medical standards

Medical examination and certification

1 Parties, in establishing seafarer medical fitness standards and provisions, should take into account the minimum physical abilities set out in table B-I/9 and the guidance given within this section, bearing in mind the different duties of seafarers.

2 Parties, in establishing seafarer medical fitness standards and provisions, should follow the guidance contained in the ILO/WHO publication *Guidelines for Conducting Pre-sea and Periodic Medical Fitness Examinations for Seafarers,* including any subsequent versions, and any other applicable international guidelines published by the International Labour Organization, the International Maritime Organization or the World Health Organization.

3 Appropriate qualifications and experience for medical practitioners conducting medical fitness examinations of seafarers may include occupational health or maritime health qualifications, experience of working as a ship's doctor or a shipping company doctor or working under the supervision of someone with the aforementioned qualifications or experience.

4 The premises where medical fitness examinations are carried out should have the facilities and equipment required to carry out medical fitness examination of seafarers.

5 Administrations should ensure that recognized medical practitioners enjoy full professional independence in exercising their medical judgement when undertaking medical examination procedures.

6 Persons applying for a medical certificate should present to the recognized medical practitioner appropriate identity documentation to establish their identity. They should also surrender their previous medical certificate.

7 Each Administration has the discretionary authority to grant a variance or waiver of any of the standards set out in table B-I/9 hereunder, based on an assessment of a medical evaluation and any other relevant information concerning an individual's adjustment to the condition and proven ability to satisfactorily perform assigned shipboard functions.

8 The medical fitness standards should, so far as possible, define objective criteria with regard to fitness for sea service, taking into account access to medical facilities and medical expertise on board ship. They should, in particular, specify the conditions under which seafarers suffering from potentially life-threatening medical conditions that are controlled by medication may be allowed to continue to serve at sea.

9 The medical standards should also identify particular medical conditions, such as colour blindness, which might preclude seafarers holding particular positions on board ship.

10 The minimum in-service eyesight standards in each eye for unaided distance vision should be at least 0.1.*

11 Persons requiring the use of spectacles or contact lenses to perform duties should have a spare pair or pairs, as required, conveniently available on board the ship. Any need to wear visual aids to meet the required standards should be recorded on the medical fitness certificate issued.

12 Colour vision testing should be in accordance with the *International Recommendation for Colour Vision Requirements for Transport,* published by the Commission Internationale de l'Eclairage (CIE 143-2001 including any subsequent versions) or equivalent test methods.

* Value given in Snellen decimal notation.

Table B-I/9

Assessment of minimum entry level and in-service physical abilities for seafarers[3]

Shipboard task, function, event or condition[3]	**Related physical ability**	**A medical examiner should be satisfied that the candidate**[4]
Routine movement around vessel: – on moving deck – between levels – between compartments *Note 1 applies to this row*	Maintain balance and move with agility Climb up and down vertical ladders and stairways Step over coamings (e.g., Load Line Convention requires coamings to be 600 mm high) Open and close watertight doors	Has no disturbance in sense of balance Does not have any impairment or disease that prevents relevant movements and physical activities Is, without assistance[5], able to: – climb vertical ladders and stairways – step over high sills – manipulate door closing systems
Routine tasks on board: – Use of hand tools – Movement of ship's stores – Overhead work – Valve operation – Standing a four-hour watch – Working in confined spaces – Responding to alarms, warnings and instructions – Verbal communication *Note 1 applies to this row*	Strength, dexterity and stamina to manipulate mechanical devices Lift, pull and carry a load (e.g., 18 kg) Reach upwards Stand, walk and remain alert for an extended period Work in constricted spaces and move through restricted openings (e.g., SOLAS regulation II-1/3-6.5.1 requires openings in cargo spaces and emergency escapes to have the minimum dimensions of 600 mm × 600 mm) Visually distinguish objects, shapes and signals Hear warnings and instructions Give a clear spoken description	Does not have a defined impairment or diagnosed medical condition that reduces ability to perform routine duties essential to the safe operation of the vessel Has ability to: – work with arms raised – stand and walk for an extended period – enter confined space – fulfil eyesight standards (table A-I/9) – fulfil hearing standards set by competent authority or take account of international guidelines – hold normal conversation
Emergency duties[6] on board: – Escape – Fire fighting – Evacuation *Note 2 applies to this row*	Don a lifejacket or immersion suit Escape from smoke-filled spaces Take part in fire-fighting duties, including use of breathing apparatus Take part in vessel evacuation procedures	Does not have a defined impairment or diagnosed medical condition that reduces ability to perform emergency duties essential to the safe operation of the vessel Has ability to: – don lifejacket or immersion suit – crawl – feel for differences in temperature – handle fire-fighting equipment – wear breathing apparatus (where required as part of duties)

Table B-I/9 *(continued)*

Notes:

[1] Rows 1 and 2 of the above table describe (a) ordinary shipboard tasks, functions, events and conditions, (b) the corresponding physical abilities which may be considered necessary for the safety of a seafarer, other crew members and the ship, and (c) high-level criteria for use by medical practitioners assessing medical fitness, bearing in mind the different duties of seafarers and the nature of shipboard work for which they will be employed.

[2] Row 3 of the above table describes (a) ordinary shipboard tasks, functions, events and conditions, (b) the corresponding physical abilities which should be considered necessary for the safety of a seafarer, other crew members and the ship, and (c) high-level criteria for use by medical practitioners assessing medical fitness, bearing in mind the different duties of seafarers and the nature of shipboard work for which they will be employed.

[3] This table is not intended to address all possible shipboard conditions or potentially disqualifying medical conditions. Parties should specify physical abilities applicable to the category of seafarers (such as "Deck officer" and "Engine rating"). The special circumstances of individuals and for those who have specialized or limited duties should receive due consideration.

[4] If in doubt, the medical practitioner should quantify the degree or severity of any relevant impairment by means of objective tests, whenever appropriate tests are available, or by referring the candidate for further assessment.

[5] The term "assistance" means the use of another person to accomplish the task.

[6] The term "emergency duties" is used to cover all standard emergency response situations such as abandon ship or fire fighting as well as the procedures to be followed by each seafarer to secure personal survival.

Section B-I/10
Guidance regarding the recognition of certificates

1 Training carried out under the STCW Convention which does not lead to the issue of a certificate of competency and on which information provided by a Party is found by the Maritime Safety Committee to give full and complete effect to the Convention in accordance with regulation I/7, paragraph 2 may be accepted by other Parties to the Convention as meeting the relevant training requirements thereof.

2 Contacted Administrations should issue the documentary proof referred to in regulation I/10, paragraph 5, to enable port State control authorities to accept the same in lieu of endorsement of a certificate issued by another Party for a period of three months from the date of issue, providing the information listed below:

.1 seafarer's name

.2 date of birth

.3 number of the original Certificate of Competency

.4 capacity

.5 limitations

.6 contact details of the Administration

.7 dates of issue and expiry.

3 Such documentary proof may be made available by electronic means.

Section B-I/11
Guidance regarding the revalidation of certificates

1 The courses required by regulation I/11 should include relevant changes in marine legislation, technology and recommendations concerning the safety of life at sea, security and the protection of the marine environment.

2 A test may take the form of written or oral examination, the use of a simulator or other appropriate means.

3 Approved seagoing service stated in section A-I/11, paragraph 1, may be served in an appropriate lower officer rank than that stated in the certificate held.

4 If an application for revalidation of a certificate referred to in paragraph 1 of regulation I/11 is made within six months before expiry of the certificate, the certificate may be revalidated until the fifth anniversary of the date of validity, or extension of the validity, of the certificate.

Section B-I/12

Guidance regarding the use of simulators

1 When simulators are being used for training or assessment of competency, the following guidelines should be taken into consideration in conducting any such training or assessment.

Training and assessment in radar observation and plotting*

2 Training and assessment in radar observation and plotting should:

.1 incorporate the use of radar simulation equipment; and

.2 conform to standards not inferior to those given in paragraphs 3 to 17 below.

3 Demonstrations of and practice in radar observation should be undertaken, where appropriate, on live marine radar equipment, including the use of simulators. Plotting exercises should preferably be undertaken in real time, in order to increase trainees' awareness of the hazards of the improper use of radar data and improve their plotting techniques to a standard of radar plotting commensurate with that necessary for the safe execution of collision-avoidance manoeuvring under actual seagoing conditions.

General

Factors affecting performance and accuracy

4 An elementary understanding should be attained of the principles of radar, together with a full practical knowledge of:

.1 range and bearing measurement, characteristics of the radar set which determine the quality of the radar display, radar antennae, polar diagrams, the effects of power radiated in directions outside the main beam, a non-technical description of the radar system, including variations in the features encountered in different types of radar set, performance monitors and equipment factors which affect maximum and minimum detection ranges and accuracy of information;

.2 the current marine radar performance specification adopted by the Organization,†

.3 the effects of the siting of the radar antenna, shadow sectors and arcs of reduced sensitivity, false echoes, effects of antenna height on detection ranges and of siting radar units and storing spares near magnetic compasses, including magnetic safe distances; and

.4 radiation hazards and safety precautions to be taken in the vicinity of antennae and open waveguides.

Detection of misrepresentation of information, including false echoes and sea returns

5 A knowledge of the limitations to target detection is essential, to enable the observer to estimate the dangers of failure to detect targets. The following factors should be emphasized:

.1 performance standard of the equipment;

* The relevant IMO Model Course(s) may be of assistance in the preparation of courses.

† See relevant/appropriate performance standards adopted by the Organization.

.2 brilliance, gain and video processor control settings;

.3 radar horizon;

.4 size, shape, aspect and composition of targets;

.5 effects of the motion of the ship in a seaway;

.6 propagation conditions;

.7 meteorological conditions; sea clutter and rain clutter;

.8 anti-clutter control settings;

.9 shadow sectors; and

.10 radar-to-radar interference.

6 A knowledge should be attained of factors which might lead to faulty interpretation, including false echoes, effects of nearby pylons and large structures, effects of power lines crossing rivers and estuaries, echoes from distant targets occurring on second or later traces.

7 A knowledge should be attained of aids to interpretation, including corner reflectors and radar beacons; detection and recognition of land targets; the effects of topographical features; effects of pulse length and beam width; radar-conspicuous and -inconspicuous targets; factors which affect the echo strength from targets.

Practice

Setting up and maintaining displays

8 A knowledge should be attained of:

.1 the various types of radar display mode; unstabilized ship's-head-up relative motion; ship's-head-up, course-up and north-up stabilized relative motion and true motion;

.2 the effects of errors on the accuracy of information displayed; effects of transmitting compass errors on stabilized and true-motion displays; effects of transmitting log errors on a true-motion display; and the effects of inaccurate manual speed settings on a true-motion display;

.3 methods of detecting inaccurate speed settings on true-motion controls; the effects of receiver noise limiting the ability to display weak echo returns, and the effects of saturation by receiver noise, etc.; the adjustment of operational controls; criteria which indicate optimum points of adjustment; the importance of proper adjustment sequence, and the effects of maladjusted controls; the detection of maladjustments and corrections of:

.3.1 controls affecting detection ranges; and

.3.2 controls affecting accuracy;

.4 the dangers of using radar equipment with maladjusted controls; and

.5 the need for frequent regular checking of performance, and the relationship of the performance indicator to the range performance of the radar set.

Range and bearing

9 A knowledge should be attained of:

.1 the methods of measuring ranges; fixed range markers and variable range markers;

.2 the accuracy of each method and the relative accuracy of the different methods;

.3 how range data are displayed; ranges at stated intervals, digital counter and graduated scale;

.4 the methods of measuring bearings; rotatable cursor on transparent disc covering the display, electronic bearing cursor and other methods;

.5 bearing accuracy and inaccuracies caused by parallax, heading marker displacement, centre maladjustment;

.6 how bearing data are displayed; graduated scale and digital counter; and

.7 the need for regular checking of the accuracy of ranges and bearings, methods of checking for inaccuracies and correcting or allowing for inaccuracies.

Plotting techniques and relative-motion concepts

10 Practice should be provided in manual plotting techniques, including the use of reflection plotters, with the objective of establishing a thorough understanding of the interrelated motion between own ship and other ships, including the effects of manoeuvring to avoid collision. At the preliminary stages of this training, simple plotting exercises should be designed to establish a sound appreciation of plotting geometry and relative-motion concepts. The degree of complexity of exercises should increase throughout the training course until the trainee has mastered all aspects of the subject. Competence can best be enhanced by exposing the trainee to real-time exercises performed on a simulator or using other effective means.

Identification of critical echoes

11 A thorough understanding should be attained of:

.1 position fixing by radar from land targets and sea marks;

.2 the accuracy of position fixing by ranges and by bearings;

.3 the importance of cross-checking the accuracy of radar against other navigational aids; and

.4 the value of recording ranges and bearings at frequent, regular intervals when using radar as an aid to collision avoidance.

Course and speed of other ships

12 A thorough understanding should be attained of:

.1 the different methods by which course and speed of other ships can be obtained from recorded ranges and bearings, including:

.1.1 the unstabilized relative plot;

.1.2 the stabilized relative plot; and

.1.3 the true plot; and

.2 the relationship between visual and radar observations, including detail and the accuracy of estimates of course and speed of other ships, and the detection of changes in movements of other ships.

Time and distance of closest approach of crossing, meeting or overtaking ships

13 A thorough understanding should be attained of:

.1 the use of recorded data to obtain:

.1.1 measurement of closest approach distance and bearing;

.1.2 time to closest approach; and

.2 the importance of frequent, regular observations.

Detecting course and speed changes of other ships

14 A thorough understanding should be attained of:

.1 the effects of changes of course and/or speed by other ships on their tracks across the display;

.2 the delay between change of course or speed and detection of that change; and

.3 the hazards of small changes as compared with substantial changes of course or speed in relation to rate and accuracy of detection.

Effects of changes in own ship's course or speed or both

15 A thorough understanding of the effects on a relative-motion display of own ship's movements, and the effects of other ships' movements and the advantages of compass stabilization of a relative display.

16 In respect of true-motion displays, a thorough understanding should be attained of:

.1 the effects of inaccuracies of:

.1.1 speed and course settings; and

.1.2 compass stabilization data driving a stabilized relative-motion display;

.2 the effects of changes in course or speed or both by own ship on tracks of other ships on the display; and

.3 the relationship of speed to frequency of observations.

Application of the International Regulations for Preventing Collisions at Sea, 1972, as amended

17 A thorough understanding should be attained of the relationship of the International Regulations for Preventing Collisions at Sea, 1972, as amended, to the use of radar, including:

.1 action to avoid collision, dangers of assumptions made on inadequate information and the hazards of small alterations of course or speed;

.2 the advantages of safe speed when using radar to avoid collision;

.3 the relationship of speed to closest approach distance and time and to the manoeuvring characteristics of various types of ships;

.4 the importance of radar observation reports and radar reporting procedures being well defined;

.5 the use of radar in clear weather, to obtain an appreciation of its capabilities and limitations, compare radar and visual observations and obtain an assessment of the relative accuracy of information;

.6 the need for early use of radar in clear weather at night and when there are indications that visibility may deteriorate;

.7 comparison of features displayed by radar with charted features; and

.8 comparison of the effects of differences between range scales.

Training and assessment in the operational use of Automatic Radar Plotting Aids (ARPA)

18 Training and assessment in the operational use of automatic radar plotting aids (ARPA) should:

.1 require prior completion of the training in radar observation and plotting or combine that training with the training given in paragraphs 19 to 35 below;*

* The relevant IMO Model Course(s) and resolution MSC.64(67), as amended, may be of assistance in the preparation of courses.

.2 incorporate the use of ARPA simulation equipment; and

.3 conform to standards not inferior to those given in paragraphs 19 to 35 below.

19 Where ARPA training is provided as part of the general training under the 1978 STCW Convention, masters, chief mates and officers in charge of a navigational watch should understand the factors involved in decision-making based on the information supplied by ARPA in association with other navigational data inputs, having a similar appreciation of the operational aspects and of system errors of modern electronic navigational systems, including ECDIS. This training should be progressive in nature, commensurate with the responsibilities of the individual and the certificates issued by Parties under the 1978 STCW Convention.

Theory and demonstration

Possible risks of over-reliance on ARPA

20 Appreciation that ARPA is only a navigational aid and:

.1 that its limitations, including those of its sensors, make over-reliance on ARPA dangerous, in particular for keeping a look-out; and

.2 the need to observe at all times the Principles to be observed in keeping a navigational watch and the Guidance on keeping a navigational watch.

Principal types of ARPA systems and their display characteristics

21 Knowledge of the principal types of ARPA systems in use; their various display characteristics and an understanding of when to use ground- or sea-stabilized modes and north-up, course-up or head-up presentations.

IMO performance standards for ARPA

22 An appreciation of the IMO performance standards for ARPA, in particular the standards relating to accuracy.*

Factors affecting system performance and accuracy

23 Knowledge of ARPA sensor input performance parameters – radar, compass and speed inputs and the effects of sensor malfunction on the accuracy of ARPA data.

24 Knowledge of:

.1 the effects of the limitations of radar range and bearing discrimination and accuracy and the limitations of compass and speed input accuracies on the accuracy of ARPA data; and

.2 factors which influence vector accuracy.

Tracking capabilities and limitations

25 Knowledge of:

.1 the criteria for the selection of targets by automatic acquisition;

.2 the factors leading to the correct choice of targets for manual acquisition;

.3 the effects on tracking of "lost" targets and target fading; and

.4 the circumstances causing "target swap" and its effects on displayed data.

---

* See relevant/appropriate performance standards adopted by the Organization.

Processing delays

26 Knowledge of the delays inherent in the display of processed ARPA information, particularly on acquisition and re-acquisition or when a tracked target manoeuvres.

Operational warnings, their benefits and limitations

27 Appreciation of the uses, benefits and limitations of ARPA operational warnings and their correct setting, where applicable, to avoid spurious interference.

System operational tests

28 Knowledge of:

- **.1** methods of testing for malfunctions of ARPA systems, including functional self-testing; and
- **.2** precautions to be taken after a malfunction occurs.

Manual and automatic acquisition of targets and their respective limitations

29 Knowledge of the limits imposed on both types of acquisition in multi-target scenarios, and the effects on acquisition of target fading and target swap.

True and relative vectors and typical graphic representation of target information and danger areas

30 Thorough knowledge of true and relative vectors; derivation of targets' true courses and speeds, including:

- **.1** threat assessment, derivation of predicted closest point of approach and predicted time to closest point of approach from forward extrapolation of vectors, the use of graphic representation of danger areas;
- **.2** the effects of alterations of course and/or speed of own ship and/or targets on predicted closest point of approach and predicted time to closest point of approach and danger areas;
- **.3** the effects of incorrect vectors and danger areas; and
- **.4** the benefit of switching between true and relative vectors.

Information on past positions of targets being tracked

31 Knowledge of the derivation of past positions of targets being tracked, recognition of historic data as a means of indicating recent manoeuvring of targets and as a method of checking the validity of the ARPA's tracking.

Practice

Setting up and maintaining displays

32 Ability to demonstrate:

- **.1** the correct starting procedure to obtain the optimum display of ARPA information;
- **.2** the selection of display presentation; stabilized relative-motion displays and true-motion displays;
- **.3** the correct adjustment of all variable radar display controls for optimum display of data;
- **.4** the selection, as appropriate, of required speed input to ARPA;
- **.5** the selection of ARPA plotting controls, manual/automatic acquisition, vector/graphic display of data;
- **.6** the selection of the timescale of vectors/graphics;

.7 the use of exclusion areas when automatic acquisition is employed by ARPA; and

.8 performance checks of radar, compass, speed input sensors and ARPA.

System operational tests

33 Ability to perform system checks and determine data accuracy of ARPA, including the trial manoeuvre facility, by checking against basic radar plot.

Obtaining information from the ARPA display

34 Demonstrate the ability to obtain information in both relative- and true-motion modes of display, including:

.1 the identification of critical echoes;

.2 the speed and direction of target's relative movement;

.3 the time to, and predicted range at, target's closest point of approach;

.4 the courses and speeds of targets;

.5 detecting course and speed changes of targets and the limitations of such information;

.6 the effect of changes in own ship's course or speed or both; and

.7 the operation of the trial manoeuvre facility.

Application of the International Regulations for Preventing Collisions at Sea, 1972, as amended

35 Analysis of potential collision situations from displayed information, determination and execution of action to avoid close-quarters situations in accordance with the International Regulations for Preventing Collisions at Sea, 1972, as amended, in force.

Training and assessment in the operational use of Electronic Chart Display and Information Systems (ECDIS)

Introduction

36 When simulators are being used for training or assessment in the operational use of Electronic Chart Display and Information Systems (ECDIS), the following interim guidance should be taken into consideration in any such training or assessment.

37 Training and assessment in the operational use of the ECDIS should:

.1 incorporate the use of ECDIS simulation equipment; and

.2 conform to standards not inferior to those given in paragraphs 38 to 65 below.

38 ECDIS simulation equipment should, in addition to meeting all applicable performance standards set out in section A-I/12 of the STCW Code, as amended, be capable of simulating navigational equipment and bridge operational controls which meet all applicable performance standards adopted by the Organization, incorporate facilities to generate soundings and:

.1 create a real-time operating environment, including navigation control and communications instruments and equipment appropriate to the navigation and watchkeeping tasks to be carried out and the manoeuvring skills to be assessed; and

.2 realistically simulate "own ship" characteristics in open-water conditions, as well as the effects of weather, tidal stream and currents.

39 Demonstrations of, and practice in, ECDIS use should be undertaken, where appropriate, through the use of simulators. Training exercises should preferably be undertaken in real time, in order to increase trainees' awareness of the hazards of the improper use of ECDIS. Accelerated timescale may be used only for demonstrations.

General

Goals of an ECDIS training programme

40 The ECDIS trainee should be able to:

.1 operate the ECDIS equipment, use the navigational functions of ECDIS, select and assess all relevant information and take proper action in the case of a malfunction;

.2 state the potential errors of displayed data and the usual errors of interpretation; and

.3 explain why ECDIS should not be relied upon as the sole reliable aid to navigation.

Theory and demonstration

41 As the safe use of ECDIS requires knowledge and understanding of the basic principles governing ECDIS data and their presentation rules as well as potential errors in displayed data and ECDIS-related limitations and potential dangers, a number of lectures covering the theoretical explanation should be provided. As far as possible, such lessons should be presented within a familiar context and make use of practical examples. They should be reinforced during simulator exercises.

42 For safe operation of ECDIS equipment and ECDIS-related information (use of the navigational functions of ECDIS, selection and assessment of all relevant information, becoming familiar with ECDIS man–machine interfacing), practical exercises and training on the ECDIS simulators should constitute the main content of the course.

43 For the definition of training objectives, a structure of activities should be defined. A detailed specification of learning objectives should be developed for each topic of this structure.

Simulator exercises

44 Exercises should be carried out on individual ECDIS simulators, or full-mission navigation simulators including ECDIS, to enable trainees to acquire the necessary practical skills. For real-time navigation exercises, navigation simulators are recommended to cover the complex navigation situation. The exercises should provide training in the use of the various scales, navigational modes and display modes which are available, so that the trainees will be able to adapt the use of the equipment to the particular situation concerned.

45 The choice of exercises and scenarios is governed by the simulator facilities available. If one or more ECDIS workstations and a full-mission simulator are available, the workstations may primarily be used for basic exercises in the use of ECDIS facilities and for passage-planning exercises, whereas full-mission simulators may primarily be used for exercises related to passage-monitoring functions in real time, as realistic as possible in connection with the total workload of a navigational watch. The degree of complexity of exercises should increase throughout the training programme until the trainee has mastered all aspects of the learning subject.

46 Exercises should produce the greatest impression of realism. To achieve this, the scenarios should be located in a fictitious sea area. Situations, functions and actions for different learning objectives which occur in different sea areas can be integrated into one exercise and experienced in real time.

47 The main objective of simulator exercises is to ensure that trainees understand their responsibilities in the operational use of ECDIS in all safety-relevant aspects and are thoroughly familiar with the system and equipment used.

Principal types of ECDIS systems and their display characteristics

48 The trainee should gain knowledge of the principal types of ECDIS in use; their various display characteristics, data structure and an understanding of:

- **.1** differences between vector and raster charts;
- **.2** differences between ECDIS and ECS;
- **.3** differences between ECDIS and RCDS;*
- **.4** characteristics of ECDIS and their different solutions; and
- **.5** characteristics of systems for special purposes (unusual situations/emergencies).

Risks of over-reliance on ECDIS

49 The training in ECDIS operational use should address:

- **.1** the limitations of ECDIS as a navigational tool;
- **.2** potential risk of improper functioning of the system;
- **.3** system limitations, including those of its sensors;
- **.4** hydrographic data inaccuracy; limitations of vector and raster electronic charts (ECDIS *vs* RCDS and ENC *vs* RNC); and
- **.5** potential risk of human errors.

Emphasis should be placed on the need to keep a proper look-out and to perform periodical checking, especially of the ship's position, by ECDIS-independent methods.

Detection of misrepresentation of information

50 Knowledge of the limitations of the equipment and detection of misrepresentation of information is essential for the safe use of ECDIS. The following factors should be emphasized during training:

- **.1** performance standards of the equipment;
- **.2** radar data representation on an electronic chart, elimination of discrepancy between the radar image and the electronic chart;
- **.3** possible projection discrepancies between an electronic and paper charts;
- **.4** possible scale discrepancies (overscaling and underscaling) in displaying an electronic chart and its original scale;
- **.5** effects of using different reference systems for positioning;
- **.6** effects of using different horizontal and vertical datums;
- **.7** effects of the motion of the ship in a seaway;
- **.8** ECDIS limitations in raster chart display mode;
- **.9** potential errors in the display of:
  - **.9.1** the own ship's position;
  - **.9.2** radar data and ARPA and AIS information;
  - **.9.3** different geodetic coordinate systems; and

* See SN/Circ.207/Rev.1 – Differences between RCDS and ECDIS.

.10 verification of the results of manual or automatic data correction:

.10.1 comparison of chart data and radar picture; and

.10.2 checking the own ship's position by using the other independent position-fixing systems.

51 False interpretation of the data and proper action taken to avoid errors of interpretation should be explained. The implications of the following should be emphasized:

.1 ignoring overscaling of the display;

.2 uncritical acceptance of the own ship's position;

.3 confusion of display mode;

.4 confusion of chart scale;

.5 confusion of reference systems;

.6 different modes of presentation;

.7 different modes of vector stabilization;

.8 differences between true north and gyro north (radar);

.9 using the same data reference system;

.10 using the appropriate chart scale;

.11 using the best-suited sensor to the given situation and circumstances;

.12 entering the correct values of safety data:

.12.1 the own ship's safety contour,

.12.2 safety depth (safe water), and

.12.3 events; and

.13 proper use of all available data.

52 Appreciation that RCDS is only a navigational aid and that, when operating in the RCDS mode, the ECDIS equipment should be used together with an appropriate portfolio of up-to-date paper charts:

.1 appreciation of the differences in operation of RCDS mode as described in SN.1/Circ.207/Rev.1, Differences between RCDS and ECDIS; and

.2 ECDIS, in any mode, should be used in training with an appropriate portfolio of up-to-date charts.

Factors affecting system performance and accuracy

53 An elementary understanding should be attained of the principles of ECDIS, together with a full practical knowledge of:

.1 starting and setting up ECDIS; connecting data sensors: satellite and radio navigation system receivers, radar, gyro-compass, log, echo-sounder; accuracy and limitations of these sensors, including effects of measurement errors and ship's position accuracy, manoeuvring on the accuracy of course indicator's performance, compass error on the accuracy of course indication, shallow water on the accuracy of log performance, log correction on the accuracy of speed calculation, disturbance (sea state) on the accuracy of an echo-sounder performance; and

.2 the current performance standards for electronic chart display and information systems adopted by the Organization.*

* See relevant/appropriate performance standards adopted by the Organization.

Practice

Setting up and maintaining display

54 Knowledge and skills should be attained in:

- **.1** the correct starting procedure to obtain the optimum display of ECDIS information;
- **.2** the selection of display presentation (standard display, display base, all other information displayed individually on demand);
- **.3** the correct adjustment of all variable radar/ARPA display controls for optimum display of data;
- **.4** the selection of convenient configuration;
- **.5** the selection, as appropriate, of required speed input to ECDIS;
- **.6** the selection of the timescale of vectors; and
- **.7** performance checks of position, radar/ARPA, compass, speed input sensors and ECDIS.

Operational use of electronic charts

55 Knowledge and skills should be attained in:

- **.1** the main characteristics of the display of ECDIS data and selecting proper information for navigational tasks;
- **.2** the automatic functions required for monitoring ship's safety, such as display of position, heading/gyro course, speed, safety values and time;
- **.3** the manual functions (by the cursor, electronic bearing line, range rings);
- **.4** selecting and modification of electronic chart content;
- **.5** scaling (including underscaling and overscaling);
- **.6** zooming;
- **.7** setting of the own ship's safety data;
- **.8** using a daytime or night-time display mode;
- **.9** reading all chart symbols and abbreviations;
- **.10** using different kinds of cursors and electronic bars for obtaining navigational data;
- **.11** viewing an area in different directions and returning to the ship's position;
- **.12** finding the necessary area, using geographical coordinates;
- **.13** displaying indispensable data layers appropriate to a navigational situation;
- **.14** selecting appropriate and unambiguous data (position, course, speed, etc.);
- **.15** entering the mariner's notes;
- **.16** using north-up orientation presentation and other kinds of orientation; and
- **.17** using true- and relative-motion modes.

Route planning

56 Knowledge and skills should be attained in:

- **.1** loading the ship's characteristics into ECDIS;

.2 selection of a sea area for route planning:

.2.1 reviewing required waters for the sea passage, and

.2.2 changing over of chart scale;

.3 verifying that proper and updated charts are available;

.4 route planning on a display by means of ECDIS, using the graphic editor, taking into consideration rhumb line and great-circle sailing:

.4.1 using the ECDIS database for obtaining navigational, hydro-meteorological and other data;

.4.2 taking into consideration turning radius and wheel-over points/lines when they are expressed on chart scale;

.4.3 marking dangerous depths and areas and exhibiting guarding depth contours;

.4.4 marking waypoints with the crossing depth contours and critical cross-track deviations, as well as by adding, replacing and erasing of waypoints;

.4.5 taking into consideration safe speed;

.4.6 checking pre-planned route for navigational safety; and

.4.7 generating alarms and warnings;

.5 route planning with calculation in the table format, including:

.5.1 waypoints selection;

.5.2 recalling the waypoints list;

.5.3 planning notes;

.5.4 adjustment of a planned route;

.5.5 checking a pre-planned route for navigational safety;

.5.6 alternative route planning;

.5.7 saving planned routes, loading and unloading or deleting routes;

.5.8 making a graphic copy of the monitor screen and printing a route;

.5.9 editing and modification of the planned route;

.5.10 setting of safety values according to the size and manoeuvring parameters of the vessel;

.5.11 back-route planning; and

.5.12 connecting several routes.

Route monitoring

57 Knowledge and skills should be attained in:

.1 using independent data to control ship's position or using alternative systems within ECDIS;

.2 using the look-ahead function:

.2.1 changing charts and their scales;

.2.2 reviewing navigational charts;

.2.3 vector time selecting;

.2.4 predicting the ship's position for some time interval;

.2.5 changing the pre-planned route (route modification);

.2.6 entering independent data for the calculation of wind drift and current allowance;

.2.7 reacting properly to the alarm;

.2.8 entering corrections for discrepancies of the geodetic datum;

.2.9 displaying time markers on a ship's route;

.2.10 entering ship's position manually; and

.2.11 measuring coordinates, course, bearings and distances on a chart.

Alarm handling

58 Knowledge and ability to interpret and react properly to all kinds of systems, such as navigational sensors, indicators, data and charts, alarms and indicator warnings, including switching the sound and visual alarm signalling system, should be attained in case of:

.1 absence of the next chart in the ECDIS database;

.2 crossing a safety contour;

.3 exceeding cross-track limits;

.4 deviation from planned route;

.5 approaching a waypoint;

.6 approaching a critical point;

.7 discrepancy between calculated and actual time of arrival to a waypoint;

.8 information on under-scaling or over-scaling;

.9 approaching an isolated navigational danger or danger area;

.10 crossing a specified area;

.11 selecting a different geodetic datum;

.12 approaching other ships;

.13 watch termination;

.14 switching timer;

.15 system test failure;

.16 malfunctioning of the positioning system used in ECDIS;

.17 failure of dead reckoning; and

.18 inability to fix vessel's position using the navigational system.

Manual correction of a ship's position and motion parameters

59 Knowledge and skills should be attained in manually correcting:

.1 the ship's position in dead-reckoning mode, when the satellite and radio navigation system receiver is switched off;

.2 the ship's position, when automatically obtained coordinates are inaccurate; and

.3 course and speed values.

Records in the ship's log

60 Knowledge and skills should be attained in:

.1 automatic voyage recording;

.2 reconstruction of past track, taking into account:

.2.1 recording media;

- **.2.2** recording intervals;
- **.2.3** verification of database in use;

- **.3** viewing records in the electronic ship's log;
- **.4** instant recording in the electronic ship's log;
- **.5** changing ship's time;
- **.6** entering the additional data;
- **.7** printing the content of the electronic ship's log;
- **.8** setting up the automatic record time intervals;
- **.9** composition of voyage data and reporting; and
- **.10** interface with a voyage data recorder (VDR).

Chart updating

61 Knowledge and skills should be attained in:

- **.1** performing manual updating of electronic charts. Special attention should be paid to reference-ellipsoid conformity and to conformity of the measurement units used on a chart and in the correction text;
- **.2** performing semi-automatic updating of electronic charts, using the data obtained on electronic media in the electronic chart format; and
- **.3** performing automatic updating of electronic charts, using update files obtained via electronic data communication lines.

In the scenarios where non-updated data are employed to create a critical situation, trainees should be required to perform *ad hoc* updating of the chart.

Operational use of ECDIS where radar/ARPA is connected

62 Knowledge and skills should be attained in:

- **.1** connecting ARPA to ECDIS;
- **.2** indicating target's speed vectors;
- **.3** indicating target's tracks;
- **.4** archiving target's tracks;
- **.5** viewing the table of the targets;
- **.6** checking alignment of radar overlay with charted geographic features;
- **.7** simulating one or more manoeuvres;
- **.8** corrections to own ship's position, using a reference point captured by ARPA; and
- **.9** corrections using the ARPA's cursor and electronic bar.

See also section B-I/12, Guidance regarding the use of simulators (pertaining to radar and ARPA), especially paragraphs 17 to 19 and 36 to 38.

Operational use of ECDIS where AIS is connected

63 Knowledge and skills should be attained in:

- **.1** interface with AIS;

.2 interpretation of AIS data;

.3 indicating target's speed vectors;

.4 indicating target's tracks; and

.5 archiving target's tracks.

Operational warnings, their benefits and limitations

64 Trainees should gain an appreciation of the uses, benefits and limitations of ECDIS operational warnings and their correct setting, where applicable, to avoid spurious interference.

System operational tests

65 Knowledge and skills should be attained in:

.1 methods of testing for malfunctions of ECDIS, including functional self-testing;

.2 precautions to be taken after a malfunction occurs; and

.3 adequate back-up arrangements (take over and navigate using the back-up system).

Debriefing exercise

66 The instructor should analyze the results of all exercises completed by all trainees and print them out. The time spent on the debriefing should occupy between 10% and 15% of the total time used for simulator exercises.

Recommended performance standards for non-mandatory types of simulation

67 Performance standards for non-mandatory simulation equipment used for training and/or assessment of competence or demonstration of skills are set out hereunder. Such forms of simulation include, but are not limited to, the following types:

.1 navigation and watchkeeping;

.2 ship handling and manoeuvring;

.3 cargo handling and stowage;

.4 reporting and radiocommunications; and

.5 main and auxiliary machinery operation.

Navigation and watchkeeping simulation

68 Navigation and watchkeeping simulation equipment should, in addition to meeting all applicable performance standards set out in section A-I/12, be capable of simulating navigational equipment and bridge operational controls which meet all applicable performance standards adopted by the Organization,* incorporate facilities to generate soundings and:

.1 create a real-time operating environment, including navigation control and communications instruments and equipment appropriate to the navigation and watchkeeping tasks to be carried out and the manoeuvring skills to be assessed;

.2 provide a realistic visual scenario by day or by night, including variable visibility, or by night only as seen from the bridge, with a minimum horizontal field of view available to the trainee in viewing sectors appropriate to the navigation and watchkeeping tasks and objectives;

* See relevant/appropriate performance standards adopted by the Organization.

.3 realistically simulate "own ship" dynamics in open-water conditions, including the effects of weather, tidal stream, currents and interaction with other ships; and

.4 realistically simulate VTS communication procedures between ship and shore.

Ship handling and manoeuvring simulation

69 In addition to meeting the performance standards set out in paragraph 37, ship handling simulation equipment should:

.1 provide a realistic visual scenario as seen from the bridge, by day and by night, with variable visibility throughout a minimum horizontal field of view available to the trainee in viewing sectors appropriate to the ship handling and manoeuvring training tasks and objectives;* and

.2 realistically simulate "own ship" dynamics in restricted waterways, including shallow-water and bank effects.

70 Where manned scale models are used to provide ship handling and manoeuvring simulation, in addition to the performance standards set out in paragraphs 68.3 and 69.2, such equipment should:

.1 incorporate scaling factors which present accurately the dimensions, areas, volume and displacement, speed, time and rate of turn of a real ship; and

.2 incorporate controls for the rudder and engines, to the correct timescale.

Cargo handling and stowage simulation

71 Cargo handling simulation equipment should be capable of simulating cargo handling and control equipment which meets all applicable performance standards adopted by the Organization† and incorporate facilities to:

.1 create an effective operational environment, including a cargo-control station with such instrumentation as may be appropriate to the particular type of cargo system modelled;

.2 model loading and unloading functions and stability and stress data appropriate to the cargo-handling tasks to be carried out and the skills to be assessed; and

.3 simulate loading, unloading, ballasting and deballasting operations and appropriate associated calculations for stability, trim, list, longitudinal strength, torsional stress and damage stability.*

GMDSS communication simulation

72 GMDSS communication simulation equipment should be capable of simulating GMDSS communication equipment which meets all applicable performance standards adopted by the Organization‡ and incorporate facilities to:

.1 simulate the operation of VHF, VHF-DSC, NAVTEX, EPIRB and watch receiver equipment as required for the Restricted Operator's Certificate (ROC);

.2 simulate the operation of INMARSAT-A, -B and -C ship earth stations, MF/HF NBDP, MF/HF-DSC, VHF, VHF-DSC, NAVTEX, EPIRB and watch receiver equipment as required for the General Operator's Certificate (GOC);

.3 provide voice communication with background noise;

.4 provide a printed text communication facility; and

---

* The relevant IMO Model Course(s) may be of assistance in the preparation of courses.

† No standards have as yet been adopted by the Organization.

‡ See relevant/appropriate performance standards adopted by the Organization.

.5 create a real-time operating environment, consisting of an integrated system, incorporating at least one instructor/assessor station and at least two GMDSS ship or shore stations.

Main and auxiliary machinery operation simulation

73 Engine-room simulation equipment should be capable of simulating a main and auxiliary machinery system and incorporate facilities to:

- **.1** create a real-time environment for seagoing and harbour operations, with communication devices and simulation of appropriate main and auxiliary propulsion machinery equipment and control panels;
- **.2** simulate relevant subsystems that should include, but not be restricted to, boiler, steering gear, electrical power general and distribution systems, including emergency power supplies, and fuel, cooling water, refrigeration, bilge and ballast systems;
- **.3** monitor and evaluate engine performance and remote sensing systems;
- **.4** simulate machinery malfunctions;
- **.5** allow for the variable external conditions to be changed so as to influence the simulated operations: weather, ship's draught, seawater and air temperatures;
- **.6** allow for instructor-controlled external conditions to be changed: deck steam, accommodation steam, deck air, ice conditions, deck cranes, heavy power, bow thrust, ship load;
- **.7** allow for instructor-controlled simulator dynamics to be changed: emergency run, process responses, ship responses; and
- **.8** provide a facility to isolate certain processes, such as speed, electrical system, diesel oil system, lubricating oil system, heavy oil system, seawater system, steam system, exhaust boiler and turbo generator, for performing specific training tasks.*

Section B-I/13
Guidance regarding the conduct of trials

(No provisions)

Section B-I/14
Guidance regarding responsibilities of companies and recommended responsibilities of masters and crew members

Companies

1 Companies should provide ship-specific introductory programmes aimed at assisting newly employed seafarers to familiarize themselves with all procedures and equipment relating to their areas of responsibility. Companies should also ensure that:

- **.1** all seafarers on a ship fitted with free-fall lifeboats should receive familiarization training in boarding and launching procedures for such lifeboats;
- **.2** prior to joining a ship, seafarers assigned as operating crew of free-fall lifeboats should have undergone appropriate training in boarding, launching and recovering of such lifeboats, including participation on at least one occasion in a free-fall launch; and

* The relevant IMO Model Course(s) may be of assistance in the preparation of courses.

.3 personnel who may be required to operate the GMDSS equipment receive GMDSS familiarization training, on joining the ship and at appropriate intervals thereafter.

2 The familiarization training required by paragraph 3 of section A-I/14 should at least ensure attainment of the abilities that are appropriate to the capacity to be filled and the duties and responsibilities to be taken up, as follows:

Design and operational limitations

.1 Ability to properly understand and observe any operational limitations imposed on the ship, and to understand and apply performance restrictions, including speed limitations in adverse weather, which are intended to maintain the safety of life, ship and cargo.

Procedures for opening, closing and securing hull openings

.2 Ability to apply properly the procedures established for the ship regarding the opening, closing and securing of bow, stern, and side doors and ramps and to correctly operate the related systems.

Legislation, codes and agreements affecting ro–ro passenger ships

.3 Ability to understand and apply international and national requirements for ro–ro passenger ships relevant to the ship concerned and the duties to be performed.

Stability and stress requirements and limitations

.4 Ability to take proper account of stress limitations for sensitive parts of the ship, such as bow doors and other closing devices that maintain watertight integrity, and of special stability considerations which may affect the safety of ro–ro passenger ships.

Procedures for the maintenance of special equipment on ro–ro passenger ships

.5 Ability to apply properly the shipboard procedures for maintenance of equipment peculiar to ro–ro passenger ships such as bow, stern and side doors and ramps, scuppers and associated systems.

Loading and cargo securing manuals and calculators

.6 Ability to make proper use of the loading and securing manuals in respect of all types of vehicles and rail cars where applicable, and to calculate and apply stress limitations for vehicle decks.

Dangerous cargo areas

.7 Ability to ensure proper observance of special precautions and limitations applying to designated dangerous cargo areas.

Emergency procedures

.8 Ability to ensure proper application of any special procedures to:

.8.1 prevent or reduce the ingress of water on vehicle decks;

.8.2 remove water from vehicle decks; and

.8.3 minimize effects of water on vehicle decks.

3 The familiarization training required by paragraph 4 of section A-I/14 should at least ensure attainment of the abilities that are appropriate to the capacity to be filled and the duties and responsibilities to be taken up, as follows:

Design and operational limitations

.1 any operational limitations imposed on the ship, and to understand and apply performance restrictions, including speed limitations in adverse weather, which are intended to maintain the safety of life, ship and cargo.

Legislation, codes and agreements affecting passenger ships

.2 Ability to understand and apply international and national requirements for passenger ships relevant to the ship concerned and the duties to be performed.

Master

4 The master should take all steps necessary to implement any company instructions issued in accordance with section A-I/14. Such steps should include:

.1 identifying all seafarers who are newly employed on board the ship before they are assigned to any duties;

.2 providing the opportunity for all newly arrived seafarers to:

.2.1 visit the spaces in which their primary duties will be performed;

.2.2 get acquainted with the location, controls and display features of equipment they will be operating or using;

.2.3 activate the equipment when possible, and perform functions, using the controls on the equipment; and

.2.4 observe and ask questions of someone who is already familiar with the equipment, procedures and other arrangements, and who can communicate information in a language which the seafarer understands; and

.3 providing for a suitable period of supervision when there is any doubt that a newly employed seafarer is familiar with the shipboard equipment, operating procedures and other arrangements needed for the proper performance of his or her duties.

Crew members

5 Seafarers who are newly assigned to a ship should take full advantage of every opportunity provided to become familiar with the shipboard equipment, operating procedures and other arrangements needed for the proper performance of their duties. Immediately upon arriving on board for the first time, each seafarer has the responsibility to become acquainted with the ship's working environment, particularly with respect to new or unfamiliar equipment, procedures or arrangements.

6 Seafarers who do not promptly attain the level of familiarity required for performing their duties have the obligation to bring this fact to the attention of their supervisor or to the attention of the crew member designated in accordance with section A-I/14, paragraph 2.2, and to identify any equipment, procedure or arrangement which remains unfamiliar.

Section B-I/15

Guidance regarding transitional provisions

(No provisions)

Chapter II
Guidance regarding the master and the deck department

Section B-II/1
Guidance regarding the certification of officers in charge of a navigational watch on ships of 500 gross tonnage or more

Training

1 Every candidate for certification as officer in charge of a navigational watch should have completed a planned and structured programme of training designed to assist a prospective officer to achieve the standard of competence in accordance with table A-II/1.

2 The structure of the programme of training should be set out in a training plan which clearly expresses, for all parties involved, the objectives of each stage of training on board and ashore. It is important that the prospective officer, tutors, ships' staff and company personnel are clear about the competences which are to be achieved at the end of the programme and how they are to be achieved through a combination of education, training and practical experience on board and ashore.

3 The mandatory periods of seagoing service are of prime importance in learning the job of being a ship's officer and in achieving the overall standard of competence required. Properly planned and structured, the periods of seagoing service will enable prospective officers to acquire and practice skills and will offer opportunities for competences achieved to be demonstrated and assessed.

4 Where the seagoing service forms part of an approved training programme, the following principles should be observed:

.1 The programme of onboard training should be an integral part of the overall training plan.

.2 The programme of onboard training should be managed and coordinated by the company which manages the ship on which the seagoing service is to be performed.

.3 The prospective officer should be provided with a training record book* to enable a comprehensive record of practical training and experience at sea to be maintained. The training record book should be laid out in such a way that it can provide detailed information about the tasks and duties which should be undertaken and the progress towards their completion. Duly completed, the record book will provide unique evidence that a structured programme of onboard training has been completed which can be taken into account in the process of evaluating competence for the issue of a certificate.

.4 At all times, the prospective officer should be aware of two identifiable individuals who are immediately responsible for the management of the programme of onboard training. The first of these is a qualified seagoing officer, referred to as the "shipboard training officer", who, under the authority of the master, should organize and supervise the programme of training for the duration of each voyage. The second should be a person nominated by the company, referred to as the "company training officer", who should have an overall responsibility for the training programme and for coordination with colleges and training institutions.

.5 The company should ensure that appropriate periods are set aside for completion of the programme of onboard training within the normal operational requirements of the ship.

* The relevant IMO Model Course(s) and a similar document produced by the International Shipping Federation may be of assistance in the preparation of training record books.

Roles and responsibilities

5 The following section summarizes the roles and responsibilities of those individuals involved in organizing and conducting onboard training:

.1 The company training officer should be responsible for:

.1.1 overall administration of the programme of training;

.1.2 monitoring the progress of the prospective officer throughout; and

.1.3 issuing guidance as required and ensuring that all concerned with the training programme play their parts.

.2 The shipboard training officer should be responsible for:

.2.1 organizing the programme of practical training at sea;

.2.2 ensuring, in a supervisory capacity, that the training record book is properly maintained and that all other requirements are fulfilled; and

.2.3 making sure, so far as is practicable, that the time the prospective officer spends on board is as useful as possible in terms of training and experience, and is consistent with the objectives of the training programme, the progress of training and the operational constraints of the ship.

.3 The master's responsibilities should be to:

.3.1 provide the link between the shipboard training officer and the company training officer ashore;

.3.2 fulfil the role of continuity if the shipboard training officer is relieved during the voyage; and

.3.3 ensure that all concerned are effectively carrying out the onboard training programme.

.4 The prospective officer's responsibilities should be to:

.4.1 follow diligently the programme of training as laid down;

.4.2 make the most of the opportunities presented, be they in or outside working hours; and

.4.3 keep the training record book up to date and ensure that it is available at all times for scrutiny.

Induction

6 At the beginning of the programme and at the start of each voyage on a different ship, prospective officers should be given full information and guidance as to what is expected of them and how the training programme is to be organized. Induction presents the opportunity to brief prospective officers about important aspects of the tasks they will be undertaking, with particular regard to safe working practices and protection of the marine environment.

Shipboard programme of training

7 The training record book should contain, amongst other things, a number of training tasks or duties which should be undertaken as part of the approved programme of onboard training. Such tasks and duties should relate to at least the following areas:

.1 steering systems;

.2 general seamanship;

.3 mooring, anchoring and port operations;

.4 life-saving and fire-fighting appliances;

.5 systems and equipment;

.6 cargo work;

.7 bridge work and watchkeeping; and

.8 engine-room familiarization.

8 It is extremely important that the prospective officer is given adequate opportunity for supervised bridge watchkeeping experience, particularly in the later stages of the onboard training programme.

9 The performance of the prospective officers in each of the tasks and duties itemized in the training record book should be initialled by a qualified officer when, in the opinion of the officer concerned, a prospective officer has achieved a satisfactory standard of proficiency. It is important to appreciate that a prospective officer may need to demonstrate ability on several occasions before a qualified officer is confident that a satisfactory standard has been achieved.

Monitoring and reviewing

10 Guidance and reviewing are essential to ensure that prospective officers are fully aware of the progress they are making and to enable them to join in decisions about their future programme. To be effective, reviews should be linked to information gained through the training record book and other sources as appropriate. The training record book should be scrutinized and endorsed formally by the master and the shipboard training officer at the beginning, during and at the end of each voyage. The training record book should also be examined and endorsed by the company training officer between voyages.

Assessment of abilities and skills in navigational watchkeeping

11 A candidate for certification who is required to have received special training and assessment of abilities and skills in navigational watchkeeping duties should be required to provide evidence, through demonstration either on a simulator or on board ship as part of an approved programme of shipboard training, that the skills and ability to perform as officer in charge of a navigational watch in at least the following areas have been acquired, namely to:

- **.1** prepare for and conduct a passage, including:
  - **.1.1** interpreting and applying information obtained from charts;
  - **.1.2** fixing position in coastal waters;
  - **.1.3** applying basic information obtained from tide tables and other nautical publications;
  - **.1.4** checking and operating bridge equipment;
  - **.1.5** checking magnetic and gyro-compasses;
  - **.1.6** assessing available meteorological information;
  - **.1.7** using celestial bodies to fix position;
  - **.1.8** determining the compass error by celestial and terrestrial means; and
  - **.1.9** performing calculations for sailings of up to 24 hours;
- **.2** operate and apply information obtained from electronic navigation systems;
- **.3** operate radar, ARPA and ECDIS and apply radar information for navigation and collision avoidance;
- **.4** operate propulsion and steering systems to control heading and speed;
- **.5** implement navigational watch routines and procedures;
- **.6** implement the manoeuvres required for rescue of persons overboard;
- **.7** initiate action to be taken in the event of an imminent emergency situation (e.g., fire, collision, stranding) and action in the immediate aftermath of an emergency;
- **.8** initiate action to be taken in event of malfunction or failure of major items of equipment or plant (e.g., steering gear, power, navigation systems);
- **.9** conduct radiocommunications and visual and sound signalling in normal and emergency situations; and
- **.10** monitor and operate safety and alarm systems, including internal communications.

12 Assessment of abilities and skills in navigational watchkeeping should:

.1 be made against the criteria for evaluating competence for the function of navigation set out in table A-II/1;

.2 ensure that the candidate performs navigational watchkeeping duties in accordance with the Principles to be observed in keeping a safe navigational watch (section A-VIII/2, part 4-1) and the Guidance on keeping a navigational watch (section B-VIII/2, part 4-1).

Evaluation of competence

13 The standard of competence to be achieved for certification as officer in charge of a navigational watch is set out in table A-II/1. The standard specifies the knowledge and skill required and the application of that knowledge and skill to the standard of performance required on board ship.

14 Scope of knowledge is implicit in the concept of competence. Assessment of competence should, therefore, encompass more than the immediate technical requirements of the job, the skills and tasks to be performed, and should reflect the broader aspects needed to meet the full expectations of competent performance as a ship's officer. This includes relevant knowledge, theory, principles and cognitive skills which, to varying degrees, underpin all levels of competence. It also encompasses proficiency in what to do, how and when to do it, and why it should be done. Properly applied, this will help to ensure that a candidate can:

.1 work competently in different ships and across a range of circumstances;

.2 anticipate, prepare for and deal with contingencies; and

.3 adapt to new and changing requirements.

15 The criteria for evaluating competence (column 4 of table A-II/1) identify, primarily in outcome terms, the essential aspects of competent performance. They are expressed so that assessment of a candidate's performance can be made against them and should be adequately documented in the training record book.

16 Evaluation of competence is the process of:

.1 collecting sufficient valid and reliable evidence about the candidate's knowledge, understanding and proficiency to accomplish the tasks, duties and responsibilities listed in column 1 of table A-II/1; and

.2 judging that evidence against the criteria specified in the standard.

17 The arrangements for evaluating competence should be designed to take account of different methods of assessment which can provide different types of evidence about candidates' competence, e.g.:

.1 direct observation of work activities (including seagoing service);

.2 skills/proficiency/competency tests;

.3 projects and assignments;

.4 evidence from previous experience; and

.5 written, oral and computer-based questioning techniques.*

18 One or more of the first four methods listed should almost invariably be used to provide evidence of ability, in addition to appropriate questioning techniques to provide evidence of supporting knowledge and understanding.

* The relevant IMO Model Course(s) may be of assistance in the preparation of courses.

.2 procedures for using propagation-prediction information to establish optimum frequencies for communications;

.3 radiocommunication watchkeeping relevant to all GMDSS subsystems, exchange of radiocommunication traffic, particularly concerning distress, urgency and safety procedures, and radio records;

.4 use of the international phonetic alphabet;

.5 monitoring a distress frequency while simultaneously monitoring or working on at least one other frequency;

.6 ship reporting systems and procedures;

.7 radiocommunication procedures of the International Aeronautical and Maritime Search and Rescue (IAMSAR) Manual;

.8 radio medical systems and procedures; and

.9 causes of false distress alerts and means to avoid them.*

Practical

35 Practical training should be given in:

.1 correct and efficient operation of all GMDSS subsystems and equipment under normal propagation conditions and under typical interference conditions;

.2 safe operation of all the GMDSS communications equipment and ancillary devices, including safety precautions;

.3 accurate and adequate keyboard skills for the satisfactory exchange of communications; and

.4 operational techniques for:

.4.1 receiver and transmitter adjustment for the appropriate mode of operation, including digital selective calling and direct-printing telegraphy;

.4.2 antenna adjustment and realignment as appropriate;

.4.3 use of radio life-saving appliances; and

.4.4 use of emergency position-indicating radio beacons (EPIRBs).

Miscellaneous

36 Knowledge of, and/or training in:

.1 the English language, both written and spoken, for the satisfactory exchange of communications relevant to the safety of life at sea;

.2 world geography, especially the principal shipping routes, services of rescue coordination centres (RCCs) and related communication routes;

.3 survival at sea, the operation of lifeboats, rescue boats, liferafts, buoyant apparatus and their equipment, with special reference to radio life-saving appliances;

.4 fire prevention and fire fighting, with particular reference to the radio installation;

.5 preventive measures for the safety of ship and personnel in connection with hazards related to radio equipment, including electrical, radiation, chemical and mechanical hazards;

.6 first aid, including heart-respiration revival techniques; and

.7 coordinated universal time (UTC), global time zones and the international date line.

* See COM/Circ.127 and IMO Assembly resolution A.814(19) – *Guidelines for the avoidance of false distress alerts*.

Training related to the Restricted Operator's Certificate

General

37 The requirements of medical fitness, especially as to hearing, eyesight and speech, should be met by the candidate before training is commenced.

38 The training should be relevant to the provisions of the STCW Convention, the Radio Regulations and the SOLAS Convention currently in force, with particular attention given to provisions for the global maritime distress and safety system (GMDSS). In developing training guidance, account should be taken of at least the knowledge and training given in paragraphs 39 to 44 hereunder.*

Theory

39 Knowledge of the general principles and basic factors, including VHF range limitation and antenna height effect necessary for safe and efficient use of all subsystems and equipment required in GMDSS in sea area A1, sufficient to support the training given in paragraph 43 below.

40 Knowledge of the use, operation and service areas of GMDSS sea area A1 subsystems, e.g., navigational and meteorological warning systems and the appropriate communication circuits.

Regulations and documentation

41 Knowledge of:

.1 those parts of the SOLAS Convention and the Radio Regulations relevant to sea area A1, with particular emphasis on:

.1.1 distress, urgency and safety radiocommunications;

.1.2 avoiding harmful interference, particularly with distress and safety traffic; and

.1.3 prevention of unauthorized transmissions;

.2 other documents relating to operational and communication procedures for distress, safety and public correspondence services, including charges, navigational warnings and weather broadcasts in the Maritime Mobile Service in sea area A1; and

.3 use of the International Code of Signals and the IMO Standard Marine Communication Phrases.

Watchkeeping and procedures

42 Training should be given in:

.1 communication procedures and discipline to prevent harmful interference in GMDSS subsystems used in sea area A1;

.2 VHF communication procedures for:

.2.1 radiocommunication watchkeeping, exchange of radiocommunication traffic, particularly concerning distress, urgency and safety procedures, and radio records;

.2.2 monitoring a distress frequency while simultaneously monitoring or working on at least one other frequency; and

.2.3 the digital selective calling system;

.3 use of the international phonetic alphabet;

.4 ship reporting systems and procedures;

* The relevant IMO Model Course(s) may be of assistance in the preparation of courses.

.5 VHF radiocommunication procedures of the International Aeronautical and Maritime Search and Rescue (IAMSAR) Manual;

.6 radio medical systems and procedures; and

.7 causes of false distress alerts and means to avoid them.*

Practical

43 Practical training should be given in:

.1 correct and efficient operation of the GMDSS subsystems and equipment prescribed for ships operating in sea area A1 under normal propagation conditions and under typical interference conditions;

.2 safe operation of relevant GMDSS communication equipment and ancillary devices, including safety precautions; and

.3 operational techniques for use of:

.3.1 VHF, including channel, squelch, and mode adjustment, as appropriate;

.3.2 radio life-saving appliances;

.3.3 emergency position-indicating radio beacons (EPIRBs); and

.3.4 NAVTEX receivers.

Miscellaneous

44 Knowledge of, and/or training in:

.1 the English language, both written and spoken, for the satisfactory exchange of communications relevant to the safety of life at sea;

.2 services of rescue coordination centres (RCCs) and related communication routes;

.3 survival at sea, the operation of lifeboats, rescue boats, liferafts, buoyant apparatus and their equipment, with special reference to radio life-saving appliances;

.4 fire prevention and fire fighting, with particular reference to the radio installation;

.5 preventive measures for the safety of ship and personnel in connection with hazards related to radio equipment, including electrical, radiation, chemical and mechanical hazards; and

.6 first aid, including heart-respiration revival techniques.

Training related to maintenance of GMDSS installations on board ships

General

45 Reference is made to the maintenance requirements of SOLAS Convention regulation IV/15, and to IMO resolution A.702(17) on Radio maintenance guidelines for the GMDSS related to sea areas A3 and A4, which includes in its annex the following provision:

> "4.2 The person designated to perform functions for at-sea electronic maintenance should either hold an appropriate certificate as specified by the Radio Regulations, as required, or have equivalent at-sea electronic maintenance qualifications, as may be approved by the Administration, taking into account the recommendations of the Organization on the training of such personnel."

* See COM/Circ.127 and IMO Assembly resolution A.814(19) – *Guidelines for the avoidance of false distress alerts.*

46 The following guidance on equivalent electronic maintenance qualifications is provided for use by Administrations as appropriate.

47 Training as recommended below does not qualify any person to be an operator of GMDSS radio equipment who does not hold an appropriate Radio Operator's Certificate.

Maintenance training equivalent to the First-Class Radioelectronic Certificate

48 In determining training equivalent to the elements of the listed First-Class Radioelectronic Certificate:

.1 the theory content should cover at least the subjects given in paragraphs 3 to 10;

.2 the practical content should cover at least the subjects given in paragraph 13; and

.3 the miscellaneous knowledge included should cover at least the subjects given in paragraph 14.

Maintenance training equivalent to the Second-Class Radioelectronic Certificate

49 In determining training equivalent to the maintenance elements of the Second-Class Radioelectronic Certificate:

.1 the theory content should cover at least the subjects given in paragraphs 17 to 24;

.2 the practical content should cover at least the subjects given in paragraph 27; and

.3 the miscellaneous knowledge included should cover at least the subjects given in paragraph 28.

Chapter V
Guidance regarding special training requirements for personnel on certain types of ships

Section B-V/1
Guidance regarding the training and qualifications of tanker personnel

Person with immediate responsibility

1 The term "person with immediate responsibility" as used in paragraphs 3 and 5 of regulation V/1-1 and paragraph 3 of regulation V/1-2 means a person being in a decision-making capacity with respect to loading, discharging, care in transit, handling of cargo, tank cleaning or other cargo-related operations.

Familiarization training for all tanker personnel

2 All tanker personnel should undergo familiarization training on board and, where appropriate, ashore before being assigned to shipboard duties, which should be given by qualified personnel experienced in the handling and characteristics of oil, chemical or liquefied gas cargoes, as appropriate, and the safety procedures involved. The training should at least cover the matters set out in paragraphs 3 to 8 below.

Regulations

3 Knowledge of the ship's rules and regulations governing the safety of personnel on board a tanker in port and at sea.

Health hazards and precautions to be taken

4 Dangers of skin contact; inhalation and accidental swallowing of cargo; the harmful properties of the cargoes carried, personnel accidents and associated first aid; lists of do's and don'ts.

Fire prevention and fire fighting

5 Control of smoking and cooking restrictions; sources of ignition; fire and explosion prevention; methods of fire fighting; portable fire extinguishers and fixed installations.

Pollution prevention

6 Procedures to be followed to prevent air and water pollution and measures which will be taken in the event of spillage.

Safety equipment and its use

7 The proper use of protective clothing and equipment, resuscitators, escape and rescue equipment.

Emergency procedures

8 Familiarization with the emergency plan procedures.

Proof of qualification

9 The master of every oil, chemical and liquefied gas tanker should ensure that the officer or the person primarily responsible for the cargo possesses the appropriate certificate, issued or endorsed or validated as required by regulation V/1-1, paragraph 3; regulation V/1-1, paragraph 5 or regulation V/1-2, paragraph 3, as appropriate, and has had adequate recent practical experience on board an appropriate type of tanker to permit that officer or person to safely perform the duties assigned.

Guidance regarding approved onboard training

General

10 The purpose of qualifying shipboard service is to provide training and knowledge for the safe carriage of specific tanker cargoes.

11 To satisfy the experience appropriate to their duties on the type of tanker on which they serve referred to in regulation V/1-1, paragraph 4.2.2, regulation V/1-1, paragraph 6.2.2, and regulation V/1-2, paragraph 4.2.2, onboard training should:

.1 emphasize practical "hands on experience" and be related to the employment of the seafarer, i.e. the training of deck and engineering departments may be different;

.2 be under the supervision of personnel qualified and experienced in the handling, characteristics and safety procedures of the cargoes being carried by the vessel;

.3 be on board the tanker carrying products relative to the tanker Certificate of Proficiency/Endorsement being sought and should be such that the specialist equipment is brought into operation but may be on a ballast passage between cargoes for part of that period;

.4 take part in at least three loading and discharge operations;* and

.5 at least cover the matters set out in "Onboard training criteria" in paragraph 19.

12 The onboard training programme must in no way affect the safe running or the seaworthiness of the vessel.

Onboard training programme

13 The trainee should be carried in a supernumerary capacity (i.e. the trainee will have no other duties than that of undertaking the training programme and emergency duties).

14 The programme of onboard training should be managed and coordinated by the company which manages the ship on which the seagoing service is to be performed and be a vessel nominated by the company as a training vessel.†

15 At all times, the trainee should be aware of two identifiable individuals who are immediately responsible for the management of the programme of onboard training. The first of these is a qualified seagoing officer, referred to as the "shipboard training officer", who, under the authority of the master, should organize and supervise the programme of training. The second should be a person nominated by the company, referred to as the "company training officer", who should have an overall responsibility for the training programme and for coordination with training organizations.

* A loading or discharging operation is considered to be the loading or discharge of more than 60% of the total cargo tank capacity of the vessel. Loading/discharges of less than this quantity may be summed together to be equivalent to this quantity.

† A nominated training vessel is a trading vessel named by the company that is suitable for the purpose of this guidance, as applicable.

16 The trainee should be provided with an approved training record book to enable a comprehensive record of practical training and experience at sea to be maintained. The approved training record book should be laid out in such a way that it can provide detailed information about the tasks and duties which should be undertaken and the progress towards their completion. Duly completed and countersigned by the master, the approved record book will provide unique evidence that a structured programme of onboard training has been completed leading towards the issue of a relevant Certificate in Advanced Training for Tanker Cargo Operations.

17 During the approved onboard training programme the trainee should be instructed in the loading, discharging, care in transit, handling of cargo, tank cleaning or other cargo-related operations of the tanker to ensure that the experience gained is at least equal to that which would be obtained in three months' normal service.

18 If the three-loading and three-unloading criteria cannot be achieved within the one-month onboard training period, then the period of onboard training should be extended until these criteria have been satisfactorily achieved.

Onboard training criteria

19 The onboard training should at least provide knowledge and experience, relevant to the applicable tanker type, of the following:

- **.1 Safety**
  - **.1.1** All tanker types
    - **.1** Ship's safety-management system
    - **.2** Cargo-specific fire-fighting equipment and procedures
    - **.3** Cargo-specific first-aid procedures, including the Medical First Aid Guide for Use in Accidents Involving Dangerous Goods (MFAG)
    - **.4** Ship-/cargo-specific hazards, including smoking regulations, oxygen-depleted atmospheres, cargo hydrocarbon narcosis and toxicity
    - **.5** Risk assessment systems
    - **.6** Permit to work, including hot work and enclosed spaces entry procedures
    - **.7** Use of personal protective equipment
  - **.1.2** Additional for liquefied gas tankers
    - **.1** Dangers and precautions related to handling and storage of cargoes at cryogenic temperatures
- **.2 Construction, cargo, cargo tanks and pipelines**
  - **.2.1** All tanker types
    - **.1** Hull/tank construction and limitations
    - **.2** Cargo connections
    - **.3** Properties and hazards associated with the types of cargo being carried, including use of Material Safety Data Sheets
    - **.4** The risks that cargo operations (such as purging/gas-freeing/tank cleaning) may have on the accommodation ventilation systems and actions to mitigate these risks
    - **.5** Configuration of cargo and ballast system
    - **.6** Pumps and associated equipment
    - **.7** Specialist equipment associated with the cargo operations
    - **.8** Particulars of the tanker's construction and how this affects the cargo operations
  - **.2.2** Additional for liquefied gas tankers
    - **.1** Use of segregation, separation and airlocks to maintain gas-safe areas
    - **.2** Cargo tank, inter-barrier, insulation spaces, and pipeline relief valves and vapour venting systems
    - **.3** Cargo vapour compressors and associated equipment

.3 **Trim and stability**

.3.1 All tanker types

.1 Tanker's stability information and calculating equipment

.2 Importance of maintaining stress levels within acceptable limits

.3 Dangers of free surface effect and "sloshing" effect

.4 **Cargo operations**

.4.1 All tanker types

.1 Pre-planning of loading/in-transit care, discharge/ballast operations

.2 Record keeping

.3 Start up/stopping procedures, including emergency shutdown

.4 Attention required for mooring arrangements during cargo operations

.5 Purging and inerting requirements and associated hazards

.6 Loading cargo, including topping-off operations

.7 Discharging cargo, including draining and stripping operations

.8 Monitoring of cargo during loading/discharging operations, including sampling where applicable

.9 Tank gauging and alarm systems

.10 Dangers from electrostatic discharge and its prevention

.11 Ballasting and deballasting operations

.12 Maintenance requirements, including coating inspections

.4.2 Additional for chemical tankers

.1 Polymerization, cargo compatibility, tank coating compatibility and other reactions

.2 Functions of inhibitors and catalysts

.3 Vapour/gas dispersion

.4.3 Additional for liquefied gas tankers

.1 Polymerization, cargo compatibility, tank coating compatibility and other reactions

.2 Functions of inhibitors and catalysts

.3 Causes of backpressure and pressure surge effects

.4 Use of boil-off gas as a fuel

.5 Vapour/gas dispersion

.6 Purging and cool-down operations

.7 Operation and maintenance of reliquefaction equipment

.8 Understanding and use of the custody transfer system

.4.4 Additional for oil tankers

.1 Crude oil washing systems

.5 **Tank washing/cleaning**

.5.1 All tanker types

.1 Tank cleaning systems and equipment fitted on the tanker

.2 Pre-planning of tank washing/cleaning operations

.3 Tank washing procedures, including purging and inerting

.4 Control of slops/waste product

.5 Electro-static hazards

.6 Cleanliness requirements

.7 Maintenance requirements

.5.2 Additional for chemical tankers

.1 Removal of inhibitors and residues

.2 Use of absorption, cleaning agents and detergents

.5.3 Additional for liquefied gas tankers

.1 Hot-gassing/boil-off of liquid residues and regassification process

.6 Inert gas systems

.6.1 All tanker types

.1 Inerting system(s) and equipment fitted to the tanker

.2 Hazards associated with inerting of spaces, with particular reference to safe entry into tanks

.3 Purging, maintaining inert atmosphere and gas-freeing operations

.4 Maintenance requirements

.7 Pollution prevention and control

.7.1 All tanker types

.1 International, flag State and company regulations, documentation and plans

.2 Operation of the tanker's pollution-prevention systems and equipment, including discharge monitoring

.3 Operation of the tanker's pollution-containment equipment

.8 Gas-detection equipment and instruments

.8.1 All tanker types

.1 Use and calibration of personal, portable and fixed gas analysers, with particular reference to oxygen and hydrocarbon monitoring equipment

.2 Operation, maintenance and limitation of cargo tank level measuring, level alarm and temperature-measuring systems

.8.2 Additional for liquefied gas tankers

.1 Operation and maintenance of hull temperature measurement

.9 Publications

.9.1 All tanker types

.1 International, flag State and company publications relevant to the operation of the tanker, including SOLAS, MARPOL and applicable guidance manuals

.2 Operating and maintenance manuals specific to the equipment on board

.3 Established industrial standards and code of safe working practice (e.g., ICS, OCIMF, SIGTTO)

Section B-V/1-1

Guidance regarding training and qualifications of masters, officers and ratings on oil and chemical tankers

Oil tanker training

20 The training required by paragraphs 2.2 and 4.3 of regulation V/1-1 in respect of oil tankers should be set out in a training plan which clearly expresses, for all parties involved, the objectives of the training. Training may be given on board or ashore, where appropriate. It should be supplemented by practical instruction on board and, where appropriate, in a suitable shore-based installation. All training and instruction should be given by properly qualified and suitably experienced personnel.*

* The relevant IMO Model Course(s) may be of assistance in the preparation of courses.

21 As much use as possible should be made of shipboard operation and equipment manuals, films and suitable visual aids, and the opportunity should be taken to introduce discussion of the part to be played by the safety organization on board ship and the role of safety officers and safety committees.

Chemical tanker training

22 The training required by paragraphs 2.2 and 6.3 of regulation V/1-1 in respect of chemical tankers should be set out in a training plan which clearly expresses, for all parties involved, the objectives of the training. Training may be given on board or ashore, where appropriate. It should be supplemented by practical instruction on board and, where appropriate, in a suitable shore-based installation. All training and instruction should be given by properly qualified and suitably experienced personnel.*

23 As much use as possible should be made of shipboard operation and equipment manuals, films and suitable visual aids, and the opportunity should be taken to introduce discussion of the part to be played by the safety organization on board ship and the role of safety officers and safety committees.

Section B-V/1-2

Guidance regarding training and qualifications of masters, officers and ratings on liquefied gas tankers

24 The training required by paragraphs 2.2 and 4.3 of regulation V/1-2 in respect of liquefied gas tankers should be set out in a training plan which clearly expresses, for all parties involved, the objectives of the training. Training may be given on board or ashore, where appropriate. It should be supplemented by practical instruction on board and, where appropriate, in a suitable shore-based installation. All training and instruction should be given by properly qualified and suitably experienced personnel*.

25 As much use as possible should be made of shipboard operation and equipment manuals, films and suitable visual aids, and the opportunity should be taken to introduce discussion of the part to be played by the safety organization on board ship and the role of safety officers and safety committees.

Section B-V/2

Guidance regarding training of seafarers on passenger ships

Enhanced fire fighting

1 For officers and crew on passenger ships, additional training should be provided highlighting the difficulties of fighting fires, including access to confined spaces and prevention of the spread of fire to adjoining spaces.

Damage control

2 In developing standards of competency given in sections A-II/1, A-II/2 and A-III/2 to achieve the necessary level of theoretical knowledge, understanding and proficiency in damage control and watertight integrity, companies and training institutions should take into account the minimum knowledge, understanding and proficiency for damage control and watertight integrity as given below:

Competence

Minimize the risk of flooding and maintain a state of readiness to respond to emergency situations involving damage to the watertight integrity of the ship.

Knowledge, understanding and proficiency

Shipboard damage control plans and organization.

Damage control systems, equipment (lockers) and emergency escape routes

The key elements in maintaining stability and watertight integrity.

Importance of securing flooding and maintaining watertight boundaries.

Actions to be taken aboard a ship in the event of an explosion, grounding, collision or fire

Damage control techniques consistent with equipment found on board including the ship bilge systems and pumps.

Section B-V/3

Guidance regarding the training and qualifications of masters, officers, ratings and other personnel on ships subject to the IGF Code

Person with immediate responsibility

1 The term "person with immediate responsibility" as used in regulation V/3, paragraphs 7 and 9 means a person being in a decision-making capacity with respect to handling of fuel addressed by the IGF Code or other fuel-related operations.

Proof of qualification

2 The master of every ship subject to the IGF Code should ensure that the officer or the person with immediate responsibility for the fuel on board possesses the appropriate certificate, issued or endorsed or validated as required by regulation V/3, and has had adequate recent practical experience on board an appropriate type of ship to permit that officer or person to safely perform the duties assigned.

Guidance regarding seagoing service

3 The purpose of qualifying shipboard service is to provide training and knowledge for the safe use of fuels addressed by the IGF Code.

4 To satisfy the experience appropriate to their duties on the ship on which they serve as referred to in regulation V/3, onboard training should:

- **.1** emphasize practical "hands on experience" and be related to the employment of the seafarer, i.e. the training of deck and engineering departments may be different;
- **.2** be under the supervision of personnel qualified and experienced in the handling, characteristics and safety procedures of the fuels being used by the ship; and
- **.3** be on board a ship carrying fuels relative to the Certificate of Proficiency being sought and should be such that the specialized equipment is brought into operation for the use of the fuels addressed by the IGF Code.

5 The onboard training programme must in no way affect the safe running or the seaworthiness of the ship.

Section B-V/a*

Guidance regarding additional training for masters and chief mates of large ships and ships with unusual manoeuvring characteristics

1 It is important that masters and chief mates should have had relevant experience and training before assuming the duties of master or chief mate of large ships or ships having unusual manoeuvring and handling

* Note there are no corresponding regulations in the Convention or sections in part A of the Code for sections B-V/a, B-V/b, B-V/c, B-V/d, B-V/e, B-V/f and B-V/g.

characteristics significantly different from those in which they have recently served. Such characteristics will generally be found in ships which are of considerable deadweight or length or of special design or of high speed.

2 Prior to their appointment to such a ship, masters and chief mates should:

.1 be informed of the ship's handling characteristics by the company, particularly in relation to the knowledge, understanding and proficiency listed under ship manoeuvring and handling in column 2 of table A-II/2 – Specification of the minimum standard of competence for masters and chief mates on ships of 500 gross tonnage or more; and

.2 be made thoroughly familiar with the use of all navigational and manoeuvring aids fitted in the ship concerned, including their capabilities and limitations.

3 Before initially assuming command of one of the ships referred to above, the prospective master should have sufficient and appropriate general experience as master or chief mate, and either:

.1 have sufficient and appropriate experience manoeuvring the same ship under supervision or in manoeuvring a ship having similar manoeuvring characteristics; or

.2 have attended an approved ship handling simulator course on an installation capable of simulating the manoeuvring characteristics of such a ship.*

4 The additional training and qualifications of masters and chief mates of dynamically supported and high-speed craft should be in accordance with the relevant guidelines of the IMO Code of Safety for Dynamically Supported Craft and the IMO International Codes of Safety for High-Speed Craft (1994 HSC Code and 2000 HSC Code), as appropriate.

Section B-V/b*

Guidance regarding training of officers and ratings responsible for cargo handling on ships carrying dangerous and hazardous substances in solid form in bulk

1 Training should be divided into two parts, a general part on the principles involved and a part on the application of such principles to ship operation. All training and instruction should be given by properly qualified and suitably experienced personnel and cover at least the subjects given in paragraphs 2 to 14 hereunder.

Principles

Characteristics and properties

2 The important physical characteristics and chemical properties of dangerous and hazardous substances, sufficient to give a basic understanding of the intrinsic hazards and risks involved.

Classification of materials possessing chemical hazards

3 IMO dangerous goods classes 4 to 9 and the hazards associated with each class; and materials hazardous only in bulk (MHB) outlined in the International Maritime Solid Bulk Cargoes (IMSBC) Code.

Health hazards

4 Dangers from skin contact, inhalation, ingestion and radiation.

Conventions, regulations and recommendations

5 General familiarization with the relevant requirements of chapters II-2 and VII of the 1974 SOLAS Convention, as amended.

* The relevant IMO Model Course(s) may be of assistance in the preparation of courses.

6 General use of and familiarization with the International Maritime Solid Bulk Cargoes (IMSBC) Code, with particular reference to:

.1 safety of personnel, including safety equipment, measuring instruments, their use and practical application and interpretation of results;

.2 hazards from cargoes which have a tendency to shift; and

.3 materials possessing chemical hazards.

Shipboard application

Class 4.1 – Flammable solids
Class 4.2 – Substances liable to spontaneous combustion
Class 4.3 – Substances which, in contact with water, emit flammable gases

7 Carriage, stowage and control of temperature to prevent decomposition and possible explosion; stowage categories; general stowage precautions, including those applicable to self-reactive and related substances; segregation requirements to prevent heating and ignition; the emission of poisonous or flammable gases and the formation of explosive mixtures.

Class 5.1 – Oxidizing substances

8 Carriage, stowage and control of temperature to prevent decomposition and possible explosion; stowage categories; general stowage precautions and segregation requirements to ensure separation from combustible material, from acids and heat sources to prevent fire, explosion and the formation of toxic gases.

Class 6.1 – Toxic substances

9 Contamination of foodstuffs, working areas and living accommodation and ventilation.

Class 7 – Radioactive material

10 Transport index; types of ores and concentrates; stowage and segregation from persons, undeveloped photographic film and plates and foodstuffs; stowage categories; general stowage requirements; special stowage requirements; segregation requirements and separation distances; segregation from other dangerous goods.

Class 8 – Corrosive substances

11 Dangers from wetted substances.

Class 9 – Miscellaneous dangerous substances and articles

12 Examples and associated hazards; the hazards of materials hazardous only in bulk (IMSBC Code); general and specific stowage precautions; working and transport precautions; segregation requirements.

Safety precautions and emergency procedures

13 Electrical safety in cargo spaces; precautions to be taken for entry into enclosed spaces that may contain oxygen-depleted, poisonous or flammable atmospheres; the possible effects of fire in shipments of substances of each class; use of the Emergency Response Procedures for Ships Carrying Dangerous Goods; emergency plans and procedures to be followed in case of incidents involving dangerous and hazardous substances and the use of individual entries in the International Maritime Solid Bulk Cargoes (IMSBC) Code, as appropriate, in this respect.

Medical first aid

14 The IMO Medical First Aid Guide for Use in Accidents Involving Dangerous Goods (MFAG) and its use and application in association with other guides and medical advice by radio.

Section B-V/c*

Guidance regarding training of officers and ratings responsible for cargo handling on ships carrying dangerous and hazardous substances in packaged form

1 Training should be divided into two parts, a general part on the principles involved and a part on the application of such principles to ship operation. All training and instruction should be given by properly qualified and suitably experienced personnel and cover at least the subjects given in paragraphs 2 to 19 hereunder.

Principles

Characteristics and properties

2 The important physical characteristics and chemical properties of dangerous and hazardous substances, sufficient to give a basic understanding of the intrinsic hazards and risks involved.

Classification of dangerous and hazardous substances and materials possessing chemical hazards

3 IMO dangerous goods classes 1 to 9 and the hazards associated with each class.

Health hazards

4 Dangers from skin contact, inhalation, ingestion and radiation.

Conventions, regulations and recommendations

5 General familiarization with the relevant requirements of chapters II-2 and VII of the 1974 SOLAS Convention and of Annex III of MARPOL 73/78, including its implementation through the IMDG Code.

Use of and familiarization with the International Maritime Dangerous Goods (IMDG) Code

6 General knowledge of the requirements of the IMDG Code concerning declaration, documentation, packing, labelling and placarding; freight container and vehicle packing; portable tanks, tank containers and road tank vehicles, and other transport units used for dangerous substances.

7 Knowledge of identification, marking and labelling for stowage, securing, separation and segregation in different ship types mentioned in the IMDG Code.

8 Safety of personnel, including safety equipment, measuring instruments, their use and practical application and the interpretation of results.

Shipboard application

Class 1 – Explosives

9 The six hazard divisions and 13 compatibility groups; packagings and magazines used for carriage of explosives; structural serviceability of freight containers and vehicles; stowage provisions, including specific

* Note there are no corresponding regulations in the Convention or sections in part A of the Code for sections B-V/a, B-V/b, B-V/c, B-V/d, B-V/e, B-V/f and B-V/g.

arrangements for on-deck and under-deck stowage; segregation from dangerous goods of other classes within class 1 and from non-dangerous goods; transport and stowage on passenger ships; suitability of cargo spaces; security precautions; precautions to be taken during loading and unloading.

Class 2 – Gases (compressed, liquefied, or dissolved under pressure), flammable, non-flammable, non-toxic and toxic

10 Types of pressure vessels and portable tanks, including relief and closing devices used; stowage categories; general stowage precautions, including those for flammable and poisonous gases and gases which are marine pollutants.

Class 3 – Flammable liquids

11 Packagings, tank containers, portable tanks and road tank vehicles; stowage categories, including the specific requirements for plastics receptacles; general stowage precautions, including those for marine pollutants; segregation requirements; precautions to be taken when carrying flammable liquids at elevated temperatures.

Class 4.1 – Flammable solids
Class 4.2 – Substances liable to spontaneous combustion
Class 4.3 – Substances which, in contact with water, emit flammable gases

12 Types of packagings; carriage and stowage under controlled temperatures to prevent decomposition and possible explosion; stowage categories; general stowage precautions, including those applicable to self-reactive and related substances, desensitized explosives and marine pollutants; segregation requirements to prevent heating and ignition, the emission of poisonous or flammable gases and the formation of explosive mixtures.

Class 5.1 – Oxidizing substances
Class 5.2 – Organic peroxides

13 Types of packagings; carriage and stowage under controlled temperatures to prevent decomposition and possible explosion; stowage categories; general stowage precautions, including those applicable to marine pollutants; segregation requirements to ensure separation from combustible material, from acids and heat sources to prevent fire, explosion and the formation of toxic gases; precautions to minimize friction and impact which can initiate decomposition.

Class 6.1 – Toxic substances
Class 6.2 – Infectious substances

14 Types of packagings; stowage categories; general stowage precautions, including those applicable to toxic, flammable liquids and marine pollutants; segregation requirements, especially considering that the characteristic common to these substances is their ability to cause death or serious injury to human health; decontamination measures in the event of spillage.

Class 7 – Radioactive material

15 Types of packagings; transport index in relation to stowage and segregation; stowage and segregation from persons, undeveloped photographic film and plates and foodstuffs; stowage categories; general stowage requirements; segregation requirements and separation distances; segregation from other dangerous goods.

Class 8 – Corrosive substances

16 Types of packagings; stowage categories; general stowage precautions, including those applicable to corrosive, flammable liquids and marine pollutants; segregation requirements, especially considering that the characteristic common to these substances is their ability to cause severe damage to living tissue.

Class 9 – Miscellaneous dangerous substances and articles

17 Examples of hazards, including marine pollution.

Safety precautions and emergency procedures

18 Electrical safety in cargo spaces; precautions to be taken for entry into enclosed spaces that may contain oxygen-depleted, poisonous or flammable atmospheres; the possible effects of spillage or fire in shipments of substances of each class; consideration of events on deck or below deck; use of the IMO Emergency Response Procedures for Ships Carrying Dangerous Goods; emergency plans and procedures to be followed in case of incidents involving dangerous substances.

Medical first aid

19 The IMO Medical First Aid Guide for Use in Accidents Involving Dangerous Goods (MFAG) and its use and application in association with other guides and medical advice by radio.

Section B-V/d*

Guidance on application of the provisions of the STCW Convention to mobile offshore units (MOUs)

1 The provisions of the STCW Convention apply to the maritime personnel of self-propelled MOUs proceeding on voyages.

2 The provisions of the STCW Convention do not apply to non-self-propelled MOUs or to MOUs on station.

3 When considering appropriate standards of training and certification when an MOU is on station, the country of registry should take account of relevant IMO recommendations. In particular, all maritime crew members on self-propelled MOUs and, where required, on other units should meet the requirements of the STCW Convention, as amended.

4 Self-propelled MOUs proceeding on international voyages are required to carry safe manning documents.

5 MOUs on station are subject to the national legislation of the coastal State in whose Exclusive Economic Zone (EEZ) they are operating. Such coastal States should also take account of relevant IMO recommendations and should not prescribe higher standards for MOUs registered in other countries than the standards applied to MOUs registered in that coastal State.

6 All special personnel employed on board MOUs (whether or not self-propelled) should be provided with appropriate familiarization and basic training in accordance with relevant IMO recommendations.

Section B-V/e†

Guidance regarding training and qualifications of masters and officers in charge of a navigational watch on board offshore supply vessels

1 It is important that masters and officers involved in offshore supply operations should have relevant experience or training before assuming their duties on offshore supply vessels. The focus should be on onboard operational experience or a combination of operational experience and simulator training.

* Note there are no corresponding regulations in the Convention or sections in part A of the Code for sections B-V/a, B-V/b, B-V/c, B-V/d, B-V/e, B-V/f and B-V/g.

† Note there are no corresponding regulations in the Convention or sections in part A of the Code for sections B-V/a, B-V/b, B-V/c, B-V/d, B-V/e, B-V/f and B-V/g.

2 Masters and officers should understand the unique manoeuvring and handling characteristics common to offshore supply vessels.

3 Prior to performing offshore supply operations, the master and officers should:

.1 have knowledge of the offshore industry and the terms used in the various operations;

.2 understand the importance of maintaining a safe working distance at all times when working in an offshore location/installation;

.3 have knowledge of vessel manoeuvring and station-keeping under various weather conditions;

.4 understand the specific design parameters of the vessels; and

.5 understand the need to have unrestricted oversight and views of work areas.

4 While on board an offshore supply vessel, the master and officers should:

.1 have knowledge of the handling characteristics and behaviour of vessels fitted with various propulsion arrangements; and

.2 be capable of operating the offshore supply vessel in close proximity to an offshore installation and other vessels.

5 Masters should understand the need for other personnel on board who are involved in performing offshore supply operations to be familiarized with their duties.

Offshore supply vessels performing anchor-handling operations

6 It is important that masters and officers in charge of a navigational watch on board offshore supply vessels involved in anchor-handling operations have relevant experience and training.

7 Prior to performing anchor-handling operations, masters and officers in charge of a navigational watch should:

.1 be well informed of the ship's handling characteristics in relation to anchor-handling, including, but not limited to:

.1.1 navigation and position-holding;

.1.2 ship-handling;

.1.3 thorough knowledge of the stability of offshore supply vessels, in particular the combination of low GZ_{max}, low open deck and large external forces. Use of loading calculators and the conflict between a rigid and stiff ship and good work environment on deck. Potential reduction of stability from use of anti-rolling devices; and

.1.4 operations in hazardous oil-field areas, including locating any pipelines or other structures on the seabed in the area where anchors or other mooring equipment is likely to be used; and

.2 be made thoroughly familiar with the use of all instruments and systems fitted in the ship concerned and involved in anchor-handling, including their capabilities and limitations, including, but not limited to:

.2.1 use of various thrusters, conventional or azimuth propulsion;

.2.2 pickup, handling, heavy lifting, towing out, anchor-handling and laying of anchors for offshore rigs, barges and installations;

.2.3 towing of rigs, barges and other vessels;

.2.4 operation of lifting and towing winches with up to 600 metric tons bollard pull;

.2.5 detailed thorough knowledge of the basis of operation of towing- and anchor-handling winches; in particular, functions of load-limiting devices and release systems and associated equipment as towing pins and stoppers; and

.2.6 the significant difference between emergency release of towing hooks and winches.

8 Masters and officers in charge of a navigational watch when in charge of anchor-handling should have sufficient and appropriate training and experience by having been supervised during a number of Rig-moves, as deemed appropriate by the Administration. Training may be supplemented by appropriate simulator training.

Section B-V/f*

Guidance on the training and experience for personnel operating dynamic positioning systems†

1 Dynamic positioning is defined as the system whereby a self-propelled vessel's position and heading is automatically controlled by using its own propulsion units.

2 Personnel engaged in operating a Dynamic Positioning (DP) system should receive relevant training and practical experience. Theoretical elements of this training should enable Dynamic Positioning Operators (DPOs) to understand the operation of the DP system and its components. Knowledge, understanding and experience gained should enable personnel to operate vessels safely in DP, with due regard for safety of life at sea and protection of the marine environment.

3 The content of training and experience should include coverage of the following components of a DP system:

.1 DP control station;

.2 power generation and management;

.3 propulsion units;

.4 position reference systems;

.5 heading reference systems;

.6 environmental reference systems; and

.7 external force reference systems, such as hawser tension gauges.

4 Training and experience should cover the range of routine DP operations, as well as the handling of DP faults, failures, incidents and emergencies, to ensure that operations are continued or terminated safely. Training should not be limited to DPOs and DP masters only; other personnel on board, such as electro-technical and engineer officers, may require additional training and experience to ensure that they are able to carry out their duties on a DP vessel. Consideration should be given to conducting appropriate DP drills as a part of onboard training and experience. DPOs should be knowledgeable of the type and purpose of documentation associated with DP operations, such as operational manuals, Failure Modes and Effects Analysis (FMEAs) and capability plots.

5 All training should be given by properly qualified and suitably experienced personnel.

6 Upon appointment to a vessel operating in DP mode, the master, DPOs and other DP-trained personnel should be familiarized with the specific equipment fitted on and the characteristics of the vessel. Particular consideration should be given to the nature of the work of the vessel and the importance of the DP system to this work.

---

* Note there are no corresponding regulations in the Convention or sections in part A of the Code for sections B-V/a, B-V/b, B-V/c, B-V/d, B-V/e, B-V/f and B-V/g.

† Refer to MSC.1/Circ.738/Rev.2 on Guidelines for Dynamic Positioning System (DP) operator training for training and experience of key DP personnel

Section B-V/g*

Guidance regarding training of masters and officers for ships operating in polar waters†

1 It is important that masters, officers in charge of a navigational watch and officers in charge of an engineering watch on board ships operating in polar waters should have relevant experience and training, as follows:

- **.1** Prior to being assigned duties on board such ships:
  - **.1.1** For masters and officers in charge of a navigational watch, the training should provide basic knowledge on at least the subjects given in paragraphs 2 to 11 hereunder; and
  - **.1.2** For officers in charge of an engineering watch, the training should provide basic knowledge on at least the subjects given in paragraphs 3, 6, 10 and 11 hereunder.
- **.2** Masters and Chief Engineer Officers should have sufficient and appropriate experience in operating ships in polar waters.

Ice characteristics – ice areas

2 Interpretation of different ice-charts and awareness of limitations in meteorology and oceanography data, ice physics, formation, growth, ageing and stage of melt; ice types and concentrations; ice pressure; friction from snow-covered ice; implications of spray-icing and icing up; precautions against icing up and mitigation of consequences; ice regimes in different regions and different seasons, including the differences between the Arctic and the Antarctic; recognition of consequences of rapid change in ice and weather conditions; movement of icebergs and pack ice.

Ship's performance in ice and cold climate

3 Vessel characteristics; vessel types, hull designs; ice-strengthening requirements; ice-class of different classification societies – polar class and local regulations; limitations of ice-classes; winterization and preparedness of vessel; low-temperature system performance.

Voyage and passage planning for a ship in ice‡

4 Development of safe routeing and passage planning to avoid ice where possible, including interpreting various forms of ice imagery and data to assist in the preparation of a strategic passage planning; entering ice from open water to avoid icebergs and dangerous ice conditions; navigation, determining when it is safe or not safe to enter areas containing ice or icebergs due to darkness, swell, fog or pressure ice.

Operating and handling a ship in ice

5 Preparations and risk assessment before approaching ice-infested waters; unassisted operation of vessels with different ice-class in different ice-types; safe speed in the presence of ice and icebergs; communications with an icebreaker and other vessels; navigation in various ice concentrations and coverage; awareness of the increase in energy of movement; use of icebergs for shelter and access through packed ice.

6 Use of different type of propulsion system and rudder, including awareness of system strength and capacity limitations; use of heeling and trim systems, engine loads and cooling problems.

---

* Note there are no corresponding regulations in the Convention or sections in part A of the Code for sections B-V/a, B-V/b, B-V/c, B-V/d, B-V/e, B-V/f and B-V/g.

† Refer to IMO Assembly resolution A.1024(26) on *Guidelines for ships operating in polar waters*.

‡ Refer to IMO Assembly resolution A.999(25) on *Guidelines on voyage planning for passenger ships operating in remote areas*.

Regulations and recommendations

7 Local requirements for entering different regions, including the Antarctic Treaty; international regulations and recommendations.

Equipment limitations

8 Use of and hazards associated with terrestrial navigational aids in polar waters; high-latitude compass errors; discrimination of radar targets and ice-features in ice-clutter; limitations of electronic positioning systems at high latitude; limitations in nautical charts and pilot descriptions; limitations in communication systems.

Safety precautions and emergency procedures

9 Availability of hydrographic data sufficient for safe navigation; precautions when navigating in poorly charted waters; limitations of search and rescue readiness and responsibility, including GMDSS area A4 and its SAR communication facility limitation; awareness of contingency planning; knowledge of towing procedures; value of contact with other ships and local SAR organization; recognizing dangers when crews are exposed to low temperatures; procedures and techniques for abandoning the ship and survival on the ice; crew-fatigue problems due to noise and vibrations; carriage of additional resources such as bunkers, food and extra clothing; awareness of the additional severity of consequences of incidents in polar waters.

10 Establishing safe working procedures; awareness of the most common hull and equipment damages and how to avoid them; fire-fighting systems limitations.

Environmental considerations

11 Sensitive sea areas regarding discharge; areas where shipping is prohibited or should be avoided; Special Areas in MARPOL; oil-spill equipment limitations; plan for coping with increased volumes of garbage, bilge water, sludge, sewage, etc.; consequences of pollution in a cold climate.

Chapter VI
Guidance regarding emergency, occupational safety, security, medical care and survival functions

Section B-VI/1
Guidance regarding mandatory requirements for safety familiarization and basic training and instruction for all seafarers

Fire prevention and fire fighting

1 The training in fire prevention and fire fighting required by section A-VI/1 should include at least the theoretical and practical elements itemized in paragraphs 2 to 4 hereunder.*

Theoretical training

2 The theoretical training should cover:

.1 the three elements of fire and explosion (the fire triangle): fuel; source of ignition; oxygen;

.2 ignition sources: chemical; biological; physical;

.3 flammable materials: flammability; ignition point; burning temperature; burning speed; thermal value; lower flammable limit (LFL); upper flammable limit (UFL); flammable range; inerting; static electricity; flashpoint; auto-ignition;

.4 fire hazard and spread of fire by radiation, convection and conduction;

.5 reactivity;

.6 classification of fires and applicable extinguishing agents;

.7 main causes of fire on board ships: oil leakage in engine-room; cigarettes; overheating (bearings); galley appliances (stoves, flues, fryers, hotplates, etc.); spontaneous ignition (cargo, wastes, etc.); hot work (welding, cutting, etc.); electrical apparatus (short circuit, non-professional repairs); reaction, self-heating and auto-ignition; arson; static electricity;

.8 fire prevention;

.9 fire- and smoke-detection systems; automatic fire alarms;

.10 fire-fighting equipment, including:

.10.1 fixed installations on board and their locations; fire mains, hydrants; international shore connection; smothering installations, carbon dioxide (CO_2), foam; pressure water spray system in special category spaces, etc.; automatic sprinkler system; emergency fire pump; emergency generator; chemical powder applicants; general outline of required and available mobile apparatus; high-pressure fog system; high-expansion foam; new developments and equipment;

.10.2 firefighter's outfit, personal equipment; breathing apparatus; resuscitation apparatus; smoke helmet or mask; fireproof lifeline and harness; and their location on board; and

.10.3 general equipment, including fire hoses, nozzles, connections, fire axes; portable fire extinguishers; fire blankets;

* The relevant IMO Model Course(s) may be of assistance in the preparation of courses.

.11 construction and arrangements, including escape routes; means for gas-freeing tanks; Class A, B and C divisions; inert gas systems;

.12 ship fire-fighting organization, including general alarm; fire control plans, muster stations and duties of individuals; communications, including ship–shore when in port; personnel safety procedures; periodic shipboard drills; patrol systems;

.13 practical knowledge of resuscitation methods;

.14 fire-fighting methods, including sounding the alarm; locating and isolating; jettisoning; inhibiting; cooling; smothering; extinguishing; reflash watch; smoke extraction; and

.15 fire-fighting agents, including water, solid jet, spray, fog, flooding; high-, medium- and low-expansion foam; carbon dioxide (CO_2); aqueous-film-forming foam (AFFF); dry chemical powder; new developments and equipment.

Practical training

3 The practical training given below should take place in spaces which provide truly realistic training conditions (e.g., simulated shipboard conditions), and whenever possible and practical should also be carried out in darkness as well as by daylight and should allow the trainees to acquire the ability to:

.1 use various types of portable fire extinguishers;

.2 use self-contained breathing apparatus;

.3 extinguish smaller fires, e.g., electrical fires, oil fires and propane fires;

.4 extinguish extensive fires with water (jet and spray nozzles);

.5 extinguish fires with either foam, powder or any other suitable chemical agent;

.6 enter and pass through, with lifeline but without breathing apparatus, a compartment into which high-expansion foam has been injected;

.7 fight fire in smoke-filled enclosed spaces, wearing self-contained breathing apparatus;

.8 extinguish fire with water fog or any other suitable fire-fighting agent in an accommodation room or simulated engine-room with fire and heavy smoke;

.9 extinguish an oil fire with fog applicator and spray nozzles; dry chemical powder or foam applicators; and

.10 effect a rescue in a smoke-filled space, wearing breathing apparatus.

General

4 Trainees should also be made aware of the necessity of maintaining a state of readiness on board.

Elementary first aid*

5 The training in elementary first aid required by regulation VI/1 as part of the basic training should be given at an early stage in vocational training, preferably during pre-sea training, to enable seafarers to take immediate action upon encountering an accident or other medical emergency until the arrival of a person with first-aid skills or the person in charge of medical care on board.

* The relevant IMO Model Course(s) may be of assistance in the preparation of courses.

Chapter VIII
Guidance regarding watchkeeping

Section B-VIII/1
Guidance regarding fitness for duty

Prevention of fatigue

1 In observing the rest period requirements, "overriding operational conditions" should be construed to mean only essential shipboard work which cannot be delayed for safety, security or environmental reasons or which could not reasonably have been anticipated at the commencement of the voyage.

2 Although there is no universally accepted technical definition of fatigue, everyone involved in ship operations should be alert to the factors which can contribute to fatigue, including, but not limited to, those identified by the Organization,* and take them into account when making decisions on ship operations.

3 In applying regulation VIII/1, the following should be taken into account:

.1 provisions made to prevent fatigue should ensure that excessive or unreasonable overall working hours are not undertaken. In particular, the minimum rest periods specified in section A-VIII/1 should not be interpreted as implying that all other hours may be devoted to watchkeeping or other duties;

.2 the frequency and length of leave periods, and the granting of compensatory leave, are material factors in preventing fatigue from building up over a period of time; and

.3 the provisions may be varied for ships on short sea voyages, provided special safety arrangements are put in place.

4 Exceptions provided for in section A-VIII/1, paragraph 9, should be construed to mean the exceptions laid down by the ILO Convention on Seafarers' Hours of Work and the Manning of Ships, 1996 (No.180) or the Maritime Labour Convention, 2006, when it enters into force. The circumstances under which such exceptions are applied should be defined by the Parties.

5 Based on information received as a result of investigating maritime casualties, Administrations should keep their provisions on prevention of fatigue under review.

Prevention of drug and alcohol abuse

6 Drug and alcohol abuse directly affect the fitness and ability of a seafarer to perform watchkeeping duties or duties that involve designated safety, prevention of pollution and security duties. Seafarers found to be under the influence of drugs or alcohol should not be permitted to perform watchkeeping duties or duties that involve designated safety, prevention of pollution or security duties, until they are no longer impaired in their ability to perform those duties.

7 Administrations should ensure that adequate measures are taken to prevent alcohol and drugs from impairing the ability of watchkeeping personnel and those whose duties involve designated safety, prevention of pollution and security duties, and should establish screening programmes as necessary which:

.1 identify drug and alcohol abuse;

* See the annex to IMO Assembly resolution A.772(18) on *Fatigue factors in manning and safety*, paragraphs 2 to 4.4.1, and MSC/Circ.1014 on Guidance on fatigue mitigation and management.

.2 respect the dignity, privacy, confidentiality and fundamental legal rights of the individuals concerned; and

.3 take into account relevant international guidelines.

8 Companies should consider the implementation of a clearly written policy of drug and alcohol abuse prevention, including prohibition to consume alcohol within four hours prior to serving as a member of a watch either by inclusion in the company's quality-management system or by means of providing adequate information and education to the seafarers.

9 Those involved in establishing drug and alcohol abuse prevention programmes should take into account the guidance contained in the ILO publication *Drug and Alcohol Prevention Programmes in the Maritime Industry (A Manual for Planners),*[*] as may be amended.

Section B-VIII/2

Guidance regarding watchkeeping arrangements and principles to be observed

1 The following operational guidance should be taken into account by companies, masters and watchkeeping officers.

Part 1 – Guidance on certification

(No provisions)

Part 2 – Guidance on voyage planning

(No provisions)

Part 3 – Watchkeeping principles in general

(No provisions)

Part 4 – Guidance on watchkeeping at sea

Part 4-1 – Guidance on keeping a navigational watch

Introduction

2 Particular guidance may be necessary for special types of ships as well as for ships carrying hazardous, dangerous, toxic or highly flammable cargoes. The master should provide this operational guidance as appropriate.

3 It is essential that officers in charge of the navigational watch appreciate that the efficient performance of their duties is necessary in the interests of the safety of life, security and property at sea and of preventing pollution of the marine environment.

Anchor watch

4 The master of every ship at an unsheltered anchorage, at an open roadstead or any other virtually "at sea" conditions in accordance with chapter VIII, section A-VIII/2, part 4-1, paragraph 51, of the STCW Code,

[*] Annex III of this manual includes Guiding principles on drug and alcohol testing procedures for worldwide application in the maritime industry. These guiding principles were adopted by the Joint ILO/WHO Committee on the Health of Seafarers (May 1993).

should ensure that watchkeeping arrangements are adequate for maintaining a safe watch at all times. A deck officer should at all times maintain responsibility for a safe anchor watch.

5 In determining the watchkeeping arrangements, and commensurate with maintaining the ship's safety and security and the protection of the marine environment, the master should take into account all pertinent circumstances and conditions such as:

.1 maintaining a continuous state of vigilance by sight and hearing as well as by all other available means;

.2 ship-to-ship and ship-to-shore communication requirements;

.3 the prevailing weather, sea, ice and current conditions;

.4 the need to continuously monitor the ship's position;

.5 the nature, size and characteristics of anchorage;

.6 traffic conditions;

.7 situations which might affect the security of the ship;

.8 loading and discharging operations;

.9 the designation of stand-by crew members; and

.10 the procedure to alert the master and maintain engine readiness.

Part 4-2 – Guidance on keeping an engineering watch

6 Particular guidance may be necessary for special types of propulsion systems or ancillary equipment and for ships carrying hazardous, dangerous, toxic or highly flammable materials or other special types of cargo. The chief engineer officer should provide this operational guidance as appropriate.

7 It is essential that officers in charge of the engineering watch appreciate that the efficient performance of engineering watchkeeping duties is necessary in the interest of the safety of life and property at sea and of preventing pollution of the marine environment.

8 The relieving officer, before assuming charge of the engineering watch, should:

.1 be familiar with the location and use of the equipment provided for the safety of life in a hazardous or toxic environment;

.2 ascertain that materials for the administration of emergency medical first aid are readily available, particularly those required for the treatment of burns and scalds; and

.3 when in port, safely anchored or moored, be aware of:

.3.1 cargo activities, the status of maintenance and repair functions and all other operations affecting the watch, and

.3.2 the auxiliary machinery in use for passenger or crew accommodation services, cargo operations, operational water supplies and exhaust systems.

Part 4-3 – Guidance on keeping a radio watch

General

9 Among other things, the Radio Regulations require that each ship radio station is licensed, is under the ultimate authority of the master or other person responsible for the ship and is only operated under the control of adequately qualified personnel. The Radio Regulations also require that a distress alert shall only be sent on the authority of the master or other person responsible for the ship.

10 The master should bear in mind that all personnel assigned responsibility for sending a distress alert must be instructed with regard to, be knowledgeable of, and be able to operate properly all radio equipment on the ship, as required by regulation I/14, paragraph 1.5. This should be recorded in the deck or radio log-book.

Watchkeeping

11 In addition to the requirements concerning radio watchkeeping, the master of every seagoing ship should ensure that:

.1 the ship's radio station is adequately manned for the purpose of exchanging general communications – in particular public correspondence, taking into account the constraints imposed by the duties of those authorized to operate it; and

.2 the radio equipment provided on board and, where fitted, the reserve sources of energy are maintained in an efficient working condition.

12 Necessary instruction and information on use of radio equipment and procedures for distress and safety purposes should be given periodically to all relevant crew members by the person designated in the muster list to have primary responsibility for radiocommunications during distress incidents. This should be recorded in the radio log.

13 The master of every ship not subject to SOLAS, 1974, should require that radio watchkeeping is adequately maintained as determined by the Administration, taking into account the Radio Regulations.

Operational

14 Prior to sailing, the radio operator designated as having primary responsibility for radiocommunications during distress incidents should ensure that:

.1 all distress and safety radio equipment and the reserve source of energy are in an efficient working condition, and that this is recorded in the radio log;

.2 all documents required by international agreement, notices to ship radio stations and additional documents required by the Administration are available and are corrected in accordance with the latest supplements, and that any discrepancy is reported to the master;

.3 the radio clock is correctly set against standard time signals;

.4 antennae are correctly positioned, undamaged and properly connected; and

.5 to the extent practicable, routine weather and navigational warning messages for the area in which the ship will be navigating are updated together with those for other areas requested by the master, and that such messages are passed to the master.

15 On sailing and opening the station, the radio operator on watch should:

.1 listen on the appropriate distress frequencies for any possible existing distress situation; and

.2 send a traffic report (name, position and destination, etc.) to the local coast station and any other appropriate coast station from which general communications may be expected.

16 While the station is open, the radio operator on watch should:

.1 check the radio clock against standard time signals at least once a day;

.2 send a traffic report when entering and on leaving the service area of a coast station from which general communications might be expected; and

.3 transmit reports to ship reporting systems in accordance with the instructions of the master.

17 While at sea, the radio operator designated as having primary responsibility for radiocommunications during distress incidents should ensure the proper functioning of:

.1 the digital selective calling (DSC) distress and safety radio equipment by means of a test call at least once each week; and

.2 the distress and safety radio equipment by means of a test at least once each day but without radiating any signal.

The results of these tests should be recorded in the radio log.

18 The radio operator designated to handle general communications should ensure that an effective watch is maintained on those frequencies on which communications are likely to be exchanged, having regard to the position of the ship in relation to those coast stations and to coast earth stations from which traffic may be expected. When exchanging traffic, radio operators should follow the relevant ITU recommendations.

19 When closing the station on arrival at a port, the radio operator on watch should advise the local coast station and other coast stations with which contact has been maintained of the ship's arrival and of the closing of the station.

20 When closing the radio station, the radio operator designated as having primary responsibility for radiocommunications during distress incidents should:

.1 ensure that transmitting antennae are earthed; and

.2 check that the reserve sources of energy are sufficiently charged.

Distress alerts and procedures

21 The distress alert or distress call has absolute priority over all other transmissions. All stations which receive such signals are required by the Radio Regulations to immediately cease all transmissions capable of interfering with distress communications.

22 In the case of a distress affecting own ship, the radio operator designated as having primary responsibility for radiocommunications during distress incidents should immediately assume responsibility for following the procedures of the Radio Regulations and relevant ITU-R Recommendations.

23 On receiving a distress alert:

.1 the radio operator on watch should alert the master and, if appropriate, the radio operator designated as having primary responsibility for radiocommunications during distress incidents; and

.2 the radio operator designated as having primary responsibility for radiocommunications during distress incidents should evaluate the situation and immediately assume responsibility for following the procedures of the Radio Regulations and relevant ITU-R Recommendations.

Urgency messages

24 In cases of urgency affecting own ship, the radio operator designated as having responsibility for radiocommunications during distress incidents should immediately assume responsibility for following the procedures of the Radio Regulations and relevant ITU-R Recommendations.

25 In cases of communications relating to medical advice, the radio operator designated as having primary responsibility for radiocommunications during distress incidents should follow the procedures of the Radio Regulations and adhere to the conditions as published in the relevant international documentation (see paragraph 14.2) or as specified by the satellite service provider.

26 In cases of communications relating to medical transports, as defined in the Protocol additional to the Geneva Conventions of 12 August 1949, and relating to the protection of victims of international armed conflicts (Protocol I), the radio operator designated as having primary responsibility for radiocommunication during distress incidents should follow the procedures of the Radio Regulations.

27 On receiving an urgency message, the radio operator on watch should alert the master and, if appropriate, the radio operator designated as having primary responsibility for radiocommunications during distress incidents.

Safety messages

28 When a safety message is to be transmitted, the master and the radio operator on watch should follow the procedures of the Radio Regulations.

29 On receiving a safety message, the radio operator on watch should note its content and act in accordance with the master's instructions.

30 Bridge-to-bridge communications should be exchanged on VHF channel 13. Bridge-to-bridge communications are described as "Intership Navigation Safety Communications" in the Radio Regulations.

Radio records

31 Additional entries in the radio log should be made in accordance with paragraphs 10, 12, 14, 17 and 33.

32 Unauthorized transmissions and incidents of harmful interference should, if possible, be identified, recorded in the radio log and brought to the attention of the Administration in compliance with the Radio Regulations, together with an appropriate extract from the radio log.

Battery maintenance

33 Batteries providing a source of energy for any part of the radio installation, including those associated with uninterrupted power supplies, are the responsibility of the radio operator designated as having primary responsibility for radiocommunications during distress incidents and should be:

- **.1** tested on-load and off-load daily and, where necessary, brought up to the fully charged condition;
- **.2** tested once per week by means of a hydrometer where practicable, or, where a hydrometer cannot be used, by a suitable load test; and
- **.3** checked once per month for the security of each battery and its connections and the condition of the batteries and their compartment or compartments.

The results of these tests should be recorded in the radio log.

Part 5 – Guidance on watchkeeping in port

(No provisions)

Revised Edition

Great Sand Dunes National Park and Preserve

VALLEY *of the* DUNES

PHOTOGRAPHY BY Bob Rozinski AND Wendy Shattil

TEXT BY Audrey DeLella Benedict

FOREWORD BY Former Senator Ken Salazar

CLOUD RIDGE PUBLISHING

I have always told people that the San Luis Valley is more than home to me.

IT IS A SPIRITUAL PLACE UNLIKE ANY OTHER ON EARTH.

The smell of the earth and the sight of the mountains at Los Rincones take me back to my childhood, and beyond. My family helped settle the San Luis Valley in the mid-1800s after first helping to settle the City of Faith, Santa Fe, more than 400 years ago. My ancestors traveled north into the Sangre de Cristo Mountains until they came to the valley where my family's ranch still stands today, near the Rio Grande.

One of the strongest impressions anyone takes from the valley is the overwhelming sense of majestic age. The Sangre de Cristos are not young mountains; they have stood silent watch as ages have passed. Emanating from these mountains and clearings, one can feel the wisdom of patience, fortitude, and strength.

But nowhere is that majestic patience more obvious than at Great Sand Dunes National Park and Preserve. These dunes were built grain by grain by the winds blowing hundreds of miles up the valley over tens of thousands of years.

Throughout the years, the Great Sand Dunes have proved more than simply a notable landmark. Their establishment as a national monument and later as a national park has helped stimulate the economy in the San Luis Valley, providing jobs to many of us both at the park and through the generated tourism. They have attracted visitors from around the world, allowing us to share our unique culture and values with all who care to learn.

San Luis Valley

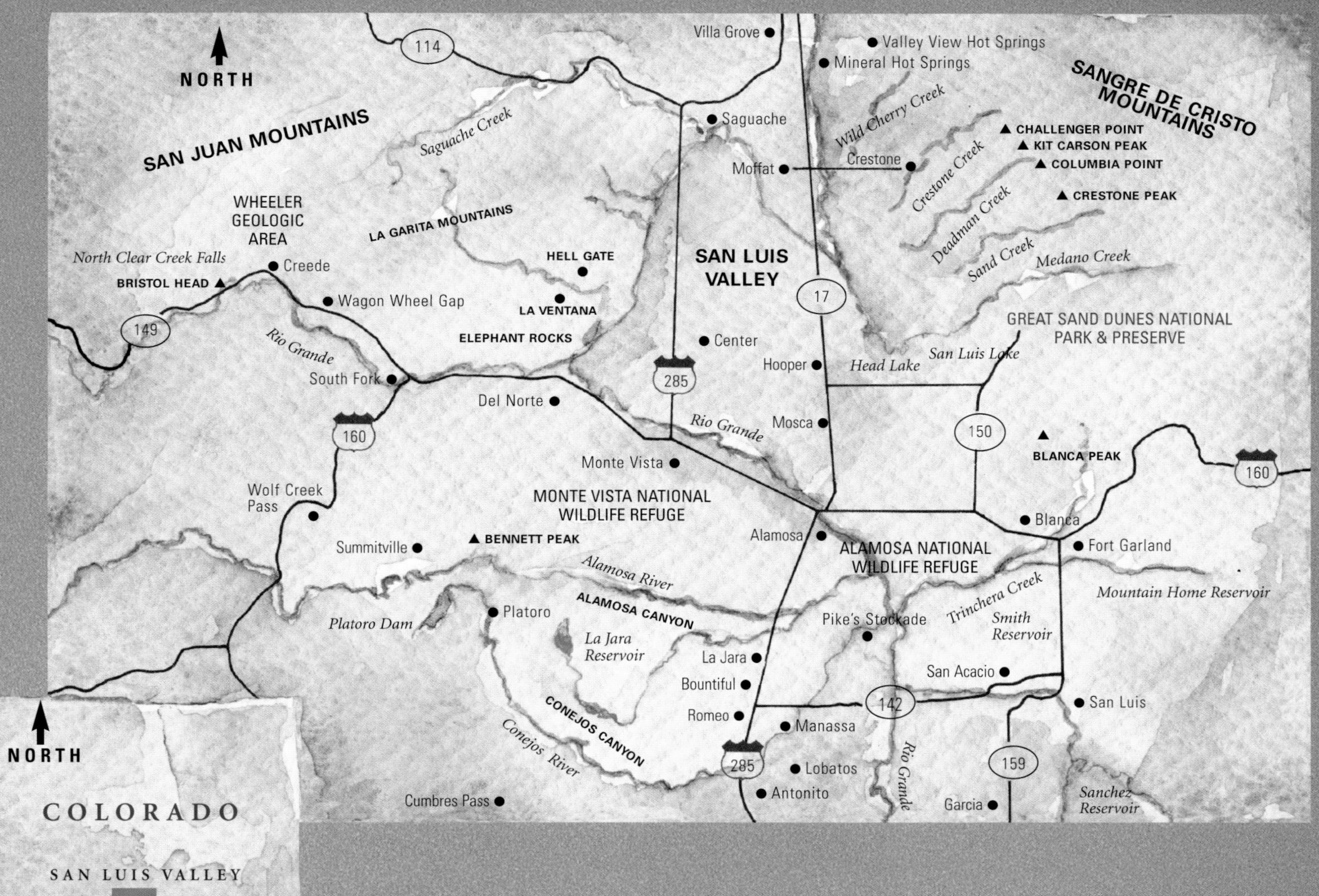

In 1932, when the Great Sand Dunes were first designated a national monument, the thirty square miles of land were finally protected after a decade of disregard by gold miners flocking into the nearby mountains.

On November 22, 2000, President Clinton signed into law the Great Sand Dunes National Park and Preserve Act. With the stroke of his pen, the monument was expanded into a national park and preserve to include the towering peaks and placid alpine lakes bordering the dunes. The dunes, and their neighbors, were forever protected for all to enjoy.

The Great Sand Dunes are the shifting sentinels of the San Luis Valley: changing yet constant, emblems of deliberate creation and a methodical Creator. They are unlike any other place on Earth, as witnessed by the thousands of visitors the dunes receive every year.

I invite you to join us, through the photographs and words in this book, to enjoy the most breathtaking and glorious places in the San Luis Valley. I promise you will be as enrapt as I am, drawn to witness them in person. And then you will begin to understand the majesty of my home.

They say that nothing of beauty can ever be rushed. Truly, the San Luis Valley and the Great Sand Dunes bear witness to this statement. And now you can too.

—Former Senator Ken Salazar, Colorado

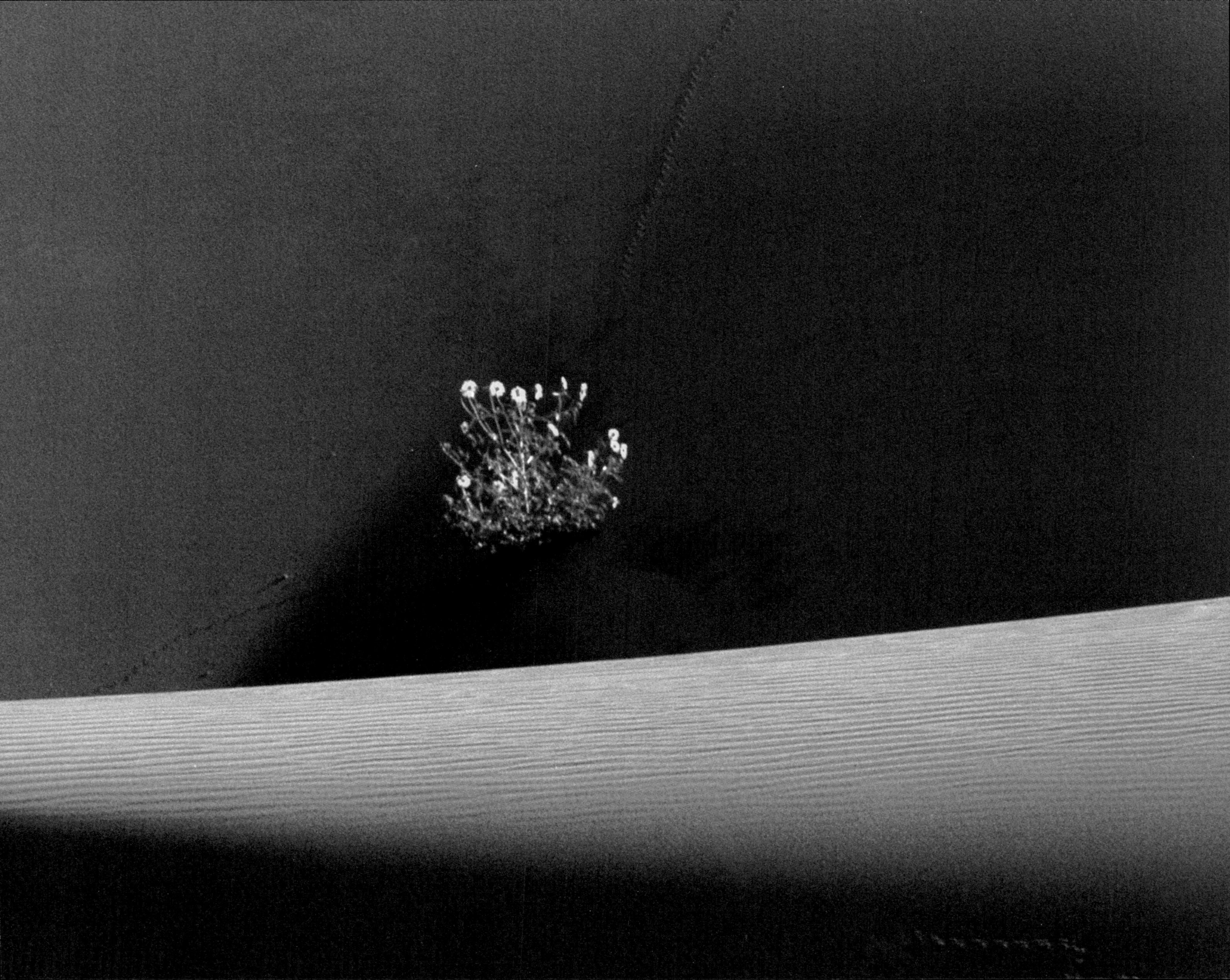

6

TIERRA INCOGNITA

Different places on earth
have different vital effluence,
different vibration,
different chemical exhalation,
and different polarity with different stars:
call it what you like.
But the spirit of place is a great reality.

—*D. H. Lawrence,* The Spirit of Place

There is euphoria in spaciousness—

A SEA OF SILVERED SAGE

shimmering beneath an azure vault of sky.

Open country resonates, the refrain ever-changing with the seasons. In the San Luis Valley, the richly aromatic scent of big sage after a rain, the flashing white tail-flag of a pronghorn racing the wind, the trumpeting calls of sandhill cranes returning to night roosts, and the very quality of the light, lavender at dusk and saffron at dawn, have the ability to seduce even the most determined urbanite. When explorer and geologist John Wesley Powell first surveyed the Rocky Mountains, he was so struck by the sweeping parklike expanses strung between the southernmost ranges of the Rockies like a string of pearls that he gave the name "Park Mountains" to the region we now refer to as the Southern Rockies. The San Luis Valley is but one glistening pearl, albeit the largest one, in that string.

From the Rio Grande near the Colorado–New Mexico border, the view to the north spans fifty miles across the San Luis Valley.

The San Luis Valley is truly a land apart—A MOSAIC OF DUNE AND HIGH DESERT LANDSCAPES bordered along their eastern edge by the haze-blue wall of the Sangre de Cristo Range and, nearly sixty-five miles to the west, by the rugged snowcapped massifs of the San Juan Mountains.

The Sangre de Cristos and San Juans meet along the valley's northernmost edge at Poncha Pass, a welcoming route through the maze of choppy swells that divides the Atlantic and Pacific watersheds. Uncompromisingly flat and nearly three times the size of Delaware, the San Luis Valley sweeps south from Poncha Pass for more than 150 miles to straddle the Colorado–New Mexico border north of the broken volcanic country of the Taos Plateau. Along the valley's eastern edge, in an otherwise unremarkable *rincón* created by three low notches in the imposing barrier of the Sangre de Cristos, a giant dunefield—Great Sand Dunes—rises to nearly 750 feet above the valley floor; it is the highest dunefield in North America. Covering nearly 150,000 acres, Great Sand Dunes National Park and Preserve is one of the most stunningly beautiful and unusual national parks on the continent.

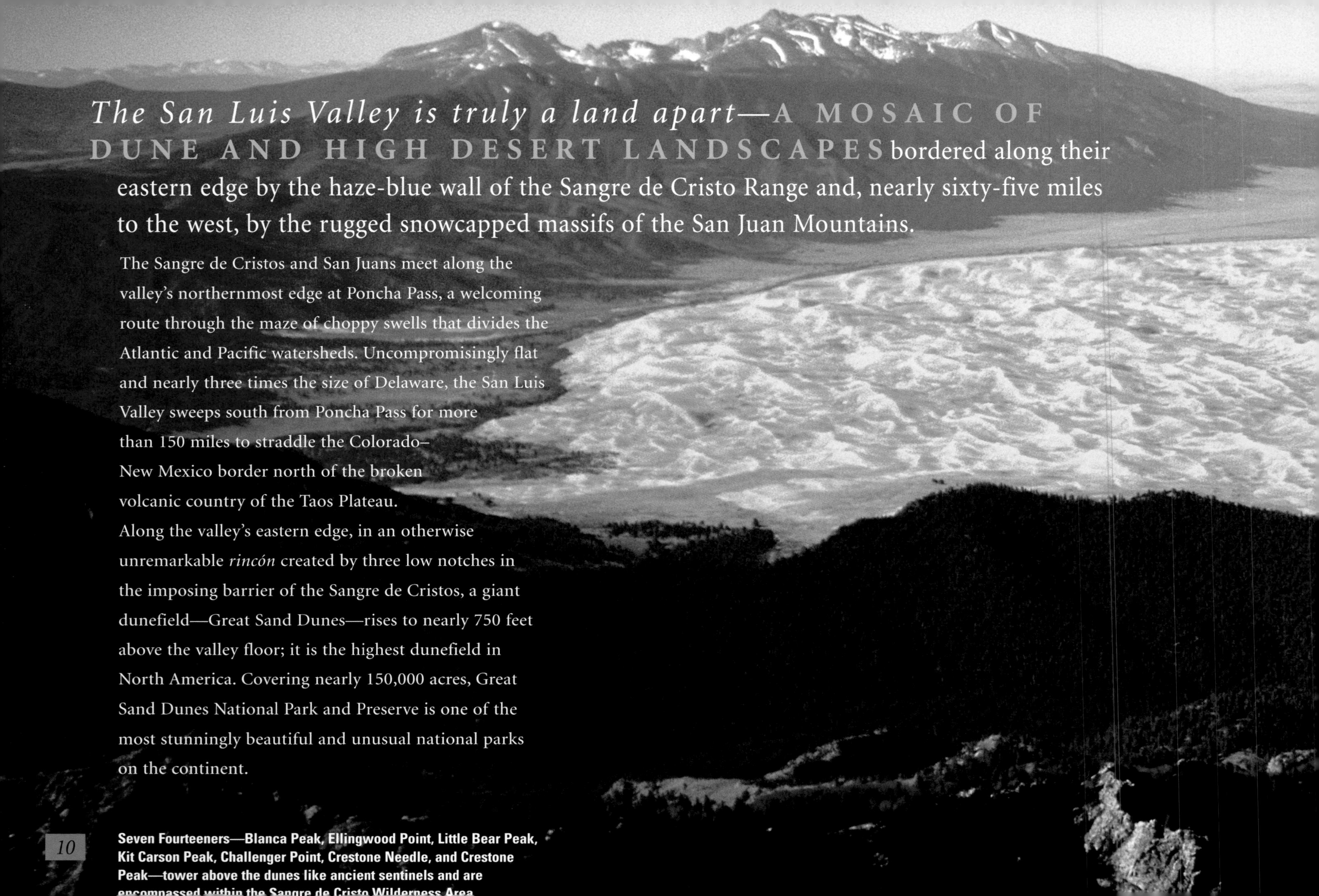

Seven Fourteeners—Blanca Peak, Ellingwood Point, Little Bear Peak, Kit Carson Peak, Challenger Point, Crestone Needle, and Crestone Peak—tower above the dunes like ancient sentinels and are encompassed within the Sangre de Cristo Wilderness Area.

The San Luis Valley is dry country—
SOME MIGHT EVEN DESCRIBE IT AS STARK AND UNCOMPROMISING.

The valley floor averages less than eight inches of precipitation a year—making it the highest and largest desert in North America. From a vantage point along the valley's northern rim, an embroidered tapestry—French-knotted with shrubs the color of verdigris and pale jade—rolls out before me, fraying along the distant horizon. The vital essence of "El Valle," a place where the seasonal dance of light and color speaks to all the senses, requires more than a fleeting acquaintance. Dry country, yes, but with the power to embrace all who come to know it well.

The landscapes and lifeways
OF THE SAN LUIS VALLEY AND GREAT SAND DUNES
have evolved in the heart of a rain shadow.

When faced with dramatic changes in climate, plants and animals have had little choice but to adapt—or perish trying. For human inhabitants, life in a rain shadow requires remarkable fortitude and resilience, possibly even some sand and grit in the soul. The Navajo, no strangers to dry places, believe that the desert's parching winds etched the whorls on their fingertips. Blanca Peak, or Sis Naajiní, is one of the four sacred compass points of the Navajo world. According to Navajo creation mythology, First Man and First Woman attached Sis Naajiní to the Earth with a bolt of white lightning and then decorated the peak with white shells, white lightning, black clouds, and male rain. Setting geologic realities aside for a moment, I've always wondered if First Man and First Woman showered any of their magic on the valley that lies at the base of their sacred peak. I suspect they did.

A sandstorm envelops the dunes in a topaz haze.

Scenes of long-vanished mountains, smoking volcanoes, and rivers of glacial ice—shape-shifting on an almost unimaginable scale—can be read from the thousands of feet of rock debris deposited on the floor of the San Luis Valley. The basic recipe for landscape evolution—time, water, wind, and geology—looks deceptively simple to the unaccustomed eye. The sensuous poetry of dune shapes and the hypnotic tapestry of earth tones belie the magnitude of the San Luis Valley's turbulent geologic history—events nearly unparalleled in the geologic saga of the Southern Rockies. It is a history reckoned in hundreds of millions of years—a timescale difficult to appreciate for those of us who think in terms of decades, centuries, or even millennia.

Beginning about 65 million years ago and lasting for nearly 32 million years, tectonic shock waves generated from deep within the Earth swept across the western half of North America. Along the entire Rocky Mountain chain, wave after wave of compressive force caused immense blocks of the Earth's crust to buckle, break, fold, and collapse; geologists refer to this unprecedented tectonic storm as the Laramide Orogeny.

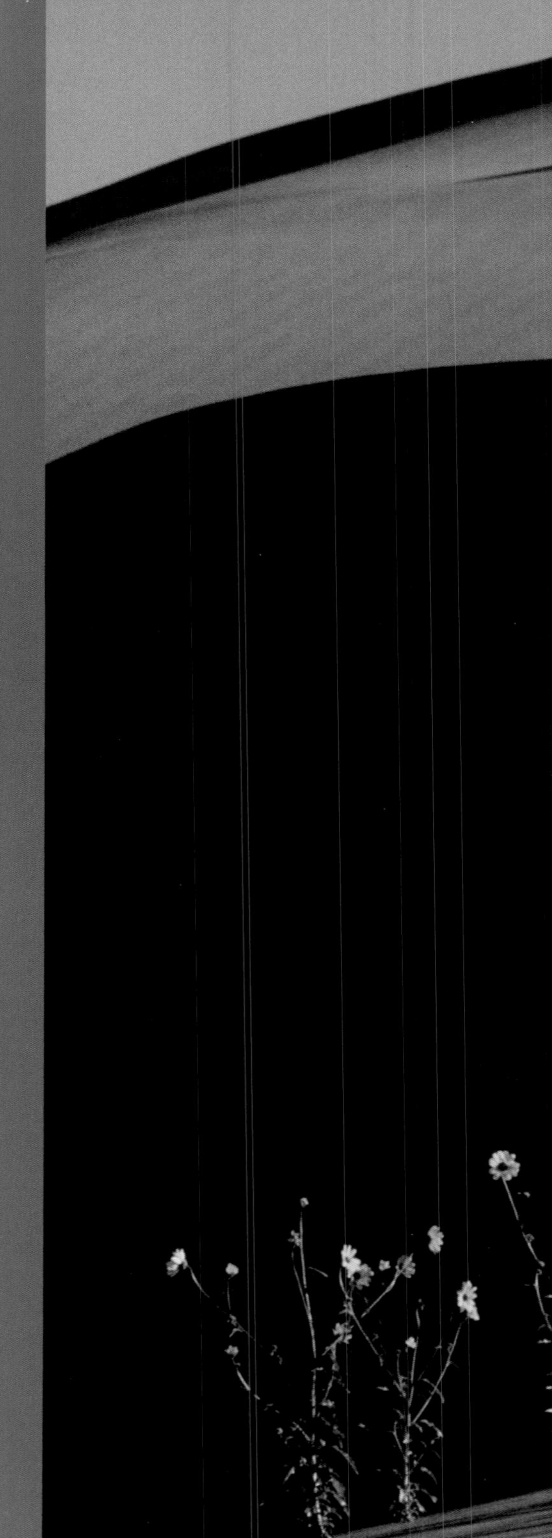

(INSETS) TOP: A dramatic sweep of columnar-jointed basalt forms Hell Gate in La Garita hills. BOTTOM: La Ventana, Spanish for "the window"

OPPOSITE: "The poetry of earth is never dead."
—John Keats, *On the Grasshopper and the Cricket*

Laramide tectonic events exposed the primal roots of the Southern Rockies, transfiguring and exhuming ancient mountain ranges that had been buried in their own debris. As quickly as the Laramide uplifts rose skyward, rivers and streams once again resumed the task of wearing them down to insignificance.

With Laramide dust barely settled, the direction and magnitude of compressive forces changed dramatically. This shift in direction triggered the cataclysmic rupturing of the Earth's crust along a 500-mile-long zone of weakness known as the Rio Grande Rift, which begins in the upper Arkansas Valley near Leadville and extends through the San Luis Valley southward to New Mexico and west Texas before disappearing into the bedrock terranes of northern Mexico. Along the rift's axis, immense blocks of the Earth's crust plunged downward along a series of deep bounding faults. Geologists refer to these downdropped blocks as *grabens*. The San Luis Valley portion of the Rio Grande Rift consists of several linked half grabens.

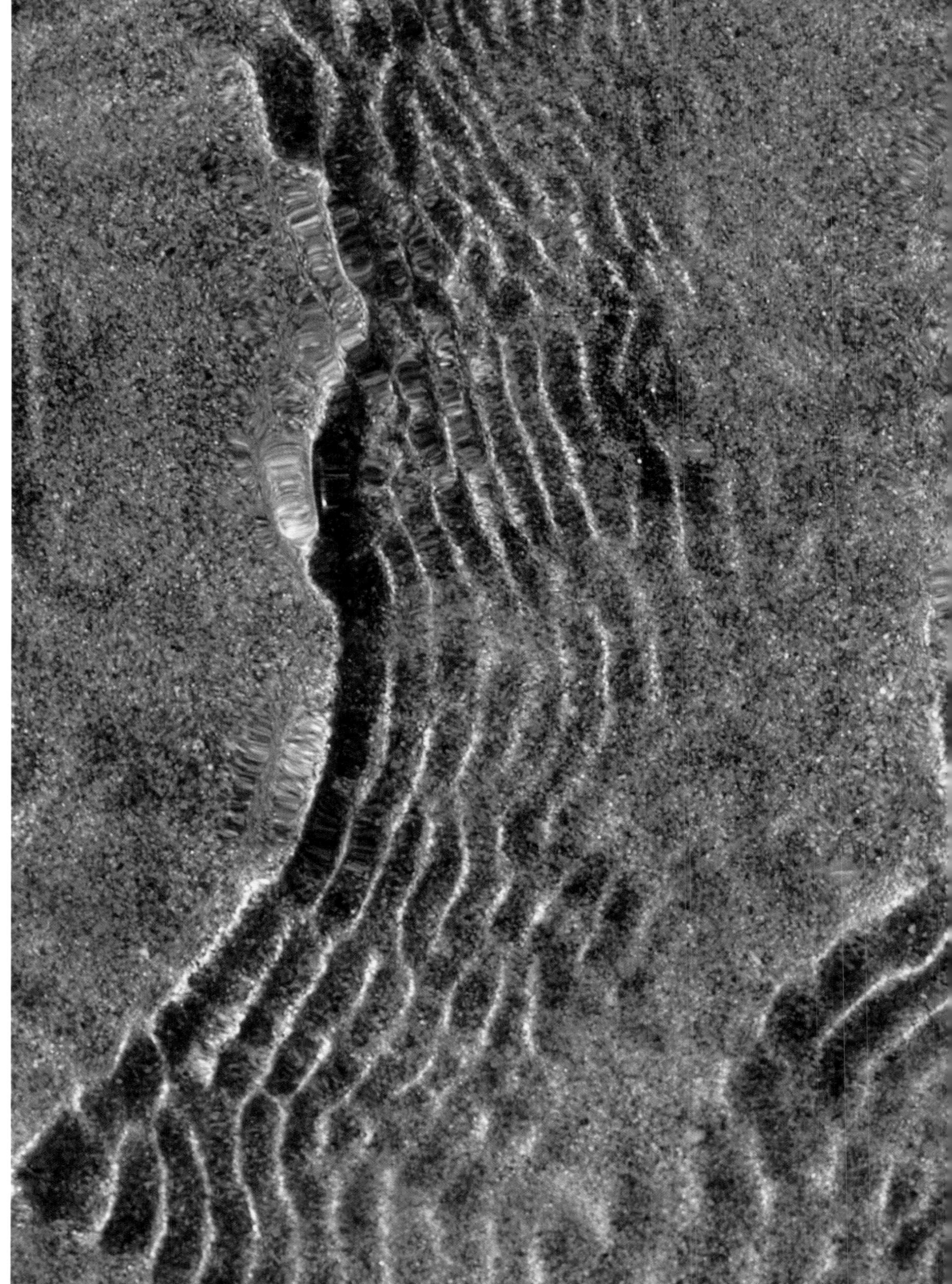

Sand grains—the memories of ancient mountains

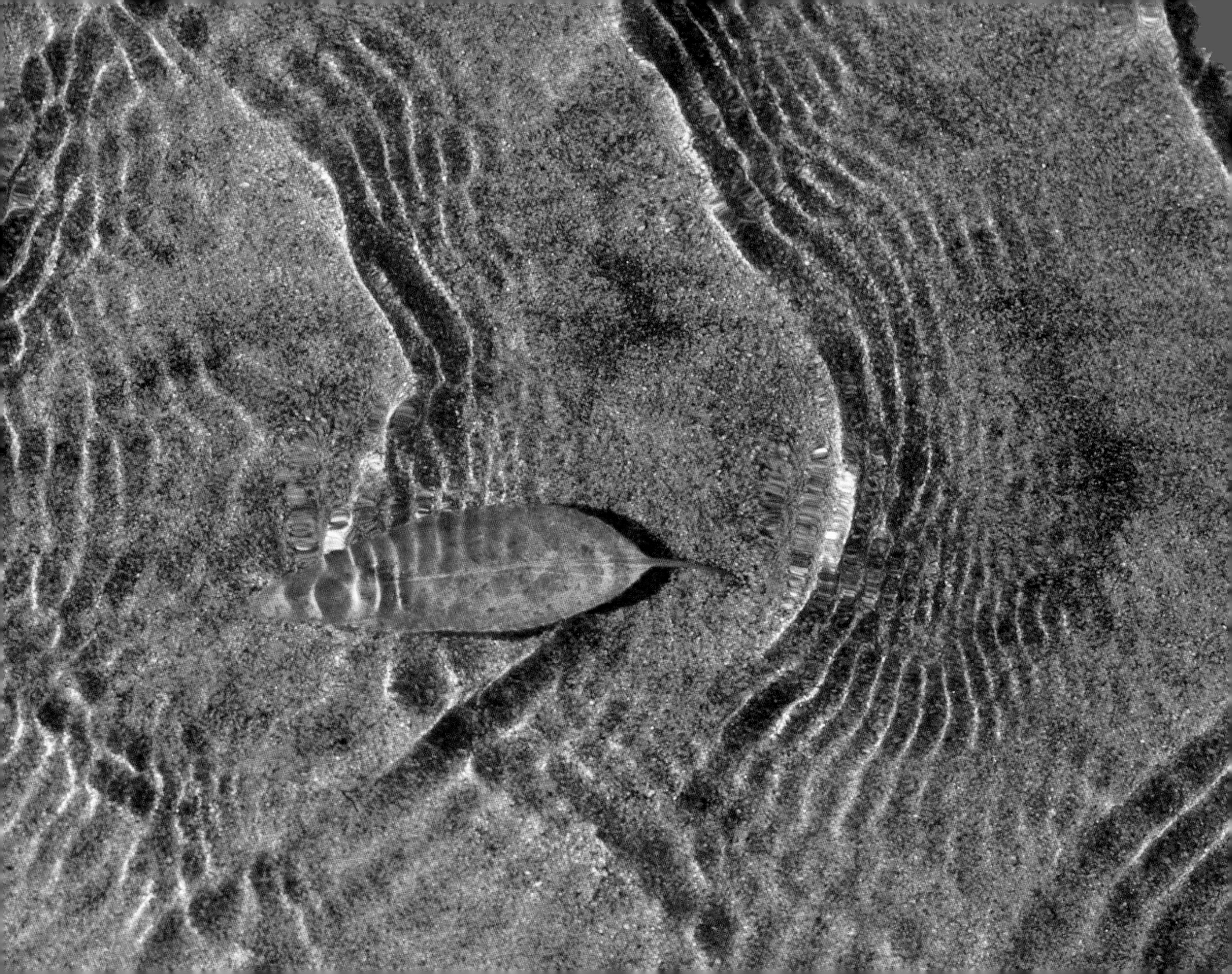

The Rio Grande Rift, like a sleeping dragon, is still geologically active. Seismic profiles reveal that a body of molten magma, called a thermal plume, is detectable along the axis of the rift. Hot springs, such as those near Villa Grove and those that heat public swimming pools near Alamosa, emerge along active fault traces. Small triangular-shaped fault scarps seen along the lower flanks of the Sangre de Cristos provide further evidence that movement along the rift is still going on. The Rio Grande breaks free of the rocky embrace of the San Juan foothills near the town of Del Norte and quickly slows its tempo to an idle, charting a gentle arc through the valley's midsection and along the trend of the rift as it travels south—the beginning of the river's long and sometimes troubled love affair with the Southwest and her people.

The canyon of the Rio Grande cuts through the rough volcanic country of the San Luis Hills near La Sauses. The Rio Grande, at 1,887 miles (180 miles in Colorado), is the second longest river in the continental United States.

The Rio Grande Rift is deepest and broadest in the San Luis Valley, where subsidence of the rift's northern segment coincided with a firestorm of volcanic eruptions in the San Juan Mountains and with block-faulting and massive igneous intrusions in the Sangre de Cristos. Volcanic eruptions occurred repeatedly along the trend of the rift, resulting in extensive flows of basaltic lava that are as much as 650 feet thick in Rio Grande Gorge. When basalt cools, it tends to fracture into tall hexagonal columns, such as those you see in the gorge or at Wagon Wheel Gap near Creede. Just to the north of Rio Grande Gorge, flat-lying basalt flows cap the starkly beautiful San Luis Hills, and a cluster of twelve volcanic cones and the larger domed volcanoes of San Antonio Peak and Los Mogotes dominate the otherwise flat floor of the valley.

Miniature landscapes pattern the bed of Medano Creek.

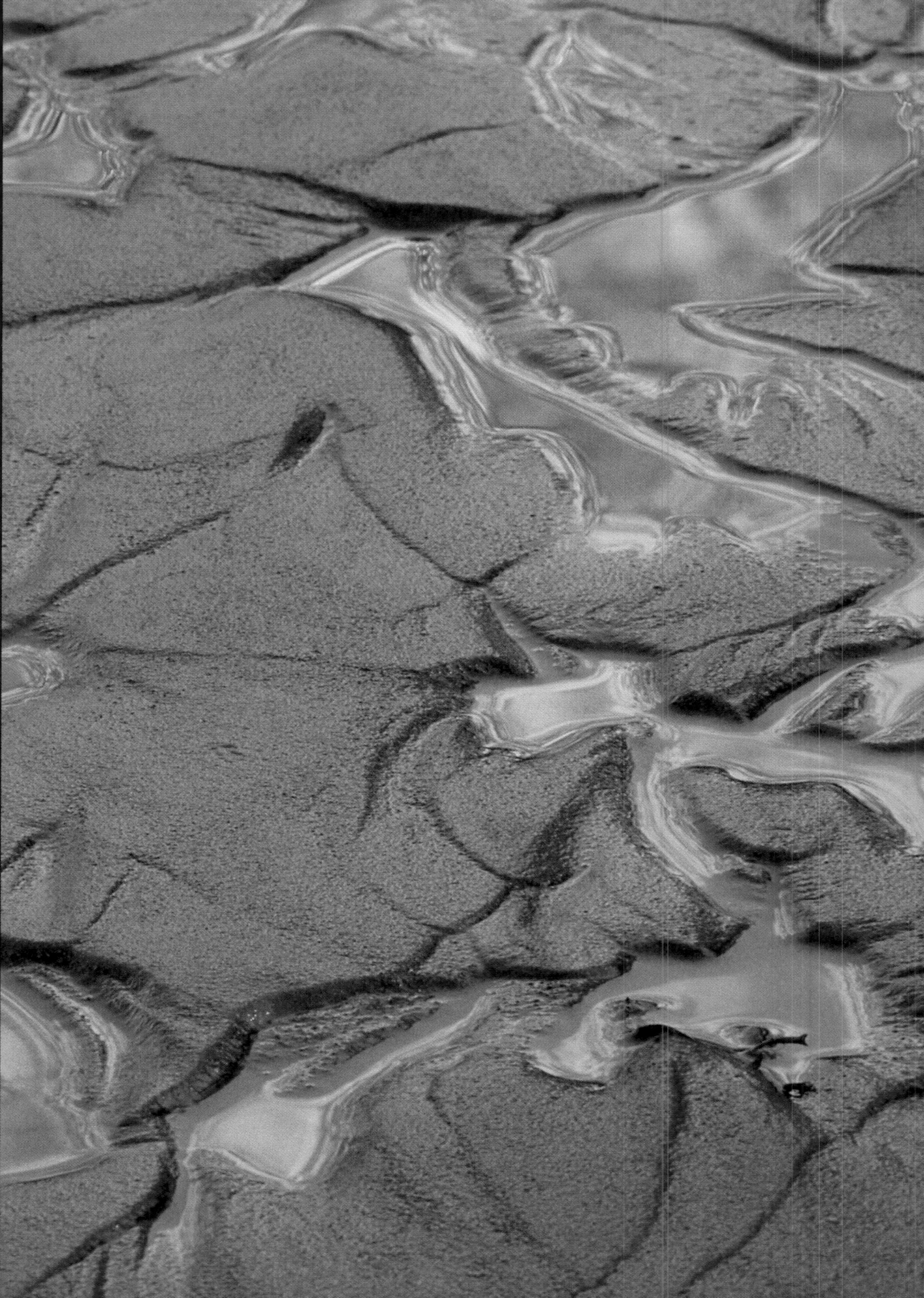

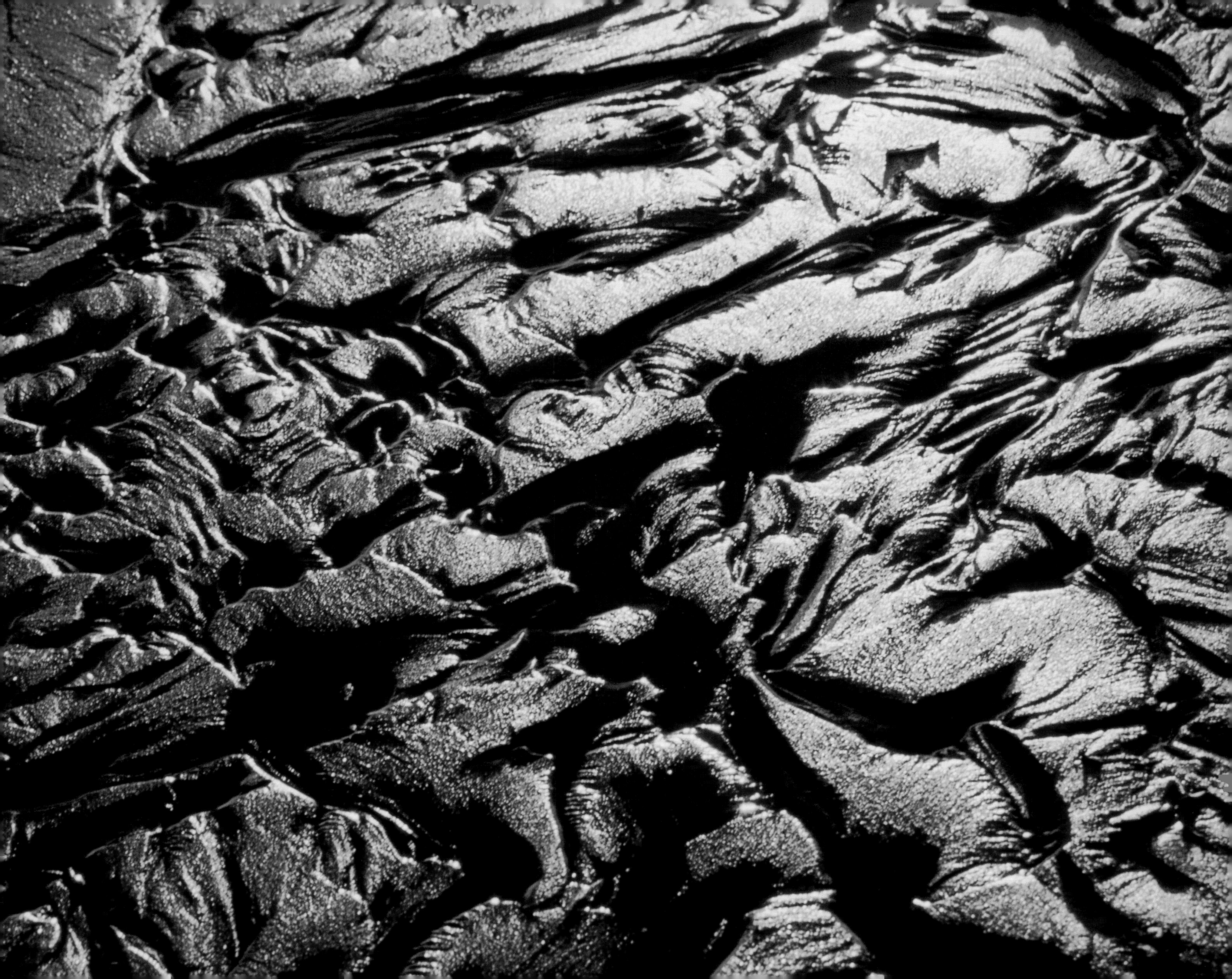

The small volcanoes and craters that dot the southern end of the San Luis Valley are dwarfed by the magnitude of the volcanic violence that occurred in the nearby San Juan Mountains. Geologists estimate that during the peak of volcanic activity, volcanoes in the San Juans produced more than 20,000 times the volume of ash and volcanic rocks ejected by the 1980 eruption of Mount Saint Helens—a minor incident by San Juan standards. Many of the highest peaks in the San Juans are carved from thousands of feet of layered volcanic rock.

Nodules and vein deposits of turquoise, a bluish green volcanic gemstone, were mined in both prehistoric and historic times in the San Luis Hills near Manassa. Ancient Puebloan peoples coveted this turquoise and made regular trips to the valley to quarry it for ceremonial purposes, for use in making jewelry, and as a valuable trade item. Though deposits of King Manassa turquoise have largely been depleted, it is still sought after by Navajo and Hopi silversmiths because of its unusual color and rarity.

At Wheeler Geologic Area, near Creede, a fairyland of lavender-and-white spires and other fanciful shapes has been eroded from more than eight different layers of volcanic tuff and ash flow deposits.

It would have been a dismal time
TO BE A HIKER IN THE DUNES.

Violent sandstorms occurred repeatedly during much of the Pleistocene, building the towering twenty-eight-square-mile dunefield we know as Great Sand Dunes.

Modern estimates suggest that the main dunefield contains between 13 and 16 billion cubic yards of sand. Dunes of this magnitude require an enormous supply of loose dry sand, frequent strong winds, and conditions that stop wind-transported sand from traveling onwards, causing it to accumulate where it falls. During Pleistocene glacial times, when the majority of the sand was deposited on the floor of the San Luis Valley, the prevailing southwesterly and westerly winds sent gritty clouds of silt, clay, and sand scudding across the valley on a collision course with the Sangre de Cristos. During the Holocene, episodes of sandstorm activity, though less significant than those of the Pleistocene, occurred during nonglacial intervals in response to a lowering of the regional water table. The fortuitous conjunction of three low passes—Music, Medano, and Mosca—generated sufficient turbulence to slow these winds and force them to drop the majority of their load in the natural sand trap at the base of the mountains. Storm winds, roaring out of the northeast, periodically piled the dunes' crests back upon themselves, contributing to their height and keeping them from lapping against the flanks of the mountains. Photographs taken of Great Sand Dunes more than a century ago show remarkably little change from what we see today, a testament to the continued importance of these northeasterly winds.

Great Sand Dunes is simply one part of a complex system of sand deposits that covers nearly 350 square miles and extends from the Rio Grande northeastward to the Sangre de Cristo Mountains. A relatively flat expanse of wind-deposited sand—the sand sheet—surrounds the active dunefield. Where the sand sheet approaches the flanks of the Sangre de Cristos, loose ramps of sand and climbing dunes often lap against the mountains, especially in the area of Castle Creek and Little Medano Creek. The most stable portions of the sand sheet are tethered to Earth by drought-resistant shrubs, tussock-forming grasses, and an assortment of tenacious wildflowers.

Wherever the vegetation has lost its foothold on the sand as a result of wind scour or other types of disturbance, the sand is freed from its lashing of roots and moves at the whim of the wind. Along the low-lying western margin of the sand sheet, wherever a high water table enhances evaporation, a mineralized hardpan, called the *sabkha,* has formed over about 120 square miles as a result of the upward movement and evaporative concentration of salts and other minerals at or near the surface.

A sand ramp climbs the western flank of the Sangre de Cristos.

OPPOSITE: Dunes do occasionally "escape" when drought conditions or a persistent shift in wind direction prevail. Actively advancing dunes may migrate as much as thirty-five feet a year; the speediest escape dune was reported to have traveled twenty feet in only forty days. The Ghost Forest, a grove of ponderosa pines almost completely smothered by encroaching dunes, is a reminder that neither trees nor human structures stand a chance against a determined escape dune.

Few people can resist a dunefield—

THE MISCHIEF AND ARTISTRY OF THE WIND

beckon the child in each of us.

The sand has stories to tell—geologic sagas of epic proportions and enduring fascination. Viewed from a distance, Great Sand Dunes often appears as monochromatic as a camel's fleece. Next time you visit the dunes, scoop up a handful of sand and use a magnifier to reveal the gemlike beauty that lies within. You'll see a kaleidoscope of colors: the metallic black of magnetite, the diamondlike sparkle of zircon, the frosty white of quartz, the bluish sheen of sanidine, the topaz yellow of citrine, and the pistachio green of epidote. You'll also see tiny bits of rock—granite, basalt, volcanic glass, and chert—each with their own rough-and-tumble tales. No two grains of sand are exactly alike. In fact, the spectacular diversity inherent in dune and beach sands around the world has inspired a unique group of collectors who call themselves arenophiles, or "sand-lovers," a word derived from Latin and Greek.

The birth of a sand grain is a microcosmic event—

ONE THAT OFTEN BEGINS WITHIN THE MOLTEN DEPTHS OF THE EARTH'S CRUST AND CONTINUES

over the eons when the rock is exposed to conditions at the Earth's surface.

All rocks undergo mechanical and chemical weathering, even those that solidified as glittering matrices of crystals (for example, granite). Chemical weathering, less obvious to our eye, is triggered by differences in the chemical stability of individual minerals. The results of weathering are often dramatic. At Great Sand Dunes, the sand you hold in your hand symbolizes the death of distant mountains—and their subsequent "rebirth" in a stunning new landscape.

Scientists love to measure the age of almost everything. The discovery of radioactivity, the phenomenon by which naturally occurring radioactive elements (such as uranium) are transformed (or "decay") into other elements as a consequence of their inherent instability, led physicists to unravel the secrets behind the Earth's natural clock—the most reliable timekeeper of all. The transformative process that uranium and other radioactive elements undergo is called radioactive decay. Zircon, which contains uranium, is the mineral of choice for dating the Earth's oldest rocks because of its extreme durability and chemical stability over the vast span of geologic time. Using a remarkable device called an ion microprobe, geologists are now able to determine a zircon crystal's age and therefore estimate the age of the rock from which it came.

Fulgurites are a rare discovery at the dunes. These strange glassy crusts and tubes form when lightning strikes the sand and the intense heat of the electrical current melts the silica-rich sand. This cross-sectional view of a tubular fulgurite shows the partially melted sand that forms the glassy interior wall of the tube and the empty space where the lightning vaporized the sand.

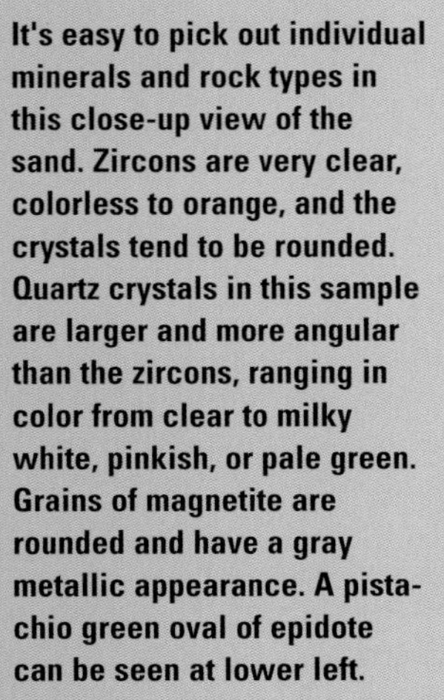

It's easy to pick out individual minerals and rock types in this close-up view of the sand. Zircons are very clear, colorless to orange, and the crystals tend to be rounded. Quartz crystals in this sample are larger and more angular than the zircons, ranging in color from clear to milky white, pinkish, or pale green. Grains of magnetite are rounded and have a gray metallic appearance. A pistachio green oval of epidote can be seen at lower left.

Where did all the sand come from? Beginning with THE HAYDEN SURVEY IN 1873, GEOLOGISTS HAVE LOOKED at the minerals in the sand for the answer.

Geologic differences between the two potential source areas are striking. The San Juan Mountains consist almost entirely of volcanic rocks that have been radiometrically dated at between 18 and 35 million years in age. The Sangre de Cristos have crystalline Precambrian rocks at their core, mostly dating between 1.0 and 2.5 billion years old. Many geologists have noted that the preponderance of bits of volcanic rock and minerals associated with volcanic rocks point to the San Juans as the primary sand source. But many of these minerals, such as zircon and magnetite, are found in both volcanic and intrusive igneous rocks. Once again, the answer lies in the sand.

Putting zircon to the test, scientists John Aleinikoff, Rich Madole, and Joe Romig dated zircon crystals from four localities at Great Sand Dunes. They found the majority of the zircons in all samples to be from Tertiary-age volcanic rocks from the San Juans. Only a small percentage of the zircons could be traced to Precambrian-age rocks from the Sangre de Cristos. They were also able to establish that seasonal meltwater runoff from Pleistocene glaciers and snowfields in the San Juans transported vast quantities of sand to the floor of the San Luis Valley, spreading it out across an expanse of intermittently dry stream channels and playa lakes well north of the modern Rio Grande floodplain. Most importantly, Madole and Romig provided compelling evidence that Great Sand Dunes began forming much earlier than previously believed, whenever dry sand was available and windy conditions prevailed—perhaps prior to 130,000 years ago.

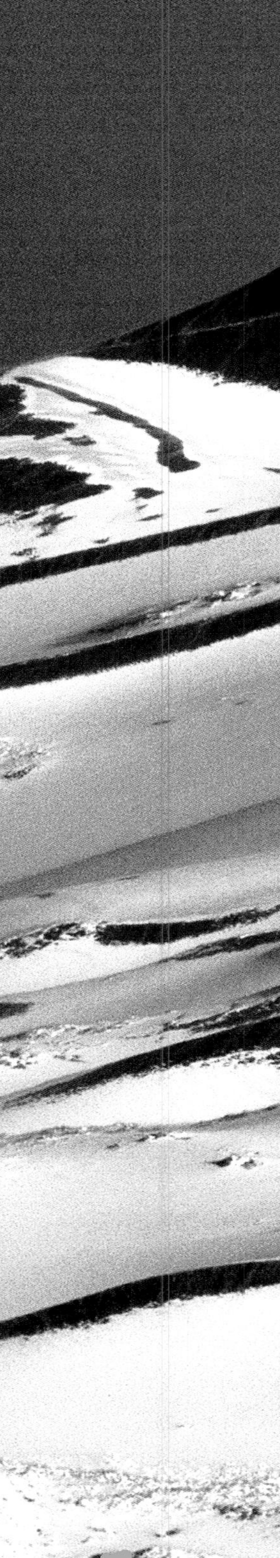

Fresh snow on the dunes is an ephemeral delight to be savored for its rarity.

Exploring Great Sand Dunes on a windy day **IS A REMARKABLE EXPERIENCE.**

Even as the sandy grit invades your clothes and stings your eyes,

you feel the absolute power of wind as a landscape force. With the Sangre de Cristos enveloped in a topaz-colored haze, sand banners unfurling from the peaks and ridges of the highest dunes, you see individual grains, frosted like sea glass, dance across the dune surfaces. The sand grains bounce a foot or so into the air, fall, and ricochet as they climb the windward slope of a dune—choreography by saltation. Along the dune crest, the addition of new sand quickly exceeds the angle of repose, sending thin sheets of sand cascading down the dune's leeward slope, or slip-face. If the winds persist, the dune creeps imperceptibly downwind as layer after layer of sand is scoured from the dune's windward slope and deposited on the slip-face.

Every dune has its own story—the shapes reflecting differences in slope angle, wind direction, and wind velocity. On gently sloping or flat surfaces of sand, saltating sand grains fall into a distinct rhythm and produce the most common of all dune deposits—ripple marks. Crescent-shaped dunes, or *barchans*, are formed by consistent unidirectional winds and always open in the downwind direction. *Barchan* is the Arabic word for "ram's horn," a perfect description of their shape. In contrast, parabolic dunes have much longer "arms" that trail behind their flanks as they migrate downwind.

Transverse dunes, which dominate the central portion of Great Sand Dunes, form at right angles to the prevailing winds, their slip-faces standing in sharp relief. Large reversing dunes, called Chinese walls, form when a northeasterly storm system prevails, folding the ridges of the dunes back upon themselves.

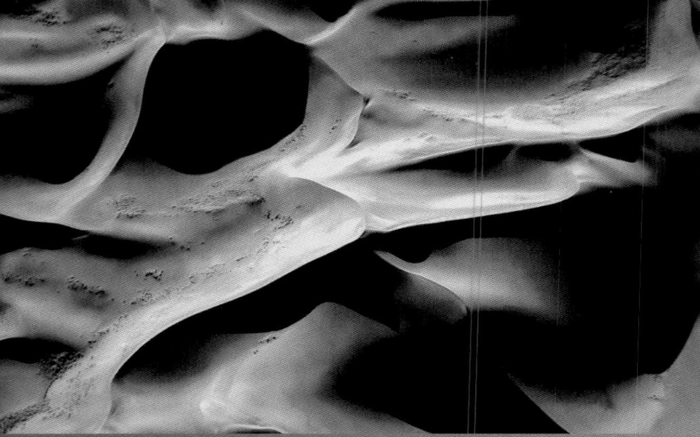

A dune shaped like a three- or four-armed starfish is created when sand-laden winds blow from several directions at different times of the year. Star Dune, shown here in an aerial photograph, formed in this way. Rising more than 750 feet above the valley floor, it is considered the tallest dune in the dunefield.

Coppice dunes form when a shrub or small tree generates sufficient turbulence to cause a dune to form around the base and downwind side of the impediment.

I'm sitting on the crest of a dune in the moonlight.

The omnipresent ghosts of wind and water seem content to rest from their labors. Even the dust devils that swirl their mischief by day on the valley floor are sleeping. Shadows deepen to matte black, and the sinuous curves of the dunes sharpen and turn luminous with moon glow. The shroud of silence that envelops me is so profound I imagine I can hear the silken hiss of Sand Creek as it disappears into the sand. A shooting star streaks across the night sky, its golden core burning as brightly as a Fourth of July sparkler. Beneath a diaphanous spray of Indian ricegrass, the tracks of high-stepping kangaroo rats still pattern the dance floor of last night's harvest ball. Coyotes sing to each other in the distance, a dolorous cantata that seems amplified somehow beneath the dome of stars. With the transforming light of dawn, the improbable geography of the dunefield loses its sharp edges in a haze of lavender-blue. As the sun rises from behind the Sangre de Cristos, a rose blush tints the highest peaks and burnishes the dunes with a copper patina. The *quork* of a raven greets the coming day, and I answer in turn.

Moonrise over Head Lake

OPPOSITE: Tracks of Ord's kangaroo rat pattern the sand

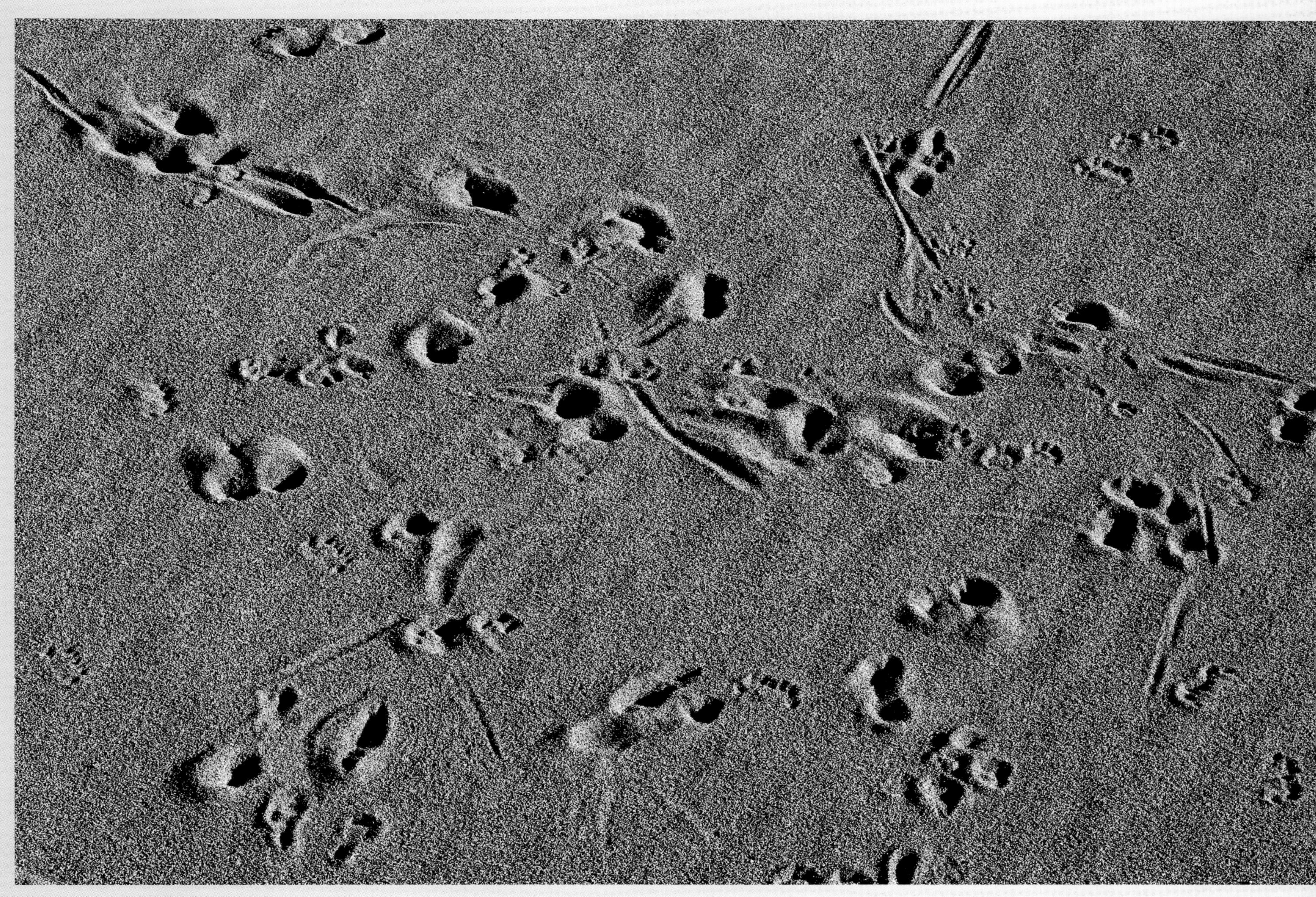

I wade into the cold surprise of Sand Creek—

AND MY FEET DISTURB TINY RIPPLES OF SAND

that form along the stream's sandy bottom, triggering a pulse of surge waves that break above my ankles.

Although I don't smell salt water, Sand Creek has the feel of a tidal stream rejoining the sea. The moist sand along the creek's edge hides nothing, reveals everything—the tracks of purposeful coyotes, the heart-shaped intaglio of a mule deer, and the quill-brushed toe pads of a porcupine are mysteries to interpret. Black swirls of magnetite-rich sand create a marbled pattern in an abandoned stream channel. Above me, the buds and glistening new leaves of a narrow-leaf cottonwood perfume the air with their smoky, resinous aroma. With the sun now high overhead, I look back on a dunefield the color of a Bedouin's sun-bleached robes, heat shimmering beneath an impossibly blue sky.

Great Sand Dunes is one of the few places in the world where you can experience "sand waves" and the tide-like phenomenon known as "surge flow." Surge flow occurs only along sandy-bottomed, low-gradient streams or rivers where sand ripples form along the streambed perpendicular to the direction of flow. The cyclic building and collapse of these tiny ripple "dams" generate the surge waves we see. Sand waves are common along Sand Creek and Medano Creek from April through July, when spring runoff transports enormous amounts of sand. Both creeks eventually disappear into the gravel of the valley floor, leaving behind their load of sand to be recycled by the prevailing winds.

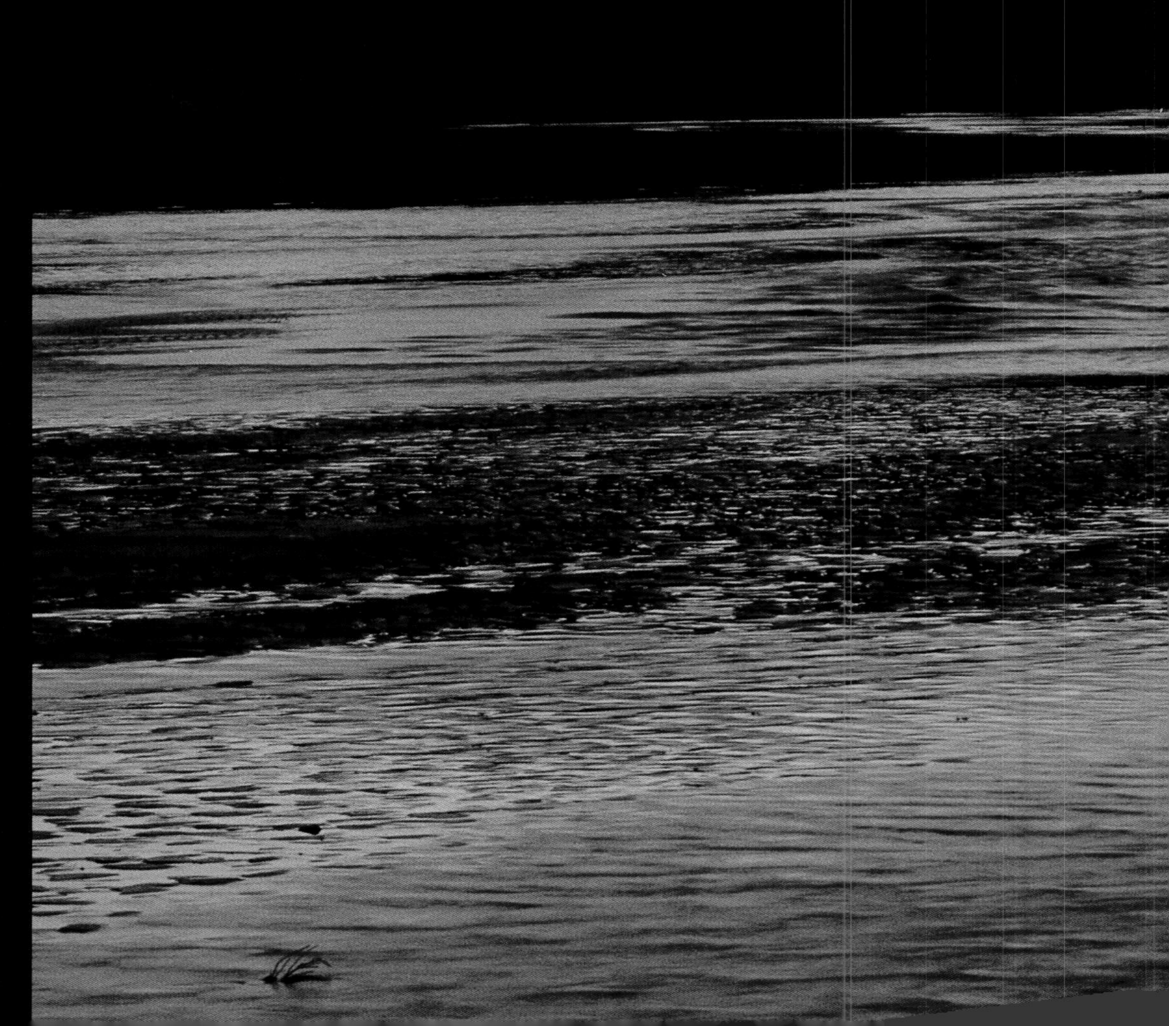

When I gaze across the dusty green shrubland and tawny undulations of the dunes, it is hard to imagine that one of the West's largest underground reservoirs—the San Luis Valley Aquifer—lies sequestered beneath tons of erosional debris on the valley floor. Nourished primarily by snowmelt streams and rivers originating in the highest watersheds of the mountains that flank the valley, the San Luis Valley Aquifer is believed to contain at least 2 billion acre-feet of water—fifty times the combined capacity of Lake Powell and Lake Mead. With the exception of the Rio Grande and its major tributaries, which include the Conejos River and the Alamosa River, streams flowing into the valley along its perimeter sink into layer after layer of sand and gravel. Precipitation on the valley floor adds relatively little to the "water bank," except during summers when moisture associated with the Arizona monsoon pushes northward into Colorado.

Meanders along Sand Creek

Scientists continue to reveal the aquifer's secrets—drill core by drill core. Coring and seismic studies provide a cross-sectional view of the thousands of feet of rock rubble and sand that lie beneath the shrub-dotted floor of the San Luis Valley. These depositional layers, like the entries in an accountant's ledger, provide a detailed record of geologic events spanning several million years. The topmost unit of the San Luis Aquifer—the "unconfined aquifer"—consists of unconsolidated Pleistocene-age erosional debris and is less than 200 feet thick in most areas. Due to its shallow nature and the valley's arid climate, the unconfined aquifer may lose as much as 86 percent of its annual recharge to evapotranspiration. The deeper subterranean reservoir—the "confined aquifer"—ranges between 5,000 and 30,000 feet in thickness, is separated from the unconfined aquifer by discontinuous layers of impermeable clays and volcanic flows, and is underlain by Precambrian crystalline rocks. Radiocarbon dating of groundwater in the combined aquifer suggests that it may be as old as 30,000 years. The degree to which these two parts of the San Luis Aquifer "communicate" with one another remains an intriguing question.

Secretive and difficult to see except during the breeding season, a pair of Wilson's snipe forages along the reedy edge of a wetland, oblivious to the scolding trill of a marsh wren (inset).

The hydrology of the San Luis Valley is key to understanding its unique biological diversity—and its human history. The most unusual aspect of the aquifer is the way in which water moves and behaves once it enters this enormous groundwater system. The northern half of the aquifer, a 2,900-square-mile area known as the Closed Basin, lies to the north and east of the Rio Grande and includes the Great Sand Dunes. Encompassing roughly 35 percent of the San Luis Valley, the Closed Basin resembles a shallow bowl—a natural water impoundment—within the otherwise flat and gently sloping valley. Because the Closed Basin lacks any outlet to the Rio Grande or to the southern half of the valley, streams entering the aquifer from the mountains to the west and east are forced to migrate along a network of natural conduits—confined by clay lenses and indurated layers of gravel—until they eventually reach a low point in the vicinity of the San Luis lakes.

Willow leaves and deer tracks

OPPOSITE: Enough for all—mule deer and sandhill cranes take advantage of spring's bounty in the fields at Monte Vista National Wildlife Refuge.

The very existence of Great Sand Dunes— **ITS PERSISTENCE IN PLACE OVER TIME—** depends on the annual recharge of the unconfined aquifer by Medano Creek and Sand Creek.

Water from these creeks enters the Closed Basin and flows beneath the main dunefield, emerging many years later at Big Spring and Little Spring creeks. Adding yet another amazing detail to the story, geologists have determined that it takes more than sixty years for a single drop of water from either Medano or Sand Creek to make the journey to the springs from which it eventually emerges. Some scientists who have studied the complex hydrology of the Closed Basin believe that the presence of moist sand, nourished by upwardly mobile groundwater from the unconfined aquifer, provides the “glue” that keeps the entire system in place. Along the western edge of the dunefield, wherever the wind has scoured depressions in the sand deep enough to tap an artesian spring, interdunal wetlands and ponds provide a flagrantly green contrast to the tawny sweep of the sand sheet.

Several families of great horned owls have been reared in this goose nesting box at Blanca Wetlands.

OPPOSITE: American white pelicans are increasingly uncommon in the West because of habitat loss, pesticide use, and human disturbance. These distinctive, gregarious birds do not fish by diving, as does the brown pelican, but by working cooperatively to surround schools of small fish in shallow water, scooping them up with their capacious bills.

The surprise of a dune-encircled wetland is A SENSUAL DELIGHT— an experience to be savored.

As I top the final rise on my way to Little Spring, lion-colored dunes suddenly give way to a sward of pure Irish green. A spiked fringe of sedges and bulrushes—a painter's palette of shimmering greens—frames the dark silvered water. Amidst a sward of Baltic rush, I spot the delicate magenta-colored blossoms of the slender spiderflower. The water is clear enough that I can see snails creeping along the bottom, oblivious to the shadows cast by water striders skating the surface tension. Sapphire-colored dragonflies patrol the periphery of the spring, hunting on the wing with quick darting movements. As I circle the shoreline, I startle several pairs of yellow-headed blackbirds, which take wing in a burst of exotic color, trilling their strident *kek-kek-kek* as they whirl overhead. Of the more than forty interdunal ponds noted in a 1959 study, only a handful remain. Careful monitoring of these endangered oases over the years suggests that several factors—drought, dune migration, or a lowering of the water table—may play a role in their disappearance.

Interdunal areas adjacent to coppice dunes often exhibit prominent ripple marks in the sand.

Ephemeral saline lakes, known as playas, dot the upwind margins of the sand sheet. Most are shallow depressions that receive seasonal moisture or have an unusually high water table. During periods of drought, playas shrink dramatically in size because of evaporation until they are little more than salt-encrusted circlets of sun-baked hardpan. Hoarfrost-like excrescences of salt form a crystal tracery on the stems and leaves of plants growing in areas of greatest evaporite concentration. The groundwater resources of the Closed Basin are dynamic and highly sensitive to hydrologic changes. Well-watered playas and wetlands, such as those at Mishak, Russell, and San Luis lakes and at the Blanca Wetlands, were much more common during the Pleistocene, a time when the climate was cooler and moister than it is today. Though the Pleistocene playas were seldom more than a few feet deep, the largest supported several species of fish, such as the now-extinct buffalofish, as well as brine shrimp and other invertebrates and several species of freshwater clams and snails. Today, remnants of these wetlands provide critical migratory and nesting habitat for shorebirds, ducks, ibis, sandhill cranes, and a host of other wildlife species.

A great blue heron—intent and motionless—fishes in the shallows at Dollar Lake. Nearby, a flock of American avocets preens and gossips.

All they could see was
SKY, WATER, BIRDS, LIGHT, AND CONFLUENCE.
It was the whole morning world. —Eudora Welty, *The Optimist's Daughter*

With the coming of spring, the San Luis Valley's wetlands welcome tens of thousands of northbound avian travelers—sandhill cranes, herons, white-faced ibis, geese, ducks, grebes, shorebirds and songbirds of every stripe. The skies are alive with continual arrivals and departures, endless lifting and settling of ducks, and the splendid cacophony of a thousand different voices.

My spring ritual—conducted with binoculars in hand—always involves a March migration to Monte Vista National Wildlife Refuge to mark winter's end with a spirit-lifting infusion of sandhill crane music. The refuge, which hosts nearly 20,000 migrating sandhill cranes and has the highest nesting densities of ducks in North America, combines a network of irrigated wetlands and fields planted solely to support resident breeders as well as migrants. For several weeks each spring and fall, the San Luis Valley serves as a staging ground and "refueling" stop for the cranes along a migratory pathway that may be millions of years old.

Gilded with the colors of a February sunrise, hundreds of ducks and Canada geese rise from the marshes, the crescendo of their voices echoing down the ages.

The crane family (Gruidae) is one of the oldest bird families in the world, having made its first appearance roughly 65 million years ago. Fossil wing bones of sandhill cranes (*Grus canadensis*) exactly identical to those we see today have been found in Wyoming and Nebraska and are thought to be at least 9 million years old—making the sandhill crane the oldest modern bird species on Earth.

We know that prehistoric people hunted sandhill cranes in the San Luis Valley for thousands of years and that the Spanish explorers referred to the nearby San Juan Mountains as *las sierras de las grullas* or "mountains of the cranes." In a rock shelter above Limekiln Creek, along the southwestern edge of the valley, the image of a large flying bird—undoubtedly a sandhill crane—has been pecked into the smoke-blackened wall of the shelter. Though the age of this rock art panel is unknown, the small geometric design below the bird is thought to be a Puebloan crane clan symbol. Sandhill cranes were held in such high regard by Puebloan peoples up and down the Rio Grande that lessons drawn from the crane's lifeway and habits are found in traditional "teaching" stories told to children. Cranes also play a signal role in secret rituals practiced by the Tewas, the Zuni, and the Hopi.

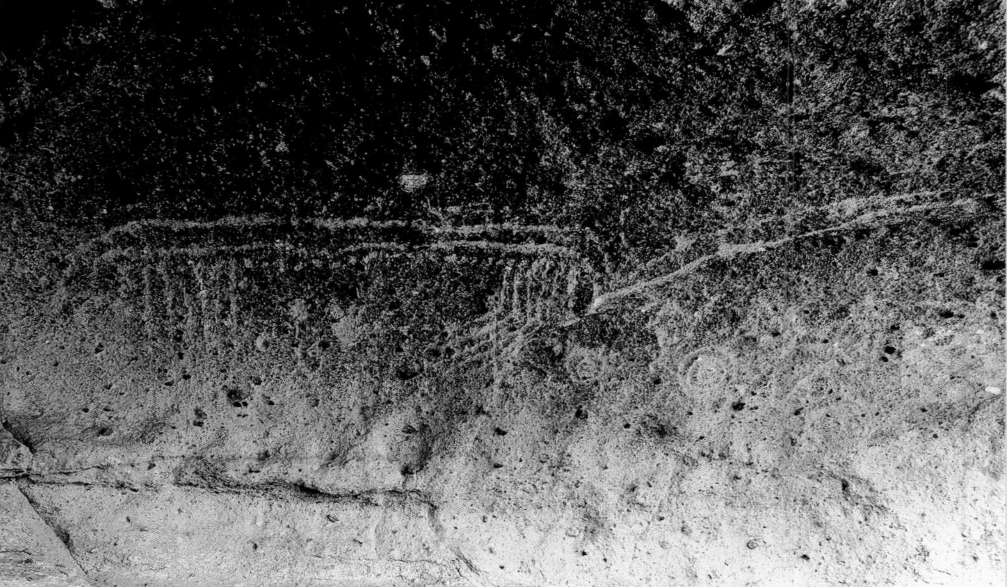

BOTTOM: Art panel approximately 2,000 years old bears an image of a sandhill crane

Though the sandhill cranes are still a long way off,
I CAN HEAR THE FIRST ARMADA CALLING
before I actually see them—
a formidable, dignified procession across the dusk-stilled sky.

Soon, a single trumpetlike horn note reverberates from overhead, and the cranes begin swirling down like parachutists to land in the field directly before me. In the distance I can see and hear hundreds more in the fading light, long wavering lines of cranes coming from every direction to spend the night within the safety of their legions. The sandhill cranes will spend several weeks alternating flights to traditional sites each evening for roosting and to farm fields and meadows each dawn to forage and build fat reserves for the final flight to the nesting grounds. There is much chattering between them as the cranes settle in for the night, the din diminishing as sleep comes to the flock, heads gracefully tucked under their wings. As the moon rises and cold settles like a blanket over the fields, I see thousands of crane shapes illuminated in silvered moonlight, and I leave them to their well-deserved rest.

The world?
MOONLIT WATER DROPS
from the crane's bill.

—Zen Master Dogen, thirteenth-century Japan

Writing in "Marshland Elegy," Aldo Leopold described the voice of the sandhill crane as "the trumpet in the orchestra of evolution." His eloquent words speak not only to the antiquity of cranes but also to an anatomical adaptation that lies at the heart of the crane's remarkable voice. Birds produce sounds at the base of the trachea (windpipe), not at the top, as mammals do. In general, bigger birds have longer tracheas and a deeper timbre to their voices—especially among those species whose calls must travel across vast distances. The sandhill crane's long trachea, acting much like a French horn, serves to increase the harmonic range of the vocalizations and improve acoustical transmission. The voices of calling cranes embody the very spirit of wilderness—and a time when the whole world turned on seasonal rhythms.

The spring migratory stopover provides sandhill cranes with an opportunity to reestablish pair bonds and to engage in the elaborate courtship displays that have been celebrated in dance, prose, and legend in cultures throughout the world. Perhaps emboldened by the ancient energy of their rituals, sandhill cranes engage in animated "dance" maneuvers that include dipping, bowing, wing flapping, and leaps of twelve or more feet into the air. Dancing activity is most intense among the younger birds, subadults who have yet to breed. At times, a frenzy of dancing will spread contagiously through the flock, creating a spectacular and unforgettable show. As the urgency to move north to the breeding areas overcomes them, a few cranes at a time will launch themselves into the air with a great flapping of wings. Others follow until the whole sky seems filled with sandhill cranes—an aerial ballet, with birds climbing skyward on the spiraling thermals, their voices diminishing as they vanish amidst the mare's tails and blue sky on the northward journey.

A male sandhill crane enlivens his dance maneuvers by tossing a dirt clod as part of his display while a female looks on.

OPPOSITE: A migratory flock of pintails fills the sky with sound and motion.

Desert country can be prickly, **SPINY, AND UNFORGIVING.**

But there is an essential, transcending beauty in the range of adaptations that permits plants and animals to survive in a landscape that offers only a slender margin for life. In the sun-drenched heart of the San Luis Valley, a gray-green haze of shrubs yields little to the simmering heat of midday. Afternoon thunderstorms are building to the west and I anticipate the scent of rain to come—welcome wetness greening the drought. Everywhere I look, gnarled shrubs and sturdy herbaceous plants wear their resilience on their leaves, reflecting back what heat they can or conserving what moisture they have. Wildflowers add occasional splashes of color to the desert palette. Spring-blooming species, such as Easter daisy, larkspur, copper mallow, yellow puccoon, prickly pear, and Indian paintbrush, have given way to the midsummer hues of sand verbena, Rocky Mountain beeplant, golden aster, and gilia. By the end of summer, the seasonal mélange will include masses of prairie sunflowers, golden rabbitbrush, snakeweed, and mounds of white and purple asters—a baroque mosaic fashioned from gold, amethyst, and pearl.

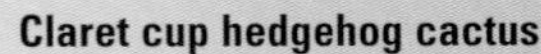

Claret cup hedgehog cactus

Plants must endure whatever comes their way—months or years of drought, drenching cloudbursts, searing heat, freezing cold, and desiccating winds. Persistent scarcity and sudden ephemeral abundance are woven into the fabric of life. For anyone schooled in the saturated greens of a northeastern forest, sagebrush may be an acquired taste. Yet from a naturalist's perspective, sagebrush is a masterpiece of perseverance—stubborn in its insistence on life and a zealot when it comes to conserving water.

Coping with an environment that can evaporate more water than it delivers clearly extracts an evolutionary price. The leaves of most plant species on the valley floor are remarkably small—a critical strategy for reducing water loss. Waxy coatings on the leaves and stems of some species, such as mountain mahogany, showy four-o'clock, and yucca, serve to "waterproof" delicate tissues and restrict evaporative losses. Cacti, such as prickly pear and claret cup, store large quantities of water in their tissues and have spines rather than leaves to further reduce water loss. Many plants have evolved a dense coat of fine, silvery, velvety hairs that provide thermal protection from both heat and cold, reflecting excess light and maintaining optimum leaf surface temperatures.

A female broad-tailed hummingbird nectar-feeding on Rocky Mountain beeplant

OPPOSITE: A late-summer display of sunflowers, alkali muhly, and snakeweed

Leaves are the factories for photosynthesis—the sun-powered chemical process that manufactures the sugars plants need for growth and development. Tiny respiratory structures in the leaves, called stomata, must remain open during photosynthesis to permit gas exchange with the atmosphere. For desert plants, the amount of water lost from the stomata must be balanced against moisture availability. When leaf temperatures are too high or when moisture is severely limited, photosynthesis shuts down. Highly reflective leaves, such as those of sagebrush and winterfat, maintain optimal leaf temperatures, allowing photosynthesis to proceed no matter what the air temperature. Additionally, sagebrush retains its gray-haired and light-reflective leaves year-round. As I examine one of the tiny trilobed leaves with my hand lens, I see stomata on both sides of the leaf rather than on only one surface, an adaptation that greatly increases photosynthetic efficiency. By adjusting the rate of photosynthesis to match the availability of moisture, sagebrush is able to micromanage its own survival.

Fine hairs protect the leaves and floral buds of checker-mallow (*Sidalcea neomexicana*).

A light breeze dances across the dune where I'm sitting—the first hint of storm clouds building along the western horizon. Shifting sands pose a special challenge to plants. Weather records at Great Sand Dunes describe a storm that deposited thirty inches of sand in one spot during a twenty-four-hour gale. Within this gritty, highly mobile world, only four plant species—scurfpea, Indian ricegrass, blowout grass, and prairie sunflower—are able to withstand the wind's mischief. To cope with sand on the move, these plants exhibit a range of adaptations that include rapid growth, specialized modes of photosynthesis that conserve water, and the ability to reproduce by vegetative means. Scurfpea, like most legumes, is host to nitrogen-fixing bacteria that live in specialized nodules on its roots; this bacteria converts atmospheric nitrogen into forms that can be used by plants to increase growth rates in high-stress environments. Indian ricegrass also makes use of nitrogen-fixing bacteria, forming sand-cemented sheaths around its root tips in which to house the bacteria. Most dune-adapted plants have extensive spreading root systems, called rhizomes, which can elongate rapidly and initiate the growth of new shoots as needed. White tangles of dead rhizomes often thread the sand in areas where plants are "on the move."

Desert plants are anything but passive when it comes to defending themselves from insects and other herbivores. Some have evolved spines, thorns, or irritating prickles to protect their delicate tissues. Chemical deterrents are also a frontline defense. Many plants—sagebrush, rabbitbrush, greasewood, lupine, and several others—synthesize volatile resins and other noxious compounds as a by-product of metabolism. The pungent aroma of big sagebrush, especially aromatic after a rain, is produced by the emanation of the volatile terpenes camphor and cineole from its leaves. Prickly pear and greasewood contain large amounts of oxalic acid, a compound toxic to most animals. Species that routinely utilize these plants for food and as a source of water—jackrabbits, pocket gophers, and pronghorn—have evolved a means of metabolizing oxalic acid without harmful side effects.

Though domestic livestock eat sagebrush sparingly, this terpene-rich shrub is a staple food for Gunnison's sage grouse and an important supplementary browse for pronghorn, mule deer, and elk. These animals have coevolved with sagebrush and have digestive adaptations that serve to detoxify and isolate the harmful compounds.

Mule deer bucks amidst a late-summer display of prairie sunflowers

In the San Luis Valley, the *sabkha* provides the harshest habitat of all in which to successfully germinate and establish new plants. The word *sabkha* is Arabic and is used to describe the wind-resistant hardpan that develops wherever surface sands or silt have become cemented together by evaporite salts. Even though sufficient soil moisture may be available to plants, high levels of soluble salts disrupt the normal osmotic balance that enables these plants to absorb water through their root systems. Next time you drive along Lane 6 on your way to the dunes, notice that the farms end where the *sabkha* begins. In areas of extreme salinity, salt-tolerant plants, such as salt grass and alkali muhly, reproduce vegetatively, sending out an extensive network of rhizomes that give rise to new shoots. Saltbush and greasewood cope with excess salt by increasing its concentration in their cell sap until it exceeds that of its soil moisture supply. Saltbush goes one step further, transporting excess salt to specialized storage glands that function like minute salt reservoirs. Once the storage glands are filled to capacity, they burst and release their contents to the leaf surface.

Pronghorn are built to run and have been clocked at speeds in excess of sixty miles per hour. During the rut (September–early October), pronghorn bucks vigorously defend their territory by chasing off rivals.

A dawn visit to Blanca Wetlands is very much like wandering

A TIDAL FLAT ALONG A DESERT COASTLINE.

As the first southwesterly breeze of the morning sweeps across the playa, the alkali mudflats exhale a similar briny aroma. Black terns swoop and glide over the shallowest water, darting here and there to feed on aquatic insects—airborne pirates on a mission of surprise. A squadron of Wilson's phalaropes, wings flashing like semaphores, performs a brilliantly choreographed series of flight maneuvers. Once the phalaropes land on the surface, they begin spinning frenetically—often as many as sixty revolutions per minute. This unique foraging strategy is thought to create a whirlpool that either draws in insects from the surface or stirs them up from the bottom. Perhaps because they seem so delicate, I find it hard to reconcile the fact that these diminutive little shorebirds make the long journey to brackish wetlands in southern South America to spend the winter. I've often wondered if any of the Wilson's phalaropes that I see on the Patagonian lakes I've visited, twirling in the company of Andean flamingos, spent the Northern Hemisphere summer in the San Luis Valley.

Each spring, Wilson's phalaropes arrive on their breeding grounds in the San Luis Valley after wintering in the Altiplano of Bolivia, Chile, or Argentina. Female phalaropes have brighter breeding plumage than males and exhibit polyandrous mating behavior (mate with more than one male). The male constructs the nest, develops two brood patches to incubate the eggs, and rears the young. The female phalarope stands sentry at the nest, sometimes providing a lookout for two adjacent nests, and abandons the male shortly after the young fledge.

OPPOSITE: A migratory flock of Wilson's phalaropes

In this world of muted greens and browns, the pale blue legs of American avocets always come as a surprise. Along the shore of the playa, a group of avocets appears to be foraging cooperatively, swishing their slim up-curved bills back and forth just below the surface, their rust-pink heads and black-and-white bodies moving in unified purpose. The only other North American member of the Recurvirostridae clan, the black-necked stilt, has long reddish pink legs that would make a chorus girl blush. These species may nest in close proximity to one another; avocets and stilts share the same diet of aquatic invertebrates and crustaceans and also rely on aggressive behaviors rather than camouflage to protect their nest sites and young. Looking equally exotic, a white-faced ibis uses its elegantly down-curved bill to probe for insects in the midst of a chartreuse sward of Baltic rush.

INSETS FROM LEFT TO RIGHT: American avocets, black-necked stilts, white-faced ibis

At the far end of the playa,
A FLOCK OF SNOWY PLOVERS
skitters along the shore, bills poking here and there
in search of brine flies in the shallows.

These delicate little plovers will nest in loose colonies—each bird making a simple scrape in soft sand, unshaded and close to water. Like most of the shorebirds that share this harsh habitat, the snowy plover has no special physiological adaptations for coping with heat or excess salt in its diet. Left unattended, plover eggs would quickly bake in the sun. Both parents must stand vigil, taking turns sitting on the nest or standing over it to shade it—hour after hour. On especially hot days, the parents will submerge their breast feathers in water periodically, returning to the nest to drip water on the eggs, while at the same time benefiting from enhanced evaporative cooling. As the heat abates in late afternoon, both parents will leave the nest to forage for food. The noontime sun is almost directly overhead as I leave the refuge, and heat shimmers have already obscured the horizon. Clearly, the rigors and challenges of incubating eggs and rearing a brood on this stark alkali flat are better left to these brave, resilient little shorebirds.

Snowy plovers, Blanca Wetlands

Life in the Sahara-like world OF THE DUNES PROVIDES A striking contrast to that of the playa.

I particularly enjoy the soft light that follows dawn, when the sand is a fresh canvas to be explored. My tracks mingle in the sand with dozens of others, both large and small. Strong winds during the night have left behind the near-perfect arcs scribed by blades of blowout grass. As I walk toward the golden river of cottonwoods that defines Sand Creek, several game trails converge at a circlet of soft sand—a bison dust bath. Woolly brown clumps of fur dot the branches of the surrounding shrubs. The tracks of the bison are almost perfectly round, impossible to confuse with elk, mule deer, or pronghorn. Minute tick marks in the sand lead me to a circus beetle, busily foraging amidst the bison dung. Like most darkling beetles, this one tips its abdomen skyward in a defensive posture to warn me to stay away.

Two dark shadows trace the corrugations of the dunes,

AND I LOOK UP

to see a pair of ravens headed toward Sand Creek.

At my feet I notice the tracks of a large bird, most likely a great horned owl. As I look more closely, the sand appears scuffed with wing marks, and I find tufts of short soft fur beside a small dimpled runway. Hoping to learn the victim's identity, I follow the runway into the damp sand of the creek bed, where the tiny tracks are more clearly defined; it seems most likely that last night's drama involved a silky pocket mouse, the smallest of the valley's rodents.

On the other side of Sand Creek, a black-tailed jackrabbit sits amidst golden sprays of rabbitbrush and lavender asters, its backlit ears pink as rose quartz and threaded with dark veins. On a hot day, those ears, which are one-fifth the size of its body, radiate about one-third of the jackrabbit's body heat through vasodilation.

Tracing a strange zipperlike trail to a tangled thatch of scurfpea, I surprise a tiger beetle scavenging the much larger, still-moist carcass of a ten-lined June beetle. Tiger beetles are often seen darting across the sandy spaces between patches of vegetation, actively hunting for small insects on the sand or capturing them in flight. As I look more closely at the ivory pattern that borders the metallic green forewings of this beetle, I'm able to identify this handsome individual as a Great Sand Dunes tiger beetle.

The Great Sand Dunes tiger beetle, *Cicindela theatina* Rotger, was first described and named by Father Bernardo Rotger, a young Spanish priest assigned to the rural missions and chapels of the San Luis Valley. Rotger was an avid amateur entomologist who spent most of his spare time collecting insects and writing articles for professional journals. Almost nothing was known of the insect fauna of the San Luis Valley when Father Rotger began his fieldwork. His legacy includes a collection of some 42,000 specimens that are now part of the Entomology Museum at the University of Colorado.

TOP: Beautiful tiger beetle (*C. formosa*)

BOTTOM: The wolf spider, another common nocturnal predator in and around the dunes, uses the silk it produces to stabilize the sandy walls of its burrow and to bind the sand it removes from the burrow during excavation. This fascinating spider is distinguished by its large prominent eyes, which reflect a greenish light in the beam of a flashlight.

OPPOSITE: Six species of tiger beetles are found in the dunes, but only the Great Sand Dunes tiger beetle (*C. theatina*) is found exclusively in the San Luis Valley and nowhere else in the world.

I'm curious about several sets of converging tracks that lead to the threshold of a tiny cone-shaped depression in the sand—quite possibly the burrow of a giant sand treader camel cricket. These fascinating insects are omnivorous and begin foraging at dusk on plant matter, other insects, or mammal scat. Individuals have been known to travel more than 650 feet a night to forage. As their name would suggest, giant sand treader camel crickets are superbly equipped for digging and moving about on the sand. Their large hind legs are armored with horny growths called sand baskets that enable them to excavate a burrow with lightning speed. Surprisingly, the sexual habits of camel crickets are especially intriguing. The male digs a burrow in the evening, hoping to attract several females to enter and join his harem. Romance is a short-term affair for camel crickets, but males will aggressively defend their burrows and harems against interlopers, often using their hind-leg armature to drive off other males. Hoping last night's revelers are still in residence, I gently scoop away the sand. I'm too late—the harem master and his harem have gone on to other digs.

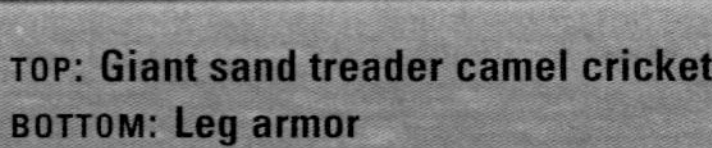

TOP: Giant sand treader camel cricket
BOTTOM: Leg armor

Tally the physiological and behavioral adaptations—
THE EVOLUTIONARY FINE-TUNING
necessary for living dry, and the list includes endless variations in strategy,

from the simple to the remarkable. As I climb the windward slope of a dune, being a biped seems a distinct disadvantage. With some chagrin, I notice the graceful tracks of another biped—Ord's kangaroo rat—paralleling my own furrowed trail. With its long bushy-tipped tail extended for balance, its small legs and feet tucked up under its chin, and the pistonlike spring action of its huge hind feet, this "master jumper" appears to ricochet across the sea of sand. This style of locomotion makes it difficult for a predator to anticipate the kangaroo's next move, making life just a bit safer for this desert speedster.

Ord's kangaroo rat is, for me, the most fascinating of all desert rodents. Despite its common name, this beautiful cinnamon-and-white silky-furred mammal is neither rat nor mouse. It is a member of a distinctive 40-million-year-old family of desert-dwelling rodents known as the Heteromyidae, which includes only the kangaroo rats and the pocket mice. Ord's kangaroo rat, like its cousins the plains pocket mouse and the silky pocket mouse, prefers sandy sparsely vegetated habitat—easy to navigate and as close as possible to a good supply of seeds.

Ord's kangaroo rat has evolved an array of physiological adaptations that helps it cope with moisture stress. It has little use for free water because it is able to make water from the foods it eats as a by-product of metabolism.

All members of this family have external fur-lined cheek pouches that open alongside the mouth, a trait they share with only one other rodent family, the pocket gophers. Kangaroo rats use their cheek pouches like recyclable grocery sacks to carry plant foods, typically high-protein seeds, back to the safety of the burrow. In a surprisingly deft and efficient manner, the kangaroo rat uses its dexterous forepaws to turn the cheek pouches inside out for cleaning and then pops them back into place for the next grocery delivery.

Curiously enough, the kangaroo rat has little tolerance for heat; it has honed the strategy of avoidance to perfection. A prodigious digger, it uses its powerful and versatile hind feet to excavate an elaborate burrow system with a labyrinthine network of tunnels and storage, waste, and sleeping chambers. Kangaroo rats are largely nocturnal, spending the majority of their time in the cool, moist environment of the burrow. Plugs of dirt are used to seal off access and maintain a high humidity level in the burrow, conserving precious moisture and providing protection from predators.

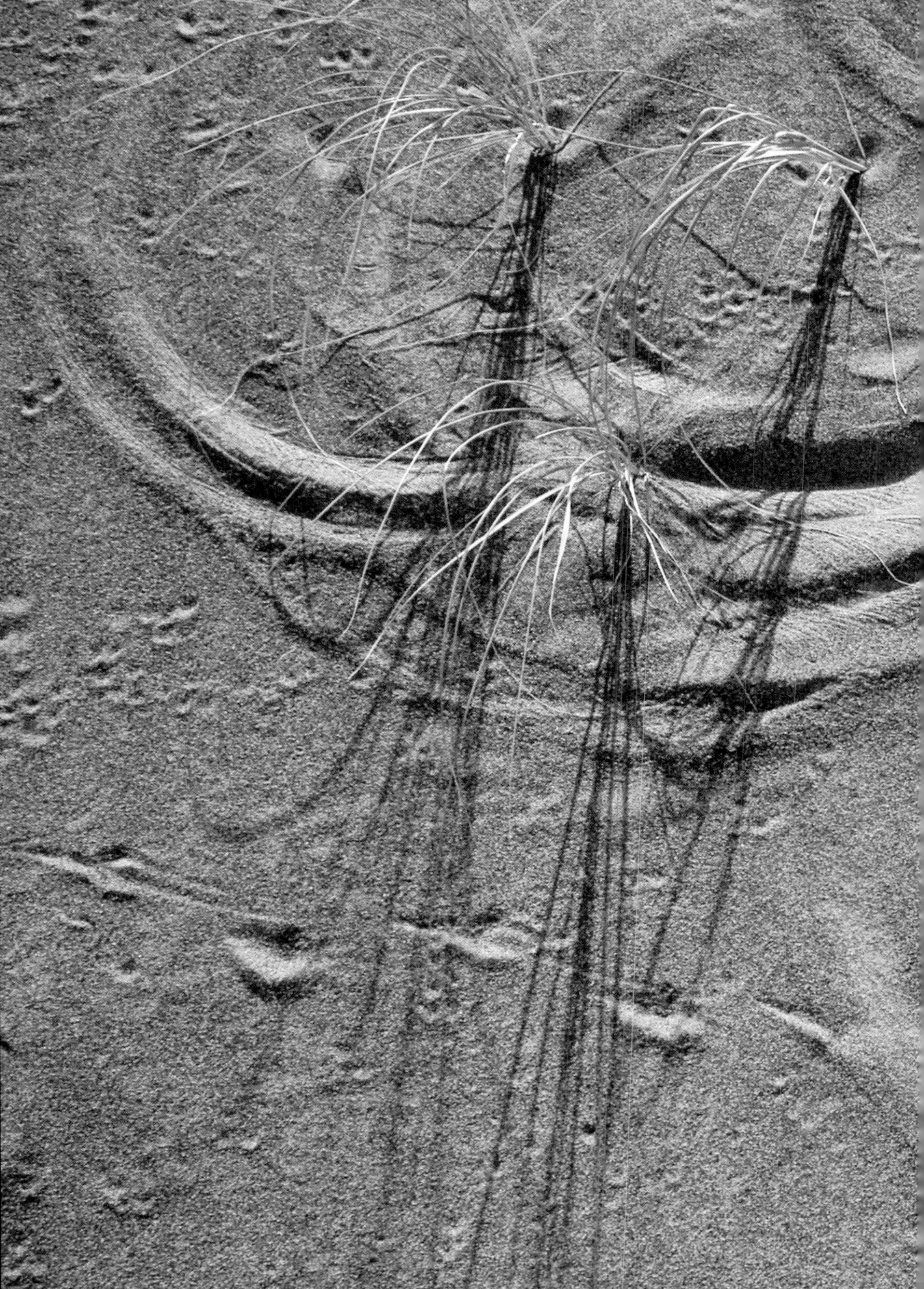

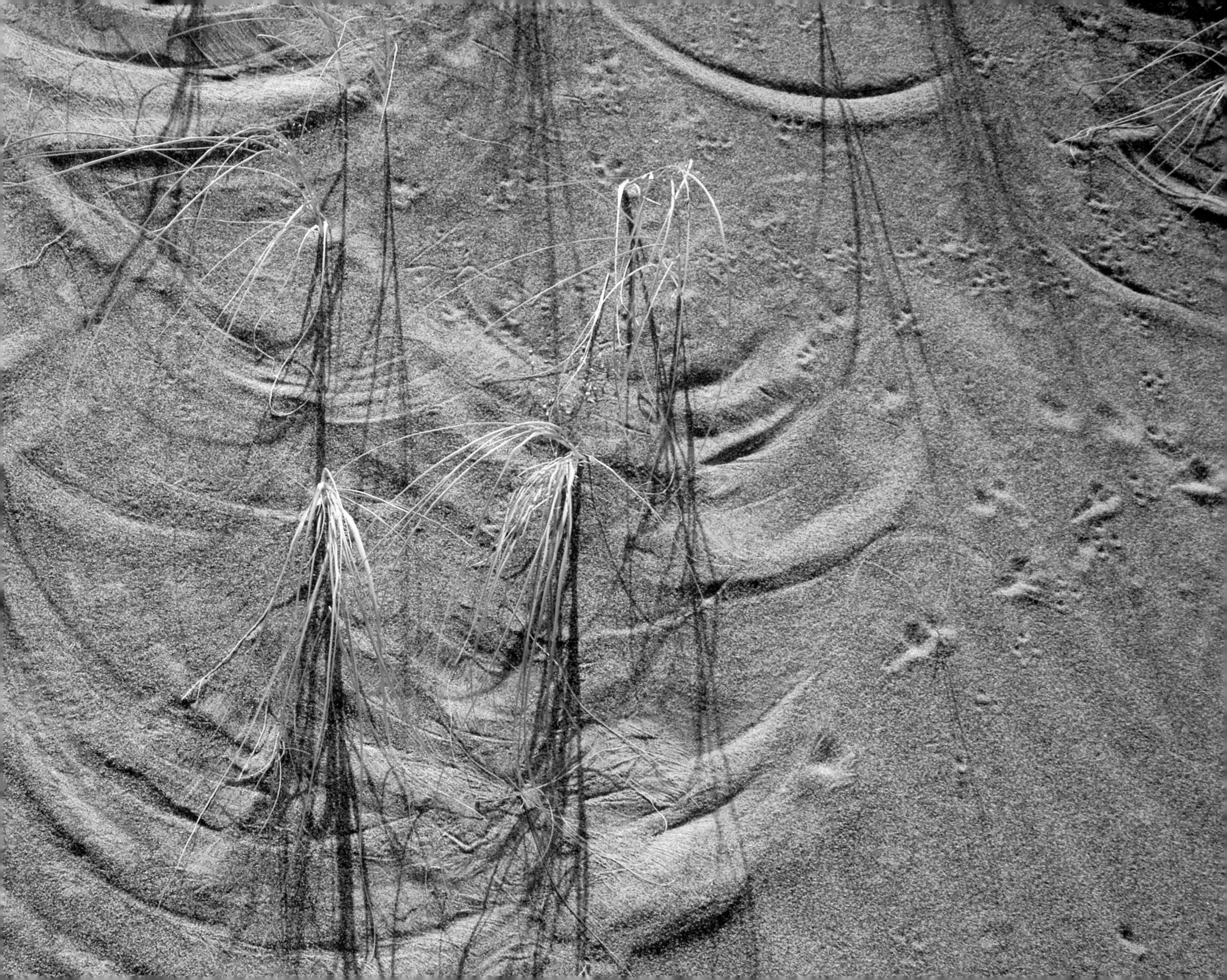

On a summer's day,
THE SUN HIGH OVERHEAD,
the temperature in the San Luis Valley is often hot enough to send birds and mammals heading for the shade or a cool burrow.

In contrast, nighttime temperatures may drop as much as fifty degrees on clear nights—a challenge to any animal that relies on solar heating for energy rather than on its own internal combustion. The body temperature of solar-powered animals—reptiles, amphibians, fish, and most invertebrates—tends to conform to their physical environment. For mammals and birds that remain active year-round, the energetic cost of internal metabolic combustion is exceedingly high. The porcupine relies on a variety of physiological and behavioral adaptations to maintain an optimal body temperature both winter and summer. Though seemingly clumsy and slow moving on the ground, porcupines are agile tree climbers, using their long curved claws for gripping and their stout spine-armored tail for balance and support. Porcupines spend most of their time in the branches of cottonwoods, aspens, or pines and feed on a seasonally shifting diet of buds, leaves, seeds, and sweet inner bark (cambium) of trees to meet their energy requirements.

A porcupine finds both food and protection from predators in a narrow-leaf cottonwood.

OPPOSITE: Porcupines will travel great distances through the dunes when moving between foraging areas.

At my feet, a small piece of the desert floor suddenly rises. As I watch, a short-horned lizard miraculously reconstitutes itself before my eyes, scale by scale. This wide-bodied, low-slung lizard is so perfectly camouflaged I might never have seen it if it hadn't moved. A fringe of thick spines projects backward from the flattened head, like the nape guard of a miniature stegosaurus; a line of enlarged scales extends along each side of the body and the tail, blurring the shape of the lizard's body against the sand. Though short-horned lizards may look a bit pugnacious at first glance, their scaly spine-armored skin significantly reduces evaporative losses and makes them virtually invisible to predators. As is true for all desert dwellers, water conservation provides the key to survival for horned lizards. By burrowing underground, they minimize evaporative water losses through the skin. Horned lizards replace lost water with water obtained from the foods they eat (mostly ants) and will drink water whenever and in whatever form it is available. Unlike all other Colorado lizards, the short-horned lizard gives birth to live young rather than laying its eggs in a nest. By allowing the eggs to develop internally, the female short-horned lizard is able to protect her offspring from predators and speed their development.

A sunning lizard burns five to ten times fewer calories than a resting bird or mammal that is maintaining the same body temperature. By waiting to emerge until the temperature is "lizard perfect," orienting their bodies in relation to the sun's rays, moving to warmer or cooler microenvironments as needed, and varying the amount of time spent in these locations, lizards achieve outstanding energy savings.

All landscapes have a history ...

THERE ARE DISTINCT VOICES, LANGUAGES THAT BELONG TO PARTICULAR AREAS.

There are voices inside rocks, shallow washes, shifting skies; they are not silent. —Joy Harjo, *Secrets from the Center of the World*

The human history of the San Luis Valley spans nearly 12,000 years—an extraordinary saga that begins with the arrival of the first Paleo-Indian hunters. This is truly a land apart—no canyon walls narrow the sky or cut off the view. From almost any vantage point, I find it impossible to look out across these gnarled greasewood flats without trying to envision what the valley would have looked like to the first nomadic hunters—the Clovis people. As I watch the dust trail kicked up by a modern herd of Medano Ranch bison, my imagination transports me to a time when the tracks of Columbian mammoths and long-horned bison would have intermingled along the shores of the valley's playa lakes.

Dense swards of moisture-loving grasses and shrubs would have extended to the far horizon. Except for the mountains that rim the edges of the valley, the scene in my mind's eye most closely resembles the East African veldt—a Pleistocene spin on a North American version of the Masai Mara. Emerging from the swirls of dust that rise along the edge of the dunefield, I imagine a small herd of ancient bison trailing behind a shaggy matriarch as she follows a well-worn path to a mud wallow near an artesian spring. I can feel the rush of anticipation the Paleo-Indian hunters must have experienced, waiting in ambush, their spears held in readiness. What I cannot imagine, in a landscape that lacks even a tree to hide behind, are the skills that would have been required to kill one of these giants at close range. As the first spear hurtles through the air of my imaginary hunt, I remember the exquisite artistry of a group of Paleo-Indian projectile points I once saw. They were larger than I'd expected, with a single flute along their midsection and finely flaked edges, so spare of form and mass that they were almost transparent—deceptively delicate, yet superbly lethal.

The slender spiderflower (*Cleome multicaulis*) (right) and Rocky Mountain beeplant (*Cleome serrulata*) (left) are rarely found in the same habitat. Both species are annuals—blooming, producing fruit, and dying in a single season. The distribution of slender spiderflower once extended from Central Mexico to southern Wyoming, but this alkali wetland–loving species has disappeared from nearly 90 percent of its former range. Prehistoric and modern Puebloan peoples boiled the stems and leaves of Rocky Mountain beeplant to produce a black paint, which was used to decorate their pottery and baskets. This pigment has endured on artifacts dating from at least the fourteenth century.

OPPOSITE: A cattle egret squares off with a curious bison.

Dryness DID NOT ALWAYS DEFINE the San Luis Valley as it does today.

Archeologists and geologists continue to shed light on the ways in which sequential prehistoric cultures adapted to the unique ecosystems of the San Luis Valley and to the dramatic climatic changes that imposed new challenges on subsistence lifeways—a story replete with lessons for both present and future inhabitants. In the absence of a written narrative, changes in stone tool technologies, especially projectile point styles, are used to differentiate among prehistoric cultural groups during the thousands of years prior to the introduction of pottery. Although more than a thousand archeological sites have been recorded in the San Luis Valley, only a small number have been excavated. Hundreds more no doubt lie hidden beneath the valley's shifting sands—a unique "prehistory savings account" for future archeologists to decipher. Of the hundred or so Paleo-Indian sites, the majority are post-Clovis in age.

Despite the abundance of both mammoth and bison bone beds, the best evidence of Clovis artifacts in direct association with mammoth bones comes from the Zapata Mammoth Site, located along the edge of an ancient wetland just to the west of Great Sand Dunes.

Cooler temperatures and increased precipitation coincided with the ascendancy of the Folsom culture, between about 12,790 and 11,910 years B.P. Increased snowfall at higher elevations resulted in the expansion of mountain glaciers, and lake levels rose throughout the San Luis Valley. At least thirty-nine Folsom sites have been reported in the valley, their distribution suggesting that Folsom people hunted and spent the majority of their time in the Closed Basin, as well as along streams and springs in the foothills and at higher elevations in the San Juan Mountains.

Deadman Creek meanders and cottonwoods

Over the past thirty years, Smithsonian archeologists Dennis Stanford and Pegi Jodry have focused their efforts on several of the San Luis Valley's most important Folsom sites: Linger, Zapata, Stewart's Cattle Guard, and Black Mountain. Stewart's Cattle Guard is the most extensively excavated Folsom site in North America. In what appears to be a single event, Folsom hunters either killed or trapped at least forty-nine bison within the arc formed by a large parabolic dune. Excavations at the site reveal three distinct activity areas: the location where the bison were killed and butchered for transport, a nearby campsite with associated hearths and waste flakes from toolmaking and repair, and a work area where meat, bones, and hides were processed. The Black Mountain site is uniquely situated along a converging network of prehistoric travel routes that would have taken Folsom people north over the Continental Divide to the Gunnison River country, southwest to potential wintering areas in the San Juan Basin, or a few miles downstream to the Rio Grande and the varied resources of the San Luis Valley.

Cotton Lake

One can easily imagine Folsom women scraping hides beside a small campfire or preparing the medicinal roots of *oshá* for drying and transport to a winter camp in the lowlands. In a nearby men's work area, brightly colored concentrations of waste flakes—bits of Mosca chert and chalcedony, black obsidian, burgundy-colored jasper, and quartzite—litter the ground around a scrap of bison hide on which a Folsom flintknapper sits as he pressure-flakes the edges of tools that have become dull from use.

Climatic change is a powerful force in shaping human economies.

The shift from Pleistocene to modern climates, vegetation patterns, and fauna was marked by a dramatic shift in the lifeways of indigenous people. Beginning about 7,500 years ago and lasting for nearly 6,000 years, during the cultural period known as the Archaic, the Paleo-Indian tool kit was replaced by stemmed and notched projectile point styles scaled to the size of the intended prey and to the method of hunting. Large game—elk, deer, antelope, and mountain sheep—as well as rabbits, ducks, sandhill cranes, and wild turkeys, became increasingly important in the diet.

A herd of cow elk and yearlings. The Colorado Division of Wildlife reports that more than 2,000 elk use the San Luis Valley.

At the Dry Lakes site, preliminary excavations of a prehistoric midden suggest that Archaic people took advantage of lower lake levels to harvest large numbers of buffalofish. Cordage nets made from twisted plant fibers or animal sinew might have been used to capture rabbits, shorebirds, and ducks. Blankets were "woven" by wrapping strips of rabbit fur around yucca cords and then binding them together in close parallel rows. Architectural features such as rock shelters and stone foundations for brush- or hide-covered dwellings suggest that some Archaic groups established seasonal camps in the valley or returned repeatedly to the same areas. The discovery of a beautiful stone-drilled pendant and a trail of carbon-darkened sand near Indian Spring led to the excavation of a primitive dwelling and central hearth dated at around 4,500 years B.P. This intriguing site, which has yielded hundreds of pottery shards, waste flakes, several stone tools, and grinding stones, provides our first real window into the domestic lives of Archaic people living in the San Luis Valley.

Hand stones (manos) and grinding slabs (metates) were used to prepare a wide variety of plant and animal foods, the most common being ricegrass, piñon nuts, juniper berries, saltbush, chokecherries, dried fish, and meat.

OPPOSITE: A snowy egret fishes in shallow water. These native egrets may be distinguished from the introduced cattle egret by their black legs and yellow feet.

There is a magical quality about Indian Spring

THAT TRANSCENDS TIME—

its beauty difficult to describe or define.

It is not surprising that in desert country, natural springs are often imbued with sacred meaning and transformational power by indigenous peoples. This extraordinary ellipse-shaped spring is the source, the lifeblood, of Big Spring Creek. In all but the driest years, the creek's sinuous meanders run bank full, crystal clear, and cold. If you sit quietly on the sweep of dune that encircles Indian Spring and look down into the reflecting pool, you can watch the end of a day mirrored in its glassy surface. Sunset colors—amber, amethyst, and pearl gray—swirl across the water with each soft breath of wind. In the waning light, as the sun disappears behind the western mountains, Indian Spring turns from sapphire to ebony—Earth's eye fringed with lashes of coyote willow.

Sunset at Indian Spring

Each of us harbors a native homeland in our hearts; we draw strength from it, just as we would from a talisman. For some, it is an actual place; for others, it is a memory-place for spiritual or personal renewal. Among Native Americans, rich oral traditions—stories of creation and emergence—link the past with the present, story by story, generation after generation. The Utes—the Blue Sky People—regard Indian Spring as sacred in their creation mythology. Several Puebloan groups trace their spiritual origins to a sacred place in the San Luis Valley. Various Puebloan creation stories relate how their ancestors emerged from the dark underworld into the sunshine through a symbolic passageway, which they call the *sipapu*; it is also said that when you die, your spirit returns to the underworld by way of the *sipapu*. According to Tewa mythology, The People emerged from a lake (their *sipapu*); the name for this lake in the Tewa language means "lake at the sandy place." Might the Tewa's sacred *sipapu* be Indian Spring or one of the San Luis lakes? We will never know for certain. Another Puebloan creation story describes their ancestors emerging from the underworld near the summit of Blanca Peak, possibly from one of the small alpine lakes.

Big Spring Creek, its banks lushly green with watercress, meanders across the sand sheet before disappearing into the sands and gravels of the valley floor.

In contrast to Puebloan mythology, the Navajo paint their creation story with a broader brush, placing their spiritual homeland within the boundaries delimited by four sacred mountains; Blanca Peak is considered to be the Sacred Mountain of the East. Traditional Navajos still travel to the mountain to collect soil, plants, and spring water to be used in special ceremonies. The Wheeler-Hayden surveys of 1874–1875 reported a large circular stone wall on the summit of Blanca Peak that might have served as a vision-quest site or as an eagle trap. At the base of Blanca Peak, a Native American burial of uncertain age was accidentally unearthed by a farmer's plow many years ago; the corpse was in a seated position facing west, with an abalone shell placed over his face and secured with a leather thong.

Coyotes are opportunists when they hunt for small prey, combining their finely tuned ability to hear the slightest sound with an amazing sense of smell. In this rare photo, the coyote has detected the presence of a mouse or vole beneath the snow and has launched itself in a perfectly aimed arc to strike the killing blow, using its front paws to break through the snow. With a quick bite, it will capture the exposed prey.

OPPOSITE: Cow elk

Although no evidence of Ancestral Puebloan dwellings has been discovered in the San Luis Valley, Taos Pueblo legends describe bird-hunting and turquoise expeditions to the valley beginning about 1300. Large numbers of small delicately made Puebloan-style points have been found near the San Luis lakes and around other wetlands. Ducks, shorebirds, and possibly sandhill cranes are known to have provided an important source of food as well as a supply of colorful feathers for ceremonial garments and clan rituals.

Spanish exploration and conquest in the New World left an indelible imprint on the land and indigenous peoples of the Southwest. The journals of Spanish explorers provide us with the first written descriptions of the Puebloan villages and Indian encampments they encountered as they explored "Tierra Incognita"—the mysterious northern frontier of Nueva España. In 1598, Don Juan de Oñate took possession of "The Kingdom and Province of New Mexico" for the Spanish crown. Spanish ambitions for the northern frontier were now clearly focused on the territory drained by the northern Rio Grande and its tributaries, which included the San Luis Valley and much of southern Colorado.

Bison, Medano-Zapata Ranch

From the Puebloans, the Spaniards learned of large herds of bison in a broad valley to the north—today's San Luis Valley. Oñate dispatched his most competent vaqueros to capture some of these wild "cows" for domestication. Though the bison roundup was a miserable failure, Oñate's misadventures in animal husbandry provide us with the first recorded description of the San Luis Valley and the Utes. In his report to the Mexican viceroy, Oñate describes a probable Ute hunting camp at the base of the Sangre de Cristos in surprising detail. The camp included at least fifty large bell-shaped tents made of expertly tanned bison hides painted in bright colors. The Spaniards seemed impressed by the ease with which the Utes were able to move the entire camp from place to place. Families would disassemble their tents, make travois (sleds) out of the hides and the tent poles, attach a heavy bundle of dried meat and pinole (corn), and hitch the travois to a shaggy medium-sized dog. The dogs would trot along at a steady gait beside their owners, one travois after another, toward the next encampment.

Coyote tracks mimic the shadow of a sunflower.

Oñate described a Ute bison hunt with considerable awe, the "Indios" hiding in simple brush blinds at the watering holes and killing the bison with a single flint-tipped arrow shot from a large bow at close range. The Utes have long been considered the primary inhabitants of the San Luis Valley from the time of Spanish contact until the late 1800s.

For 250 years, the fortunes of the Spanish waxed and waned in the far-flung corners of Nueva España. As Spanish dreams of empire began to fade, French and American traders, followed by U.S. Army explorers and surveyors, began arriving in the region in ever-increasing numbers. With Europe in turmoil, Napoleon offered the United States the Louisiana Territory for $15 million. President Thomas Jefferson wasted no time in closing the deal—sight unseen, geography unknown. Though the actual geographic boundaries of the purchase were hazy at best, Jefferson believed that the territory encompassed all the land west of the Mississippi River as far south as the Arkansas River's drainage and north to Canada; everything south of the Arkansas, including all of the San Luis Valley, the Sangre de Cristos, and the San Juans, remained under the control of the Spanish territorial government in Santa Fe.

A bachelor gathering amid the sunflowers

In 1806, in what may have been a deliberate provocation to test Spanish resolve, the army dispatched Lt. Zebulon Pike and a small exploring party to trace the headwaters of the Arkansas River and the Red River.

Crossing the High Plains on a crisp November day,
PIKE'S EXPEDITION SPOTTED A STRANGE APPARITION,
"a small blue cloud" on the distant horizon—
the cloud, of course, would one day be called Pikes Peak.

From this point onward, Pike's miscalculations went from bad to worse. Winter found Pike and his men in the mountains, struggling through snowdrifts, bitterly cold, and near starvation. On January 28, 1807, the expedition finally reached Medano Pass in the Sangre de Cristos. The view from the pass must have seemed like a strange mirage to the weary men. In Pike's own words:

> The sand hills extended up and down at the foot of the White Mountains, about 15 miles and appeared to be about five miles in width. Their appearance was exactly that of a sea in a storm (except for color) not the least sign of vegetation thereon.

The expedition camped for the night near Medano Creek, and Pike was able to climb "one of the largest hills of sand." From the top of this pinnacle he could see a large river in the distance, which he wrongly identified as the Red River. The river in question was undoubtedly the Rio Grande, and Pike and his men were eventually arrested by the Spanish and taken to Santa Fe.

Fearing continued encroachment by the Americans, the Mexican and Spanish governments renewed their efforts to increase settlement in southern Colorado. New Mexico's territorial governors were encouraged to give large tracts of land, or *mercedes*, to individuals who promised to establish permanent settlements between Taos and the Arkansas River. The practice continued even after Mexico declared its independence from Spain in 1821. The last of the territorial governors, Manuel Armijo, completed most of the grants before 1848, when the San Luis Valley became an American territory. Land grants in the San Luis Valley were among the largest of all. They were set up as *ejidos*, in accordance with Spanish colonial law, which allowed for private ownership of small farms in conjunction with large tracts of communal lands that were intended to be used for livestock grazing, wood gathering, hunting, and fishing.

Aspen and piñon with fresh snow

Hispanic settlers—*los primeros pobladores*—began arriving in the San Luis Valley in significant numbers in the 1840s and 1850s. The first permanent settlement in Colorado, San Luis, was established in 1852. The earliest homes were simple log and adobe structures made by setting cottonwood posts upright in the ground and filling the crevices with mud. Little by little, as peace with the valley's indigenous groups allowed, the rustic homes were replaced by adobe homes constructed with thick walls and flat roofs. Many settlers built simple single-family ranchos along the valley's streams and rivers. The ruins of a few of these remote outposts can still be seen today in the southern half of the valley. Because of the need for mutual protection and to provide a better sense of community on the frontier, settlers would often conjoin several individual adobe room blocks to form a large square or rectangle—a plaza—which was entered through an opening at each end. Today, descendents of these hardy colonists are represented in both federal and state government, in education, medicine, science, and the arts. In fact, wherever you go in the valley you can feel the enduring spirit and cultural presence of these Hispanic settlers.

Autumn cottonwoods

The Colorado gold rush of 1858–1859 shifted the balance of power and changed the face of the San Luis Valley forever. Following the Civil War, the political rhetoric of Manifest Destiny sent wave after wave of Euro-Americans scudding westward in ever-increasing numbers. In slow, bitter increments, treaty by treaty, the Utes lost their claim to their beloved Blue Sky country and were eventually confined to a dusty corner of southwestern Colorado. Competition for grazing land and town sites intensified and sometimes turned violent, significantly slowing the pace of Hispanic settlement. Following annexation, U.S. courts confirmed fewer than 10 percent of the legitimate Mexican land grant claims, forcing many Hispanic settlers off lands that they believed to be legally theirs. Many of these land grants were subsequently sold to eager buyers, such as William Gilpin, first governor of the Territory of Colorado, an unabashed promoter of investment opportunities in what he called "Bayou San Luis." Nearly a hundred years later, two of the land grants, the Zapata and the Baca, would play a pivotal role in the battle to preserve the ecological diversity and extraordinary landscapes of the San Luis Valley for future generations.

Juvenile great horned owl at the old Medano Ranch headquarters

Water—
A SCARCE COMMODITY IN DESERT COUNTRY—has been the single most pervasive force in the geologic, natural, and human history of the San Luis Valley.

For more than 150 years, beginning with the granting of Colorado's first water right—the San Luis People's Ditch—the economic realities of ranching and farming in the valley have been driven by the availability of water and by the legal doctrine of prior appropriation: "first in time, first in right." The arcane vocabulary of western water law—junior rights, senior rights, ditch rights, surface rights, subsurface rights—has become common parlance among farmers, ranchers, and environmentalists. To obtain a water right, the appropriator had to first "divert" the water—physically take it out of a stream or river—and put it to "beneficial use." The court's definition of beneficial use was that the diversion be consumptive (extractive), and that once diverted and put to use, the water could not be "wasted." As decreed by Colorado law, returning water to the original stream or river from which it had come or using it to maintain wildlife habitat or natural ecosystems did not constitute a beneficial use.

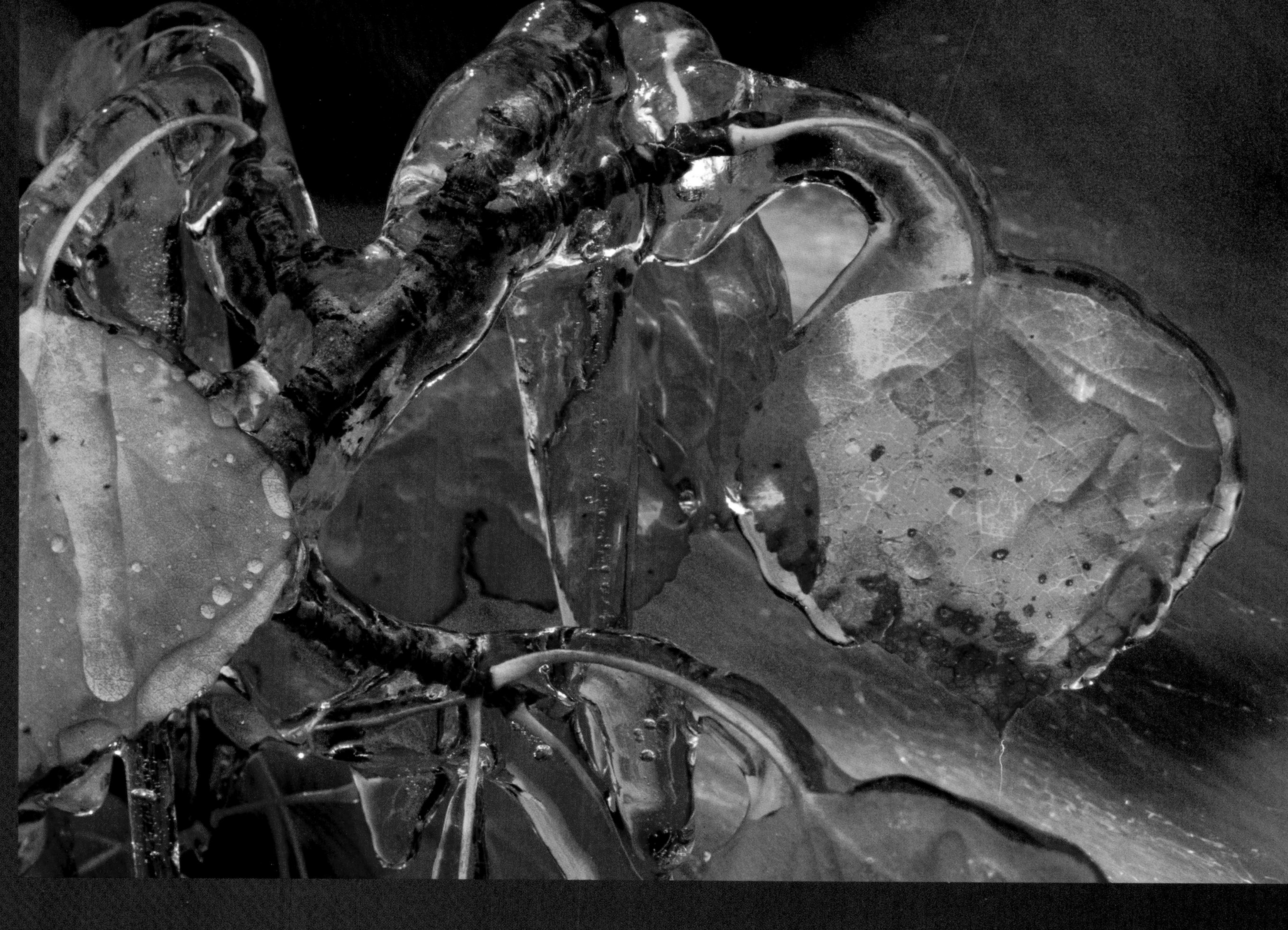

Pressures to develop the water in the Closed Basin have billowed like storm clouds on the horizon for nearly a quarter of a century. Encompassing about 2,940 square miles, the Closed Basin serves as the principal source of irrigation water for ranching and for the rotating boom sprinklers, or center pivots, that delimit the valley's agricultural lands. From the air, a vast checkerboard pattern of center pivots—more than 2,000 quarter-mile circles of potatoes, malt barley, lettuce, and alfalfa—defines the southern half of the Closed Basin. In addition, the Closed Basin Project, a forty-two-mile network of narrow cement-lined canals and pump stations, removes as much as 40,000 acre-feet of groundwater annually from the unconfined aquifer and diverts it to the Rio Grande in compliance with the 1939 Rio Grande Compact, a complex legal agreement between the states of Colorado, New Mexico, and Texas. The Closed Basin aquifer is the lifeblood that nurtures not only human endeavors and cultural traditions throughout the valley but also the intricate ecological relationships and landscape processes that are unique to Great Sand Dunes.

Center pivots

Water battles seem to come in waves—and for two decades the fight for San Luis Valley water focused on the historic Baca Ranch. The 100,000-acre ranch is situated just to the north of Great Sand Dunes and encompasses most of the Luis Maria Cabeza de Baca Grant No. 4, one of the original Mexican land grants. Hydrologists believed the ranch, which includes two Fourteeners and multiple watersheds along the flanks of the Sangre de Cristos, to be the last private landholding in the northern half of the valley large enough to support a major groundwater mining and exportation project. Two consortiums of ambitious investors—American Water Development, Inc. (AWDI) in the 1980s and Stockman's Water in the 1990s—set their sights on the Baca with the intent of mining the underlying aquifer and selling the water to the highest bidder. Canadian businessman Maurice Strong, who bought the Baca in 1986 and founded AWDI, wanted to sell water to urban markets in Los Angeles, Phoenix, or any one of several thirsty cities along the Colorado Front Range.

The long-billed dowitcher visits the San Luis Valley only during migration and may be seen skittering through the shallows of the playa, probing in the mud for food with rapid sewing machine–like movements of its bill.

OPPOSITE: Bitterns align with the grass blades in perfect concealment.

Opposition to AWDI spread like a sandstorm across the San Luis Valley and beyond. The Department of the Interior moved quickly to secure a Federal Reserve Water Right for Great Sand Dunes. With so much at stake, both environmentally and economically, a remarkable alliance of public and private partners joined forces against the water developers. In 1991, AWDI was soundly defeated in the Colorado Supreme Court. In an effort to lay the groundwork for long-term protection of the valley's water, Tim Wirth, who represented Colorado in the U.S. Senate at the time, added critical language to a draft water bill making its way through Congress. The amended bill gave the Interior secretary critical approval rights on any proposal that involved water mining or export over or under any federally owned lands or via a federal facility. To ready the war chest for the next water battle, scientists embarked on a series of research projects whose principal aim was to better understand dune and valley hydrology.

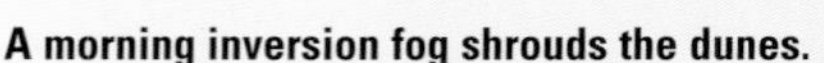

A morning inversion fog shrouds the dunes.

OPPOSITE: A red-winged blackbird greets the morning with a frosty song.

In 1995, with the purchase of the Baca Ranch by valley native Gary Boyce and his Cabeza de Baca Company, which included San Francisco–based Farallon, a new water exportation scheme—Stockman's Water—landed on the table. Ken Salazar, then Colorado's attorney general and a fifth-generation native of the valley, voiced the state's opposition to Cabeza's plans in clear unequivocal language. The resounding defeat of two Cabeza de Baca–sponsored ballot initiatives in 1998 sounded the death knell for Stockman's Water.

The need to turn a battleground into common ground was urgent. In 1999, The Nature Conservancy purchased the historic 100,000-acre Medano-Zapata Ranch, another of the San Luis Valley's biological "hot spots," from its conservation-minded owner, Hisa Ota. Government officials and local community leaders joined The Nature Conservancy in a groundbreaking bipartisan partnership to secure national park status for Great Sand Dunes through the acquisition of the Baca Ranch and to move toward lasting protection for the unique hydrological system of the Closed Basin.

Colorado's congressional delegation sponsored the long-awaited legislation required for the federal government's purchase of the Baca Ranch, and with the enthusiastic support of the Clinton administration, the Great Sand Dunes National Park and Preserve Act passed in 2000. The Nature Conservancy assumed the critical role of banker for the federal government until Congress appropriated the $33 million purchase price of the ranch through the Land and Water Conservation Fund. In addition to the expansion of Great Sand Dunes, the legislation created the 92,500-acre Baca National Wildlife Refuge and placed the mountainous portion of the Baca (including Kit Carson Peak) under the jurisdiction of Rio Grande National Forest.

But a new threat—posed by Lexam Explorations, a Canadian company that bought the mineral rights to the Baca Ranch in the 1990s—moved to center stage. In 2006, welcomed by the energy-friendly Bush administration, Lexam announced plans to begin drilling for gas and oil on the nation's newest and largest wildlife refuge. Wasting no time, the San Luis Valley Ecosystem Council filed a lawsuit to stop Lexam in its tracks. Its position was soon joined by representatives of the environmentally friendly Obama administration and Interior Secretary Ken Salazar, the National Park Service, the EPA, Colorado Governor Bill Ritter, the San Luis Valley Water Protection Coalition, the Colorado State Historic Preservation Office, the Hopi Tribe, and many other agencies and organizations. In 2010, Lexam stepped back, agreeing to sell the mineral rights to the federal government for $9.7 million—a resolution that will ensure that these rights are permanently retired on behalf of the American public. At long last, the journey that began more than seventy-five years earlier to protect one of Colorado's most unique landscapes and to establish Great Sand Dunes National Park and Preserve—our fifty-eighth national park—brings to a close one of the greatest conservation success stories of all time.

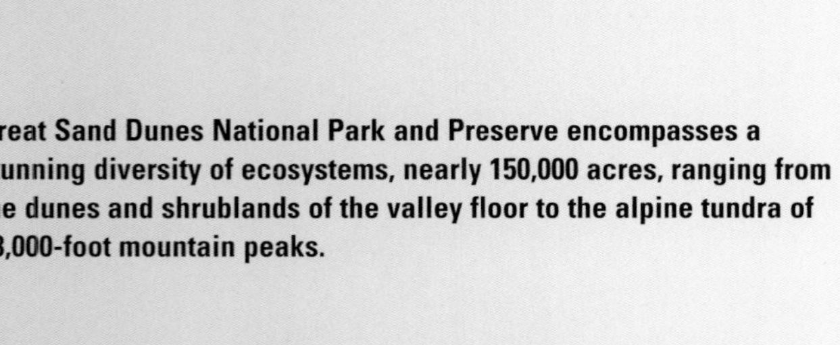

Great Sand Dunes National Park and Preserve encompasses a stunning diversity of ecosystems, nearly 150,000 acres, ranging from the dunes and shrublands of the valley floor to the alpine tundra of 13,000-foot mountain peaks.

There is something about the San Luis Valley THAT AFFECTS PEOPLE as surely as it breeds resilience in every plant and animal.

The places to which we are drawn enter our hearts and minds through our senses: the smell of sagebrush after a rain, the sound of sandhill cranes trumpeting down the wind, the sensuous shapes of dunes washed in pastel light, or the golden blaze of cottonwood leaves backlit by the sun. These experiences may last only minutes, but the feelings they invoke may be with us for a lifetime. As you begin to know a place, you learn the rhythm of the days and the seasons, the lifeways of its animals; you learn where the snowy plovers nest, when the Clark's nutcrackers begin harvesting piñon nuts, and when the elk begin bugling each autumn. Slowly, the unknown becomes familiar, and the familiar becomes a part of you—more precious for the knowing.

For me,
THE JOY IN LEARNING ANY LANDSCAPE
lies in figuring out how all the parts fit together to make the whole.

You lose one piece and the thread of the story changes. The ability of life to adapt to change, to seize opportunities, and to re-create itself lies at the very heart of what makes the San Luis Valley so special. Achieving lasting stewardship of this extraordinary landscape requires that we understand that economic stability and the permanence of human communities on the land are intertwined with the health of the surrounding land, water, and wildlife.

In the San Luis Valley, it's not the sound of cement flowing inexorably across the land in the name of development that should worry us—it's the probability that the voices of sandhill cranes and countless other wild things will fade away if we fail to remember how inextricably linked this valley is to every other place.

DEDICATION

To my parents, Sig and Arlene Shattil, who enriched my life, supported my passion for nature photography, and taught me that I could achieve any goal I set for myself.

—WS

In memory of Gitzo, our beloved four-legged friend, who brought joy to our lives, forgave our absences, and who will never be forgotten.

—RR

To my husband, Jim Benedict, who has been a beloved touchstone in my life for nearly forty years, and who taught me—by example—that writing with integrity and purpose can be one of the best contributions we can make to future generations.

—ADB

ISBN 978-0-9845257-0-6

Printed in Manitoba, Canada
Friesens Corporation
The text and cover paper meet the requirements of the Forest Stewardship Council (www.fsc.org)

10 9 8 7 6 5 4 3 2 1

Originally published by Fulcrum Publishing in 2005.
Revised edition published by Cloud Ridge Publishing in 2010.

Editor, Cloud Ridge edition: Alice Levine
Editor, Fulcrum edition: Faith Marcovecchio
Design: Ann W. Douden
Cover image: Bob Rozinski and Wendy Shattil

CLOUD RIDGE PUBLISHING
8297 Overland Road
Ward, Colorado 80481
(303) 459-3248
www.CloudRidge.org

Bob Rozinski and **Wendy Shattil** are the rarest of species—full-time professional nature photographers. They have worked individually and as a photographic team since 1981, capturing unique images of nature on film and digital media. Bob and Wendy are known worldwide for their award-winning work and reputation as conservation photographers of threatened and endangered species and at-risk ecosystems throughout North America. This book highlights at least twenty-five years of intense photographic work in the San Luis Valley—a labor of love and an unparalleled passion for place. Their images were used to introduce members of the U.S. Congress to the beauty of Great Sand Dunes during the struggle to achieve national park status, and now grace the visitor center at the dunes. Bob and Wendy have produced twelve books, and their images have appeared in *National Wildlife*, *Audubon*, *Nature Conservancy*, *BBC Wildlife*, *Nature's Best*, National Geographic publications, and others. Wendy was the first woman awarded Grand Prize in the worldwide BBC Wildlife Photographer of the Year competition, and the team has won numerous other prestigious contests. Rozinski and Shattil received the Philip Hyde Grant for Environmental Photography, the Environmental Stewardship Award from Denver Audubon, and the Conservationist of the Year and Business of the Year awards from the Colorado Wildlife Federation. They have been artists in residence at Rocky Mountain National Park as well as department associates at the Denver Museum of Nature and Science. Their adherence to photographic integrity and ethical practice is apparent in everything they do. As Fellows of the International League of Conservation Photographers, they have participated in several Rapid Assessment Visual Expeditions, documenting areas of critical environmental concern, ranging from the impacts on the wildlife of the border wall in the Lower Rio Grande Valley to the effects of gas field development on wildlife in Wyoming's Red Desert.

Audrey DeLella Benedict is a naturalist, a writer, and a passionate advocate for the conservation of Colorado's mountain landscapes. She is the author of *The Naturalist's Guide to the Southern Rockies: Colorado, Southern Wyoming, and Northern New Mexico* as well as the natural history essay "Leaf Dance: Aspen Forests of the Rockies" in Linde Waidhofer's *Forests of Light: The Romance of Rocky Mountain Aspens*. Audrey is the founder and director of Cloud Ridge Naturalists, a nonprofit natural history education organization that is now in its fourth decade. Her fascination with the myriad adaptations of species living in high altitude, Arctic, Antarctic, and marine ecosystems inspires her love for natural history. Benedict served for nine years as a trustee for the Colorado chapter of The Nature Conservancy and was actively involved in conservation efforts in Colorado's San Luis Valley and in the Ecuadoran Andes, for which she received TNC's prestigious One Conservancy Award in 2003. She lives in the Colorado Front Range, near the eastern border of the Indian Peaks Wilderness Area, with her geoarcheologist husband, Jim Benedict, and her ever-patient Labrador, Scruggs.